Abstracts of Current Studies 1983

The World Bank Research Program

The World Bank
Washington, D.C. 20433, U.S.A.

ISSN 0253-9535
ISBN 0-8213-0280-9

Foreword

The World Bank's research program is intended to contribute
to a deeper insight into the development process and the policies
affecting it, to introduce new techniques or methodologies into
the Bank's operational and analytical work at country, sectoral,
and project levels, and to help strengthen indigenous research
capacity in developing member countries. Now in its fourteenth
year, the program covers a broad range of development-oriented
issues in about sixty countries, with most research undertaken by
the Bank's own staff. To the extent possible, collaborators from
client countries are also actively involved in the research process.
The wide-ranging topical interest of the research portfolio is a
reflection of the types of policy advice and information that are
sought by member countries, according to their needs and
priorities, and of the data requirements of the Bank as a leading
development institution.

Within *Abstracts*, the objectives, methodology, achievements,
and sources of detailed information on ongoing or nearly completed research projects are set forth. This basic information is
presented to keep development practitioners and researchers well
informed of the Bank's research activities, with the intention of
maintaining and expanding the dialogue on development issues.

Anne O. Krueger
Vice President
Economics and Research Staff

3

The Abstracts were compiled and edited by Sharon Blinco in the Office of the Vice President, Economics and Research Staff. Margaret de Tchihatchef of the Publications Department was responsible for the production of the book.

Contents

List of Abstracts of Current Studies, by Functional Category

1. Development Policy and Planning

1-A. Income Distribution

1-B. Planning, Growth, and Country Economic Analysis

2. International Trade and Finance

3. Agriculture and Rural Development

4. Industry

5. Transportation and Telecommunications

6. Energy

7. *Urbanization and Regional Development*

8. *Population and Human Resources*

8-A. Education

8–B. Labor and Employment

8–C. Population, Health, and Nutrition

Introduction

This compilation of *Abstracts* provides a summary of work undertaken in the World Bank's central research program through September 1983.[1] Research has always been an integral part of the Bank's economic work, and the growing diversification of the Bank's lending operations has induced further expansion of research activities.

To give wider dissemination to the results of its research, the Bank also publishes a newsletter, entitled *World Bank Research News*, three times a year. The newsletter supplements the *Abstracts* by reporting on completed projects, by describing projects that are in the pipeline, not yet included here, and by listing new and forthcoming publications related to the Bank's research. Each issue of *Research News* includes an article that describes various aspects of the Bank's research program in some detail.

The Bank has designed its research program in the light of four major objectives:

- To support all aspects of the World Bank's operations, including the assessment of development progress in member countries.
- To broaden understanding of the development process.
- To improve the Bank's capacity to provide advice to member countries.
- To assist in developing indigenous research capacity in member countries.

To these ends, the World Bank has initiated research projects that develop the data base, construct analytical tools, and extend the Bank's understanding of rural and urban development, industry,

---

[1] This does not include research related to specific projects that are funded by loans and credits to member governments and other, generally short-term, studies carried out by the Bank's staff. Also, completed or discontinued research projects are not generally includes in the *Abstracts*.

trade, economic growth, and social conditions. While the immediate purpose of the research program is to support the Bank's own activities, most studies of importance to the operations of the World Bank are relevant to planning and operational agencies in developing countries, as well as to other development finance institutions.

The design and implementation of research can be used to build and strengthen indigenous research capacity in developing countries. The Bank, therefore, stresses collaborative research with individuals and institutes in those countries. Finally, the World Bank's research program may serve to stimulate others to finance studies on topics of particular interest and to improve the coordination of such research.

The Current Research Program

The 122 projects now in the research program are briefly described in this book. The studies are grouped into eight functional categories and, within each category, appear in numerical order by reference number. Applications of existing research or tried research methodologies to new areas or case studies are identified by the letter "A" following the reference number of the project and appear in numerical order within each category.

The first category, *Development Policy and Planning,* which is divided into two subsections—"Income Distribution" and "Planning, Growth, and Country Economic Analysis"—represents the core of the Bank's effort to improve country economic analysis. The causes, processes, and consequences of aggregate economic development are analyzed with respect to intersectoral linkages and broad social objectives. Various planning and modeling techniques, such as social accounting matrices and general equilibrium and programming models, provide the tools with which issues of structural adjustment facing the developing countries in the 1980s are examined. "The Living Standards Measurement Study" is also to be found in this section.

The second category, *International Trade and Finance,* includes studies that examine the institutional and structural factors underlying changes in the direction of developing countries' trade, particularly in manufactured goods, and their policy implications.

The third category, *Agriculture and Rural Development,* focuses on the design of rural development strategies, particularly on the role of the small farmer in agricultural production. Some studies address planning and policy aspects of agricultural development, such as the design and operation of irrigation projects and the role of technical and financial services in the adoption of agricultural innovations. Others consider the consequences of risk for agricultural policy and the impact of rural development on employment.

The fourth category, *Industry*, is concerned with the sources and patterns of industrial growth and with initiating policies and techniques for efficient industrial development. The use of programming techniques for sector analysis and project design is studied, as are issues of appropriate technology in the manufacturing sector. Also included in this category are studies on the managerial characteristics of public enterprises and the evolution of small-scale enterprises.

The fifth category, *Transportation and Telecommunications*, is concerned with the design, implementation, and management of transportation and sanitation systems. Of special importance in this section are the studies on highway design and maintenance.

Research on *Energy*, the sixth category, includes the study of tools for analyzing investment policies in the energy sector and the pricing of indigenous energy resources.

Studies in the seventh category, *Urbanization and Regional Development*, seek to improve understanding of the spatial and economic effects of policy intervention in cities of the developing world. Identifying appropriate technologies and pricing policies for urban services, including housing and water supply and sanitation systems, is a significant component among a number of the studies.

The eighth category, *Population and Human Resources*, has three subsections—"Education," "Labor and Employment," and "Population, Health, and Nutrition." Studies on education are evaluating the efficacy of alternative modes of transmission (for example, educational radio) and measuring the impact of facilities and programs designed to improve the quality of education. The labor market studies focus on the informal urban sector and its relation to rural-urban migration. The studies on population consider the determinants of fertility and the economics of household size; those on health, the influence of augmented food intake and efficient disease control on workers' nutrition and productivity.

Correspondence

Requests for information on specific research projects should be addressed to the director of the World Bank department listed within the "Responsibility" section of each abstract. The completion date is only an estimate.

Reports stemming from the research projects are listed at the end of individual abstracts. Informal documents, such as divisional or departmental discussion papers or mimeographed and draft papers, are generally available through the responsible department or through the recently established Bank Research Documentation Center (BRDC) in the Office of the Vice President, Economics and Research Staff, The World Bank, Room I-8-203, in Washington D.C. at the address below.

World Bank Staff Working Papers, Country Reports, and other official series that are published by the Bank are listed in *The World Bank Catalog of Publications*, which provides detailed ordering instructions and a price list. The catalog may be obtained by writing to:

> The World Bank
> Publications Distribution Unit
> 1818 H Street, N.W.
> Washington, D.C. 20433, U.S.A.

> The World Bank
> European Office
> 66, avenue d'Iéna
> 75116 Paris, France

1
Development Policy and Planning
1-A. Income Distribution

The Living Standards Measurement Study

Ref. No. 620-47

The Living Standards Measurement Study (LSMS) is an exploration into ways of improving the type and quality of household data collected in developing countries. Its principal goal is to foster increased use of household data as a basis for policymaking. Specifically, LSMS seeks better ways to monitor progress in raising standards of living, to identify the consequences of past and proposed government policies, and to improve communications between statisticians and analysts on the one hand and policymakers on the other.

The first phase of LSMS's work program, now near completion, reviewed existing theory and methodologies to identify what data were necessary to meet LSMS's objectives. General conclusions from this background work are that identification of incomes by source and of household expenditure patterns must be central elements of a living standards study. Further, these data must be complemented by data on human development and on demographic change. Both income and expenditures must be built up from highly disaggregated information and the two sides of the household's accounts must be closely integrated to improve the accuracy of the survey. Employment is the major source of income for most households, so what is typically regarded as a labor force survey will be integral to the overall design.

A volume now in preparation will illustrate the uses to which LSMS data can be put in five policy areas: identification of poverty and inequality; expenditure analysis; the human development dimension of living standards; manpower, employment, and earnings analysis; and income distribution and national accounts.

LSMS's first field trial is now under way in the Ivory Coast in conjunction with "The Distribution of Welfare in the Ivory Coast" (Ref. No. 673-22 in this category). Discussions are under way in several other countries concerning the possibility of further trial Living Standards Surveys.

Responsibility: Development Research Department—Dennis De Tray, Christiaan N. Grootaert, and Timothy King, with the participation of a large number of Bank staff from other departments and of several consultants.

Completion date: June 1984.

Reports

Pyatt, F. Graham. "Some Conceptual Problems of Measuring Living Standards, or: How Do We Find Out Who is Benefiting from Development?" Paper presented at the meeting of the International Statistical Institute, Manila, Philippines, December 1979.

Living Standards Measurement Study (LSMS), Working Papers Nos. 1-20, available through the World Bank's Development Research Department:

  1. Chander, Ramesh; Grootaert, Christiaan N.; and Pyatt, F. Graham. "Living Standards Surveys in Developing Countries." October 1980.
  2. Visaria, Pravin. "Poverty and Living Standards in Asia: An Overview of the Main Results and Lessons of Selected Household Surveys." October 1980.
  3. Altimir, Oscar, and Sourrouille, Juan. "Measuring Levels of Living in Latin America: An Overview of Main Problems." October 1980.
  4. United Nations Statistical Office. "Towards More Effective Measurement of Levels of Living, and Review of Work of the United Nations Statistical Office (UNSO) Related to Statistics of Levels of Living." October 1980.
  5. Chander, Ramesh; de André, Paulo T. A.; and Scott, Christopher. "Conducting Surveys in Developing Countries: Practical Problems and Experience in Brazil, Malaysia, and the Philippines." October 1980.
  6. Booker, William; Savane, Landing; and Singh, Parmeet. "Household Survey Experience in Africa." October 1980.

7. Deaton, Angus. "Measurement of Welfare: Theory and Practical Guidelines." October 1980.
8. Mehran, Farhad. "Employment Data for the Measurement of Living Standards." October 1980.
9. Wahab, Mohammed Abdul. "Income and Expenditure Surveys in Developing Countries: Sample Design and Execution." October 1980.
10. Grootaert, Christiaan N., and Saunders, Christopher. "Reflections on the LSMS Group Meeting." October 1980.
11. Deaton, Angus. "Three essays on a Sri Lanka Household Survey." October 1981.
12. Musgrove, Philip. "The ECIEL Study of Household Income and Consumption in Urban Latin America: An Analytical History." February 1982.
13. Martorell, Reynaldo. "Nutrition and Health Status Indicators: Suggestions for Surveys of the Standard of Living in Developing Countries." February 1982.
14. Birdsall, Nancy. "Child Schooling and the Measurement of Living Standards." February 1982.
15. Ho, Teresa J. "Measuring Health As A Component of Living Standards." April 1982.
16. Sullivan, Jeremiah M.; Cochrane, Susan H.; and Kalsbeek, William D. "Procedures for Collecting and Analyzing Mortality Data in LSMS." June 1982.
17. Grootaert, Christiaan N. "The Labor Market and Social Accounting: A Framework of Data Presentation." July 1982.
18. Acharya, Meena. "Time Use Data and the Living Standards Measurement Study." July 1982.
19. Grootaert, Christiaan N. "The Conceptual Basis of Measures of Household Welfare and Their Implied Survey Data Requirements." October 1982.
20. Grootaert, Christiaan N.; Cheung, K. F.; Fung, H. W.; and Tam, S. M. "Statistical Experimentation for Household Surveys: Two Case Studies of Hong Kong." November 1982.

Studies on Brazilian Distribution and Growth

Ref. No. 672-21

Brazil is the world's most often cited example of rapid, but inequitable growth. While acknowledging rapid growth, there is little agreement on how the benefits of that growth have been distributed and, particularly, on whether the poor have gained much in absolute terms. Difficulties in the interpretation of data abound and, in the absence of a common interpretation, little progress has been made in understanding the economic, social, and demographic mechanisms that have generated the Brazilian combination of growth and inequality.

Recognition of the important role of demographic factors, especially at the household level, in assessing the relationship between growth and inequality is increasing, yet much work remains to be done in analyzing the interrelationships.

The recent release by the Brazilian Census Bureau of a one percent sample of the 1970 population census has made it possible to pursue several issues at the household level. The census tape contains data on about 910,000 individuals, cross-classified into 176,000 households and 117 identifiable geographical areas. This research project comprises three interrelated sets of studies, each designed to explore the links between demographic variables at the household level and income distribution. These studies are now nearing completion.

The first set of studies has been essentially descriptive. It has focused on a hitherto neglected aspect (because published data were not available and special tabulations were costly) of the Brazilian income distribution issue: the relation of household size and composition (age of the head of the household, age structure and work status of members) to inequality, and household responses, particularly in terms of labor supply, to the economic pressures that have been created by an allegedly unequal growth process. The studies have allocated labor force members by household and described the extent to which the low wages of individual workers are compensated for by earnings of other family members.

In part, through the other two sets of studies, explained below, the first project has made it possible to link differences in income across households to other welfare indicators and has contributed to the definition of socioeconomic groups. Finally, it has established a base line for comparison with the 1980 census.

The second set of studies has examined the important question of human capital formation at the household level, focusing on the schooling decision. One objective has been to clarify the relative importance of family characteristics, on the one hand, and the availability of schools, on the other hand, in determining schooling for children. The distribution of schooling among today's children has a significant influence on tomorrow's distribution of income. A key issue is the extent to which public interventions to increase access to schooling are made more or less effective by individual family resources and the capacity of poor families to use school systems. Children from poor families may not have access to school, either because schools are not available or because they work to supplement family incomes. In this way, poverty may be transmitted from one generation to the next, unless the link between poverty and schooling is modified by public policy. In addition, research on the benefit of schooling in terms of adult income has been geared to examining how differences in availability and quality of schools across regions of Brazil have affected adult income and to considering the efficiency and equity of public schooling investments between rural and urban areas and between expansion versus quality improvements.

The third set of studies has examined infant and child mortality as aspects of distribution of income. Important indicators of household welfare, mortality differentials also raise major questions about the relative importance of policy interventions to alleviate poverty vis-à-vis social, economic, and demographic characteristics of households. These influences have been examined at the regional and household level.

Responsibility: Country Policy Department and *Development Research Department*—Nancy Birdsall (currently assigned to the *World Development Report*) and Constantino P. Lluch, respectively, in collaboration with Thomas W. Merrick of Georgetown University and Jere R. Behrman of the University of Pennsylvania (consultants).

Completion date: September 1983; the completion report is in process.

Reports

Behrman, Jere R., and Birdsall, Nancy. "The Quality of Schooling: Quantity Alone is Misleading." *American Economic Review*, vol. 73, no. 5 (December 1983).

"Three Studies in the Economics of Education Using Brazilian Data." Country Policy Discussion Paper No. 1983-1. The World Bank, February 1983.

Birdsall, Nancy. "Public Inputs and Child Schooling in Brazil." *Journal of Development Economics* (forthcoming).

Birdsall, Nancy, and Fox, M. Louise. "Why Males Earn More: Location and Training of Brazilian Schoolteachers." *Economic Development and Cultural Change* (forthcoming, 1984).

Birdsall, Nancy, and Meesook, Oey Astra. "Child Schooling, Number of Children and the Intergenerational Transmission of Inequality: A Simulation." Population and Human Resources Division Discussion Paper No. 81-19. The World Bank, May 1981.

Fox, M. Louise. "Income Distribution Analysis in Brazil: Better Numbers and New Findings." Mimeo. The World Bank: Development Research Department, 1982.

Jen, C. "Urban Female Labor Force Participation in Brazil." Ph.D. dissertation. State University of New York at Buffalo, 1983.

Lluch, Constantino P. "Income Distribution and Family Characteristics in Brazil." Mimeo. The World Bank: Development Research Department, August 1981.

_____. "On Measures of Income from the Censuses and National Accounts in Brazil." *Pesquisa e Planejamento Econômico*, vol. 12 (1) (April 1982):133-48.

_____. "On Poverty and Inequality in Brazil." *Pesquisa e Planejamento Econômico*, vol. 11 (3) (December 1981):757-82.

Merrick, Thomas W. "The Effect of Piped Water on Early Childhood Mortality in Urban Brazil, 1970 to 1976." World Bank Staff Working Paper No. 594, 1983.

Income Formation and Expenditures of Poor Urban Households

Ref. No. 672-57

The project is designed to yield more definitive information on the real resources at the command of urban families and, thus, on their ability to afford shelter and other essential services. It has often been assumed by policymakers and researchers alike that one of the effects of urbanization has been to break the ties of the urban household with the extended family group and to eliminate many of the supportive functions that are carried out by family networks in rural areas. Based on these assumptions, the designers of urban development projects have tended to see the potential participant household as a discrete entity and its labor market earnings as the indicator of what it could afford to pay for services. In projects that must cover their recurrent costs, this assumption has tended to lead to the exclusion of households who receive a significant proportion of their income from nonlabor market earnings. One consequence has been to introduce a potential bias against groups such as female-headed households who may receive regular monetary or in-kind transfers from other households.

Background work done by the World Bank in El Salvador and the Philippines has shown that an important part of the total income of many poor families comes from other households. For instance, 58 percent of the households in the lowest-earnings decile in the city of Santa Ana, El Salvador, receive income transfers. For recipient households in that decile, transfers make up one-third of total income. Results from both countries suggest that poor families headed by women and/or with women who are not working are most likely to receive income transfers.

In studies of household expenditure behavior, it has been customary to use the level of total income as one of the main explanatory variables. The possibility that the composition of income may affect expenditure behavior—with receipts from different sources earmarked for different types of expenditure—has largely been overlooked. So has the possibility that a household's income may rise in response to specific opportunities for expenditure or investments. The background work for the present study shows that the structure of income does affect the pattern of expenditures. A significant proportion of transfer income appears to be earmarked to meet basic needs (food, health care, education, and shelter). The results from El Salvador suggest that a poor household receiving most of its income in the form of transfers will spend 75 percent of its income on basic needs, 10 percent on other expenditures, and save the remaining 15 percent. An equally poor household that derives most of its income from earnings will devote only 62 percent to basic needs.

Furthermore, the studies in El Salvador and the Philippines suggest that other things being equal, a household directly affected by an urban development project will receive more transfer income than a comparable household that is not so affected. If households with the prospect of benefiting from a project can elicit additional income, this will have important implications for project planning.

The present study is examining the sources of income and types of expenditure of urban households in low-income areas of Cartagena, Colombia. It seeks a better understanding of the determinants of income transfers, the motivation of these transfers, and the rights and obligations associated with them. It is hoped that the study will yield important insights into the capacity to pay for housing and related services and into the appropriate criteria for selecting project beneficiaries.

The results are likely to shed light on a number of allocative and distributive issues. For example, by studying the interactions among the family network, it should be possible to assess how exchanges between households affect the overall distribution of welfare among the urban poor. Second, investigating the sources of, and motivations for, income transfers, their reliability, and the uses to which they are put by recipients will improve knowledge of the role of the family network as a substitute for imperfect formal capital markets.

The research is being conducted in the low-income areas of Cartagena (the Zona Sur Oriental) where an urban development project is supported by the Bank. A questionnaire which investigates in detail the patterns and uses of income transfers has been applied to a random sample of approximately 520 households. The survey was complemented by anthropological case studies on six households that were observed intensively over a period of several months. Econometric techniques, similar to those used in El Salvador, were applied in the analysis of the survey data.

Initial findings reveal that for the lowest-income earnings quintile in Cartagena, 61.8 percent of male-headed and 66.7 percent of female-headed households received income transfers, which represented 40.3 percent and 51.6 percent, respectively, of total household income. However, unlike in the earlier studies in El Salvador and the Philippines, households in Cartagena directly affected by an urban development project did not receive more transfer income than comparable households outside the project area. The apparent reason is that the project had developed more slowly than expected and, at the time of the study, households did not perceive that returns to such an investment would be high and consequently were either unable or unwilling to obtain additional transfers for this purpose.

Responsibility: Water Supply and Urban Development Department—Michael Bamberger and Daniel Kaufmann, assisted by

Lisa Peattie, Scott Parris, and Anna Sant'Anna (consultants). The sample survey and preparation of the initial data were conducted by the Instituto SER de Investigación in Bogota (Colombia).

Completion date: December 1983; the completion report is in process.

Reports

The following background reports relating to earlier work in El Salvador and the Philippines are available:

Kaufmann, Daniel. "Social Interactions as a Strategy for Survival among the Urban Poor: A Theory and Some Evidence." Ph.D. dissertation. Cambridge, Massachusetts: Harvard University, 1982.

Kaufmann, Daniel, and Lindauer, David. "Basic Needs, Inter-household Transfers and the Extended Family." Urban and Regional Report No. 80–15. The World Bank: Urban and Regional Economics Division, 1980.

Reforma, Mila, and Obusan, Ricci. "Household Networks and Survival Strategies among the Urban Poor: Monetary and Non-monetary Transfers among Selected Families in Tondo." Urban and Regional Report No. 81–22. The World Bank: Urban and Regional Economics Division, 1981.

"A Study of Income and Expenditure Patterns of Households in the Tondo Foreshore Area." Summary of a report prepared by the Research and Analysis Division, National Housing Authority, Philippines, 1981.

The Distribution of Welfare in the Ivory Coast

Ref. No. 673-22

This investigation of welfare levels in the Ivory Coast is the World Bank's first in-depth monitoring of the distribution of welfare on a national or regional basis in a sub-Saharan African country. The project's first phase will analyze data from a nation-wide consumption and income survey involving 1,980 households in 1979; its second phase will establish, in collaboration with the Ivory Coast's Direction de la Statistique (STAT), a permanent household survey with the capability of monitoring market and household activities among Ivorian families. Data from this second phase will be used to measure welfare changes over time and across regions and to analyze sources of welfare differentials.

In the first phase, a World Bank team in collaboration with Ivorian researchers, based in the Direction de la Statistique in the Ivory Coast's Ministry of Planning and Industry and in the Centre ivoirien de recherche économique et sociale (CIRES), will prepare a comprehensive baseline description of the distribution of welfare among Ivorian households in 1979. This analysis will also serve as the basis for planning and pretesting elements of the new household survey to be initiated in 1984. Further objectives are to establish standard analytical procedures for the 1984 survey that will yield policy-relevant information for the government and identify shortcuts in data processing that reduce the time lag between survey activities and usable data.

The 1979 survey was conducted by the Ivorian government in order to refine its understanding of the relationship between development and growth. The country's growth rate has been 2.5 percent per capita annually over the past two decades, yet the government has perceived an increasingly uneven distribution of welfare between urban and rural regions and among socioeconomic groups. Its intention is to use the household survey, in part, to identify policy instruments that will benefit welfare across regions and over time for identifiable groups in the Ivorian economy.

In the 1979 survey, each of the 1,980 households surveyed was visited biweekly for a year. The data covered three modules—an inventory of durable and semidurable goods in the household, along with a description of housing conditions regarding the availability of water, electricity, and other amenities; data on food consumption; and detailed information on economic activities of the household.

Analysis of the 1979 survey will focus on consumption-based measures of welfare. However, since the high cost of a detailed consumption survey prohibits regular repetition, the investigators will also explore to what extent comparisons based on various income concepts correlate with those based on consumption data. Two welfare measures based on income will be developed: total cash income, which is the easiest measure to obtain, and cash income plus the value of income in kind and home-produced consumption items.

The project's second phase will draw on recommendations from the World Bank's "Living Standards Measurement Study" (LSMS) (Ref. No. 620–47, in this category) to establish a permanent household survey in the Ivory Coast. The survey's principal objective will be to improve the information base on which Ivorian policy decisions rest. The planning ministry's Direction de la Statistique will carry out the survey, interviewing 1,500 households each year. The survey will operate on a "rolling panel" principle in which one half of the sample households are replaced with new households each year.

The first waves of the permanent survey will serve as the basis for work on three research topics: (1) a comparative analysis of Ivorian welfare distribution based on the 1979 and 1984 data; (2) an exploration of underlying causes of welfare differentials with special emphasis on labor market activities in the Ivory Coast's "informal" sector; and (3) an analysis of survey activities aimed at refining LSMS's recommendations for future living standard surveys.

The project is cosponsored by the World Bank's Living Standards Measurement Study which is developing improved methods for measuring welfare in developing countries. LSMS will use information from the 1979 survey to adapt prototype questionnaires to the informational needs of the proposed permanent survey.

Responsibility: Development Research Department—Jacob Van Der Gaag and Dennis De Tray, in collaboration with E. Yai, Direction de la Statistique (STAT), Ministry of Planning and Industry of the Ivory Coast, and A. Atsain, Centre ivoirien de recherche économique et sociale (CIRES).

Completion date: June 1984.

1–B. Planning, Growth, and Country Economic Analysis

International Comparison Project

Ref. Nos. 670–68 and 671–91

The International Comparison Project (ICP) is a cooperative effort, begun in 1968 under the aegis of the United Nations, to establish a reliable system of comparisons of real product and the purchasing power of currencies. The World Bank joined the ICP in 1969 and has been a major supporter since that time. In addition to the United Nations and the World Bank, the Ford Foundation and a number of governments have made direct contributions to the work; every participating country has contributed significantly by providing resources for collecting data on its own economic activity.

The ICP has two main objectives: first, to work out the methods required for a system of international comparisons and, second, to apply these methods to a gradually expanding sample of countries with the intention of eventually establishing global coverage. The project has advanced in well-defined stages. In Phase I, the results of which were published in 1975, the essential features of the methodology were formulated and detailed comparisons were produced for ten countries, varying significantly in type, stage of development, and location, for the year 1970 (and for six of these countries for 1967 as well). The Phase II report, published in 1978, added six countries, including four developing countries, to the original ten and included estimates for 1973 as well as 1970. In Phase III of the study the list of countries covered was expanded to 34 and the entire data base was updated to 1975. More than half of the countries covered in the final stage are developing countries.

The project has produced a set of price and per capita quantity comparisons for gross domestic product (GDP), its three main expenditure subaggregates (consumption, investment, and government), and 36 major components for each country and year covered. These estimates are both base country invariant and transitive, characteristics which were established at the outset of the study as being highly desirable. The underlying detailed data are provided in the reports to enable researchers to aggregate the quantity data in alternative ways of their own choice.

Work on the initial research phase of the ICP was concluded with the completion of the Phase III study and the associated data base for 34 countries in June 1981. The report on the third phase was published in 1982. With support provided under research project Ref. No. 671-91, arrangements have been completed for transfer of the basic work on the ICP on a permanent basis to the United Nations Statistical Office. The benchmark estimates will be kept up to date, and additional countries will be brought into the data base. Under Phase IV, which began in 1980 under UN auspices, comparisons will be made for some 60–65 countries, including most of the countries covered in Phase III, with new countries concentrated primarily in Africa, Asia, and Latin America.

Responsibility: Economic Analysis and Projections Department —Sultan Ahmad, with the previous substantive contribution of Robert A. McPheeters, Jr. Professor Irving B. Kravis, University of Pennsylvania, is director of the project; the United Nations Statistical Office is responsible for the ICP at the United Nations.

Completion date: The completion report on Phase III is in process.

Reports

Heston, Alan. "A Comparison of Some Short-Cut Methods of Estimating Real Product per Capita." *The Review of Income and Wealth* 19 (March 1973):79–104.

Kravis, Irving B.; Heston, Alan; and Summers, Robert. "International Comparison of Real Product and its Composition: 1950–77." *The Review of Income and Wealth* (March 1980):19–66.

————. *Phase II: International Comparisons of Real Product and Purchasing Power.* Baltimore and London: The Johns Hopkins University Press, 1978.

————. *Phase III: World Product and Income: International Comparisons of Real Gross Product.* Baltimore and London: The Johns Hopkins University Press, 1982.

————. "Real GDP per Capita for More than 100 countries." *The Economic Journal* (June 1978).

————. "The Role of Regionalization in a Worldwide System of International Product Comparisons." Paper prepared for a Conference on Purchasing Power and Real Product Comparisons at the Economic Comission for Europe, Geneva (Switzerland), May 1979.

Kravis, Irving B.; Kenessey, Zoltan; Heston, Alan; and Summers, Robert. *Phase I: A System of International Comparisons of Gross Product and Purchasing Power.* Baltimore and London: The Johns Hopkins University Press, 1975.

Summers, Robert. "International Price Comparisons Based Upon Incomplete Data." *The Review of Income and Wealth* 19 (March 1973):1–16.

A complete bibliography, covering the main ICP research reports, status and planning reports, documentation and manuals for data collection, and miscellaneous reports and studies, most of which have been published, is available from the Economic Analysis and Projections Department, The World Bank.

Social Accounts and Development Models

Ref. No. 671-27

Macroeconomic analysis of the development process has been restricted mainly to two-gap models of resource needs and input output models of industrial structure. This framework is inadequate for studying policies that deal with problems of the generation of employment, redistribution of income, and eradication of poverty. This study attempts to provide a basis for macroeconomic models, which permits analysis of the trade-offs between alternative policy goals. The analysis focuses simultaneously on the causes of poverty and inequality and their measurement and on the determination of both prices and quantities in a model framework. The study involves an attempt to construct a social accounting matrix (SAM) for Malaysia and to develop an economywide model based on the SAM.

Data needs are identified on the basis of the United Nations system of standardized national accounts, which presents annual data in a SAM framework. Since the UN system imposes a heavy burden on the statistical offices of developing countries, the research begins with specific country studies on the feasibility of obtaining basic data in modified versions of the UN format. At the same time, some extensions of the standardized UN system are required to encompass questions of income distribution, employment, basic needs, and poverty in an integrated framework. Systems of classification (for example, the level of disaggregation) and methods of reconciling data from various sources are studied in order to make the system more relevant for planning.

The elaboration of data requirements is paralleled by research on model structures within the SAM framework. The model being developed generalizes the linear (input-output) models by allowing for price substitution. Through extensive use of CES functions, the basic model provides a general and flexible framework that includes a wide range of existing models as special cases. A major feature is the specification of two-way causal links between income distribution and the structure of production, both of which are endogenous.

A conference has been held as part of the project, bringing together a number of individuals with practical experience in SAM construction and applications. The papers delivered at this conference will be published in a volume; two further volumes are being drafted on the specific work on Malaysia.

Responsibility: Development Research Department—F. Graham Pyatt, in collaboration with Jeffery Round and Frank Lysy (consultants). The Department of Statistics and the Economic Planning Unit of Malaysia have been closely involved in the work.

Completion date: December 1983.

Reports

Ahluwalia, Montek, and Lysy, Frank. "Multipliers under Alternative Model Structures." *Journal of Policy Modeling* (September 1979).

Byron, R. J. "The Estimation of Large Social Accounting Matrices." *Journal of The Royal Statistical Society*, Series A, vol. 141 (1978). Also World Bank Reprint Series: Number Sixty-five.

Chander, R; Gnasegarah, S.; and Round, J. I. "Social Accounts and the Distribution of Income: The Malaysian Economy in 1970." *Review of Income and Wealth*, vol. 26, no. 1 (March 1980). Also World Bank Reprint Series: Number 143.

King, B. B. "What is SAM? A Layman's Guide to Social Accounting Matrices." World Bank Staff Working Paper No. 463, June 1981.

Lahiri, Sajal, and Pyatt, F. Graham. "On the Solution of Scale-Dependent Input-Output Models." *Econometrica*, vol. 48, no. 7 (November 1980).

Pyatt, F. Graham, and Round, J. I. "Accounting and Fixed Price Multipliers in a Social Accounting Matrix Framework." *The Economic Journal* 89 (December 1979):874–96. Also World Bank Reprint Series: Number 125.

————. "Social Accounting Matrices for Development Planning." *The Review of Income and Wealth*, Series 23 (December 1977). Also World Bank Reprint Series: Number Seventy-four.

A General Algebraic Modeling System (GAMS)

Ref. Nos. 671-58 and 673-06

Mathematical modeling has developed into one of the major tools of strategic planning. Its potential power and relevance in sectoral and economywide applications have been demonstrated convincingly over the last decade in a research-oriented environment. Despite this general acceptance, few mathematical models are being built outside the research laboratory. Many problems can be attributed to the current approach to model building, which requires a variety of technical skills and fails to address problems of documentation, communication, and dissemination of mathematical models. The existing solution algorithms also require inputs that are not compatible with each other; this results in different representations of the same model.

The project explores a machine-intensive route to modeling and aims at a dramatic reduction in the time needed to develop a model, in the technical skills required, and in the total cost associated with existing modeling and data systems. GAMS is a system that provides a formal framework for the specification, manipulation, generation, and reporting of models and their associated data.

The two main components of GAMS are the definition of a uniform notation (formal language) to allow unambiguous representations of models and data, and a modeling system that automatically analyzes and translates models from one representation into another, as required by different solution processes.

A number of large-scale models developed in the World Bank have been used as test cases and form the nucleus of a uniform model library. The series, The Planning of Investment Programs (see "Programming in the Manufacturing Sector," Ref. No. 670–24, in category 4—Industry), has adopted the GAMS representation to guarantee consistency and replicability of all models and their data throughout the series.

Phase I of the project concentrated on language definitions, the integration of a relational data base into the system, and the automatic interface to commercial linear programming systems. Phase II was developed on the basis of responses and recommendations from users. The major thrust was in the area of large nonlinear models that use new concepts in automatic recognition of structures and the facilities of an extended data base. A prototype model for Control Data Corporation computers has been operational in production environments of several universities and research institutes since 1981.

The project is now in Phase III which plans to make the system available for a large number of computer and operating systems to permit wider distribution in developing countries. Phase III is jointly sponsored by the World Bank and the Communication and Computer Science Department of Exxon Corporation.

Responsibility: Development Research Department—Alexander Meeraus and Arne Drud, in collaboration with Paul van der Eijk and Charlene Bashford of Exxon Corporation (consultants).

Completion date: June 1985.

Reports

Bisschop, J., and Meeraus, A. "Matrix Augmentation and Partitioning in the Updating of the Basis Inverse." *Mathematical Programming,* vol. 13 (3) (1977):241–54.

_____. "Matrix Augmentation and Structure Preservation in Linearly Constrained Control Problems." *Mathematical Programming,* vol. 18 (1) (1980):7–15.

_____. "On the Development of a General Algebraic Modeling System in a Strategic Planning Environment." *Mathematical Programming Study 20* (1982):1–29.

_____. "Selected Aspects of a General Algebraic Modeling Language." In *Proceedings of the 9th IFIPS Conference on Optimization.* Berlin and Heidelberg: Springer Verlag, 1980.

_____. "Towards Successful Modeling Applications in a Strategic Planning Environment." In G. Dantzig, M. Dempsler, and M. Kellio, (eds.), *Large-Scale Linear Programming.* Vienna: International Institute for Applied Systems Analysis, 1981.

Drud, A. "Adding Algorithms to Existing Modeling Systems." *Journal of Economic Dynamics and Control,* vol. 5 (1983).

_____. "Combining an Optimal Control Program with the Time Series Processor System." In J. M. L. Jannsen, L. F. Pau, and A. J. Straszak, (eds.), *Dynamic Modeling and Control of National Economics.* Oxford: Pergamon Press, 1981.

_____. "The Implications of Modeling Systems on Large-Scale Nonlinear Optimization Codes." In M. J. D. Powell (ed.), *Nonlinear Optimization 1981.* London and New York: Academic Press, 1982.

_____. "A Survey of Modeling Systems." *Journal of Economic Dynamics and Control,* vol. 5 (1983).

Kendrick, D.; Meeraus, A.; and Suh, J. "Oil Refining Modeling and the GAMS Language." Research Report No. 14. Austin: Center of Energy Studies, The University of Texas, 1981.

Lasdon, L., and Meeraus, A. "Solving Nonlinear Economic Plan-
ning Models Using GRG Algorithms." In *Proceedings of the
International Symposium of Systems Optimization and Analysis.*
Berlin and Heidelberg: Springer Verlag, 1979.

Meeraus, A. "An Algebraic Approach to Modeling." *Journal of
Economic Dynamics and Control,* vol. 5 (1983).

———. "GAMS—User's Guide." The World Bank: Development
Research Department, 1982.

A Series of Technical Notes that addresses specific issues
related to the development of GAMS is available from the World
Bank's Development Research Department.

Research Support for the World Development Report

Ref. No. 671–66

The object of this study is to develop a price-endogenous,
interregional model for the world economy, in support of the
World Bank's global model of trade and capital flows.

Since 1974, the World Bank has been engaged in global
modeling to identify the major constraints affecting the growth
of developing countries and to explore alternative strategies for
development.

In the Bank's early global modeling work (SIMLINK or Mark I),
the problem of describing the interdependence between various
parts of the world was simplified by adopting four rather heroic
assumptions. The first was that the growth of developing countries was constrained principally by a shortage of foreign exchange. The second was that the availability of foreign exchange
depended largely on the industrialized countries, through the
impact of their growth on the markets for raw materials and
exports of manufactured goods from developing countries and
through their aid policies. The third assumption was that this
causal relation was unilateral: developed countries influenced the
developing world but there was no feedback. The last assumption
was that it was reasonable to divide the countries of the world into
four income groups: low income countries, middle-income countries, oil-exporting developing economies, and developed market
economies.

As the SIMLINK framework provided little scope for independent action by the developing countries to improve their situation,

other than their efforts at trade promotion, a beginning was made, in 1977, to design a new model.

The Bank's monitoring of problems in developing countries in 1976–77 clearly suggested that the developing world was moving toward a situation where many different constraints are at work. The natural way of taking these into account was to introduce all of the alternative constraints into the model as inequalities, thus switching from the set of recursive equations of SIMLINK to a representation of the world economy by linked linear programming models.

The resulting Mark II model, used in the first three editions of the *World Development Report*, is substantially larger than SIMLINK; it is also far more complex, since a system of linked linear programs is more difficult to manage than a system of recursive equations. The paradigm described by the model is that of a world of closely managed developing economies, whose governments seek the best course of development subject to the constraints on their balance of payments, savings, and industrial capacity.

But this modeling approach raises three interconnected types of problems. The first one is the fundamental question of whether it is appropriate to describe the behavior of developing countries by regional optimizing models. The second is whether the scheme linking the submodels dovetails the components of the system as correctly as possible. The third problem is that of specifying constraints so that the resulting system clearly interprets economic behavior.

The Mark III series of models emerging from the present study is designed to address a number of these problems. The models have tried to capture the economic realism in a mixed economy where some features of behavior correspond to the competitive equilibrium, while others reflect the existing market rigidities. In either case, the normative decisions of the economic agents play a major role in the mechanics of the solution processes.

In the initial two years of the project (fiscal years 1979 and 1980), the focus was on the construction of the model: basic econometric estimation work, experimentation with the various trial versions of the model, and streamlining of the solution algorithms. In the third year, Mark III was used extensively in sensitivity runs for *World Development Report 1981*. In these runs, it explored the mechanics of adjustment between the two cases traced by the older Mark II model. The two cases are described in detail in the Report. This combination proved to be a useful blend of the two most recent generations of the Bank's global models.

Since then, the model has been continuously upgraded to emphasize the supply aspects of growth, the role of price and income rigidities in hampering adjustment to external shocks, and the balance between agricultural and nonagricultural growth. A version of the current model includes a disaggregated representation of world agriculture and of world agricultural policies. These successive versions of the model were used for background global simulation work for the *World Development Report* in 1982 and in 1983.

The project is essentially completed, and its final output is being written and disseminated.

Responsibility: Economic Analysis and Projections Department —Peter Miovic and John D. Shilling. The research is being undertaken largely at the Free University of Brussels (Belgium) under the direction of Jean Waelbroeck.

Completion date: January 1984

Reports

Burniaux, J. M. "First Experiments with a World Agricultural Model in a General Equilibrium Framework." Center for Econometrics and International Economics (CEME) Discussion Paper 8205. Brussels (Belgium): Free University of Brussels, 1982.

_____. "Impact of Growth and Price Policies on the Pattern of World Trade." In O. Havrylyshyn, ed., *Proceedings of the World Bank-sponsored Conference on South-South or South-North Trade: Does the Direction of the Developing Countries' Trade Matter?* Brussels (Belgium), February 28–March 1, 1983 (forthcoming).

Carrin, G.; Gunning, J. W.; and Waelbroeck, J. "A General Equilibrium Model for the World Economy: Some Preliminary Results." In B. Hickman, ed., *Global Modelling.* Amsterdam: North Holland, 1980.

Gunning, J. W. "Rationing in an Open Economy: Fix-Price Equilibrium and Two Gap Models." Center for Econometrics and International Economics (CEME) Working Paper 8002. Brussels (Belgium): Free University of Brussels, June 1980.

Gunning, J. W.; Carrin, G.; Waelbroeck, J.; *et al*. "Growth and Trade of Developing Countries: A General Equilibrium Analysis." Center for Econometrics and Mathematical Economics (CEME) Discussion Paper 8212. Brussels (Belgium): Free University of Brussels, 1982.

Waelbroeck, J. "A Global Development Model: the M3 Model of Developing and Developed Countries." Center for Econometrics and International Economics (CEME) Discussion Paper 7901. Brussels (Belgium): Free University of Brussels, 1979.

Research Dissemination: A Computable General Equilibrium Model of Turkey

Ref. No. 672-04

In recent years, the World Bank has sponsored a number of research projects to improve the specification of multisector, economywide models for studying a variety of issues in developing countries. In particular, a model of Turkey has been developed that focuses on issues of growth, trade policy, and industrial structure. This model is in the family of computable general equilibrium (CGE) models. It is highly nonlinear and determines product prices, factor prices, and the exchange rate endogenously so as to clear the markets for commodities, labor, and foreign exchange. Market clearing is achieved by varying prices to equate supply and demand in the various markets, while the behavior of the different "actors" in the economy—producers, consumers, government, and the rest of the world—is specified separately.

In the application to Turkey, a version of the model was specified in which the exchange rate was fixed, and the adjustment to foreign payments imbalances was made through a combination of quantitative import restrictions by sector and economywide import rationing by means of import premia that equilibrate the market for foreign exchange. The model has been used for a variety of reports within the Bank. It has also provided projections which aided in policy analysis for the report of the Special Economic Mission to Turkey in April 1979.

The development and application of CGE models has aroused interest in a number of academic and policymaking institutions in developing countries. This research project was initiated in response to a request from the Institute of Economic and Social Research at the Middle East Technical University, Ankara, to acquire the CGE modeling framework developed for the Bank's model of Turkey. The original goal of the project was to transfer the modeling technology, including the computer program, to the institution in Ankara. This has been successfully completed, enabling staff of the institute to use the model for policy-conditional forward projections for the Turkish economy and undertake more detailed empirical studies based on the model framework.

In a second phase of the project, the scope was expanded to include consideration of macroeconomic features that are traditionally absent from CGE models but are of paramount importance in many developing countries. This phase involved continued collaboration with researchers at the Middle East Technical University on model design, incorporation of macroeconomic mechanisms into the CGE model, and a study of inflation in Turkey. Also, the CGE modeling technology has been transferred to the research department of the Turkish Industrial Development Bank (TSKB), where the staff has begun linking the CGE model to a macroeconometric model of the Turkish economy.

Responsibility: Development Research Department and Europe, Middle East, and North Africa Projects Department II—Sherman Robinson (on leave at the University of California at Berkeley) and Jayanta Roy, respectively, in collaboration with Merih Celasun and Ataman Aksoy, Middle East Technical University, Ankara, and Fahrettin Yagci, Turkish Industrial Development Bank (TSKB), Istanbul.

Completion date: September 1983; the completion report is in process.

Reports

Aksoy, M. Ataman. "Structural Aspects of Turkish Inflation." World Bank Staff Working Paper No. 540, 1982.

Celasun, Merih. "Extension of the Data Base for the Sources of Growth: Study on the Turkish Economy." Mimeo. Ankara: Middle East Technical University, May 1981.

Celasun, M.; Guven, S.; and Yaprak, T. "The Transfer of the General Equilibrium Modelling Framework to Turkey." Mimeo. Ankara: Middle East Technical University, June 1982.

Dervis, Kemal, and Robinson, Sherman. "The Foreign Exchange Gap, Growth and Industrial Strategy in Turkey:

1973-1983." World Bank Staff Working Paper No. 306, November 1978.

Dubey, Vinod; Faruqi, Shakil; et al. *Turkey: Policies and Prospects for Growth.* A World Bank Country Study. The World Bank, March 1980.

Lewis, Jeffrey D., and Urata, Shujiro. "Turkey: Recent Economic Performance and Medium Term Prospects, 1978-1990." World Bank Staff Working Paper No. 602, 1983.

Reduced Information Methods of International Real Income Comparisons

Ref. No. 672-16

It is generally recognized that intercountry comparisons of relative levels of income should be carried out with national income converted to a common currency using purchasing power parity (PPP) instead of exchange rates. Unfortunately, reliable estimates of PPPs are available for only a handful of countries because the standard benchmark method of estimating them requires a very substantial commitment of time and resources.

With financial support from the World Bank, the International Comparison Project (ICP) (see Ref. No. 670-68 in this category) has, in three phases extending over 12 years, produced PPP estimates for 34 countries and laid the foundation for developing a worldwide system of real income comparisons. During Phase IV, ending in 1984, the ICP expects to extend coverage to over 60 countries.

The amount of time and resources required for a full-scale comparison of the ICP type is so large that a system of comparison covering all countries of the world is regarded as infeasible. Attempts have been made to use shortcut methods that seek to predict real incomes on the basis of some physical or monetary indicators. The World Bank has also been funding research in this direction—for example, through the research project "Real Product and World Income Distribution" (Ref. No. 671-87 in this category). But shortcut estimates, although good on the average, are found to have unacceptably large residual errors for individual countries. It is now apparent that in order to succeed in developing a truly universal system of real income comparisons, a reduced information method must be found that will produce real income comparisons quickly and cheaply with much less than the full set of price and expenditure information that is required by the ICP.

This research project is designed to investigate various approaches to reduced information estimates, with a view to finding one that will enable the ICP at the United Nations to extend real income comparisons to countries not covered by the full-scale ICP work and to develop annual comparisons for interbenchmark years for the countries covered by the benchmark study. Three approaches will be investigated:

1. Working with data regularly collected by national statistical organizations for their published price indices.
2. Selecting a small sample of prices based on the judgment of experts.
3. Determining analytically (for example, with multiple regression) the best subset of items that will predict the PPPs at various levels of gross domestic product aggregation.

These data will be collected in a sample of countries and the results will be compared with those produced by the ICP Phase IV benchmark study of the ICP. In Asia, India and Indonesia, and in Africa, Kenya, Nigeria, Tanzania, and Zimbabwe will be directly surveyed by the World Bank. Four Central American countries—Costa Rica, Dominican Republic, Guatemala, and Panama—will be surveyed by consultants in Guatemala. The European Economic Community has agreed to provide data for Morocco, Senegal, and Tunisia. Data for all these countries will be processed at the World Bank.

The principal output of the project will be a report on reduced information methodology and estimates for the sample of countries, and two reports on the integration of reduced information results with other regional and global estimates.

Responsibility: Economic Analysis and Projections Department —Sultan Ahmad, in collaboration with Professors Irving Kravis, Alan Heston, and Robert Summers of the University of Pennsylvania, and the Centro de Estudios Centroamericanos de Integración y Desarrollo (ECID), Guatemala.

Completion date: September 1983; the completion report is in process.

Reports

Ahmad, Sultan. "Approaches to Purchasing Power Parity Comparisons Using Shortcuts and Reduced Information." World Bank Staff Working Paper No. 418, September 1980.

_____. "Seminar on Appraisal of ICP Results for World Bank Application—Summary of Proceedings." Comparative Analysis and Data Division Working Paper No. 1983-1. The World Bank: Economic Analysis and Projections Department, 1983.

_____. "Shortcut Methods of International Comparisons of Real Product and Purchasing Power of Currencies." Ph.D. dissertation. Philadelphia: University of Pennsylvania, 1978.

Development of a SAM Basis for Planning and Modeling in Egypt

Ref. No. 672-25A

The Egyptian economy is going through a period of profound structural change requiring careful economic management. Consequently, there is a pressing need to put the process of decision-making on a sound factual basis. This project is intended to fulfill this need for the Government of the Arab Republic of Egypt both directly and through a collaborative effort with the Development Research and Technical Planning Center (DRTPC) of Cairo University. It aims at strengthening the capacity of the DRTPC to build social accounting matrices (SAMs) and to develop and maintain SAM-based models for development planning.

The major issues facing the Egyptian economy in the 1980s relate to (1) income distribution, (2) pricing policies, (3) inflation, (4) mobilization of resources, and (5) allocation of investments. The identification of the data and the choice of disaggregations are designed to shed light on these issues. In gathering and organizing the data, the problem is that reliable information is available only for time periods several years in the past. However, in order to be relevant for policymakers, it is necessary to have access to the most up-to-date data sources.

The project is designed in two phases. The first one focused on building the data base and consolidating it in a SAM framework. Three SAMs of different levels of disaggregation were completed. The second phase of the project is concerned with the development of economywide models using the SAM as their data base, including the MISR-1 model, a relatively aggregated model focusing on demand management issues; the MISR-2 model that is designed to analyze pricing policies; and the MISR-3 model that attempts to capture instruments of monetary policy. The three models are at different stages of development. MISR-1 and

MISR-2 are already implemented, while only the framework of MISR-3 is specified. The three models are formulated according to a "transactions-value" approach, which integrates the data base and algebraic formulation of the model in a SAM framework. This approach is also being used in "The Development and Extension of Macromodeling in Relation to Thailand" (Ref. No. 672-47 in this category).

Responsibility: Development Research Department—F. Graham Pyatt and Wafik Grais, with staff participation of Arne Drud and Boris Pleskovic; *Europe, Middle East, and North Africa Programs Department*—Amarendra Bhattacharya and Sadiq Ahmed; *Industry Department*—Kemal Dervis; in collaboration with Amr Mohieldin at the Development Research and Technical Planning Center (DRTPC), Cairo University.

Completion date: December 1983.

Reports

Bhattacharya, A., and Grais, W. "A Modelling Framework for Macroeconomic Management of a Regulated Economy." Mimeo. The World Bank: Development Research Department, 1982.

Crosswell, M., and Pleskovic, B. "Social Accounting Matrices for Egypt: Outlines and Suggestions for Disaggregation of Individual Accounts." The World Bank: Development Research Department, May 1981.

Mohieldin, Amr, *et al.* "Social Accounting Matrices for Egypt." Mimeo. Cairo: Development Research and Technical Planning Center (DRTPC), Cairo University, 1983.

Multisector and Macroeconomic Models of Structural Adjustment in Yugoslavia

Ref. No. 672-26A

This project has two objectives. The first, now completed, is the construction of a computable general equilibrium (CGE) model of the Yugoslav economy designed to analyze issues of trade and industrial policy and to trace the implications for different sectors of alternative adjustment strategies over the medium term. The second objective, still in progress, is to extend the CGE modeling framework to include variables and phenomena typically handled only by macroeconomic models.

The model applied to Yugoslavia in the first phase of the project was based on an earlier model of Turkey (see Vinod Dubey, Shakil Faruqi, et al., *Turkey: Policies and Prospects for Growth*, A World Bank Country Study, March 1980, Chapter 7) and was used as part of a review of Yugoslavia's new Five-Year Plan (1981–85), carried out by the Europe, Middle East, and North Africa Country Programs Department I of the World Bank. It has also been used to generate projections and to conduct experiments on the economic outlook of Yugoslavia until 1990. The major new conceptual work in the first phase was the specification of institutional and behavioral relationships appropriate for the Yugoslav economy. The modeling technology is now being transferred to the Europe, Middle East, and North Africa Regional Office for continuing policy work. The model has also been transferred to the Federal Planning Institute in Yugoslavia where a week-long seminar was given in May 1983 to various researchers and representatives of government institutes at the federal and state levels.

CGE models have become increasingly popular because they are able to capture the responses of decentralized decisionmakers to policy actions that change the structure of incentives in both product and factor markets. At their present state of development, however, they do not adequately treat macroeconomic phenomena, such as inflation, or capture the conflict between policies to influence growth and structural change in the medium term and policies to achieve macroeconomic stabilization in the short term. Macroeconomic models, by contrast, emphasize short-run adjustments and demand management, taking an aggregate view and generally neglecting problems of supply and the structure of production.

The second phase of this project aims at breaking new ground by incorporating variables, policies, and processes that are common in macroeconomic models into the multisectoral structure of a CGE model. It is intended to explore the theoretical and empirical problems of integrating the two sets of policy concerns within a unified modeling framework. Substantively, the application to Yugoslavia is aimed at improving understanding of both equilibrium and disequilibrium processes at work in a country undergoing structural adjustment to internal and external shocks. Though Yugoslavia's economic institutions are not those of a typical developing country, the underlying economic processes at work and the interactions between macroeconomic and structural variables are fundamentally similar to those characteristic of other semi-industrial countries. Current work is focusing on rigidities in the labor market and firms' decisions about employment and capacity utilization. Special attention is being devoted to inflation and equilibrium in the flow of capital funds.

The second phase of the project is being undertaken jointly with two Yugoslav research institutes. The goal is to transfer the modeling technology to these and other research institutes so that it can be used for future policy analysis within the country and to draw on the experience and skills of local researchers.

Responsibility: Development Research Department and Europe, Middle East, and North Africa Country Programs Department I— Sherman Robinson (on leave at the University of California at Berkeley) and Suman Bery, respectively, in collaboration with Laura Tyson, University of California at Berkeley; Lovro Pfafjar, Institute of Economic Research, Ljubljana (Yugoslavia); and Joze Menzinger, Economic Institute of the Law Faculty, Ljubljana (Yugoslavia).

Completion date: July 1984.

Reports

Ginsburgh, V., and Robinson, S. "Equilibrium and Prices in Multisector Models." Development Strategy Division Working Paper No. 82-2 (revised). The World Bank: Development Research Department, August 1983.

Robinson, S. "Real and Nominal Flows in a Computable General Equilbrium (CGE) Model." Paper presented at the 4th IFAC/IFORS Conference on the Modeling and Control of National Economies, Washington, D.C., June 17–18, 1983.

Robinson, S., and Tyson, L. D. "A Computable General Equilibrium Model for Yugoslavia: Summary Description and Equations." Mimeo. The World Bank: Development Research Department, May 1982.

————. "Foreign Trade, Resource Allocation, and Structural Adjustment in Yugoslavia: 1976–80." Mimeo. The World Bank: Development Research Department, September 1983.

————. "Modeling Structural Adjustment: Micro and Macro Elements in a General Equilibrium Framework." In H. Scarf and J.

Shoven (eds.), *Applied General Equilibrium Analysis*. Cambridge (United Kingdom): Cambridge University Press (forthcoming).

Development of Social Accounts and Models for the Cyprus Five Year Plan

Ref. No. 672-38A

Under this project, the World Bank has been collaborating with the Cyprus Planning Bureau in constructing a macroeconomic framework and its associated data base for the Five-Year Development Plan for 1982–86. The project comprises two principal pieces of analysis. First, a dynamic semi-input-output model was used to examine the consistency and feasibility of medium-term economic plans for the Republic of Cyprus and to measure their implications for certain target variables. The five-year plan, as initially formulated, required a greater number of skilled workers than would be available throughout the plan period and more productive capacity than anticipated during the earlier years of the plan. It was modified, upon the advice of World Bank staff, to feature a slight reduction in the overall growth of gross domestic product (GDP) and less emphasis on capital-intensive industries based on highly skilled labor components.

Second, a dynamic linear programming model is being used to determine the optimal mix of economywide outputs over a fifteen-year period and the levels of foreign borrowing required to sustain this growth and to derive a complete set of shadow prices for project evaluation. Preliminary results indicate that a four percent rate of growth of GDP is optimal, although trade-offs between it and the debt-service ratio implicit in such a growth rate are subject to policy evaluation. Moreover, the shadow prices fluctuate considerably over the model's time period, which suggests that the timing of investment projects is a crucial element in the planning process.

Responsibility: Development Research Department—Clive L. G. Bell, and *Europe, Middle East, and North Africa Programs Department II*—Heinz B. Bachman, in collaboration with Shantayanan Devarajan, Harvard University (consultant).

Completion date: June 1984.

Reports

Bell, C. L. G., and Devarajan, S. "Appraising Development Plans for a Small, Open Economy." Paper presented at the 4th IFAC/IFORS Conference on the Modelling and Control of National Economies, Washington, D.C., June 17–19, 1983 (forthcoming in the *Proceedings*).
————. "Shadow Prices for Project Evaluation under Alternative Macroeconomic Specifications." John F. Kennedy School of Government Discussion Paper Series No. 108D. Cambridge (Massachusetts): Harvard University, September 1981. Also in *Quarterly Journal of Economics* (forthcoming).

The Development and Extension of Macromodeling in Relation to Thailand

Ref. No. 672-47

This project has two main objectives. The first is to develop an economywide framework for structural adjustment analysis for Thailand which would be available to the government and to the World Bank. The second objective is to enhance the modeling capacity of the Bank.

The first objective has lead to the joint development by the National Economic and Social Development Board (NESDB) of Thailand and by the Bank of an economywide general equilibrium model, focused on the issue of structural adjustment in production and trade patterns. This model (the SIAM model of Thailand) has the standard features of multisectoral general equilibrium models, yet it goes well beyond these models in that it takes into account the dualistic feature of the economy (formal-informal activities) and existing price rigidities—in particular, the regulated prices of energy. Formal activities, which face fixed wages and are investment driven, behave in a Keynesian way, while informal activities with flexible wages and financial constraints behave neoclassically. The two types of activities are interlinked via the supply of goods and services, income generation, distribution and consumption, as well as at the macroeconomic level. The model is now in use in Bangkok and Washington. Four parallel studies, whose purpose is to provide a better understanding of the behavior embedded in the model and to address issues of structural adjustment not covered by the model, are being conducted on (1) consumption patterns, (2) the behavior of the trade balance and the current account deficit, (3) investment savings and crowding out, and (4) the employment consequences of structural adjustment.

The second objective of enhancing the Bank's modeling capacity is leading to a systematic approach for developing and implementing economywide models. This "transactions-value" approach integrates the data base and algebraic formulation of the model in a social accounting matrix (SAM) framework. A laboratory version of software capable of handling a large class of models (from simple one-sector macroeconomic to economywide general-equilibrium models) has been developed and is now in use.

Responsibility: Development Research Department—Wafik M. Grais and Arne Drud; *Economic Analysis and Projections Department*—John D. Shilling; and *East Asia and Pacific Regional Office* —Dusan Vujovic, in collaboration with Phisit Pakkasem and Piyasawasti Amranand of the National Economic and Social Development Board of Thailand.

Completion date: December 1983.

Reports

Amranand, P., and Grais, W. "The SIAM-2 Model of Thailand." Paper presented at the Conference on Macroeconomic Management of the Thai Economy, Pattaya (Thailand), June 24–25, 1983.

Decaluwe, B., and Grais, W. "La méthode TV pour la construction de modèles empiriques d'équilibre général." Mimeo. The World Bank: Development Research Department, 1983.

Drud, A.; Grais, W.; and Pyatt, G. "The Transaction-Values Approach: A Systematic Way for Implementing and Solving Economywide Models." Paper presented at the 4th IFAC/IFORS Conference on The Modelling and Control of National Economies, Washington, D.C., June 17–18, 1983.

Development Paths for Oil Exporters: A Long-Run Macroeconomic Analysis

Ref. No. 672-49

This research project addresses the longer-run development options and problems facing the "capital deficit" oil-exporting

economies. Included in this group are: Algeria, Ecuador, the Arab
Republic of Egypt, Indonesia, Islamic Republic of Iran, Mexico,
Nigeria, Trinidad and Tobago, and Venezuela. Notwithstanding
their different structural and institutional features, it is easy to
discern a strong central theme of common concern: how to use oil
revenues that may be available only for a limited period to
promote sustained growth with acceptable distributional characteristics?

The recent experience of industrial, as well as of developing oil
exporters, suggests that to use mineral rents productively is not
easy, despite the central role played by a rich and diversified
natural resource base in the development of a number of economies. With limited linkages between a key rent-producing export
sector and the domestic economy, the problem faced by mineral
exporters is not unlike that of absorbing large, and possibly
volatile, capital inflows. Short-run market signals affected by a
rapid increase in absorption out of oil windfalls may provide an
indication to producers of investment patterns that are inappropri-
ate to longer-run developmental objectives. Appreciation of real
exchange rates, stagnant agriculture, slow growth of manufacturing, the crowding-out of the private by the public sector, and a
trend to dualism are all classic symptoms of the oil-economy
syndrome, although such effects are not inevitable.

Clearly, the rate at which oil revenues are spent, as well as the
spending pattern decided on by government, will influence the
extent to which alternative productive sectors are developed and
experience is accumulated to assist in raising productivity. Efficient, nonoil tradeable sectors are needed to supplement and
eventually replace declining oil revenues as a source of foreign
exchange and public revenue. The initial spending decisions,
which are essentially political rather than determined by market
forces, will also have a substantial impact on income distribution
and the extent to which the economy develops along dualistic
lines.

Theoretical and empirical analysis of these issues for oil exporters is of relatively recent vintage, although a considerable literature exists on the "export-enclave" economy. Most research in the
field of natural resources focuses on the fact that the resources are
exhaustible, rather than on the impact of varying resource rents on
the rest of a producing economy. In addition, while analyses of
individual producer countries naturally include the role of the oil
sector, cross country analysis has been limited.

The present research project has two components. The objective of the first, comparative part is to document, analyze, and compare the dynamic options selected by several oil exporters and the consequences for their nonoil economies. As comparators, the experience of developed oil exporters—Norway and the United Kingdom—will also be included. The point of departure in the comparative analysis is a government's decision on how to spend its revenues. This produces multiplier effects, real exchange rate and price changes, and expansion of domestic production capacity that will affect the evolution of the rest of the economy. The central difficulty—strengthening nonoil tradeable sectors in the face of a strong pull to use resources for the construction and service sectors—is common and widely acknowledged in oil-exporting economies concerned about undue dependence on a single, exhaustible source of foreign exchange. Yet, exporting countries have adopted quite divergent development strategies and sectoral priorities. Comparative analysis is a continuing exercise over the horizon of the project, extending the study undertaken by Alan H. Gelb, listed below. An element of comparative political analysis is included in this part of the study, which also will draw on the experience of the World Bank's country economists.

The second component of the project is to model formally the impact of key policy options for a particular country and to assess the development paths resulting from such choices. In addition to choices involving the selection of extraction rates and total expenditures, sectoral emphasis and trade policies are being addressed. There are some important trade-offs here. If, for example, spending is heavily directed toward infrastructure, domestic inflation is likely, at least for a period, to lead to appreciation of the real exchange rate and the squeezing-out of private manufacturing. An import-intensive investment strategy will place less stress on the domestic economy but reduce the multiplier effects of oil spending. The analysis is comparative-dynamic rather than static. Such an exercise is being undertaken for Indonesia, one of the poorest of the oil exporters, and includes the simulation of hypothetical alternative paths over a time frame of twenty years. Because of the common experience and the broad underlying problems, the modeling exercise has relevance for other oil exporters. At the same time, the comparative element will prevent research from focusing too exclusively on the special features of one country.

The research is organized in three stages. In the first stage, the data base has been set up and analyzed, and arrangements for a set of country studies are in progress. The second stage covers tuning and simulation of the model. During this stage the comparative analysis will proceed in parallel with formal modeling. In the third stage, the two components of research will be completed and written up.

Responsibility: Development Research Department—Alan H. Gelb. A number of consultants are involved in comparative analysis and data collection.

Completion date: July 1984.

Reports

Bienen, Henry. "Oil Revenues and Policy Choices in Nigeria." World Bank Staff Working Paper No. 592, May 1983.

Bowden, Roger, and Gelb, Alan H. "Testing Stylised Facts: An Application of Random Parameters Estimation." Development Strategy Division Working Paper No. 82-3. The World Bank: Development Research Department, June 1982.

Downey, Roger J.; Keuning, Steven; et al. "An Indonesian SAM." Development Strategy Division Working Paper No. 83-5. The World Bank: Development Research Department, June 1983.

Gelb, Alan H. "Capital-Importing Oil Exporters: Adjustment Issues and Policy Choice." World Bank Staff Working Paper No. 475, August 1981.

Taxation and Pricing Policies in Rural and Urban Korea

Ref. No. 672-61

Public intervention in agriculture in the developing world has stimulated much research. Theoretical advances have greatly increased understanding of the likely consequences of agricultural policies, but the analytical approaches used in research have been difficult to duplicate in practical work. The broad goal of the present study is to adapt and apply up-to-date analytical techniques to typical kinds of policy problems on which the World Bank's regional economists are asked to advise.

Since agriculture is so important to the economies of most developing countries, public intervention in agriculture can result in large changes in both the allocation of resources and the distribution of income. Such interventions serve a variety of goals, including correcting market failures, raising revenue, redistributing income, improving nutrition, or achieving national self-sufficiency in particular commodities. They include measures to influence input or product prices, quantitative controls, and the public provision of goods and services. The creation of wedges between rural and urban prices is a conspicuous and common policy; so is the subsidization or taxation of agricultural commodities. The public expenditure occasioned by these policies has often become burdensome, especially in countries that are poor in resources.

This study seeks to provide a methodology that can be used to evaluate the effects of alternative pricing policies on the various public objectives specified above. The study will draw on two bodies of previous research. The first is the considerable amount of theoretical empirical work sponsored by the Bank on the responses (of households, agricultural producers, and prices) to interventions in agriculture.[1] The second source is the set of modern public finance methodologies in which desirable policy interventions are identified by seeking the maximum increase in aggregate welfare, while meeting the public budget constraint and other exogenously specified requirements.[2]

The methodology is used to analyze selected policies in the Republic of Korea. The Korean problem to be analyzed is the following. With its past policy on rice the Government of Korea tried to fulfill three objectives: (1) to achieve self-sufficiency in rice production; (2) to maintain rural incomes in parity with urban incomes; and (3) to keep the price of rice low in the cities in order to restrain workers' demands for wage increases. Similar objectives applied to barley.

---

[1] See, for example, Howard N. Barnum and Lyn Squire, A Model of an Agricultural Household: Theory and Evidence (Baltimore and London: The Johns Hopkins University Press, 1980), and C. Ahn, I. J. Singh, and L. Squire, "A Model of an Agricultural Household in a Multi-Crop Economy: The Case of Korea," Review of Economics and Statistics, vol. LXIII, no. 4 (November 1981):520–25.

[2] See A. Atkinson and J. E. Stiglitz, Lectures on Public Economics (Maidenhead, United Kingdom: McGraw-Hill, 1980), Chapters 12, 13, 15.

In order to fulfill these objectives, the government generated wedges between the rural prices and urban prices of rice and barley through its Grain Management Fund. These wedges, which constitute price support to farmers and subsidies to urban consumers, generate large deficits. The subsidized price of rice paid by urban consumers is substantially higher than the world price of rice. In addition, fertilizers are produced domestically at a guaranteed price significantly higher than international prices. The government subsidizes the cost of fertilizer to farmers through the country's Fertilizer Fund, but the input price is also above the international price. The Korean government has decided to reduce the amount of resources spent on its Grain Management Fund and Fertilizer Fund, with the aim of eliminating them in 1986.

The study developed a methodology and assessed quantitatively the implications of different pricing policies aimed at reducing the public deficit on production and consumption of rice and barley; real income distribution, in both the rural and urban sectors; import levels of rice; self-sufficiency in rice; and the public budget.

The research and policy analysis have been completed. The methodology is currently being applied to other countries with different institutional structures, including African countries where data are scarce. The project's dissemination activities, including the production of publications and making the Korean model accessible to other users, are continuing.

Responsibility: Country Policy Department—Avishay Braverman and Jeffrey S. Hammer, in collaboration with Choong Yong Ahn, Chung Ang University (Republic of Korea); Joseph E. Stiglitz, Princeton University; and Raaj Kumar Sah, Massachusetts Institute of Technology (consultants).

Completion date: June 1984.

Reports

Braverman, A.; Ahn, C. Y.; and Hammer, J. S. "Government Deficit Reduction and Alternative Agricultural Pricing Policies in Korea." Country Policy Department Discussion Paper. The World Bank, August 1983.

Braverman, A.; Sah, R. K.; and Stiglitz, J. E. "The Town versus Country Problem: Optimal Pricing in an Agrarian Economy."

Country Policy Department Discussion Paper. The World Bank, August 1982.

Economic Consequences of the Coffee Boom in East Africa: A Comparative Analysis of Kenya and Tanzania

Ref. No. 672-65

The period 1976–78 witnessed a massive, but temporary, increase in the world price of coffee, a major smallholder cash crop in Kenya and Tanzania. While the economic structure of these two low-income African countries is similar in many respects, the policies they pursued, both before the boom in coffee prices and in response to it, were markedly different. In Tanzania, some 60 percent of the incremental coffee income was taxed away by government, while in Kenya 95 percent of the incremental income went to the smallholder coffee growers. This large, abrupt change in an important price, handled so differently in two countries with comparable economic structures, provides a rare opportunity for a quantitative analysis of a set of micro and macro questions that are of fundamental importance to our understanding of the development process, especially in the low-income and resource-poor countries of sub-Saharan Africa. The results of the analysis should have direct policy relevance to the design of government tax and expenditure policies, agricultural pricing, and projects and programs in agriculture in developing countries.

Using the "experiment" of the coffee boom and detailed modeling of the two economies, the research has the following principal objectives:

1. To evaluate alternative policies for alleviating rural poverty in East African economies, with particular emphasis on the relative efficacy of policies for the pricing of export crops and of public expenditures.
2. To attempt to garner lessons for optimal domestic policy responses to sharp, temporary changes in the world price of a major agricultural export crop, with particular attention to incorporating, in the assessment, both the temporary and the lasting consequences to the economy of the ephemeral price change.
3. To augment the quantitative analytical bases for studyingand evaluating economic structures and policies in these two

East African economies. The analytical frameworks emerging from this research could be deployed to explore a rich variety of policy simulations in the course of dialogue between the World Bank and its client countries in general, and in the context of structural adjusment operations, in particular.

The basic approach will be to build on a substantial body of research on these economies. Existing economywide models for the two countries will serve as starting points. In order to pursue the principal objectives of the research and utilize the new micro survey data sets that have emerged since the earlier models were constructed, the proposed study will:

1. Devote a major effort to modeling smallholder agriculture, using the Barnum-Squire approach and extending it to incorporate the asset-behavior of farm households and the role of remittances from urban households in facilitating the diffusion of agricultural innovation. A modest amount of sample information on smallholder coffee growers will also be gathered.

2. Specify and estimate detailed fiscal "modules," which attempt to endogenize government tax and expenditure behavior (and their economic consequences) as much as possible.

3. Integrate both these major "modules" into a computable general equilibrium framework which takes account of various indirect and feedback effects of the policy shifts (and exogenous shocks) whose consequences are to be explored.

4. Conduct a number of simulations to gauge the effects on growth and income distribution of alternative policy thrusts and responses (including exploring alternative responses to the coffee price boom) and, thus, to obtain some guidance on the principal issues motivating this research.

Responsibility: Eastern Africa Country Programs Department —David G. Greene and Robert Liebenthal. Principal researchers are Paul Collier, Keble College and the Institute of Economics and Statistics, Oxford University; David L. Bevan, St. John's College, Oxford; Arne Bigsten, Gothenberg University (Sweden); and Jan Gunning, Free University, Amsterdam (the Netherlands).

Completion date: June 1984.

Econometric Modeling of Investment and Saving in Korea

Ref. No. 672-66

With the increasing complexity of economic decisionmaking in industrial economies, a growing reliance on macro models has emerged. In such models, policymakers have found a useful tool for analyzing the effects of government actions and understanding the dynamics of the economic system. The inavailability of suitable data and the limited size of the formal market economy in many developing countries previously restrained the spread of these techniques, but in the past decade it has become desirable and possible to make econometric tools an integral part of the decision-making process in a number of developing countries. Statistical information has improved in quality and abundance; most economic activities are within the ambit of the market system and can be influenced by conventional monetary and fiscal policies; the government is less inclined to use direct controls to regulate the economy; and macropolicies are systematically used to maintain growth, minimize cyclical fluctuations, and curb inflation.

In the case of the Republic of Korea which was selected for the purposes of this research, the above conditions apply. The government has already accumulated some experience in the area of macromodeling, and World Bank economic and sector work for the country necessitates the use of more sophisticated analytical techniques. The objectives of the project are threefold: (1) to describe the pattern of investment in the manufacturing sector over the past decade and, with the aid of econometric models, to isolate the principal determinants of investment at the aggregate as well as the subsectoral levels; (2) to attempt to explain savings behavior in Korea by using theories and econometric techniques successfully applied in developed countries; and (3) to estimate some of the major structural parameters of the economy by way of a model based on the neo-Keynesian methodology.

These exercises can be seen as a small contribution towards putting macropolicymaking on a more rigourous footing. They provide an opportunity for testing the applicability of certain hypotheses, tailored primarily to the institutional circumstances of the United States in the Korean context. They should bring into sharper focus those remaining data limitations that are likely to interfere with the effective deployment of econometric models.

Responsibility: East Asia and Pacific Country Programs Department—Shahid Yusuf, in collaboration with R. Kyle Peters, Jr. of the East Asia and Pacific Regional Office and Sayeed Sadeq (consultant).

Completion date: December 1983.

Tax and Contractual Arrangements for Exploiting Natural Resources

Ref. No. 672-71

The long-term rise in oil prices and the need to adjust to it has stimulated interest in three broad areas of research at the World Bank: domestic and external macroeconomic issues, energy demand, and energy supply. Several projects on macroeconomic issues have recently been started. Among them are studies of Egypt (Ref. No. 672-25A), Thailand (Ref. No. 672-47), and Yugoslavia (Ref. No. 672-26A), all in this category; of development options in oil-exporting countries (Ref. No. 672-49 in this category); and of adjustment in oil-importing countries (Ref. No. 672-74 in category 6—Energy). In the demand area, the World Bank's Economic Analysis and Projections Department is starting work on a minimum standard model of energy demand (Ref. No. 672-63 in category 6—Energy). The present project addresses microeconomic issues related to oil supply. Its findings will also be relevant for other nonrenewable natural resources.

A vast majority of developing countries depends on imported oil. Among these are 64 countries, including some of the poorest, that depend on imports for more than 75 percent of their commercial supplies. It is vitally important for these countries to attract foreign companies to explore for oil. But it is not enough merely to attract these companies, for if no oil passes to the government or no government revenues are generated, the problem is not alleviated. It is important for these countries to provide adequate incentives to foreign companies in a way that ensures that as much benefit (or rent) accrues to the government as possible.

As stated in 1979, "Most of these (developing) countries need advice in framing or amending legislation relating to the energy sector, or in adapting policies and procedures that would improve the prospects of cooperation with foreign prospecting and production organizations."[3] In the area of natural resources generally, the Bank has long been interested in issues related to exploration, extraction, and processing, especially in many African and other small economies where mining is the dominant sector and the main source of export earnings and budgetary revenues.

The ultimate objective is to design policies for taxes and contracts that will provide sufficient incentives to attract foreign firms to explore for and produce exhaustible natural resources in developing countries, while maintaining as much of the rent for the producing country as possible. This search for optimal policies will also take account of the risks borne by the contracting parties. Inherent in the process of exploration for a natural resource in a given tract of land is the possibility of a change in the value that the firm and the government assign to the tract before and after exploration. This raises the possibility that one of the parties may want to change the terms of the contract, once exploration is completed, if the penalties for doing so are small. Such possible changes include expropriation by the government or the firm abandoning the enterprise after some initial exploration. Tax and contract terms can be designed to minimize such risks, and, consequently, to increase the (ex ante) expected benefits to both parties. Also to be taken into account are imperfections in the market for natural resources and in the knowledge available to contracting parties.

The research builds on two major bodies of work. One relates to the analysis and simulation of different forms of contract and bidding procedures in the context of uncertainty about the amount and value of the resource stock; most of this work has been done in the context of offshore leasing by the United States (Outer Continental Shelf). The other is concerned with the effect of the various taxes on the extraction of a fixed stock of a natural resource, and the simulation of the development expenditures and production profiles that firms adopt under different conditions. Again, much of this analysis refers to conditions in the developed countries.

The first phase of the research will concentrate on simulating the forms of taxation and contracts that are currently recommended, using available simulation models, including that in use

---

[3] The World Bank, "A Program to Accelerate Petroleum Production in the Developing Countries," 1979, p. 10.

by the staff of the Bank's Energy Department. The results from this analysis will be used to develop a more efficient framework for analysis that would be usable by the Bank's project staff charged with advising on taxes and contracts. In the course of the research, a typology of countries will be constructed, classified by characteristics such as the energy balance, the degree of riskiness versus possible returns as seen by extraction firms, and the degree and success of past exploration activity. Particular attention will be given to countries (many of them in sub-Saharan Africa) with little activity in exploration or production in the past.

Responsibility: Development Research Department—Arvind Virmani.

Completion date: December 1983.

Evaluation and Estimation of National Accounts Statistics of Centrally Planned Economies

Ref. No. 672-73

Centrally planned economies (CPEs) account for about one-third of the world's population and one-fifth of its output. In view of their importance in the world economy, they need to be included in international comparative studies. The World Bank has included them in several documents with universal coverage, such as the *World Development Indicators*. Further, several CPEs are members of the Bank (China, Hungary, Lao People's Democratic Republic, Romania, Viet Nam, and Yugoslavia). In order to analyze these economies, the Bank's staff needs to understand their macroeconomic accounting frameworks and price systems.

The national accounts of the CPEs are based on the concept of net material product, which differs from the concept of gross national product (GNP) used in market economies. Prices in CPEs are generally set administratively and, to a considerable extent, are independent of the scarcity of goods and services. For all aspects of the Bank's work mentioned above, it is necessary to derive GNP levels and growth rates from country data that are based on the concept of net material product.

At present, the Bank lacks sufficient understanding of the national accounting concepts being used in CPEs and has, therefore, had to use a fairly rough and mechanical methodology for translating the statistics based on them into concepts that are comparable with the United Nations System of National Accounts. Though the statistical offices of several centrally planned economies have carried out and published illustrative computations of GNP, there is no systematic effort among CPEs, or between CPEs and any international organization, to produce a consistent set of GNP figures in dollars for these countries.

The project is designed primarily to identify the best methods for computing the levels and growth rates of GNP of selected centrally planned economies. The study will concentrate on eight countries—Bulgaria, Cuba, Czechoslovakia, the German Democratic Republic, Hungary, Poland, Romania, and the USSR.

Comprehensive and internationally comparable data will be produced on the size of GNP, on the appropriate factors for converting income figures in national currencies into U.S. dollars, and on growth rates. The project should substantially advance understanding of the national accounts, development history, and development plans of CPEs.

Responsibility: Economic Analysis and Projections Department —Sang E. Lee. The principal researcher is Professor Paul Marer, Indiana University.

Completion date: The work program was completed in May 1983; the completion report is in process.

Reports

"Evaluation and Estimation of National Accounts Statistics of Selected Centrally Planned Economies." Comparative Analysis and Data Division Working Paper No. 1983-2. The World Bank: Economic Analysis and Projections Department, July 1983. Vol. 1 (Summary) by P. Marer. Vol. 2 (Exchange Rate and Country Studies) includes the following:

Wolf, T. A. "Exchange Rates, Foreign Trade Accounting and Purchasing Power Parity for Centrally Planned Economies."
van Brabant, J. M. "Exchange Rates in Eastern Europe— Types, Derivation and Application."
Singh, S., and Park, J. "National Accounts Statistics and Exchange Rates in Bulgaria."
Levcik, F., and Havlik, P. "GDP of Czechoslovakia."
Mesa-Lago, C., and Perez-Lopez, J. "Study of Cuba's MPS, Its Conversion to SNA and Estimation of GDP/capita and Growth Rates."

Collier, I. L. "Review of National Accounts Data of German Democratic Republic and Estimation of Its Gross Domestic Products and Growth Rates."

Fallenbuchl, Z. M. "Derivation of Polish Gross National Products and Growth Rates."

Hewett, E. A. "Hungarian Gross National Product—Important Issues for Comparative Research."

Jackson, M. R. "Romanian National Accounts Statistics and Estimation of Its Gross Domestic Products and Growth Rates."

Campbell, R. W. "The Conversion of Soviet National Income Data to SNA Concepts in Dollars and Estimation of Growth Rates."

Cross-Country Analysis of Growth in Sub-Saharan Africa

Ref. No. 672-75

The failure of growth in agriculture, in particular, and exports, in general, are increasingly viewed by many economists both as the proximate cause of stagnation in sub-Saharan Africa and as the result of incorrect government policies. Yet, the conviction is widespread among African thinkers and leaders that most stagnation is a result of decreasing prices of African exports or as a consequence of exploitation by the developed countries which need to maintain Africa as a source of primary commodities and of profits for transnational firms. In this perspective, development requires delinking from the world economy to reduce a detrimental dependency. Still others emphasize variables such as drought and civil strife as causes of stagnation. Such wide disparity in outlook suggests that study of just what has determined growth in Africa would be useful.

Three sets of variables appear important in such a study: (1) the effects of the external economic environment (for example, the terms of trade and the nature of African exports); (2) important noneconomic variables of the character of force majeure (civil strife, refugee movements, droughts); and (3) policy variables, that is those over which the African governments have some control, such as exports, basic prices, and investment and its structure. An analysis based on these variables, and using cross-country regressions, could develop well-grounded conclusions about the interactions of domestic policy and other important variables in affecting

African growth. The results could, therefore, be useful in the dialogue between the World Bank and African governments concerning, inter alia, the role of the external environment, pricing for foreign exchange, and pricing in agriculture.

The study uses econometric analysis in an attempt to estimate the importance of environmental and policy variables as contributing to the stagnation of output growth in sub-Saharan Africa. Environmental variables include weather, the terms of trade, international interest rates, foreign aid, civil strife, refugee flows, and economic conditions in nearby labor-importing states (for example, Ivory Coast, Nigeria, South Africa, and the Middle Eastern countries of the Persian Gulf). Policy variables under examination are those indicating the nature and degree of government intervention in international trade, intervention in domestic product and factor markets, and allocation of public expenditures. For example, they might include the degree of overvaluation, wage dualism, and distortion in interest rates. The environmental and policy variables in the study are treated as exogenous in a multi-equation structural model of the growth process. Econometric equations which link growth outcomes directly to these exogenous variables are valid reduced-form specifications that can be estimated consistently by single equation techniques. The three-phase research study encompasses:

1. Identification of superior and inferior national policy performance using a partial reduced-form model to analyze the impact of environmental variables alone.
2. Estimation of a "balanced" reduced-form model that will be a full exercise in reduced-form growth accounting, with all relevant variables included in the estimating equations.
3. Structural modeling to identify and estimate key structural relationships.

The advantage of the three-phase approach outlined above is that it throws into sharp relief the impact of the exogenous variables which are of primary interest in the debate over the sources of stagnation in sub-Saharan Africa during the 1970s. The reduced-form estimates, however, are only summaries of the total impact of forces flowing through many structural channels. The delineation of these channels in a more detailed model would in itself be extremely useful. The identification and estimation of key structural relationships in the third phase will aid in explaining the reduced-form results to policymakers and provide information about the most promising leverage points in the system.

Much of the work in the first and second phases of the project has been completed and is undergoing revision. A workshop to discuss the preliminary findings was held in August 1983. In general terms, the preliminary results indicate that both the environment—terms of trade, civil strife—and policy are important in explaining African growth in the 1970s. Recommendations from the workshop and results from other research projects in the Bank are being used in the formulation of the third phase, which commenced in the fall of 1983.

Responsibility: Western Africa Regional Office—Jacob Meerman. The research is being undertaken by Professor David R. Wheeler (consultant) of Boston University.

Completion date: September 1984.

Reports

Wheeler, David. "Sources of Stagnation in Sub-Saharan Africa: Summary of Findings." The World Bank, April 1983 (detailed version).
———. "Sources of Stagnation in Sub-Saharan Africa." Second Report. The World Bank, July 1983 (condensed version).

Medium- and Long-Run Issues in Economies with an Exhaustible Resource-Based Traded Sector

Ref. No. 672-77

This project addresses the problem of managing a country where a significant part of the total value of tradable goods produced in the economy comes from the extraction of exhaustible resources. It particularly focuses on those countries where reserves are not so large as to put exhaustion beyond the horizon defined by uncertainty and a reasonable social discount rate, or where there is a significant nonoil traded sector.

The dynamic choices faced by these countries and that will be addressed are (1) how much to save, and (2) how to allocate those savings between the different assets available to the economy: oil in the ground (decumulated via extraction), physical capital (accumulated via investment), and claims on the rest of the world (accumulated via current account surpluses).

This project will try to push the theoretical analysis further in areas where the literature is either unsatisfactory or nonexistent and to implement an applied case study providing quantitative answers for two oil-exporting countries, the Arab Republic of Egypt and Mexico.

On the theoretical side, the project departs from most of the literature on optimal extraction in two aspects. First, the resource is considered a tradable good, with its price given exogenously to the economy, in contrast to the usual emphasis on endogenously determined prices. A significant consequence of this method is to introduce a source of uncertainty that has not been adequately taken into account so far. The second major difference is that it is concerned with an economy containing other traded goods, in addition to oil, and a nontraded sector. Thus, the extraction decision is tied up with the real exchange rate, and the group of problems commonly referred to as "deindustrialization" or "Dutch-disease" is introduced. These problems induce a decline of the nonoil traded-goods sector (manufacturing) under the pressure of real appreciation induced by higher oil revenues. If high revenues are, for practical purposes, expected to last forever, there is no problem: a reallocation of factors towards nontraded goods is the efficient response to the increased availability of traded goods. However, the economies where the traded sector is based on the extraction of exhaustible resources have to face the reality that their reserves (of say, oil) will run out in the future. Their policy should, therefore, be formulated with this, possibly not so distant, event clearly in mind. Thus, for instance, if capital once installed in one sector cannot be used in the other, a forward-looking investment policy should start shifting net investment towards the traded goods sector before the oil runs out.

A further question is related to the infant industry argument. Most oil producers outside the Organisation for Economic Cooperation and Development (OECD) are in the process of starting up a manufacturing sector, a process that may be cut short by the real appreciation caused by the high influx of oil revenues. However, it is in this sector that the effects of learning by doing are thought to be most important. Does the fact that the oil revenues (and then the real exchange rate) are high now, but will be lower in the future, call for more subsidies to the manufacturing sector than would otherwise be the case?

The applied part of this project for Egypt and Mexico consists of the construction of numerical dynamic models capable of quantifying the characteristics of optimal extraction policies, the resulting time pattern of investment and the real exchange rate, and their dependence on the parameters defining social objectives and technical possibilities. For the two countries involved, this information will be useful in discussions of development strategies. In addition, the predicted time paths for the real exchange rate, oil rents, and such variables as the consumption rate of interest can be important inputs in the evaluation of investment projects.

The expected product of this research is a series of papers on some of the theoretical issues, plus the empirical models whose results will be included in the forthcoming reports on Egypt and Mexico. A monograph on the subject will be considered.

Responsibility: Development Research Department—Ricardo M. Martin and Sweder van Wijnbergen. The study on Egypt builds on previous work done by Kemal Dervis (currently of the Industry Department) and will benefit from his active collaboration.

Completion date: December 1983.

Reports

Dervis, K.; Martin, R.; and van Wijnbergen, S. "Shadow Pricing, Foreign Borrowing and Resource Extraction Policies in Egypt." Mimeo. The World Bank: Development Reearch Department, July 6, 1983.

van Wijnbergen, S. "The Dutch Disease: A Disaster After All?" *Economic Journal* (forthcoming, 1984).

————. "Inflation, Employment and the Dutch Disease in Oil Exporting Countries: A Disequilibrium Analysis." *Quarterly Journal of Economics* (forthcoming, 1984).

————. "Optimal Capital Accumulation and the Allocation of Investment between Traded and Non-Traded Sectors in Oil Producing Economies." Mimeo. The World Bank: Development Research Department, November 1982.

A Computable General Equilibrium Model for the Ivory Coast

Ref. No. 672-87A

The purpose of this research application project is to develop a computable general equilibrium (CGE) model of the economy of the Ivory Coast as one of two submodels that would be used to help formulate the key policy trade-offs in the country's process of structural adjustment and transition to an oil economy. The specification of a long-term multisector CGE model will parallel the development of a macroeconometric model for medium-term projections focusing on highly aggregated variables.

CGE models have been applied to various newly industrialized developing countries to analyze the impact of alternative trade adjustment policies (in particular, with respect to exchange rates, tariffs, quantitative import restrictions, and export subsidies) on growth, economic structure, and the distribution of income. Such models have been used as part of World Bank missions to Turkey and Yugoslavia. The current project is closely related to other projects involving those countries—see Ref. No. 672-04 ("Research Dissemination: A Computable General Equilibrium Model of Turkey") and Ref. No. 672-26A ("Multisector and Macroeconomic Models of Structural Adjustment in Yugoslavia") in this category.

This project is part of a joint work program with the Government of the Ivory Coast whose objectives are to broaden the scope of the macropolicy dialogue between the government and the Bank; to prepare the groundwork for analyzing macroeconomic policy issues arising from the emergence of the Ivorian oil sector; to reinforce administrative units responsible for macroeconomic projections within the government; and to develop collaborative arrangements with Ivorian researchers.

The need for such a joint work program has arisen from a number of considerations. The tight foreign exchange situation experienced by the Ivory Coast since the fall in prices of its primary export products has revealed the importance of the link between public investment decisions and the external debt; it has reduced the value and relevance of the government's own plan-budget model—a static input-output model used for short-term projections, which lacks a detailed financial block and specification of flow-of-funds variables. The Ivory Coast is also entering a period of rapid structural change, mainly as a result of the adjustment policies pursued by the government, especially in the industry and agriculture sectors. This structural change will be complicated by the possible emergence of net oil surpluses at the end of the 1980s.

Responsibility: The development of the CGE model for the Ivory Coast will be undertaken with the joint responsibility of the government's Directorate of Planning at the Ministry of Planning and Industry and of the World Bank's *Development Research Department*, Development Strategy Division, and its *Western Africa Programs Department*, Division 2A—Gilles Michel and Michel Noël, respectively. Sherman Robinson, currently on leave at the University of California at Berkeley, codirected the project in its first year and continues as an advisor.

Completion date: December 1983.

Reports

Michel, G., and Noël, M. "The Ivorian Economy and Alternative Trade Regimes." In C. Delgado and W. Zartman (eds.), "The Political Economy of the Ivory Coast." New York: Praeger (forthcoming, 1984).

_____. "Short-Term Responses to Trade and Incentive Policies in the Ivory Coast." Mimeo. The World Bank: Development Research Department, September 1983.

Book on Modern Tax Theory for Developing Countries

Ref. No. 672-92

The World Bank is increasingly called upon to offer policy advice to developing countries. At one extreme, it may recommend substantial tax, tariff, and public enterprise price reforms in the context of structural adjustment lending, while on the other, the Bank is engaged in a more or less continuous policy dialogue with countries at the sectoral and project level, where the social profitability of specific projects may be quite sensitive to sectoral tax, tariff, or pricing reforms. This is particularly true of agricultural projects and is increasingly the case in the energy sector, where a large number of energy pricing studies have been commissioned, either by the Bank or at its behest.

The rapid development of the theory of public finance in the last decade has had a dramatic effect on the way policy interventions are analyzed. The subject is maturing rapidly, empirical applications are becoming more common, and the techniques are beginning to be applied to developing economies. However, while an increasing number of economists have heard of the new approach, very few know whether it is applicable, whether it comes to conclusions that are different from the traditional approach, and whether to take it seriously. The aim is to produce a book that will describe the theory and its relevance to developing countries, demonstrate how it can be used, and raise questions suggested by the theory if it is to be made more useful for policy analysis.

The groundwork for this book was laid at a Workshop on Public Economics in Developing Countries, organized by the Bank's Development Research Department in June 1982. A range of leading writers on Public Economics, many of whom presented papers at the workshop, will prepare chapters for the book which is aimed at the general working economist.

The proposed contents will include: (1) a textbook exposition of the new theory, relating it to the closely allied subject of social cost-benefit analysis; (2) illustrations of the normal application of the theory to economywide tax reform; (3) a definition of the range of the theory's applicability and identification of the key assumptions that are most important in shaping policy advice; (4) application of the theory to sectoral tax reform; and (5) a discussion of taxes affecting factor markets and issues of development policy.

The draft manuscript is expected to be available in March 1984.

Responsibility: Development Research Department—Pradeep K. Mitra, in collaboration with other Bank staff in the department's Public Economics Division and in the Country Programs Department. Principal consultants and coeditors are David M. Newbery, Churchill College, Cambridge University, and N. H. Stern, Warwick University (United Kingdom).

Completion date: July 1984.

Analysis of the Tax Systems in Developing Countries: Applications to Pakistan and Mexico

Ref. No. 673-13

Governments in developing countries face severe revenue constraints and the Bank is becoming more involved in the analysis of measures to increase public revenues. One of the major instruments for raising revenue is the tax system. The problem is to raise additional revenue in a manner consistent with a government's social objectives—with respect to the distribution of income, for example—and with desired levels of production and public expenditure.

The immediate objective of this research is to study the tax systems of Pakistan and Mexico to identify the direction tax reform should take and the most efficient and equitable ways in which to raise extra revenue, as well as to provide information on the working of the current tax system of the sort needed for informed decisionmaking. The more fundamental objective is to develop a methodology of public finance so that similar studies can be undertaken in the future for a wider range of developing countries.

Although much economic theory and most empirical research has tended to treat these issues separately, modern developments in the theory of public finance explicitly link taxation, social objectives, production, and public expenditure. Although the theory has developed rapidly, it has only recently been applied in a systematic way to the analysis of the tax system of a developing country. For the past two years, Professor Nicholas H. Stern of Warwick University (United Kingdom), with the collaboration of Dr. Ehtisham Ahmad, has been conducting a study of the tax systems in India, financed largely by the British Social Science Research Council.

The question the researchers ask is a central and standard one in public finance: how should a government best design its tax system to raise a given revenue or, in its more operational form, how should the government change the present tax system to improve its structure and/or raise more revenue? This research demonstrated that the recent developments in public economics provide an effective framework for answering these questions, and that it was possible to collect and interpret the data required to make the approach operational.

In the extension of this work to Pakistan and Mexico, each country's tax structure will be described in a form useful for policy analysis, which is a major task of considerable interest to the countries and the World Bank, and improvements will be identified, given some specification of each country's objectives. Just as earlier the Bank developed a methodology for social cost-benefit analysis that could be used for project selection in a wide range of countries, it is expected that this methodology can be developed for replication in several other countries.

The study will entail analyses of the impact of indirect taxes on prices (taking account of the taxation of intermediate goods), the implicit tax component in public enterprises, tariffs, personal income tax reforms, and market structure. A number of other research projects, currently under way within the Bank, employ the same methodological framework, including "Book on Modern Tax Theory for Developing Countries" (Ref. No. 672-92 in this category) and "Pricing and Taxing Transport Fuels in Developing Countries" (Ref. No. 672-83 in category 6—Energy).

Responsibility: Development Research Department and *Country Policy Department*—Pradeep K. Mitra and Lyn Squire, respectively, with the previous substantive contribution of David M. Newbery, currently of Churchill College, Cambridge University (United Kingdom), who will continue with the project as a consultant. Other consultants are Nicholas H. Stern, Ehtisham Ahmad, and Jesus Seade, Warwick University (United Kingdom). The British Social Science Research Council is cofunding part of the study.

Completion date: June 1986.

Collaborative Research with China (Phase II)

Ref. No. 673-14

After an initial exploratory phase, now completed, the World Bank and the Institute of Economic Research at the Chinese Academy of Social Sciences have agreed on a program of collaborative research. The program has two parts.

The first part will be an analysis of the system of enterprise guidance in China: the system as it worked in the past, the effect of current reforms, and the likely effect of proposed reforms. The main source of information will be interviews with key personnel in 20 enterprises. Pilot interviews have already been completed.

The second part is concerned with structural change. While studies of other aspects of the Chinese economy are contemplated in the future, during the present phase the emphasis will be on the study of consumption patterns in China in comparison with other developing countries. In parallel, an initial attempt will be made to compare the overall structure of the Chinese economy with other large countries.

Responsibility: East Asia and Pacific Country Programs Department and *Development Research Department*—Edwin R. Lim and Gregory K. Ingram, respectively. For the Chinese Academy of Social Sciences, overall supervision of the program is being provided by Dong Furen, Deputy Director of the Institute of Economics. Gene Tidrick and William Byrd, of the East Asia and Pacific Country Programs Department, together with Chen Jiyuan and others of the Institute of Economic Research, are the principal researchers on enterprise guidance, while Benjamin King (consultant), Shujiro Urata, and Jacob Van Der Gaag of the Development Research Department, together with Li Xuezeng and others of the Institute of Economic Research, are the principal researchers on structural change.

Relative Efficiency of Public and Private Expenditures on Social Services in Chile (Small Study)

Ref. No. 673-21

As a complement to a larger-scale study of the incidence of public expenditure on social services in Argentina, Chile, Costa Rica, and Uruguay—financed by the Inter-American Development Bank—a small study is being financed by the World Bank to extend the analysis of that study only in Chile. The small study will include a limited examination of the relative efficiency and cost of education, housing, and health services that are being provided by the state, on the one hand, and by firms or semiprivate organizations, on the other hand.

This study differs from other studies of the distributive impact of social services on welfare in most Latin American countries in that analysis is not confined to the dominant public sector. The opportunity for comparison between public and private sectors exists in Chile, due to efforts by the government in the mid-1970s to "privatize" the delivery of a wide range of social services, including significant components in the education, housing, and health sectors.

The small study in Chile is being conducted by the Instituto Latinoamericano de Doctrina y Estudios Sociales (ILADES) and is a partial by-product of the much larger study in the four countries, mentioned above, that is being supervised by ECIEL (Estudios Conjuntos para la Integración Económica Latinoamericana), the consortium of national research institutions in Latin America. The

Chilean part of the larger study involves two sample surveys—one of 1,500 families in Santiago, and the other of 800 families in Colchagua—between 1982 and 1984.

The small study that is being funded by the World Bank will test the commonly held hypothesis that a state is less efficient in providing social services than private alternatives. In the analysis, consumers of social services will be distinguished by income and socioeconomic status.

Responsibility: Latin America and the Caribbean Country Programs Department I—Paul M. Meo. The coordinator and chief researcher is Jorge Rodriguez Grossi of the Instituto Latinoamericano de Doctrina y Estudios Sociales (Chile).

Completion date: September 1984.

Social-Accounting-Matrix-Based Computable General Equilibrium Model for Cameroon

Ref. No. 673-23A

Cameroon is in a unique situation: it can reasonably expect six to eight percent annual economic growth over the medium term due to significant revenues from sales of crude oil, which should continue for perhaps ten to fifteen years. Earnings from exports of crude oil should free the country from foreign exchange constraints over much of the next decade, and oil revenues should provide significant additional funds for investment in national development programs. The government faces major choices on how to use this income from oil to bring about a permanent increase in productivity, at the same time preparing for eventually decreasing reliance on oil revenues. It is particularly anxious to avoid having Cameroon's agricultural base undermined by the "Dutch disease"—the syndrome associated with a sudden export boom wherein the success of one export undermines the competitiveness of other exports from the same economy, due to upward pressure on the exchange rate, generally inducing a higher-priced economy.

The purpose of this research application project is to develop a social accounting matrix and a general equilibrium model for development planning in Cameroon that makes most use of current data, motivates improvement in the government's statistical systems, and furnishes analysis of alternative planning options.

While Cameroon maintains a good number of statistical series, these are not, with the exception of the national accounts, organized in a consistent framework.

The social accounting matrix organizes country economic data into such a framework using realistic budget constraints for individual producers and consumers. The data can then be adapted to estimate parameters for the computable general equilibrium model. The model, in turn, specifies structural and behavioral relationships for each market. It extends traditional input-output models to allow for substitution among factors in production and between domestically produced goods and competitive imports. Moreover, agents in the economy—producers and consumers—are assumed to respond to market signals in making their decisions. The resulting nonlinear set of equations is solved simultaneously so that prices, wages, outputs, and incomes are consistently and endogenously determined.

The World Bank has developed computable general equilibrium (CGE) models in Egypt, Ivory Coast, Thailand, Turkey, and Yugoslavia. They have focused on trade and industrial strategy for semi-industrial countries with foreign exchange constraints. This is the first CGE to be constructed of an oil-surplus economy with a predominantly agricultural base. The model is tailored to the Cameroonian case in that it captures certain features of the economy, such as rigidities in the labor market, capital market imperfections, and membership in the Central African Franc Zone.

This dynamic general equilibrium planning model is to be used by the government of Cameroon in formulating its Sixth Economic Plan (1986–90), because of its usefulness in simulating alternative investment programs, the costs of adopting specific policies, and their effects over the medium term. The World Bank will provide training to two researchers from Cameroon who will assist in designing and building, and later implementing, the multisectoral, price-endogenous model.

Responsibility: Western Africa Programs Department II—Derek A. White and *Development Research Department*—Sherman Robinson (on leave at the University of California at Berkeley), in collaboration with Nancy C. Benjamin, University of California at Berkeley, and Shantayanan Devarajan, Harvard University (consultants).

Completion date: June 1984.

2

International Trade and Finance

Export Incentives in Developing Countries

Ref. No. 671-35

Over the past two decades, several developing countries have expanded their exports of manufactured goods through export incentives. But export incentives have been studied only in general terms and in an aggregated industry format. To provide more useful conclusions, they must be subjected to a more detailed analysis.

The present research project serves this purpose through a cross-section investigation of major export products and a time series analysis of the effects of export promotion measures. It evaluates, in a comparative framework, the export promotion efforts of three countries—Greece, Republic of Korea, and Pakistan. All the country studies are being carried out with the support of the governments concerned.

Apart from evaluating the export promotion measures used in the three countries under study, this project should yield useful findings for other countries that contemplate the reform of a system of incentives, in general, and export promotion schemes, in particular. It should also aid the World Bank in advising developing countries on export promotion.

The main focus of the country studies is a cross-section investigation of major export products for the latest year for which data are available. Rates of export incentives are estimated and compared with the social profitability of specific exports. Carrying out the investigation at the product level permits consideration of the supply and demand constraints on export expansion, the existence of "cross-subsidization" of exports, and assessment of and reactions to export incentives by individual firms.

The product-by-product analysis is supplemented by a time series study of each country's export promotion effort and its effect on the growth of exports. Coverage includes traditional as well as nontraditional exports, and agricultural and manufactured goods within each category. Finally, the contribution of export expansion to economic growth is analyzed.

An international synthesis will provide a comparison of the results obtained in each country and for each product. The results will be used to formulate recommendations on the scope and methods of export promotion in developing countries, with emphasis on the countries under study.

Responsibility: Development Research Department—Bela Balassa. Collaborating are the following authors of the country studies: Greece—Demetrios Papageorgiou, Country Policy Department, and Evangelo Voloudakis, Bank of Greece, and Panagiotis Fylactos, Center for Planning and Economic Research, Athens; Korea—Yung Whee Rhee and Garry Pursell, Industry Department, and Suk Tai Suh, Yonsei University, Seoul; Pakistan—Mohammed Zubair Khan, International Monetary Fund.

Completion date: December 1983.

Reports

Rhee, Yung Whee. "Administrative Arrangements for Korean Export Promotion." The World Bank: Industry Department, June 1981.

Rhee, Yung Whee; Pursell, Garry; and Ross-Larson, Bruce. "Promoting Exports: Institutions, Technology, and Marketing in Korea." The World Bank: Industry Department, June 1981.

Westphal, Larry E.; Rhee, Yung Whee; and Pursell, Garry. "Foreign Influences on Korean Industrial Development." *Oxford Bulletin of Economics and Statistics*, vol. 41, no. 4 (November 1979).

―――. "Korean Industrial Competence: Where It Came From." World Bank Staff Working Paper No. 469, July 1981.

Penetration of Industrialized Country Markets by Imports of Manufactures from Developing Countries

Ref. Nos. 671-67 and 671-82

The purpose of these studies is to analyze the effects of increases in imports of manufactured goods from developing countries on product and factor markets in industrial countries (see also "Research Support for the World Development Report," Ref. No. 671-66 in category 1—Development Policy and Planning). The country focus is on Australia, Canada, the European Economic Community, Japan, Sweden, and the United States. The studies are (1) examining the extent of import penetration of markets in the industrial countries by various developing regions and countries in order to determine the market shares of particular groups of developing countries; (2) determining the impact of competition from developing countries on exports of manufactures of industrialized countries; and (3) analyzing the factors that lead to successful protectionist actions against imports from developing countries, or to high market penetration without such actions.

A major part of the studies consists of the collection and analysis of production and trade data for some 150 product groups. Various import penetration ratios have been calculated, including the share of imports in domestic production and consumption, the rate of change of these import shares, and the growth rate of consumption for an industry. The economic, social, and political factors that affect the nature of protection are being analyzed for each country and for the European Economic Community.

Whether a particular industry obtains protection against increasing imports seems to depend upon a complex set of economic and political factors relating to that industry. If generalizations of the way these factors operate can be made by analyzing previous protectionist episodes, the industrial countries could improve their adjustment planning and developing countries could be helped in planning the industrial composition of the manufactures that are selected for export increases. The studies are, thus, expected to assist both industrial and developing countries in formulating policies that will facilitate a smooth transition for expanded exports of manufactured goods by developing countries and, of course, corresponding export increases by the industrialized countries.

Responsibility: Economic Analysis and Projections Department —Helen Hughes (currently of the Australian National University, Canberra) and Vasilis Panoutsopoulos. The principal researchers and institutes associated with the project are Robert E. Baldwin, University of Wisconsin, and Jean Waelbroeck, Free University of Brussels (Belgium), who is coordinating the European Studies, which are taking place at the Overseas Development Institute (United Kingdom); University of Lille (France); Institut für

Weltwirtschaft, Kiel (Federal Republic of Germany); Institute for International Economic Studies, Stockholm, and the University of Umea (Sweden); Erasmus University, Rotterdam (the Netherlands); Centre for Development Studies, Antwerp (Belgium); and Confederazione Generale dell' Industria Italiana; Canadian-North-South Institute; Australian National University; and Japan Economic Research Center.

Completion date: March 1983. Work on the project has been completed. The monographs should be available by mid-1984.

Reports

Anderson, Kym, and Baldwin, Robert E. "The Political Market for Protection in Industrial Countries: Empirical Evidence." World Bank Staff Working Paper No. 492, October 1981.

Bale, Malcolm D., and Mutti, John H. "Output and Employment Changes in a 'Trade Sensitive' Sector: Adjustment in the U.S. Footwear Industry." World Bank Staff Working Paper No. 430, October 1980. Also in *Weltwirtschaftliches Archiv* (June 1981).

Bobe, Bernard. "Public Assistance to Industry and Trade Policy in France." World Bank Staff Working Paper No. 570, 1983.

Cable, Vincent. "Economics and Politics of Protection: Some Case Studies of Industries." World Bank Staff Working Paper No. 569, 1983.

Cable, Vincent, and Rebelo, Ivonia. "Britain's Pattern of Specialization in Manufactured Goods with Developing Countries and Trade Protection." World Bank Staff Working Paper No. 425, October 1980.

Evans, John C.; Glenday, Graham; and Jenkins, Glenn P. "Worker Adjustment to Liberalized Trade: Costs and Assistance Policies." World Bank Staff Working Paper No. 426, October 1980.

Glismann, H. H., and Weiss, F. D. "On the Political Economy of Protection in Germany." World Bank Staff Working Paper No. 427, October 1980.

Grilli, Enzo. "Italian Commercial Policies in the 1970s." World Bank Staff Working Paper No. 428, October 1980.

Hamilton, Carl. "Effects of Non-Tariff Barriers to Trade on Prices, Employment and Imports: The Case of the Swedish Textile and Clothing Industry." World Bank Staff Working Paper No. 429, October 1980.

_____. "A New Approach to Estimation of the Effects of Non-Tariff Barriers to Trade: An Application to the Swedish Textile and Clothing Industry." *Weltwirtschaftliches Archiv*, vol. 117, no. 2 (1981):298-325.

_____. "Public Subsidies to Industry: The Case of Sweden and its Shipbuilding Industry." World Bank Staff Working Paper No. 566, 1983.

Hughes, Helen, and Waelbroeck, Jean. "Can Developing-Country Exports Keep Growing in the 1980s?" *The World Economy* (June 1981):127-47.

Jenkins, Glenn P. "Costs and Consequences of the New Protectionism: The Case of Canada's Clothing Sector." North South Institute, July 1980.

Koekkoek, K. A.; Kol, J.; and Mennes, L. B. M. "On Protectionism in the Netherlands." World Bank Staff Working Paper No. 493, October 1981.

Lundberg, Lars. "Patterns of Barriers to Trade in Sweden: A Study in the Theory of Protection." World Bank Staff Paper No. 494, October 1981.

Messerlin, P. A. "The Political Economy of Protection: The Bureaucratic Case." *Weltwirtschaftliches Archiv*, vol. 117, no. 3 (1981):469-96.

Tharakan, P. K. M. "The Political Economy of Protection in Belgium." World Bank Staff Working Paper No. 431, October 1980.

Verreydt, Eric, and Waelbroeck, Jean. "European Community Protection against Manufactured Imports from Developing Countries: A Case Study in the Political Economy of Protection." World Bank Staff Working Paper No. 432, October 1980.

Waelbroeck, Jean. "The Commercal Policy and Relations with Developing Countries." In P. Quisumbing (ed.), *European Integration: A Useful Experience for ASEAN?* Manila, Philippines: University of Manila (forthcoming).

_____. "Politique commerciale commune et théorie du commerce extérieur." *Economie appliquée*, no. 2 (1983).

_____. "Protection, Employment and Welfare in a Stagflating Economy." Center for Econometrics and Mathematical Economics (CEME) Working Paper No. 8201. Brussels (Belgium): Free University of Brussels, 1982. Also in Helen Hughes (ed.), *Labor and Development*, Proceedings of Section 4 of the 1980 Congress of the International Economic Association held in Mexico (forthcoming).

_____. "Trends of EC Protection and the Prospects of ASEAN
   Trade." In N. Akrasanee and H. C. Rieger (eds.), *ASEAN-EC
   Economic Relations*. Singapore Institute for Southeast Asian
   Studies, 1982.
Waelbroeck, Jean, co-author with G. Curzon, *et al. The MFA
   Forever?* London: Trade Policy Research Center, 1981.
Weiss, Frank D. "The Structure of International Competitiveness
   in the Federal Republic of Germany: An Appraisal." World
   Bank Staff Working Paper No. 571, 1983.

Key Institutions and Expansion of Manufactured Exports

Ref. No. 671-68

Exports of manufactured goods from developing countries are growing much faster than their other exports and have become critically important for many of these countries. This project is designed to fill gaps in current knowledge by investigating the practical effects of institutional arrangements in selected areas that are crucial to the exports of manufactured goods, such as nontariff protection and marketing.

Among its objectives, the research seeks to learn more about how to expand manufactured exports and increase their value. A related aim is to gain an increased understanding of the effects of institutionally complex obstacles, such as textile quotas in industrial countries. A third purpose is to learn more about prospects of manufactured exports at the level of particular products and countries. In all these areas, the project builds on previous staff studies and related research, including "Export Incentives in Developing Countries" (Ref. No. 671-35 in this category). The findings are intended to improve the World Bank's advice and its lending operations and illuminate practical aspects of manufactured exports that have tended to be neglected in research elsewhere.

A principal focus of this project is research into marketing and related nonprice aspects of exports, by locally owned firms in developing countries, of consumer goods sold in leading industrial countries. This research studies the role in these exports of foreign buyers and intermediaries, such as importers and trading companies, together with the learning processes and expanding operations of the local firm in linking its production to consumer demand overseas. Attention is given, for example, to the shifting division of labor over time between local firms and outside buyers in such areas as contacting wholesalers and retail outlets, choosing designs, organizing delivery, packaging and shipping, and assuring quality control, and to ways in which the unit value of exports can be increased along with their volume. The research also looks at how exports are and can be institutionally promoted at a national level. Interviews for this part of the project have been conducted in Hong Kong, the Republic of Korea, the Philippines, and Thailand, and with firms and institutions involved in this trade in the United States. A study has also been made of the experience in five South American countries—Argentina, Brazil, Colombia, Peru, and Uruguay.

A second focus of the study has been textile quotas against developing countries under the Multifiber Arrangement and their effects on trade in clothing and textiles. Studies have been made of the evolution, functioning, impact, and prospects of this system of managed trade. The system is immensely complex, with several thousand quotas and numerous other details as part of an ever-changing set of agreements restricting the opportunities open to developing countries in exporting clothing and textiles. The potential for exports of these products from low-wage countries is huge and quotas are a major obstacle.

The earlier study of textile quotas completed in 1980 (see under Reports below) is being updated.

Responsibility: Eastern Africa Regional Office—Donald B. Keesing. Recent participants include Martin H. Wolf, Lawrence H. Wortzel, David Morawetz, and Camilo Jaramillo (consultants).

Completion date: June 1984.

Reports

Keesing, Donald B. "Linking Up to Distant Markets: South to North Exports of Manufactured Consumer Goods." *American Economic Review* 73 (May 1983):338–42.

Keesing, Donald B., and Wolf, Martin H. "Questions in International Trade in Textiles." *The World Economy* 1 (March 1981):79–101.

———. *Textile Quotas against Developing Countries: A Study of Managed Trade.* London: Trade Policy Research Centre, 1980.

The Direction of Developing Countries' Trade: Patterns, Trends, and Implications

Ref. No. 672-32

The potential for increased trade among developing countries, the benefits from expanding that potential, the constraints upon it, and the appropriate policy choices in this respect have become of increasing interest to analysts and policymakers. This is particularly so in view of a growing belief that prospects for growth and the concomitant expansion of export markets in developed countries are not favorable. Thus, expanded trade among developing countries is seen as a desirable option given the adverse trading environment they face.

This project seeks to analyze some of the underlying issues by examining the characteristics of trade among developing countries and the determinants of the level of their trade in different directions. In the process, some light will be shed on such debated questions as:

1. How can countries adjust to shocks in the international environment and take advantage of new trading opportunities?
2. How does the rapid industrialization of some developing countries and the increase in wealth of some mineral and fuel exporters affect the trade of other developing countries?
3. Are there biases against trade among developing countries?
4. Have policies to encourage trade among developing countries had any noticeable effect? Conversely, have policies of import substitution in developing countries been important in thwarting such trade?
5. Is a country's trade regime an important influence on the direction of its trade?
6. Is there a potential for intra-industry trade among developing countries, particularly the more industrially advanced among them?

To address some of these questions, a number of analytical techniques have been applied to trade and its determinants. These include: A "market shares analysis" for five commodity groups of changes in exports by individual developing countries to different destinations; a more detailed examination of the commodity characteristics of the different export baskets, focusing largely on manufactured goods, and using such measures as product specialization indices (revealed comparative advantage), weighted average capital-labor ratios of exports in different directions, and indices of intra-industry trade; and a "gravity model" analysis, in which the exports of a particular commodity from a country to all country destinations are regressed upon the principal determinants of trade volume—gross domestic product (GDP), GDP per capita, population, and such barriers as transport costs and protection.

The quantitative analysis has been completed. The major findings as well as their policy implications are either being written or can be found under "Reports" listed below. A summary of the major conclusions, which should be of interest to policymakers and country analysts, is as follows:

1. The Hecksher-Ohlin theory does provide a very strong explanation of the pattern of trade of developing countries. The residual can be explained by using complementary theories such as those on intra-industry trade.

2. Directionality of trade does matter in the sense that developing countries' exports to other developing countries are more capital-intensive than those to industrial countries, whereas the reverse is true for imports.

3. There is limited evidence to support the view that south-south trade provides the most dynamic opportunities for export expansion. Additionally, any inherent superiority in this type of trade is very difficult to observe.

4. There does not seem to be "too little" south-south trade at present.

A volume stemming from a World Bank-sponsored conference on "South-South or South-North Trade: Does the Direction of Developing Countries' Trade Matter?" is forthcoming.

Responsibility: Economic Analysis and Projections Department —Peter Miovic, in collaboration with Professor Oli Havrylyshyn of George Washington University (consultant).

Completion date: Phase I—January 1984.

Reports

Alikhani, Iradj, and Havrylyshyn, Oli. "The Political Economy of Protection in Developing Countries: A Case Study of Korea and Colombia." International Trade and Capital Flows Division Working Paper No. 1982-4. The World Bank: Economic Analysis and Projections Department, July 1982.

Havrylyshyn, Oli, and Alikhani, Iradj. "Is There Cause for Export Optimism? An Inquiry into the Existence of a Second-Generation of Successful Exporters." *Weltwirtschaftliches Archiv*, vol. 118, no. 4 (1982). Also in *Finance & Development* (June 1983).

Havrylyshyn, Oli, and Civan, Engin. "Determinants of Intra-Industry Trade in Developing Countries: A Cross-Country Regression Analysis." International Trade and Capital Flows Division Working Paper No. 1982-7. The World Bank: Economic Analysis and Projections Department, December 1982.

_____. "Intra-Industry Trade Among Developing Countries." International Trade and Capital Flows Division Working Paper No. 1982-6. The World Bank: Economic Analysis and Projections Department, December 1982.

Havrylyshyn, Oli, and Wolf, Martin H. "Promoting Trade Among Developing Countries: An Assessment." *Finance & Development* (March 1982). Also in *European Economic Review*, vol. 21 (1983).

_____. "Trade Among Developing Countries: Theory, Policy Issues, and Principal Trends." International Trade and Capital Flows Division Working Paper No. 1981-1. The World Bank: Economic Analysis and Projections Department, February 1981.

Khanna, Ashok. "Testing for the Directionality of India's Exports." World Bank Staff Working Paper No. 538, December 1982.

Agricultural Trade Patterns in an Expanding European Community and Their Effects on Tunisia

Ref. No. 672-33

The European Community (EC) as a bloc is the largest importer of agricultural products in the world. In particular, it is the dominant market for horticultural products. These imports originate mainly from Mediterranean countries (especially North African countries) and from certain countries in the Southern Hemisphere. But for exporters to the Community, the EC is a difficult market to penetrate. It is a "moving target" as regulations within the EC Common Agricultural Policy and membership of the EC evolve and change. This presents a problem to planners and policymakers of countries that supply products to the EC, because the market environment appears to be in a constant state of flux.

This research addresses the question of the impact of an expanded European Community (and its associated Common Agricultural Policy) on horticultural trade from nonmember countries. With the accession of Greece and possibly Portugal and Spain to the EC, it is postulated that patterns of EC horticultural trade will alter dramatically, especially for the "off-season" imports of many types of fruits and vegetables, and for cut flowers, wine, and olive oil. This new pattern of trade is being estimated under alternative policy scenarios. In addition, the effects on one country, Tunisia, are being studied in terms of alternative markets or end-products (fresh versus processed) for existing output, and alternative crops for agriculture.

Tunisia is not unique in the region as a horticultural exporter but is selected as the case study because of the current and potentially increasing importance of its horticultural exports and because it is likely to be seriously affected by the accession of new members. While the study could be enlarged to include several horticultural exporting countries in the Mediterranean region, the study is restricted to a developing country for two reasons. First, the research is testing an approach to a problem where seasonality is the crucial element. Seasonal trade studies for developing countries are basically untested. Second, the work will test whether such studies are operationally useful (and used).

Over the last few years, the World Bank has participated in agricultural projects in virtually all its client countries on the Mediterranean rim and in several African countries where the output of the project is off-season (European season) vegetables, fruit, and flowers. The major part of the output from these projects is destined for the EC market under the assumption that current trading conditions and opportunities will remain constant for the foreseeable future. With the expansion of the EC to include southern countries, this assumption is becoming increasingly suspect. Consequently, the research on the horticultural sector of the EC and Tunisia attempts to quantify some of the forthcoming changes, which are of particular interest to the Bank's regional agricultural projects departments.

The research design has two major parts. The first is a study on horticultural trade in an expanded European Community. The changed trade patterns by commodity that will result from accession of the new members is being simulated by developing a trade model disaggregated by individual fruit and vegetables, and by season. In addition to the modeling exercise, the study describes the nature of EC horticultural trade policies, their background, and internal and external pressures on them.

The second part of the research, the case study of Tunisia, contains a descriptive institutional section and a formal modeling exercise. Institutional material on current production and trade in horticulture and on problems of market access is presented along with a description of possible alternative markets and products that might be available to Tunisia. Further, a disaggregated sector model (a linear competitive equilibrium model) of Tunisian horticulture is being developed. From the model it is possible to simulate the impact on output, prices, and income of changes by product in the trading regime faced by Tunisia. The objective of the work is to provide a reasoned basis for export adjustment and promotion.

The adjustments proposed are those in response to EC policy changes, export promotion, increased production of export crops, and the optimal mix of export crops. To accomplish this means studying likely EC policy changes with respect to Tunisian horticultural exports; examining alternative uses and markets for expected production that may be diverted from the EC market; discussing the feasibility of export promotion policies and the establishment of institutions within Tunisia to coordinate and transact the merchandising of the products; and estimating the investment required to expand or convert to production of export crops.

The final product, expected by February 1984, will be a monograph integrating the two studies with a more general section on agricultural trade in the Mediterranean/EC countries.

Responsibility: Country Policy Department—Malcolm D. Bale. Principal researchers and institutes associated with the project are Professor Reimar v. Alvensleben, Institute of Horticultural Economics, University of Hannover (Federal Republic of Germany), and Claude Falgon, of Roland Olivier Conseil, Paris (France).

Completion date: February 1984.

Changes in Comparative Advantage in Manufactured Goods

Ref. No. 672-41

The factors determining international trade in manufactured goods and the future prospects for this trade are of considerable interest to country economists, the World Bank's management, and policymakers in developing countries. This research project will address itself to these questions by analyzing the pattern of, and changes in, comparative advantage in manufactured goods and prospective changes in trade flows.

The first part of the project represents a major extension and amplification of earlier work by one of the investigators on the "stages approach" to comparative advantage. The second part will focus on international specialization in a multilateral context. Both these parts will involve integrated theoretical propositions and empirical testing.

The paper on "A 'Stages Approach' to Comparative Advantage" by one of the researchers will serve as the point of departure for the first part of the research project.[1] In the course of the research, it is proposed to apply the model to data for a number of years, use time-series data for individual countries, and combine time-series and cross-section data. Bilateral trade relationships will be examined and alternative capital-labor coefficients introduced, with the inclusion of additional factor intensity and factor-endowment variables. Data on imports as well as on net exports and export-import ratios will be used for alternative formulations of variables representing international specialization. Policy variables will be introduced into the analysis and projections will be made.

The second part of the research project will analyze the determinants of international specialization in a multilateral framework by the use of econometric and simulation methods. The econometric approach to the problem will combine interactions among factor endowments and factor intensities with gravitational elements and demand factors. The employment effects of this trade will further be estimated, and trade flows and employment will be projected by the use of a simulation model.

Responsibility: Development Research Department—Bela Balassa, in collaboration with Roger J. Bowden (consultant), University of Western Australia.

Completion date: December 1983.

---

[1] Bela Balassa. "A 'Stages Approach' to Comparative Advantage," in Irma Adelman (ed.), *Economic Growth and Resources*, Proceedings of the Fifth Congress of the International Economic Association, Tokyo, Japan, 1977.

Reports

Bowden, Roger. "The Conceptual Basis of Empirical Studies of Trade in Manufactured Commodities: A Constructive Critique." *Journal of International Economics* (forthcoming).

Liberalization with Stabilization in the Southern Cone

Ref. No. 672–85

After several decades of a development strategy based on import substitution and extensive direct control of all markets, Argentina, Chile, and Uruguay introduced profound reform packages in the mid-1970s that included liberalization and stabilization policies. Spanning labor, commodity, and financial markets, these reforms are still in progress in Uruguay, are being overhauled in Argentina, and are fairly advanced in Chile. The magnitude, sequence, and outcome of the reforms in the Southern Cone countries of Latin America offer a rare opportunity to analyze the transition toward a more liberal economic environment, which the research project proposes to study. The objective is to understand how these countries are adjusting to the new environment and, thereby, to identify policy packages that minimize the costs associated with transition to a more liberal regime.

The research strategy is to identify and measure the costs and benefits of the reforms at the microeconomic level, the first task being to describe the adjustment by firms to the new environment provided by the reforms. These descriptions take into account three elements that affected the performance of firms: liberalization, market competitiveness, and stabilization. Next, models will be used to determine the sensitivity of the adjustment by firms to different reform packages, which will be determined from macroanalyses. Special attention will be given to separating avoidable from unavoidable costs, with the objective of identifying policy packages that minimize the measured adjustment costs. How these adjustments at the microeconomic level add up to economywide costs and benefits will be inferred by measuring sources of growth and structural change at the sectoral level.

A complication for the research arises from the simultaneous application of macro stabilization policies to reduce inflation and of micro-oriented liberalization policies (across all markets) to increase the efficiency and extent of resource use. The evolution of such variables as interest and exchange rates, which were crucial inputs for decisions by firms, was the result of interactions between liberalization and stablization policies. That these inter-actions are still poorly understood can be seen by the variety of explanations offered. Some observers attribute the changes in these variables to events unrelated to the reforms (bank failures and the appreciation of the dollar); others to the inconsistent application of policies, resulting in high inflation and continuing uncertainty (the maintenance of a fiscal deficit in Argentina); others to a misguided stabilization program (the assumptions underlying the monetary approach to the balance of payments); still others to stabilization policies that were too successful (in the sense of reduced inflation).

Partial accounts of experiences under the reforms are becoming available. None, however, has been undertaken in a coordinated framework: they lack either a comprehensive comparative descrip-tion of the reform packages or a comparative evaluation of the outcomes. This also applies to variables such as the real exchange rate and the real interest rate. Given the importance of these variables for decisions by firms, the research will supplement existing accounts of the reforms to fill the gaps.

The interaction between liberalization and stabilization mea-sures is best understood at the macro level. Consequently, the micro research undertaken must be complemented by macro-analysis, without which it could not be established whether adjust-ment—successful or unsuccessful—was due to the application of stabilization policies or of liberalization policies. Furthermore, the macro analysis will enrich the micro research by suggesting policy packages whose application would result in a greater net benefit during the transition.

The project will have two phases and last about four years. Phase I, which is now in progress, will consist of describing the firms' adjustment and of performing the supporting macroanalysis and sectoral analyses. The research will include a statistical de-scription of adjustment (based on existing data) for a large sample of firms and a qualitative description (based on case studies) for a small number of firms. Phase I will also include a pilot survey to determine the feasibility and design of a full-fledged survey at the firm level during Phase II. It is expected that the second phase will include, in addition to the survey, special studies to be determined during the first phase. Progress of the research will be periodically reported in working papers. At the end of Phase II, the lessons from the Southern Cone countries will be integrated in a summary volume.

Responsibility: Development Research Department—Jaime de Melo, cosponsored by the *Latin America and the Caribbean Regional Office*, and in collaboration with a number of consultants: Vittorio Corbo (co-director of the project), Instituto de Economía, Universidad Católica, in Chile; Amalio H. Petrei, Fundación Mediterránea, in Argentina; James R. Tybout of Georgetown University; Julio Galvez, Escuela de Administración, Universidad Católica, Chile; José Delfino, Universidad Nacional de Cordoba; Jaime Mezzera, PREALC, Santiago; Juan-Carlos Protasi and Ricardo Pascale, Universidad del Uruguay; Graciela Kaminsky, Boston College; Roque Fernandez, Centro de Estudios Macroeconómicos de Argentina.

Completion date: Phase I—December 1984.

Reports

Corbo, V. "Recién Desarrollos en la Economía Chilena." *Cuadernos de Economía* (April 1983).
Hanson, J., and de Melo, J. "The Uruguayan Experience with Liberalization and Stabilization: 1974–81." *Journal of Inter-American and World Affairs* (forthcoming).

The Assessment of Country Foreign Borrowing Strategies

Ref. No. 673-01

Major external changes in the international economic environment in the 1970s—some temporary and cyclical, some permanent—have necessitated adjustment in the economic management of developing countries. Foreign borrowing from commercial and multilateral sources has become a flexible instrument in macroeconomic management, but the excessive build-up of debt and associated debt-servicing obligations can create serious financial problems.

This project addresses the problem of how to choose a level of foreign borrowing appropriate for a country's economic structure and consistent with its other macroeconomic objectives, that would permit the realization of gains from using international capital markets, without unduly prejudicing future creditworthiness. It focuses on assessing the factors that should be considered in formulating a foreign borrowing strategy, identifying the welfare gains from external borrowing, and clarifying the policy options in avoiding debt crises, rather than on the narrower topic of predicting creditworthiness, which has been the goal of extensive indicator work in the World Bank and elsewhere.

The research has two main aims: to provide a methodology to assist country economists and developing country policymakers in formulating appropriate borrowing strategies, and to strengthen the Bank's analytical capability for assessing country debt-servicing capacity in the medium term. The first objective necessitates the development of a model in which the impact of alternative borrowing strategies can be simulated. The model structure will incorporate the main advantages of foreign borrowing, such as consumption smoothing, investment and insurance, and the major sources of uncertainty that may precipitate debt crises—for example, volatility in interest and inflation rates, commodity prices, and agricultural output. Major innovative features are the modeling of uncertainty and of the joint behavior of borrowers and international lenders. Within this framework, the way in which a country's economic and institutional structure affects its appropriate borrowing strategy will be analyzed.

The detailed features of the model will be drawn from the characteristics of five countries selected as case studies, Colombia, Costa Rica, Senegal, Sudan and Thailand. The choice of countries reflects a diversity of debt experience and of borrowing strategies, both among countries and over time. These countries have also used a variety of mechanisms, with varying effectiveness, to control external borrowing: examples are prior approval of foreign-financed investment, minimum maturity regulations, deposit requirements for the financing of trade, and exchange-rate guarantees. Despite these differences, there are certain similarities in their economic structure in terms of commodity composition of exports and susceptibility to terms-of-trade shocks. This variance will be used to draw inferences about the relative impact of the domestic and international environments on the debt problems.

The country case studies will also provide information on how the process of foreign borrowing can create distortions in the economy that reduce and, in some cases, negatively alter the purported benefits of external financing. For example, in some cases, foreign borrowing has led to an appreciation of the real exchange rate, aggravating future balance of payments problems. Similarly, it has been associated with monetary expansion and inflationary pressures. In addition, differential access to foreign capital may affect the distribution between public (especially parastatal) and private investment, and the sectoral allocation of investment. A taxonomy of such issues will be constructed.

The second objective of the research is to provide a country-specific means for evaluating debt-servicing capacity. From the basic methodological framework, the factors that may lead to debt crises will be identified. The empirical significance of these factors in historical reschedulings will be determined through cross-sectional analysis. This work attempts to generalize existing research on early-warning indicators by incorporating the impact of country characteristics on the weight assigned to each indicator, to show that, for example, a country in the process of liberalizing trade may suffer a short-term deterioration of its debt-service ratio but also may improve its creditworthiness at the same time.

Responsibility: Country Policy Department—Homi J. Kharas, Robert B. Myers, Zmarak Shalizi; *Economic Analysis and Projections Department*—Nicholas C. Hope; and *Development Research Department*—Arne Drud, in collaboration with Anthony Brooke, Reuven Glick, and Hisanobu Shishido (consultants).

Completion date: June 1985.

3
Agriculture and Rural Development

Programming and Designing Investment: Indus Basin

Ref. No. 671-45

Formulation of agriculture and irrigation projects often depends
on implicit policy assumptions and on complex technical relationships that are rarely explored at the appraisal stage of the World
Bank's project lending cycle. The principal objectives of this
research are (1) to test the meaningful integration of complex
physical relationships between surface water and groundwater into
an economic planning model; (2) to test the sensitivity of project
design to the inclusion of objectives other than economic efficiency; and (3) to construct an investment planning model for the
Indus Basin in Pakistan that will quantify the trade-offs between
multiple welfare objectives in investment project design and agricultural development policy.

Static linear programming is employed to characterize the
Indus Basin, using an objective function that simulates producer
response to policy intervention. The data base for the estimation
of model parameters comes principally from a parallel study
carried out by the Water and Power Development Authority
(WAPDA) of the Government of Pakistan. The study was funded
in part by a United Nations Development Programme (UNDP)
project, for which the World Bank was executing agent.

The basin-level model includes component models that are
integrated via a module representing the network of canals, reser-
voirs, and other basin-level constraints. The component models, in
turn, characterize the agricultural production and the hydrology of
the fresh and saline water aquifers of 53 different regions of the
basin. Each of these component models includes a farm-level
model to simulate producer response to changes in resource

endowment due to public investment. The farm-level models have a modular construction to facilitate efficient design of the many models of this type, including specialization of crop and livestock activities for nine different agroclimatic zones of the basin.

Thus, the basin-level model simulates the integrated use of groundwater and surface water throughout the Indus Basin. While the inclusion of groundwater greatly complicates the model structure, it is necessary if the relevant set of investment projets is to be modeled in a meaningful way. Moreover, given significant basin-level interdependence on a crucial input—water—that is neither marketed nor priced in any realistic sense, project design and appraisal are quite sensitive to the specification of the institutional arrangements for the allocation of water.

Another set of simulation experiments allows a rigorous consistency test of the hypotheses underlying planned water-related investments. In these and other experiments, the effects of alternative policies are examined via parametric programming. A range of simulations were made to assess the efficacy of alternative investment programs and policy instruments in meeting various goals. The mode of analysis is comparative-static so that sufficient microeconomic detail can be included to facilitate project design and appraisal. Technical change and some other dynamic elements, however, can be analyzed by solving the model with parameter estimates that represent various points in time.

Several components of the model family have been recast for their transfer to Pakistan and operational use by the country's Planning Division of the Water and Power Development Authority. This entailed training of WAPDA technical personnel by members of the Development Research Department.

Responsibility: Economics and Research Staff—John H. Duloy, and *Agriculture and Rural Development Department*—Gerald T. O'Mara, in collaboration with the South Asia Regional Office and the Water and Power Development Authority of Pakistan.

Completion date: December 1983.

Reports

Bisschop, J.; Candler, W.; Duloy, J. H.; and O'Mara, G. T. "The Indus Basin Model: A Special Application of Two-Level Linear Programming." *Mathematical Programming Study 20* (1982):30–38.

Duloy, J. H., and O'Mara, G. T. "Lessons from the Indus Basin Study." Mimeo. The World Bank: Development Research Department, October 1982.

Evaluation of Food Distribution Schemes

Ref. No. 671-80

This study was part of the Food Security Work Program within the Agriculture and Rural Development Department of the World Bank and follows up on a previous research project, "Projections of the Extent of Food Deficits of Target Groups under Alternative Policy Programs" (Ref. No. 671-64), now completed. In the earlier project, a methodology was developed to relate the caloric intake of different groups to income and food price levels and project the state of malnutrition under policy alternatives. This methodology was applied in eight country case studies. It demonstrated the extent to which malnutrition is a widespread and serious problem in developing countries and suggested that, in many of them, food distribution and intervention schemes will continue to be necessary.

Currently, information on the effectiveness of food distribution and intervention schemes is lacking. Further, no satisfactory method exists for (1) estimating the required scale of food distribution systems; (2) projecting their costs and benefits under alternative development strategies; and (3) evaluating the costs and benefits of basic needs programs in rural development projects. The primary objective of this research project was to study the operational aspects of food distribution systems and explore alternative approaches to evaluating their effectiveness.

The study had several parts:

1. A survey evaluating current food distribution systems and how they operate.
2. An empirical study of alternative food distribution systems, their impact on several variables and associated fiscal costs, and on economic costs and benefits.
3. The exploration of alternative methodologies for the evaluation of food distribution systems and basic needs programs.

Some of the contributions from this research are:

1. An assessment of the operational problems associated with alternative food distribution and intervention schemes.

2. Estimates of fiscal costs, losses in producer incomes, consumption by subsistence producers, and leakages to unintended beneficiaries of food distribution schemes.
3. A methodology and program for evaluating alternative food distribution systems.
4. An assessment of alternative methodologies to evaluate basic needs programs in nutrition.
5. Estimates of the social demand function for basic food needs.

Responsibility: Agriculture and Rural Development Department —Graham Donaldson, in collaboration with Odin K. Knudsen, *South Asia Projects Department*, and Gurushri Swamy, *Economic Analysis and Projections Department*, and with Lloyd Harbert (consultant).

Completion date: December 1982; the completion report is in process.

Reports

Harbert, Lloyd, and Scandizzo, Pasquale L. "Food Distribution and Nutrition Intervention: The Case of Chile." World Bank Staff Working Paper No. 512, May 1982.

Knudsen, Odin K. "Economics of Supplemental Feeding of Malnourished Children: A Case of Leakages, Benefits and Costs." World Bank Staff Working Paper No. 451, April 1981.

_____. "Nutrition and Food Needs in South Asia: A Review of Research on Magnitudes, Policy and Prospects." Working Paper presented at the IFT Annual Meeting, Atlanta (Georgia), June 1981. *Food Technology* (September 1981):105–109.

Knudsen, Odin K., and Scandizzo, Pasquale L. "The Demand for Calories in Developing Countries." Agricultural Research and Economic Policy Division Working Paper No. 26. The World Bank, October 1980.

_____. "Price Policy and Basic Needs: Implications and Estimates." Agricultural Research and Economic Policy Division Working Paper No. 41. The World Bank, April 1981.

Scandizzo, Pasquale L., and Graves, J. "The Alleviation of Malnutrition: Impact and Cost Effectiveness of Official Programs." Agricultural Research and Economic Policy Division Working Paper No. 19. The World Bank, March 1979.

Scandizzo, Pasquale L., and Knudsen, Odin K. "The Evaluation of the Benefits of Basic Needs Policies." *American Journal of*

Agricultural Economics 62 (February 1980):46–57. Also World
Bank Reprint Series: Number 138.

Scandizzo, Pasquale L., and Swamy, Gurushri. "Benefits and
Costs of Food Distribution Policies: The India Case." World
Bank Staff Working Paper No. 509, 1982.

Swamy, Gurushri. "Public Food Distribution in India." Agricultural Research and Economic Policy Division Working Paper
No. 25. The World Bank, July 1979.

India: Impact of Agricultural Development on Employment and Poverty (Phase II)

Ref. No. 671-89

The objective of Phase II of this research (Phase I, Ref. No.
671-62, has now been completed) is to produce a better understanding of some of the policy and investment alternatives for
alleviating poverty in rural India by studying their effects in a
number of specific institutional, infrastructural, and agroclimatic
contexts. In particular, policies such as investment in irrigation
works (public and private), increased availability of credit through
public lending institutions, and expansion of nonfarm employment
opportunities will be the focal points of the research. In studying
these policies' effects, it is assumed that the preexisting institutions and infrastructures are extremely important. To capture
their variations, the research will concentrate on three areas:
Andhra Pradesh, Punjab, and Bihar. Punjab, at one extreme,
represents a dynamic agriculture, based on the availability of
irrigation (private and public), increasing mechanization, and
"capitalistic" modes of production. Certain areas of Bihar represent almost a polar opposite—semifeudal, stagnant agriculture.
Andhra Pradesh falls between the two.

The second major assumption is that the impact of public
policy on rural households is filtered and possibly distorted
through the prism of an interlocked set of transactions between
households. In the absence of a complete set of smoothly functioning markets for inputs and outputs, rural households enter into
simultaneous transactions in more than one commodity or service
with each other. This linking could also reflect the distribution of
economic/political power among households. As the effects of
public policy interventions in this system may be completely

frustrated or be the opposite of their ostensible objectives, it is proposed to study these interlinkages in some detail.

While institutional changes cannot be ruled out, at least in principle, given the past history of implementation of land reform and tenancy laws, the important question is: How far can agricultural development be pushed through public policy with a favorable impact on poverty, without major institutional change? The proposed research addresses this question.

Phase I set out a tentative methodology and identified the data requirements. As the preexisting data were inadequate to test the methodology, primary data collection is one of the major tasks of Phase II.

Responsibility: Development Research Department—Clive L. G. Bell and Chalongphob Sussangkarn, with the assistance of T. N. Srinivasan (consultant) and in collaboration with the Indian Institute of Management, Ahmedabad, and the Agro-Economic Research Center, Waltair.

Completion date: June 1985.

Reports

Bell, Clive, L. G., and Braverman, A. "On the Non-Existence of 'Marshallian' Sharecropping Contracts." *Indian Economic Review*, vol. XV, no. 3 (July–September 1980).

Bell, Clive L. G., and Zusman, P. "Towards a General Bargaining Theory of Equilibrium Sets of Contracts—The Case of Agricultural Rental Contracts." Paper presented at the World Congress of the Econometric Society, Aix-en-Provence (France), August–September 1980.

Braverman, A., and Guasch, J. L. "Capital Requirements, Screening and Interlinked Sharecropping and Credit Contracts." *Journal of Development Economics* (forthcoming).

Braverman, A., and Srinivasan, T. N. "Agrarian Reforms in Developing Economies Characterized by Interlinked Credit and Tenancy Markets." World Bank Staff Working Paper No. 433, October 1980. Also in H. Binswanger and M. Rosenzweig (eds.), *Rural Labor Markets in Asia: Contractual Arrangements, Employment and Wages* (forthcoming).

———. "Credit and Sharecropping in Agrarian Societies." *Journal of Development Economics* 9:3 (December 1981):289–312.

Braverman, A., and Stiglitz, J. E. "Sharecropping and the Inter-
linking of Agrarian Markets." *American Economic Review* 72
(4) (September 1982):695–715.
Mitra, P. K. "A Theory of Interlinked Rural Transactions." *Journal
of Public Economics*, vol. 20 (March 1983).

The Construction of Econometric Models for the Supply of Perennials: A Case Study of Natural Rubber and Tea in Sri Lanka

Ref. No. 672–02

The "tree crop problem," that is, the development of well
specified structural econometric models for the supply of perennial crops, has long defied a satisfactory solution. In view of the
heavy reliance of many developing countries on perennial crops to
provide necessary foreign exchange earnings, this is an issue of
considerable importance to the World Bank. Replanting and reha-
bilitation projects for perennials have historically accounted for a
significant proportion of the Bank's agricultural investment portfolio. But the fact that demand and short-run supply functions
both are inelastic with respect to price has caused great instability
in world prices of perennial crops, and hence in the export
earnings of producers. Balancing the need of governments to
extract sufficient surplus from the export of cash crops (through
the imposition of export duties) against the need of farmers for
sufficient profits to warrant new planting and replanting with
improved clonal varieties and intensive use of fertilizers has
proved to be an extremely difficult problem. Despite the plethora
of subsidies and other incentives, such policies have rarely succeeded in stimulating the smallholder. As a result, in many
developing countries the existing stock of perennials is not only
overaged, but also contains an excessive proportion of low-yielding
clonal material.

One of the important obstacles to a thorough examination of
the tree-crop problem has been the lack of systematic data on the
age structure and clonal composition of existing stands. Unfortunately, in many of the developing countries the available data on
perennials consist only of macro time series on output, producer
prices, area under cultivation, and the array of government incentives and taxes. In some cases, data on wages and labor inputs, on
new plantings and replantings, inputs and prices of materials

(notably fertilizer), and on climatic conditions are also available. As a result of differences and gaps in the data base, researchers have been forced to specify overly simple models that fail to capture many of the important features of the problem. The inability to incorporate age structure and clonal mix in the form of a vintage model of perennial production has substantially hampered a quantitative assessment of the effects of alternative government tax and incentive schemes on replanting, new plantings, the use of inputs, and the trajectory of future output.

The objective of this pilot project is to explore the feasibility of constructing vintage models of perennial supply via a case study of the rubber and tea sectors in Sri Lanka. For both sectors, extensive published macro time-series data exist, covering upwards of forty years. In the case of rubber, these include age structure and (since 1953) clonal mix. Various surveys, within the last 10 years, of smallholders and estates in the two sectors will supplement the aggregate data. The Government of Sri Lanka has provided access to previously unpublished data obtained from individual rubber estate records covering the past 10 years.

The Bank has collaborated with the two state plantation corporations to extract data for a sample of fifty rubber estates from annual accounting statements and field record books. These records, not previously assembled in usable form, provide a wealth of detailed information on age distribution, clonal mix, labor inputs and wages, expenditures on other factors of production, fertilizer usage, and tapping systems and intensities. The data make it possible to develop vintage models of rubber and tea production that are applicable at micro and macro levels. Thus, the first phase of the project involved collaboration with the Central Bank of Ceylon to collect and organize aggregate and estate-level data on rubber and tea available from both published and unpublished sources.

As presently envisaged, the models will address the new planting and replanting decisions of estates and smallholders and their relation to producer prices, government subsidy payments, and anticipated yields; the relationship of yields to age structure, clonal mix, labor, other inputs, and climatic conditions; the depletion of existing stands over time; the use of inputs in relation to input and producer prices; tapping intensities and plucking rounds and their relation to wage rates, prices, climatic conditions, and elevation; and the effect of changes in the price structure of grades of processed output on the output mix. The models will also incorporate such policy variables as export duties, export cesses, subsidies for replanting, the use of fertilizer, and varieties of planting materials. Hence, they should permit a systematic evaluation of the consequences of alternative incentive schemes on usage of inputs, the output of crops, associated foreign exchange earnings, and the flow of government revenues for other purposes. It is hoped that the research will be of use to government planners in Sri Lanka.

To assess whether models such as these could be used in countries that do not have as complete a data base, a series of experiments will be conducted. Increasingly more complex models will be specified, estimated, and tested, in order to pinpoint the deficiencies and sources of bias in the parameter estimates and resulting projections. These experiments should provide valuable guidelines as to which are the most useful models (given the constraints of available data) and should also help in establishing priorities for the use of resources in collecting more comprehensive data in other countries.

It is expected that the project will result in a series of research papers and possibly a monograph summarizing the results obtained.

Responsibility: Development Research Department—Michael J. Hartley, in collaboration with R. Kyle Peters, Jr., East Asia and Pacific Regional Office, and Eric V. Swanson, Development Research Department. Professor Marc Nerlove, Northwestern University, and Professor Dan Etherington, Australian National University, are consultants.

Collaboration with the Government of Sri Lanka in the collection and organization of data and the administration of the rubber estate questionnaire has been coordinated by the Statistics Department of the Central Bank of Ceylon under the overall supervision of Dr. K. S. E. Jayatillake, Director of Statistics; primary responsibility for the estate questionnaire was borne by M. D. D. Gunatillake, Assistant Director of Statistics; Sunil Fernando, Senior Assistant Director and Chief of the Economic Indicators Division, was responsible for the collection of the macro data. Extraction of data from historical records at each of the estates has been organized by the two state corporations—the Sri Lanka State Plantations Corporation and the Janatha Estates Development Board.

Completion date: June 1984.

Agricultural Innovations in India: A District and Farm-Level Analysis of Fertilizer Use and HYV Adoption

Ref. No. 672-14

While similar to previous decades in aggregate terms, the growth of agricultural output in India over the last ten to fifteen years has been qualitatively different in that it has resulted largely from higher yield rather than larger cropped area. The increasingly intensive use of "modern" inputs like fertilizers and high-yielding varieties (HYV) of seeds has been mainly responsible for the improvement in yields. This study proposes to examine in depth the factors that are influencing the adoption of these "new" inputs by farmers in various parts of India.

An analysis of the determinants of the adoption of these innovations will provide answers to a range of policy-related questions. What has determined the spread of these innovations? Has nonadoption of these inputs been a function of a lack of knowledge or nonprofitability of inputs for particular farm conditions? What role have relative prices played in the adoption process? What has been the contribution of agricultural extension services to farm productivity? Thus, a major objective of this research is to assess the role that various factors farmer characteristics (e.g., education), farm characteristics (e.g., soil quality, irrigation), and policy variables such as fertilizer prices, output prices, and the provision of extension services—have played in the process of adoption. Knowledge of the economic forces determining adoption will be useful in shaping policies aimed at increasing farm production.

Answers to the above questions will be sought through analysis of household and district-level data for the years 1970–71, 1975–76, and 1976–77. The behavior of farmers growing the two major crops—wheat and rice—will be specifically examined. Analysis both at the household and district level will be conducted because the results from these analyses are complementary to an understanding of the process of adoption. Household-level analysis can indicate the role of the factors that determine adoption at a given time. District-level data for two different periods (1970–71 and 1976–77) can be used to evaluate factors determining the speed with which the new practices are adopted.

Responsibility: Development Research Department—Surjit S. Bhalla, in collaboration with Prannoy L. Roy and Kaushik Basu of the Delhi School of Economics, Delhi University; Rajendra Prasad, Indian Agricultural Research Institute; and Shymal Roy, Indian Institute of Management, Bangalore.

Completion date: February 1984.

Reports

Basu, Kaushik, and Roy, Prannoy. "Credit Markets and Their Impact on Agricultural Production—A Review." Mimeo. Development Strategy Division Working Paper. The World Bank: Development Research Department, September 1983.

Bhalla, Surjit S. "Adoption of Fertilizer and High-Yielding Varieties in India." Mimeo. Development Strategy Division Working Paper. The World Bank: Development Research Department, December 1983.

_____. "Land Quality and its Role in the Determination of Farm Size—A Theoretical Model." Mimeo. Development Strategy Division Working Paper. The World Bank: Development Research Department, October 1983.

Bhalla, Surjit S., and Roy, Prannoy. "Land Quality—The Missing Variable in Farm Productivity Equations." Mimeo. Development Strategy Division Working Paper. The World Bank: Development Research Department, September 1983.

Prasad, Rajendra. "Soil Characteristics and Their Impact on Wheat and Rice Production." Mimeo. Development Strategy Division Working Paper. The World Bank: Development Research Department, August 1983.

Roy, Shymal. "Agricultural Extension in India—A Review." Mimeo. Development Strategy Division Working Paper. The World Bank: Development Research Department, July 1983.

Food Policy Analysis for Practitioners

Ref. No. 672-18

The objective of this project was to examine, reconcile, and incorporate production and consumption issues in the process of formulating food policies in developing countries.

The work plan for the project consisted of the following steps: (1) a review of the literature on food and nutrition planning; (2) a review of a few recent studies that are particularly relevant for food planning, even though they are directed at the broader issue of policies for agricultural development; (3) a new synthesis of analytical work in other related agricultural fields, putting it into an operational context; (4) an analysis of the conceptual framework of food policies; and (5) a critical appraisal of practical approaches to preparing strategies for food development.

Responsibility: Agriculture and Rural Development Department —Graham F. Donaldson, in collaboration with Professor C. Peter Timmer of Harvard University, and Professors Walter Falcon and Scott Pearson of the Stanford Food Research Institute.

Completion date: June 1983; the completion report is in process.

Reports

Timmer, C. P.; Falcon, W.; and Pearson, S. *Food Policy Analysis.* Baltimore and London: The Johns Hopkins University Press, 1983.

Agriculture Sector Modeling Conference: A Research Application

Ref. No. 672-24A

The General Algebraic Modeling System (GAMS), now being completed in the Development Research Department, is designed to make mathematical models more generally accessible (see Ref. No. 671-58 in category 1—Development Policy and Planning). The lack of a common documentation system and shared conventions has meant that existing models are difficult to communicate and has been an important barrier to their more widespread use. GAMS uses a language comprehensible to both people and machines that stays close to the conventions of algebra and is easily transferable among different computers. Because it permits more stages to be automated in the specification and solution of models, the system also reduces the likelihood of errors and makes modeling cheaper and less demanding of highly specialized skills.

GAMS has been used very successfully for the design and operation of models in the area of industrial planning, but it has not yet been applied to models of the agriculture sector. To demonstrate its use in this area, work has begun on the "translation" into GAMS of two models: a model of the agriculture sector in India, developed by the International Institute for Applied Systems Analysis (IIASA) in Vienna (Austria), and a model of the agriculture sector in Algeria, developed by the Bureau national d'études du développement et de l'économie rurale (BNEDER) in Algiers, which is collaborating in the project. This work should render the models computationally more accessible and make their structure easier to comprehend.

Responsibility: Eastern Africa Projects Department and *Development Research Department*—Wilfred V. Candler and Alexander Meeraus, respectively.

Completion date: December 1983.

The Impact of Agricultural Extension: A Case Study of the Training and Visit Method in Haryana, India

Ref. No. 672-29

Agricultural extension is widely perceived as an important mechanism for transmitting the results of agronomic research to farmers, thus helping them to increase the productivity of the land and water at their disposal. At the same time, the feedback from farmers through the extension system can be used to ensure that agricultural research concentrates on farmers' needs.

One particular kind of extension organization, the Training and Visit (T&V) System, has been adopted in many of the Bank's member countries, as it seems to be more effective than other systems in improving farmers' performance. The essence of this system is a tightly structured work program for agents, based on a strict schedule of visits to groups of farmers, each of which includes selected contact farmers; training and updating sessions for agents; a hierarchical organizational structure, with clearly defined duties and responsibilities; and exclusive devotion to extension work. At the initial stage, the T&V extension method stresses improved practices that are likely to require additional labor rather than the increased use of costly material inputs, in the expectation that small farmers with surplus family labor will find such innovations easier to adopt. More complex changes are recommended at later stages.

- the incomes and consumption of poor households that are
  not among the projects' direct beneficiaries, as a result of
  project induced changes in relative prices and employment.

This study attempts to remedy these deficiencies for dairy
development projects by looking at the actual effects on (1)
production and labor allocation; (2) income distribution; and (3)
human nutrition of selected dairy development projects in India.
The study will:

1. Estimate the direct economic benefits produced by the
   projects.
2. Estimate how project benefits are being distributed, paying
   particular attention to the projects' impact on the incomes of
   the poor.
3. Estimate how the projects are affecting food consumption
   (including food distribution within a family) and nutrition
   among the poor and population groups that are deficient in
   calories and protein.
4. Identify and quantify the key relationships and parameters
   determining the effects of a project on production, food
   consumption, and nutrition.
5. Develop a system for evaluating the economic and nutritional effects of dairy development projects.

Data will be gathered through household surveys in two or
three separate locations in India. Preparations for field work are
well advanced in Karnataka where a primarily cross-sectional
survey will be undertaken among households that have participated in the project from one to four years, as well as non-
participating households. The sample of approximately 1,000
households will be surveyed, once each quarter, over a year.
Similar studies are being planned in Madhya Pradesh.

The analysis will attempt to estimate the direct effects of the
project on income, consumption, and nutrition. It will include
identification of the principal linkages and estimation of related
key parameters. It is anticipated that it will ultimately be possible
to identify a few key parameters and relationships that will
capture most of the observed change and, thus, provide the basis
for the use of more modest surveys and techniques in future
evaluation studies. These estimated parameters will also be used
to test the usefulness of an ex ante framework.

The analytical framework consists of three main parts. First,
the compiling of comparative data on project benefits. Second, the

testing of hypotheses, principally through regression and other statistical procedures. Third, the construction of an econometric model of a farm household that will be used to test and evaluate the effect of changes in the value of parameters that have been caused by the project or other influences. The model will have the following elements:

1. Production functions relating inputs (labor by household members, hired labor, and other agricultural inputs) to output of milk and other agricultural products.
2. Labor demand functions estimated from the production functions.
3. Labor supply functions for individual household members in milk and other production activities.
4. Demand functions for individual household members for homegrown and purchased food.
5. Estimated weights for the distribution of commodities within the family.

Responsibility: South Asia Projects Department—Odin K. Knudsen and Roger H. Slade, in collaboration with Per Pinstrup Andersen of the International Food Policy Research Institute. In India, the Center for Rural Studies, Bangalore, the monitoring and evaluation units of the Karnataka Dairy Development Corporation and the Madhya Pradesh Dairy Development Corporation, and the Institute of Rural Management, Anand, will be the main collaborating institutions.

Completion date: June 1985.

Market and Agricultural Policy Determinants of Rural Incomes

Ref. No. 672-39

Most studies of the effects of agricultural growth and technical progress on rural incomes have concentrated on changes in the distribution of incomes among farms of different sizes, resulting from different ways of adopting new farm technology in the adoption cycle and from different modes of access to production credit or irrigation facilities. While these effects are undoubtedly important, the effects of agricultural growth on food prices, wages, and real labor incomes have not been dealt with adequately, although they may be of equal or greater significance as determinants of the distribution of income.

A study designed to analyze such issues would have to adopt an approach focusing on price and wage determinants at a more aggregative level rather than being based mainly on sample surveys of farming units. This project aims at constructing aggregative models of the agriculture sectors in India that will then be used to analyze the effects of agricultural development policies and projects, trends in population and the labor force, and technical change, on the incomes of major socioeconomic groups.

The model will contain four major agroclimatic regions of India. The rural and urban populations, respectively, will be divided into four quartiles of the income distribution. Each of these quartiles is differentiated by (1) ownership pattern of agricultural factors of production from which income is derived, (2) supply behavior of factors of production, such as labor, and (3) expenditure in sharply different patterns according to income position.

The model is designed to handle a large set of issues related to agriculture. In particular, it is intended to examine how the incomes of poor laborers and residents of lagging regions can be improved by policies and programs for the rural sector. Such programs include rural works, investments in irrigation, agricultural mechanization, input subsidies, agricultural research, changes in the international trade regime governing agricultural commodities and inputs, taxes, subsidies, and direct income transfers.

The quantities and prices of agricultural outputs and factors are determined endogenously in the model. Real income of all groups depends on their supplies of agricultural factors of production and food consumption patterns, that is, because changes in food prices affect real incomes of poor groups more sharply than of rich groups.

Most econometric estimations of supply and demand parameters for all four regions have been completed. For each region and income quartile, base-year values have been estimated for their supplies of factors of production, their contribution to output, and their level of consumption and of income. A number of technical issues have been clarified in technical notes. A version of the model has been completed for the northern wheat region; it was used to analyze a number of preliminary scenarios and policy simulations. An initial set of simulations with the complete model is expected by the end of 1983 and the project should be completed by mid-1984.

Responsibility: Agriculture and Rural Development Department —Hans Binswanger, in collaboration with Jaime Quizon and with Devendra Gupta of the Institute of Economic Growth, New Delhi (consultants).

Completion date: July 1984.

Reports

Bapna, Shanti; Binswanger, Hans; and Quizon, Jaime. "Systems of Output Supply and Factor Demand Equations for Semi-Arid Tropical India." Studies in Employment and Rural Development No. 73. The World Bank, October 1981.

Binswanger, Hans; Quizon, Jaime; and Swamy, Gurushri. "The Demand for Food and Foodgrain Quality in India." Agriculture Research Unit Discussion Paper No. 6. The World Bank: Agriculture and Rural Development Department, November 1982.

Quizon, Jaime, and Binswanger, Hans. "Factor Gains and Losses in the Semi-Arid Tropics of India." Agriculture Research Unit Discussion Paper No. 9. The World Bank: Agriculture and Rural Development Department, September 1983.

_____. "Income Distribution in Agriculture: A Unified Approach." *American Journal of Agricultural Economics* (forthcoming).

Quizon, Jaime; Binswanger, Hans; and Gupta, Devendra. "The Distribution of Agricultural Incomes in India's Northern Wheat Region." Agriculture Research Unit Discussion Paper No. 10. The World Bank: Agriculture and Rural Development Department, September 1983.

Swamy, Gurushri, and Binswanger, Hans. "Flexible Consumer Demand Systems and Linear Estimations: Food in India." *American Journal of Agricultural Economics* (forthcoming).

Canal Command Model for Project Design and System Operation in the Indus Basin

Ref. No. 672-50A

This project is a research application of the project "Programming and Designing Investment: Indus Basin" (Ref. No. 671-45 in this category). Its objectives will be (1) to assist in the design and evaluation of the planned "Command Water Management (CWM)" project and (2) to help develop the analytical capability of the collaborating institution, the Water and Power Development Authority (WAPDA) of Pakistan, for effective system management and planning.

The Command Water Management project is primarily intended to bring about a substantial increase in agricultural production in selected pilot areas through improved water management backed up by the necessary agricultural supporting services and nonwater inputs. The application involved modifying the present Indus Basin modeling system to make it suitable for use in evaluating and planning components of the CWM project. These modifications were made by officers of WAPDA who thereby acquired experience in using and adapting the model system, and in disseminating it among other concerned agencies.

Specifically, the research task was to build a canal command model using components of the Indus Basin Model. The model will be used to study losses in flows from the diversion point (barrage) to the fields, additions to and subtractions from the aquifer, and farmer response to additional water and related inputs in terms of increased agricultural production. The data base for the application is unusually good, as it is the product of an extensive data gathering exercise over the past several years.

The final output of the application consists of:

1. Inputs into the CWM project, particularly planning the set of components within subprojects and the evaluation of subprojects.
2. A canal command model that can be used by WAPDA for optimal management of the system and purposes of investment appraisal.
3. An enhanced modeling capability of WAPDA.
4. A slender monograph on the application of modeling techniques to the design and appraisal of irrigation projects at the canal command level. This will be in the nature of a manual addressed to the practitioner.

Responsibility: Economics and Research Staff, Agriculture and Rural Development Department, and *Development Research Department*—John H. Duloy, Gerald T. O'Mara, and Alexander Meeraus, respectively, in collaboration with Anthony Brooke (consultant). The major collaborating institution is the Water and

Power Development Authority of Pakistan, which provided two staff members who were involved in building and applying the canal command model under the supervision of staff of the Development Research Department.

Completion date: December 1983.

Conditions for Sustained Farm Mechanization

Ref. No. 672-67

In most developing countries where farm mechanization has been introduced, there have been problems that impede potential benefits from being realized. Mechanization schemes, especially involving tractors, are continually falling short of expectations, in large part because of deficiencies in a country's supporting framework. The problems show up in poor machinery performance, short operating life, frequent breakdowns, long downtimes, high repair costs, inadequate supplies of spare parts and maintenance services. An extensive literature search has shown that these problems are pervasive and persistent, and that the mechanization process is often slowed or brought to a halt as a result.

This study addresses the question of how farm mechanization can be sustained in both the short term and the long term. It intends to identify and analyze the conditions that must be satisfied in the economic, financial, technical, social, institutional, and policy framework, if sustained mechanization is to be achieved.

The research focuses on tractors, ranging from small two-wheeled ones to larger, four-wheeled tractors. An analytical model of the sociotechnical systems framework within which mechanized farming takes place is being developed and refined by means of a case study in Thailand. The aims are: (1) to develop an operational tool that may be used widely in developing countries, (2) to elaborate strategies for farm mechanization, and (3) to plan viable projects. Of particular interest will be the examination of appropriate roles for the public sector and the private sector, as well as for external agencies, such as the World Bank, in providing technical or financial assistance.

Responsibility: Agriculture and Rural Development Department —W. Graeme Donovan. The principal investigator is Peter Delp (consultant). A field survey has been undertaken by the Center for Applied Economics Research, Kasetsart University (Thailand), and the project has the support of the National Economic and Social Development Board in Thailand.

Completion date: December 1983.

Agricultural Pricing Policies in Turkey

Ref. No. 672–78A

The formulation of agricultural development priorities in Turkey and related food security interventions has been hampered by a poorly developed statistical system and questionable methodologies for policy analysis. The purpose of this research application is to transfer methodologies developed in the research projects "Country Case Studies of Agricultural Prices and Subsidies" (Ref. No. 671–42), and "A Framework for Agriculture Sector Analysis" (Ref. No. 672–11), both now completed, to Turkey, adapting them to the country's specific environment in order to demonstrate their usefulness to the research community and the government. The methodologies would also provide prototype modeling techniques for countries with a similar mix of geoclimatic conditions and production/marketing opportunities.

The main topics addressed in this research were (1) the comparative advantages of and within agriculture; (2) the production, consumption, and trade effects of devaluation; (3) the production, consumption, and welfare effects of alternative trade regimes; and (4) alternative price stabilization and food security policies for grains, principally wheat.

For these purposes, two models were developed. A model of the mathematical programming variety of agricultural production and marketing activities was constructed to answer questions raised by the first three abovementioned topics. This model includes features such as risk aversion, price-responsive input supply, consumption and trade, and income effects. It also models production transformation possibilities in detail, including crop rotations under different geoclimatic conditions and relationships between the animal feedbase, animal production, and demands for livestock products. Under the project, a version of this model has been installed at the facility of the cooperating research institute, the Middle East Technical University in Ankara.

A second model, of the stochastic programming variety, was developed to address the fourth topic. It analyzes alternative price stabilization policies for grains in Turkey, by focusing on pricing decisions by producers, price and subsidy schemes for consumers, stocking rules, and government interventions in trade. Simple measures of variation and insecurity compare trade-offs between policies with reference to important economic indicators.

Both models have been used in the preparation of the forthcoming report of the Turkey Agricultural Sector Study Mission. In the context of discussions of the project and the sector report, an attempt will be made to promote use of the models within the Turkish government to improve its capability for agricultural policy analysis.

Responsibility: Agriculture and Rural Development Department —Graham Donaldson, with Vinh Le-Si (consultant), and *Europe, Middle East, and North Africa Regional Projects Department*—Richard Burcroff II, in collaboration with Professor Haluk Kasnakoglu of the Middle East Technical University, Ankara (Turkey).

Completion date: June 1983; the completion report is in process.

Reports

Bigman, D. "Turkey: Price Stabilization and Food Security Policies in Grains." Economics and Policy Division Working Paper No. 66. The World Bank: Agriculture and Rural Development Department, March 1983.

Evans, M. C., and Le-Si, Vinh. "Turkey Agricultural Sector Model: Further Results for the Livestock Sub-sector." Economics and Policy Division Working Paper No. 68. The World Bank: Agriculture and Rural Development Department, 1983.

Le-Si, Vinh, and Scandizzo, P. L. "Turkey Agricultural Sector Model." Economics and Policy Division Working Paper No. 67. The World Bank: Agriculture and Rural Development Department, March 1983.

A Manual of Agriculture Sector Programming Models

Ref. No. 672–80A

Agriculture Sector Models (ASM) have been constructed for a number of developing countries in the past decade, and they continue to be built. While some of the studies may not have yielded results commensurate with expectations, there is no doubt that many of them have provided valuable insights into the effects of agricultural policy, and in some cases (for example, in Chile, Mexico, and Portugal), the models have contributed direct inputs for the policy process.

The principal appeal of ASMs for policy analysis is their comprehensiveness. The models provide the opportunity to explore a large number of linkages, such as the effects of pricing policy on employment and income distribution, the consequences of freer trade policies for prices, incomes, and resource allocation, and the impact of investment on employment and the composition of the sector's output.

The objective of this project is to facilitate and improve the application of methodologies for evaluating policy options for the sector by developing a manual for the construction and use of agriculture sector models. The manual would emphasize practical approaches, and it would illustrate how to set up models for solutions that have policy relevance. While the manual will address a large number of specific technical points, the emphasis throughout will be placed on readability and ease of use.

The research tasks can be described in terms of the components of the manual:

1. A small prototype of a sector model will be presented initially, and its structure will be divided into components that can be analyzed and presented separately.

2. Several case studies will present a compact description of the models that are used, including actual numbers. The considerable advances in the procedures of model management in recent years now permit much more compact descriptions of the models than were previously possible.

3. The approach will also show the ways in which the models can be applied to policy issues and review the experience in country applications in several cases; this is obviously an important area in which many model studies are weak.

4. The design of investment projects and the use of models to study the sensitivity and trade-offs of optimal project design to different objectives and scenarios will be described. Special attention will be paid to the treatment of investments in tree crops, livestock, irrigation, marketing, and research and extension.

5. Examples will be given of how regional components of these models are applied to issues of project design for certain classes of projects, especially irrigation and mechanization projects.

Responsibility: Agriculture and Rural Development Department and *Development Research Department*—Gerald T. O'Mara and Alexander Meeraus, respectively, in collaboration with Professor Roger Norton, University of New Mexico.

Completion date: June 1984.

Agricultural Household Models: Extensions and Policy Implications

Ref. No. 672-82

Since 1975, researchers at the Food Research Institute of Stanford University and the World Bank have been developing models of agricultural households that combine producer and consumer behavior. Subsequently, various researchers have developed and applied extensions of the basic model. The intention of this project is to produce a monograph that distills the policy implications of this work and, on the basis of a comparative analyis of existing models, identifies areas for further extensions and refinements.

A large part of agriculture comprises semicommercial farms producing multiple crops. These farms or agricultural households combine two fundamental units of microeconomic analysis—the household and the firm. Traditional economic theory has dealt with these separately, but in developing countries where peasant farms dominate, it is their interdependence that is of crucial importance. The proper understanding of the economic behavior of these households requires the specification and estimation not only of complete demand systems (including leisure and hence labor supply) but also production systems (including a full range of production possibilities, such as multiple cropping and intercropping or ancillary activities). Moreover, the interdependence of consumption and production requires that this be done within an integrated framework of analysis. A substantial body of theoretical and empirical work that consistently integrates production and consumption is now available, but little has yet been done with respect to either comparative analysis of different formulations of the basic model or a compilation of cross-country results. More importantly, no systematic attempt has yet been made to derive the major policy implications of these models.

The primary purpose of the proposed monograph, therefore, is to allow the systematic extraction of the major policy conclusions deriving from as wide a range of alternative specifications and as many different countries as possible. In addition, by means of a careful scrutiny of existing extensions to the basic model and an assessment of policy priorities, it is hoped that the monograph will provide firm foundations for guiding the next round of theoretical and applied research.

Responsibility: Eastern Africa Regional Office and Country Policy Department—Inderjit Singh and Lyn Squire, respectively, in collaboration with John Strauss, University of Virginia (consultant).

Completion date: March 1984.

Direct and Indirect Effects of Irrigation: Matar Taluka, Gujarat, India

Ref. No. 672-84

Despite substantial lending programs in irrigation, there is little empirical evidence of the impact on landowners, agricultural workers, and other sectors of the economy. Few empirical studies have been carried out in this field. One reason is that such studies demand rather comprehensive and costly data collection and processing. Also, there are many unresolved methodological problems relating to quantification.

A large proportion of the World Bank's lending in irrigation has been allocated to the South Asia region, particularly to India, which is the focus of this research. The project's main thrust is to study and quantify the impact of irrigation investments in the development of the Matar Taluka area in the State of Gujarat. This particular area was selected because a large proportion of villages and households in Matar Taluka had been surveyed several times since the 1930s. Two of these surveys (1965–66 and 1974–75) were carried out by the Gujarat Institute of Area Planning. The data had been collected and processed, but they had not been used to assess the potential effects of irrigation. The project is important to the Bank because of its involvement in irrigation in Gujarat, and a major demand has been placed on using the existing data base to analyze the direct and indirect effects of irrigation.

Matar Taluka is an administrative unit, comprising 82 villages and having a land area of approximately 2,212 square miles and a population of a little over 100,000 (1960–61). In this taluka, the major source of irrigation is canal water. The region has four rivers which cross it: Shehdi, Khari, Watrak and Sabarnati. In addition to these rivers, there are three big water tanks located in Bobhalaj, Tranya Nagrama, and Pariej. Tank irrigation has declined over the years, particularly after the introduction of the Mahi canal, built in 1961–62. The impact of irrigation on production, crop diversification, income and profits, and several other economic concerns has been quite remarkable.

The area has been surveyed three times—first, in 1929, with a view to find out what was the actual tax burden of producers. The survey also included data relating to assets, debts, consumption, and employment. Another survey was undertaken in 1965 and it provided a broad picture of the changes in the economy of the taluka over three-and-one-half decades. A resurvey was undertaken in 1974, with the support of the Indian Council of Social Science Research, and was designed to reach the same households a decade later. These surveys provide a unique record of rural development at the household level over time.

The main objectives of the research project are (1) to quantify the direct and indirect benefits from irrigation, providing a framework and the empirical basis with which to assess the importance of water resource development; and (2) to enhance institution building through the development of a collaborative research relationship with the Gujarat Institute of Area Planning. Three effects of irrigation on rural households will be considered: production and income, consumption, and savings and investments. Irrigation has a direct impact on agricultural production and farm income via changes in cropping patterns, yield, and the use of inputs. It has an indirect effect on nonfarm income via an increased demand for labor and a general equilibrium effect in wage rates. The effect on consumption occurs via its effect on farms and incomes. Finally, by affecting the rates of return on agricultural investment, irrigation has an effect on investment and capital formation. Both data sets will be used to explore the effects of irrigation.

Output from the research will include a document on the quantification of direct and indirect effects of irrigation, background papers, and an assessment of the data base for farm household modeling.

Responsibility: Agriculture and Rural Development Department and South Asia Projects and Programs Departments—Alfredo Sfeir-Younis and Christoph Diewald, respectively, in collaboration with the Gujarat Institute of Area Planning.

Completion date: June 1984.

Managing African Agricultural Development: Lessons from the Tanzanian Experience

Ref. No. 673-04

Strategic questions of economic management affect the long-term agricultural prospects of Africa. These questions center on the issues of short-term versus long-term development objectives, promotion of self-sufficiency versus export promotion, and the use of aid and foreign capital versus the mobilization of domestic resources. The appropriateness of a range of instruments, including price and exchange rate policies, and the relative balance between private and public sectors are also called into question.

To explain past agricultural performance and to consider the implications of future policy, the interface of external and internal constraints with key areas of domestic policymaking need to be understood more clearly. Such knowledge can form the basis for the formulation and support of more effective agricultural strategies by governments and the community of donors.

This study aims at producing a detailed review of the experience of governments and donor agencies in managing and supporting agricultural development in Africa during the postindependence period. Based on evidence from six countries, the analysis will attempt to discuss the nature of, the reasons for, and the consequences of the major policy and institutional choices with a view to identifying the type of changes needed to induce self-sustained agricultural growth. The objective is to stimulate a dialogue among scholars, donors, and African policymakers on how governments, acting with the support of donors in the area of agricultural management, can improve agricultural performance and prospects.

The genesis of the study is the World Bank's study on the agriculture sector in Tanzania, which explored how and why a number of critical policy choices affecting the sector were made by the Tanzanian government, supported by its donors, and examined the short- and the long-run implications of these choices for overall developmental performance. While Tanzania faces many of the development dilemmas experienced by policymakers throughout the African continent, there are sufficient differences in policy and results among African countries to raise interesting questions about the relationship of agricultural performance with certain combinations of policies in the long-term strategies of specific countries. Detailed comparisons will be made in key areas of agricultural policy, constraints, and performance with regard to Tanzania and five other African countries —Cameroon, Kenya, Malawi, Nigeria, and Senegal. These countries exemplify the diversity of the continent with regard to geography, endowment of physical resources, economic structure, and agricultural policy.

The research has two parts: a series of background studies analyzing particular issues on a cross-country comparative basis and the simultaneous development of individual country profiles containing statistical and qualitative data for each country case. To the extent possible, the background studies will cover the (1) macroeconomic management experience as it affects the agriculture sector, including exchange rate and fiscal policies and management of the balance of payments; (2) foreign exchange requirements and allocations to the agriculture sector; (3) policy of public resource allocation regarding agricultural requirements, including intersectoral breakdown of expenditures; (4) interface of producer pricing policy and various kinds of marketing institutions; (5) role of donor assistance in developing agricultural potential; (6) factors affecting government decisionmaking on national development strategies and agriculture sector policies; and (7) sectoral performance and prospects for technological development based on dissemination and links between manpower-training policies and capacity for research institution building.

Data will be drawn from records of the World Bank and International Monetary Fund, recent and ongoing work from other research institutions, and field investigations in the respective countries. A final report will synthesize the findings of these studies, drawing conclusions about the types of policies that can induce agricultural growth and the necessary conditions for their implementation, including the implications for donor assistance.

Responsibility: Development Research Department and *Eastern Africa Projects Department*—Uma Lele and Wilfred Candler, respectively, in collaboration with Ellen Hanak (consultant). A team of consultants will be involved in the preparation of background studies and country profiles. The project will involve close collaboration with the Bank's operational staff and with African government officials.

Completion date: September 1985.

Agricultural Pricing Policy in Eastern Africa

Ref. No. 673–07A

Governments intervene actively in agricultural input and output markets in pursuit of such goals as efficient resource allocation, food self-sufficiency, equitable income distribution, and resource mobilization. In an earlier research project, "Taxation and Pricing Policies in Rural and Urban Korea" (Ref. No. 672–61 in category 1—Development Policy and Planning), the World Bank developed a methodology for exploring the consequences of alternative agricultural pricing policies for the Korean government's major goals. Compared with simpler, partial equilibrium approaches that rely on the techniques of consumer surplus and producer surplus, the current exercise may best be described as a limited general equilibrium analysis. It specifically incorporates the major interactions between related markets and allows the analyst to explore the consequences of simultaneous price changes in more than one market. Unlike earlier work, this analysis is based firmly on the microeconomic behavior of producers and consumers and explicitly recognizes the importance of the farm household as a microeconomic unit. The present project applies this basic approach to the analysis of agricultural pricing policy in Malawi. Other applications are being undertaken in Cyprus, Senegal (see Ref. No. 673–08A below), and Sierra Leone.

Government intervention in agricultural markets in Malawi is both extensive and effective. The producer and consumer prices of the major food crops—maize, groundnuts, rice—are set by the government. The state is also responsible for exporting the major cash crops of tobacco and cotton produced by smallholders and for importing their fertilizer. In general, the cash crops are taxed relative to world prices and the food crops are subsidized. The government marketing agency usually enjoys a net surplus. By way of contrast, the estates can sell their ourputs—tobacco, sugar, tea —directly on world markets. They are, however, subject to a tax on profits. The objective of the project is to explore the consequences of alternative pricing (including a movement towards free trade) and taxation policies for government revenue, producer incomes, consumer welfare, and food self-sufficiency.

Responsibility: Country Policy Department—Lyn Squire, and *Eastern Africa Regional Office*—Inderjit Singh.

Completion date: February 1984.

Agricultural Pricing Policy in Senegal

Ref. No. 673–08A

This research project shares a methodology and will extend to Senegal in Western Africa the application of a previously developed model that explored alternative agricultural pricing policies in the Republic of Korea.

In the case of Korea (see Ref. No. 672–61 in this category), the model identified the consequences of alternative agricultural pricing policies for the supply and demand of selected commodities, net import requirements, and the real incomes of four urban groups distinguished by income category and of six rural groups defined by size of landholding. The intent of the analysis was to ensure specified reductions in the overall budget of the government, based on alternative pricing options.

The Korean model has a microeconomic structure in that it uses simple models of farm household behavior as its building blocks. This allows for an investigation of the response by producers and consumers to externally induced changes in prices, derivation of aggregate demand and supply curves as the basis for analysis of alternative pricing policies, and precise measurement of the changes in welfare of selected socioeconomic groups following a particular market intervention.

In Senegal, where agriculture is the dominant sector of employment and a major contributor to gross domestic product and total value of exports, the government intervenes in its agricultural markets. The application of the model has potentially important implications for policymakers regarding questions about urban versus rural income distribution, parastatal efficiency, the role of private traders, the level of incentives to farmers, the budgetary cost of food subsidies, and the role of agriculture as the source of foreign exchange. The assessment of the impact of different agricultural pricing policies on all these variables is critical in generating policy recommendations.

For Senegal, the model will be modified to handle a larger number of agricultural commodities than in the Korean case and to take account of the effects of weather on the production of groundnuts, Senegal's major crop.

Responsibility: Country Policy Department—Avishay Braverman and Jeffrey Hammer, in conjunction with Christopher J. Redfern and Joseph Baah-Dwomoh of the Western Africa Country Programs Department II and Western Africa Projects Department, respectively.

Completion date: June 1984.

Reports

Braverman, A.; Hammer, J; and Levinsohn, J. "Balance of Payments, Government Deficit Reduction, and Agricultural Pricing in Senegal." Country Policy Department Discussion Paper. The World Bank, September 1983.
Hammer, J. "Subsistence First: Farm Allocation Decisions in Senegal." Draft. The World Bank: Country Policy Department, March 1983.

Workshop on the Effects of Externalities on the Efficiency of Irrigated Agriculture in Developing Countries

Ref. No. 673-09

Research on irrigation has focused attention on the significant social costs incurred when the development of irrigation neglects physical interdependencies. The core of the problem is that private agents individually do not take into account the physical externality that dependence on a common resource imposes on them collectively when allocating the resources at their disposal. In addition, decisions by government policymakers all too often neglect environmental effects that do not seem to require immediate attention—for example, the effects of canal irrigation on groundwater levels (and ultimately agricultural production) in confined or slowly draining river basins. The ultimate effect of such shortsighted decisionmaking, which underestimates the real cost of current production in irrigated agriculture, is a sharp increase in real and perceived costs of production at some future date. Regions where the neglect of environmental interdependence has begun to affect production include the North China Plain and the Indus and Ganges Plains of South Asia.

For example, interdependence between supplies of groundwater and surface water means that the levels of efficient controls on the withdrawal of groundwater depend on the allocation of surface water. While this allocation is typically controlled by the government, usually groundwater withdrawals are not. The problem of efficiently coordinating allocative decisions by public and private agents has proved to be resistent to resolution by any of the policies yet adopted by concerned governments, in spite of possible significant gains in mean agricultural production and decreased exposure to risk.

In developing countries, any of the schemes proposed to internalize efficiently the externality due to an aquifer or to its linkage with a surface water distribution system have not been applied to any significant extent, despite the incentive of significant benefits. This suggests that either the schemes have neglected one or more constraints that are operative in the real world or other social objectives, in conflict with the efficiency criterion, are dominant in practice. The strategy of this workshop was to bring the conceptualizing theorists together with engineers and administrators with operating experience in irrigation systems to reexamine the problem and find solutions that can be implemented.

The workshop was held at the World Bank between May 11 and 13, 1983, with 20 invited guests and a number of interested Bank staff participating. A staff working paper summarizing workshop discussion and conclusions will be forthcoming in the near future. A conference volume is expected to be available in about one year.

Responsibility: Agriculture and Rural Development Department —Gerald T. O'Mara.

Completion date: December 1983.

Supply Response of Aggregate Crops Output

Ref. No. 673-15

Price regimes in many developing countries discriminate substantially against agriculture. Discrimination takes the form of taxes on production or exports, or protection given to other sectors of the economy. Lending institutions, such as the World Bank, have argued that these discriminatory policies result in reducing agricultural output substantially from what it otherwise would have been, dampening agricultural, as well as overall, economic growth. Implicit in this position is the assumption that aggregate agricultural output has a high price elasticity. Most studies have found, however, that the long-run elasticity of aggregate agricultural output is very small—near to zero, in fact. A recent study has pointed out that these estimates, based on time-series data for individual countries, are invalid because they do not reflect the investment impact of changes in long-term price strategies such as those advocated in much of the World Bank's sector work.[1]

It is essential to provide a sound empirical basis for the World Bank's general position, as well as that of other development agencies, on the movement toward more rational agricultural pricing policies in developing countries. At issue is whether time-series data from an individual country provide a valid experiment for the measurement of long-run price elasticities, because countries generally pursue high or low price strategies for decades, with price peaks and troughs around these policies being maintained for only short periods. These price movements would not lead to the kind of investment response that would be seen if a country were to abandon its discriminatory stance for good.

Utilizing recent advances in the pooling of time-series and cross-sectional data and in estimation techniques for variable coefficients, this study will estimate aggregate crop supply responses to output price changes, as well as to changes in input prices, from data of a large number of countries.

---

[1] W. L. Peterson. "International Farm Prices and the Social Cost of Cheap Food Policies," *American Journal of Agricultural Economics* (February 1979), pp. 12–21.

The assembled data base for about 90 industrial and developing countries will comprise, for example, data on agricultural output by commodity, producer prices, wage rates, expenditure on research and extension, fertilizer consumption and prices, tractors, literacy rates, as well as measures of agricultural potential. This data base will allow further analysis to be carried out on aggregate livestock production response and disaggregation by regions and products.

Since the major problem areas in this study are the specification and estimation of a system of equations using pooled cross-sectional, time-series data and variable coefficient estimators, the project is employing the services of Professor Yair Mundlak, who has done considerable research using these techniques.

Responsibility: Agriculture and Rural Development Department —Hans P. Binswanger, and *Economic Analysis and Projections Department*—Ronald C. Duncan and Maw-Cheng Yang, in collaboration with Yair Mundlak (consultant) of Hebrew University (Israel).

Completion date: April 1984.

Agricultural Mechanization in Africa: Review and Prospects

Ref. No. 673-16

The driving forces of the mechanization process—scarcity of labor, abundance of land and capital, elastic demand for agricultural output, and innovation and invention by the private sector —are fairly well understood for most regions of the world. Yet, in Africa mechanization has proceeded very slowly. Hoe cultivation is tenaciously maintained in areas where labor appears to be very scarce, and successful mechanization is restricted to sharply defined areas. While recent reviews of mechanization have looked at management factors and constraints to the supply of farm machinery, this project will center on factors that determine the demand for mechanization, particularly agroclimatic and soil conditions, seasonality of crops and peaks in the demand for labor, and the final demand for agricultural products. A better understanding of these interactions will provide more reliable predictions of future patterns of mechanization.

In the study, mechanization is defined as the replacement of human labor by animal or mechanical power. The slow progress of animal traction and motorization in sub-Saharan Africa is well documented. The project aims at identifying persistent forces that govern the profitability of mechanized investments and that remain relevant when shorter-run impediments, such as sociocultural or institutional factors, could be overcome. The review is intended to assist World Bank project departments in clarifying, on a region-by-region basis, the factors that have limited mechanization and whether these factors continue to be relevant or are about to be overcome. The study will examine the evolution and extent of mechanization in twenty to thirty different areas of sub-Saharan Africa. The geographical areas selected for analysis include regions where animal traction has long been established, such as Botswana and Ethiopia; where animal traction spread shortly after World War II, such as the areas of groundnut cultivation in Senegal or of cotton cultivation in Mali; and regions where it has spread in the past 10 years, such as southwestern Upper Volta and central Ivory Coast. A similar comparative approach will be used in the case of tractors, with reference to their introduction in selected areas of northern Ivory Coast, Kenya, and Sudan.

Field visits by the researchers to selected locations in eastern and western Africa will complement the review of existing economic, agronomic, anthropological, and historical studies upon which the project is based.

Responsibility: Agriculture and Rural Development Department —Hans P. Binswanger, with the assistance of Prabhu L. Pingali (consultant), and *Eastern Africa Regional Office*—Inderjit J. Singh, in collaboration with Ives Bigot, Institut de recherches agronomiques tropicales et des cultures vivrières (IRAT), Paris (France), and Surender Virmani and N. S. Jodha, International Crops Research Center for the Semi-Arid Tropics (ICRISAT), Hyderabad (India).

Completion date: June 1984.

4

Industry

Scope for Capital-Labor Substitution in the Mechanical Engineering Industry

Ref. No. 670-23

The World Bank's Research Committee has conducted two investigations of planning methodology in the mechanical engineering industries. The investigations have demonstrated that it is feasibile to implement numerically solvable process analysis models of mechanical engineering activities (see Ref. No. 670-24 hereunder). The present study extends this methodology to permit the specification of alternative production techniques and the incorporation of product differentiation. It analyzes the scope for capital-labor substitution in mechanical engineering activities and the extent of substitution between locally produced and imported mechanical engineering products.

The first part of this study is concerned with alternative production techniques for given product specifications. The traditional approach of econometric production function analysis is not employed. Instead, to avoid ambiguities that arise through aggregation, process analysis models based on engineering data are constructed for four products: a specific model each of an electric motor, water pump, distribution transformer, and bicycle.

Each product is reduced to its components and subassemblies. The production of each component and each assembly stage is further broken down into a sequence of process stages, i.e., elementary operations performed jointly by labor and a single piece of equipment. Alternative techniques, described by engineers' estimates, are then enumerated at each process stage. For given factor prices, including the cost of capital and wages for different levels of skills, cost minimization determines the optimal technique for each individual process stage at different scales of output. This approach can analyze the sensitivity of optimal production techniques to factor prices, economies of scale, joint production and output mix, the sequential nature of production, and the degree of capacity utilization. The results indicate that there is substantial scope for capital-labor substitution in the production of these goods. The optimal choice of technique appears more sensitive to the scale of output than to factor prices, with highly labor intensive techniques being chosen at low scales and highly mechanized techniques at high scales.

The second part of this study is concerned with substitution between domestically produced and imported textile-weaving machinery in the Republic of Korea. This part of the study is also highly disaggregated in order to isolate the effects of differentials in labor skills, characteristics of individual machines, learning by doing, depreciation and obsolescence, firm organization, and product differentiation. Engineering production functions are estimated econometrically from data at the man-machine level in order to establish relationships between inputs and outputs. (In turn, the structure of prices for differentiated material inputs and outputs is determined using hedonic regression techniques, so that the impact of market structure and certain government incentive policies may be isolated.)

Technique choices are investigated by simulation to obtain the present value of the stream of net revenues associated with particular machines and product mixes. Results (see the fourth report listed below) confirm that substantial scope for capital labor substitution exists in textile weaving by choosing the degree of automation. For most product mixes, domestically produced machinery is optimal if shadow prices are used and perfect competition is assumed. On the other hand, producers have, in many cases, actually chosen more highly automated imported machinery because of incentives granted by the government, including access to suppliers' credit at lower interest rates, accelerated depreciation, and tariff exempt imports of machinery. Government incentives in the product markets appear to have altered the mix of products being produced. The hypothesis that producers are profit maximizers is tested and not found to be invalid.

Responsibility: Development Research Department—Larry E. Westphal, in collaboration with Yung Whee Rhee of the Industry

Department, and with engineers of the Korea Institute of Science and Technology.

Completion date: June 1984.

Reports

Korea Institute of Science and Technology. "Final Report on a Study of the Scope for Capital-Labor Substitution in the Mechanical Engineering Sector." (F6-400-2), February 1973.

Rhee, Yung W., and Westphal, Larry E. "Choice of Technology: Criteria, Search, and Interdependence." In Herbert Giersch (ed.), *International Economic Development and Resource Transfer: Workshop 1978* (Institut für Weltwirtschaft, Kiel). Tübingen: J.C. Mohr (Paul Siebeck), 1979. Also World Bank Reprint Series: Number 103.

_____. "Microanalytic Aspects of Complementary Intraindustry Specialization." Paper presented at the seminar on North-South Complementary Intraindustry Trade, Mexico City, August 1980. Summary in *Directors Report,* U.N. 1980, UNCTAD/MD/III, pp. 17-19.

_____. "A Micro Econometric Investigation of Choice of Technology." *Journal of Development Economics* 4 (September 1977):205-37. Also World Bank Reprint Series: Number Fifty.

Westphal, Larry E. "Research on Appropriate Technology." *Industry and Development* 2 (1978):28-46. Also World Bank Reprint Series: Number Eighty eight.

Programming in the Manufacturing Sector

Ref. No. 670-24

This research project deals with the problem of investment analysis in industries characterized by increasing returns to scale. The study focuses on improved methods for selecting investment projects from among the many alternatives in size, timing, location, technology, and output mix. The research aims at providing operationally useful and practical techniques of analysis that permit a more systematic treatment of the problem of project selection.

The research effort was begun with three empirical studies, dealing with the Eastern African fertilizer industry, the Korean mechanical engineering industry, and the Mexican heavy electrical equipment industry. In the case of the first two, mixed-integer programming models were formulated in a process analysis format which made possible an explicit recognition of various forms of interdependence within the sectors. The third study focused exclusively on the methodological problems involved in the modeling of a sector characterized by a large number of products and processes. Aggregation procedures that might be employed in such cases were developed and tested. The Korean study used some of the concepts developed in the Mexican study. The results of this analysis will be published in a monograph, entitled *Industrial Investment Analysis under Increasing Returns*, that will include a detailed and comprehensive statement of the methodology of planning in the presence of increasing returns.

In addition to the monograph, a number of separate volumes addressed to the prospective user of the planning methodology are being published under the series entitled The Planning of Investment Programs (see under "Reports" below). The series includes volumes on general methodology; investment planning in specific industrial sectors; and detailed guidelines on the use of specifically developed computer software to organize the input data, generate the appropriate planning models, and report on the results. All volumes in the series will be self-contained and will not assume prior familiarity with mathematical modeling, computer languages, or the industrial processes concerned. In addition to a general section, each volume dealing with a specific sector will contain a detailed report on an application of the methodology.

Except for the development of software, the major emphasis of this research program has gradually shifted from research to application and dissemination. Applications are carried out in various contexts. Investment planning studies were completed for the fertilizer sector in the Arab Republic of Egypt, as well as in member countries of the Association of South East Asian Nations (ASEAN) and the Andean Common Market. A detailed case study on India is under way. A planning study was made of the Mexican steel industry jointly with Mexican counterparts. The World Pulp and Paper Program of the Food and Agriculture Organization (FAO) has used the planning methodology to analyze national and multicountry investment programs in the forest industry sector. Most studies are conducted in collaboration with staff from the World Bank's Industry Department and relevant regional offices, and usually involve local institutions as well. The Andean Common Market study involved staff and financing from the Junta del Acuerdo de Cartagena and the Inter-American Development Bank.

Responsibility: Europe, Middle East, and North Africa Country Programs Department II—Ardy Stoutjesdijk, and *Development Research Department*—Alexander Meeraus and Larry E. Westphal, in collaboration with Armeane M. Choksi, Country Policy Department; Yung Whee Rhee and William F. Sheldrick, Industry Department; Harald Stier, South Asia Projects Department; and Hans Bergendorff, David Kendrick, Peter Glenshaw, Loet Mennes, and Jaime Alatorre (consultants).

Completion date: December 1983.

Reports

Balassa, Bela, and Stoutjesdijk, Ardy. "Economic Integration among Developing Countries." *Journal of Common Market Studies* 186 (September 1974):37–55. Also World Bank Reprint Series: Number Thirty.

Choksi, Armeane M.; Kendrick, David; and Meeraus, Alexander. *La Programmation des investissements industriels—Méthode et étude de cas.* Paris: Economica, 1981.

_____. "A Planning Study of the Fertilizer Sector in Egypt." World Bank Staff Working Paper No. 269, July 1977.

Meeraus, Alexander, and Stoutjesdijk, Ardy (eds.). The Planning of Investment Programs (A World Bank Research Publication series):

Vol. 1. Kendrick, David, and Stoutjesdijk, Ardy. *The Planning of Industrial Investment Programs. A Methodology.* Baltimore and London: The Johns Hopkins University Press, 1978.

Vol. 2. Choksi, Armeane M.; Meeraus, Alexander; and Stoutjesdijk, Ardy. *The Planning of Investment Programs in the Fertilizer Industry.* Baltimore and London: The Johns Hopkins University Press, 1980.

Vol. 3. Kendrick, David; Meeraus, Alexander; and Alatorre, Jaime. *The Planning of Investment Programs in the Steel Industry.* Baltimore and London: The Johns Hopkins University Press (forthcoming, 1982).

Vol. 4. Mennes, Loet B. M., and Stoutjesdijk, Ardy. *Multicountry Investment Analysis* (forthcoming).

Vol. 5. Bergendorff, Hans; Glenshaw, Peter; and Meeraus, Alexander. *The Planning of Investment Programs in the Forestry and Forest Industry Sector* (forthcoming).

Westphal, Larry E., and Cremer, Jacques. "The Interdependence of Investment Decisions' Revisited." Mimeo. The World Bank: Development Research Department, August 1983. Also in Moshe Syrquin, Lance Taylor, and Larry E. Westphal (eds.), *Economic Structure and Performance*. New York: Academic Press (forthcoming, 1984).

_____. "The Interdependence of Investment Decisions with Positive Export Prospects." Mimeo. The World Bank: Development Research Department, August 1983.

Industrial Policies and Economic Integration in Western Africa

Ref. No. 670-87

Earlier studies on incentives in developing countries concentrated on those countries that had already established an industrial base. This research project examines the policies followed by four developing Western African nations that are representative of the region and provide diversity in industrial development, location, and language: Ghana, Ivory Coast, Mali, and Senegal. The purpose of the project is to examine the choice of alternative strategies for economic growth in Western Africa, such as import substitution, export promotion, and the expansion of intraregional trade through economic integration. Attention is given to the choice between the expansion of agriculture or of industry in the individual countries. A comparison of the results for the four countries will also shed light on the possibilities for regional integration.

The country studies describe the incentives applied, including tariffs, quantitative restrictions, export taxes and subsidies, tax holidays, credit preferences, and government expenditures. These incentives are quantified in an effort to gauge their impact on particular industries or import substitution and exports, as well as on domestic and foreign investment. Information collected on individual firms and products is used to assess the economic cost of the incentive scheme applied, the comparative cost position of various industries, and the benefits of foreign investment.

Indicators of incentives, including the coefficients of effective protection and subsidy, relate the combined effects of measures of protection and of protective credit, tax, and expenditure measures, respectively, to the net gain in foreign exchange in particular activities. These indicators are calculated separately for import substitution and for exports, with further distinction made between preferential and nonpreferential export sales.

Measures of domestic resource costs relate the shadow value of domestic resources used in a particular activity to the net gain in foreign exchange. They are adjusted to take account of the foreign exchange cost of expatriates and of foreign-owned firms, and are also calculated for the case of full capacity utilization and excluding the forgone costs of capital investment.

The final output of the project, carried out by the Development Research Department in cooperation with the Western Africa Regional Office, will be a series of country studies and a comparative analysis of the results for the individual countries. All the country studies have been undertaken with the support of, and preliminary results have been discussed with, the governments concerned.

Responsibility: Development Research Department—Bela Balassa. The individual country studies have been undertaken by the following collaborators: Agricultural sections in all country studies —J. Dirck Stryker, Tufts University. Industrial sections and general evaluation: Ghana—Scott R. Pearson and Gerald C. Nelson, both of the Food Research Institute, Stanford University; Ivory Coast—Garry Pursell, Industry Department, and Terry D. Monson, formerly of the Centre ivoirien de recherche économique et sociale, Abidjan; Mali—Geoffrey Shepherd, University of Sussex, United Kingdom; Senegal—Brendan Horton (consultant) and Garry Pursell, Industry Department.

Completion date: December 1983.

Reports

Balassa, Bela. "Avantages comparés et perspectives de l'intégration économique en Afrique de l'Ouest." Paper prepared for the Colloque sur l'intégration en Afrique de l'Ouest, Dakar, Senegal, March–April 1978.

————. "The Effects Method of Project Evaluation." *Oxford Bulletin of Economics and Statistics* (November 1976):219–32. French translation in *Annales économiques* 11 (1977). Also World Bank Reprint Series: Number Fifty-five.

Monson, Terry D., and Pursell, Garry. "An Evaluation of Expatriate Labor Replacement in the Ivory Coast." Center for Research on Economic Development Discussion Paper No. 49. Ann Arbor: University of Michigan, April 1976. French translation in *L'Actualité économique* (June 1977). Revised version in *Journal of Development Economics* 6 (1979):119–39.

Pursell, Garry. "Cost-Benefit Analysis of Foreign Capital and Expatriates in the West African Community." Paper presented at the International Conference on the Economic Development of the Sahelian Countries, Montreal (Canada), October 1977.

———. "Cost-Benefit Evaluation of LDC Industrial Sectors Which Have Foreign Ownership." World Bank Staff Working Paper No. 465, July 1981.

A Comparative Study of the Sources of Industrial Growth and Structural Change

Ref. No. 671-32

Policy appraisal requires an analysis of how policy instruments and autonomous elements interact to determine the allocation of resources. Significant advances have been made over the past decade in understanding the impact of individual government policies operating through price incentives and direct interventions, especially with respect to foreign trade and allocation of investments. But, in the absence of a comprehensive analytical framework for quantitative analysis, few attempts have been made to establish explicit relationships between individual policy instruments, changes in industrial structure, and economic performance. This project is designed to contribute to the development of the analytical framework that is required to articulate these relationships.

Specifically, the present project is intended to provide the empirical basis from which quantitative models for policy analysis may be developed in subsequent projects. The relative contributions of growth of domestic demand, export expansion, import substitution, and technological change to industrial growth and structural change, using input-output data, are being determined for Colombia, Israel, Japan, Republic of Korea, Mexico, Norway, Turkey, and Yugoslavia, and for *Taiwan*, China.

Parallel to the case studies, a simulation model has been developed to assess the relative importance of universal and economy-specific influences on industrial structure and its evolution. In this model, regression analysis, based on the results of the research project, "Patterns of Industrial Development" (Ref. No. 671–05), now completed, is used to provide estimates of the share of the various aggregate demand categories and trade (exports and imports) in gross domestic product, and of the sectoral disaggregation of each of these as functions of per capita income and size of the area. An input-output matrix, the coefficients of which are obtained from comparative analysis and are dependent upon per capita income, is then used to determine the associated production levels by sector. A simulation for given per capita income, population size, and trade orientation isolates the impact of autonomous factors that are not specific of a given area.

A subsequent project, "The Sources of Growth and Productivity Change: A Comparative Analysis" (Ref. No. 671–79 in this category), involving construction of specific models for several of the areas covered in the first phase, has been initiated to exploit recent advances in the incorporation of policy instruments explicitly within planning models. Each model will be validated by ensuring that it adequately simulates the past history of an area's industrial development. The model will then be used to explore the probable consequences of having followed alternative policies through a series of ex post "what if" experiments. Here, as throughout the entire program of research, the emphasis will be on an evaluation of import substitution and export promotion strategies from a long-term, sector-by-sector perspective, stressing questions of sequencing as well as problems of transition to a different industrial structure.

Responsibility: Development Research Department—Sherman Robinson (on leave at the University of California at Berkeley), in collaboration with Larry E. Westphal, Development Research Department, Hollis B. Chenery, Harvard University, and Moises Syrquin of Bar Ilan University (Israel), who are responsible for the overall design of the research and its execution.

Responsibility for the component parts of the project: Comparative analysis—Hollis B. Chenery, Sherman Robinson, and Moises Syrquin; Colombia—Jaime de Melo, Development Research Department; Israel—Mordechai Fraenkel, Bank of Israel; Japan—Hollis B. Chenery and Yuji Kubo, Tsukuba University; Korea—Kwang Suk Kim, Korea Development Institute, Seoul; Mexico—Moises Syrquin; Norway—Bela Balassa, Development

Research Department; Turkey—Merih Celasun, Middle East
Technical University, Ankara; and *Taiwan*, China—Wan-Yong
(Shirley) Kuo, National Taiwan University, Taipei.

Completion date: June 1984.

Reports

Balassa, Bela. "Accounting for Economic Growth: The Case of
    Norway." *Oxford Economic Papers* 3 (November 1979):415–36.
    Also World Bank Reprint Series: Number 132.
Celasun, Merih. "Sources of Industrial Growth and Structural
    Change: The Case of Turkey." World Bank Staff Working
    Paper No. 614, 1983.
Chenery, Hollis B. "Transitional Growth and World
    Industrialization." Paper presented at the Nobel Symposium on
    the International Allocation of Economic Activity, Stockholm
    (Sweden), June 1976.
Chenery, Hollis B., and Syrquin, Moises. "A Comparative Analysis
    of Industrial Growth." Paper presented at the Fifth World Con-
    gress of the International Economic Association on Economic
    Growth and Resources, Tokyo (Japan), August–September 1977.
Kim, Kwang Suk. "Industrialization and Structural Change in
    Korea." Mimeo. Korea Development Institute, September 1978.
————. "Relative Price Structure and Industrial Growth Patterns
    in Korea." Mimeo. Korea Development Institute, July 1980.
Kubo, Yuji, and Robinson, Sherman. "Sources of Industrial Growth
    and Structural Change: A Comparative Analysis of Eight Coun-
    tries." Paper presented at the Seventh International Conference
    on Input-Output Techniques, Innsbruck (Austria), April 1979.
Kuo, Shirley W. Y. "Economic Growth and Structural Change in
    Taiwan." Mimeo. The World Bank: Development Research
    Department, August 1979.
Syrquin, Moises. "Sources of Industrial Growth and Change: An
    Alternative Measure." Paper presented at the European Meeting
    of the Econometric Society, Helsinki (Finland), August 1976.

Small-Scale Enterprise Development

Ref. No. 671-59

This research project follows a World Bank Sector Policy
Paper, *Employment and Development of Small Enterprises* (Febru-

ary 1978), and a World Bank Issues Paper, *Rural Enterprise and Nonfarm Employment* (January 1978). The main conclusion of these papers concerned the substantial importance of small-scale enterprises, in both urban and rural areas, as sources of employment and earnings opportunities for low income groups. In developing countries, over three-quarters of the employment outside agriculture is in small enterprises in the industrial, commercial, and service sectors. Yet, it is broadly true that policies concerned with the development of these sectors devote very limited attention and resources to small-scale enterprises, while little information is available on the nature and functioning of small enterprises and on the constraints and difficulties they face in maintaining or expanding earnings.

The project has two objectives: first, to review the existing information on small enterprises in developing economies and, through trial surveys, to attempt to define ways in which the information base can be improved; and second, to develop a basis, in the course of this work, for assessing the impact on incomes and employment of various policy options.

The research consists of:

- Case studies of patterns of small-scale enterprise development (using existing information) in Colombia, India, Japan, Republic of Korea, Nigeria, and the Philippines, and in Taiwan, China.
- A number of surveys of enterprises in manufacturing subsectors in India and Colombia to investigate entrepreneurial history, markets, capital structure, labor use, and other aspects and problems of small-scale enterprises.

The case studies also include some analysis and evaluation of policy. The surveys concentrate on about a dozen manufacturing sectors (specified at the five-digit or six-digit level) to gain detailed insights into the workings of the enterprises, their levels of efficiency, and the process of technological transformation and modernization with market development. The surveys are not, however, being restricted solely to small enterprises; interviews with medium and large enterprises are to be undertaken to examine relative efficiency, market competition, and linkages (e.g., through subcontracting).

A further issue that is being examined concerns estimation of the costs and benefits of various policies toward small-scale enterprises. It is already apparent that, for example, the implementation of credit and technical assistance programs can be quite costly in relation to the economic benefits generated. Also, a large number of small enterprises exist as an inefficient by-product of policies that depress the demands for labor in agriculture and the "modern" industrial and commercial sectors. Both these considerations make it important to develop a methodology to assess the economic efficiency of policies toward small-scale enterprises.

The major output of this research (in addition to a number of individual reports) will be monographs on Colombia and India by the principal researchers listed below and a number of papers on other countries. The draft study on Colombia is substantially complete; the monograph on India is in progress.

Responsibility: Development Research Department—Dipak Mazumdar, in collaboration with John M. Page, Jr., Industry Department, and Dennis Anderson, Western Africa Projects Department; Mariluz Cortes, Eastern Africa Projects Department; and other relevant regional offices in the World Bank; and with José F. Escandon (researcher) from Colombia; Hermina Fajardo (engineer/management consultant) in the Philippines; and R. Albert Berry (consultant). Ian Little, Emeritus Fellow, Nuffield College, Oxford University, is adviser to the project.

The following government and research institutions are collaborating in the research: Philippines—Ministry of Industry; India —Sri Ram Center for Industrial Research, New Delhi, and the Giri Institute, Lucknow; Colombia—Corporación Financiera Popular.

Completion date: June 1984.

Reports

Anderson, D. "Small Industry in Developing Countries: Some Issues." World Bank Staff Working Paper No. 518, 1982. Also, an abridged version is available in *World Development*, vol. 10, no. 11 (1982):913–48.

Anderson, D., and Khambata, Farida. "Financing Small-Scale Industry and Agriculture in Developing Countries: The Merits and Limitations of 'Commercial' Policies." World Bank Staff Working Paper No. 519, 1982.

————. "Small Enterprises and Development Policy in the Philippines: A Case Study." World Bank Staff Working Paper No. 468, July 1981.

Berry, Albert, and Pinell-Siles, Armando. "Small-Scale Enterprises in Colombia: A Case Study." Employment and Rural Development Division Paper No. 56. The World Bank, July 1979.

Cortes, Mariluz; Berry, Albert; and Ishaq, Ashfaq. "What Makes for Success in Small and Medium Scale Enterprises: The Evidence from Colombia." Draft. The World Bank: Development Research Department, June 1983.

Ho, S. P. S. "Small Scale Enterprises in Korea and Taiwan." World Bank Staff Working Paper No. 384, April 1980.

Kaneda, Hiromitsu. "Development of Small and Medium Enterprises and Policy Response in Japan: An Analytical Survey." Employment and Rural Development Division Paper No. 52. The World Bank, October 1980.

Mazumdar, Dipak. "A Descriptive Analysis of the Role of Small-Scale Enterprises in the Indian Economy." Draft. The World Bank: Employment and Rural Development Division, Part I—December 1979, Part II—May 1982.

———. "Product Quality and the Choice of Techniques." Draft. The World Bank: Development Research Department, May 1982.

———. Studies in the Small-Large Issue in the Indian Textile Industry: No. 1. "The Development of the Indian Textile Industry and its Three Sectors"; No. 2. "Relative Costs in the Handloom, Powerloom and Mill Sectors." Employment and Rural Development Division Papers Nos. 76 and 77. The World Bank, December 1981.

Page, John M., Jr. "Firm Size and Technical Efficiency: Applications of Production Frontiers to Indian Survey Data." Paper (draft), presented at the 1982 Meetings of the American Economic Association, September 1982.

———. "Firm Size, Capital-Labor Substitution and the Form of the Production Function: A Study of India's Shoe Manufacturing Industry." The World Bank: Employment and Rural Development Division, April 1981.

———. "Firm Size, the Choice of Technique, and Technical Efficiency: Evidence from India's Soap Manufacturing Industry." Employment and Rural Development Division Paper No. 59. The World Bank, December 1979.

———. "Small Enterprises in African Development: A Survey." World Bank Staff Working Paper No. 363, October 1979.

Managerial Structures and Practices:
Public Manufacturing Enterprises

Ref. No. 671-71

Government-owned and government-managed enterprises form
a significant and growing segment of the industrial sector in a
number of developing countries. This project proposes to examine
the degree to which the performance of such enterprises, in
relation to their explicit or implicit objectives, depends upon their
managerial and organizational structures and the policy environment in which they operate. The broad purpose of this research is
to identify the characteristics of the structures and the policy
environment that are consistent with the efficiency and growth of
such enterprises.

Using the analytical framework of the literature on the economics of industrial organization and drawing on organization theory
and the management sciences, two developing countries—India
and Yugoslavia—have been studied. Case studies of three or four
public manufacturing enterprises from the same broad subsector
in each country form the core of the research. In addition, a study
of the experience of a developed country—Italy—with respect to
the management, control, and performance of its public manufacturing enterprises is also a part of the research. Finally, an
examination of the evolution of the control environment for public
enterprises in India has been undertaken.

The research has made extensive use of interviews and a set of
specific hypotheses has been examined, using both quantitative
and qualitative evidence. In view of the complexity of the subject
matter and the exploratory nature of the proposed effort, the
contribution of the study to the operations of the World Bank
must be viewed from a long-term perspective. The study is
expected, nonetheless, to strengthen the Bank's ability (1) to deal
with the issues of management, organization, and policy environment that arise in its lending to industries in the public sector; (2)
to address important issues in the public-enterprise sector in
country economic analysis and sector work; and (3) to respond to
technical assistance requests by member governments on various
issues of management, organization, and accountability in public
sector enterprises. The developing countries participating in this
study are expected to benefit not only from a systematic study of
their own experiences in the management of public-sector indus-

tries, but also from the experience of other countries that will be made available to them by the proposed research.

Responsibility: Western Africa Country Programs I—Gobind T. Nankani; *Resident Staff in Indonesia*—Javad Khalilzadeh-Shirazi; and *Economic Development Institute*—Vinayak V. Bhatt; with the assistance of Martin Schrenk in the East Asia and Pacific Regional Office.

The following authors have prepared the country studies: India—P. N. Khandwalla, S. Murthy, and B. H. Dholakia of the Indian Institute of Management, Ahmedabad; Italy—Romano Prodi, formerly of the Center of Economic and Industrial Policy, University of Bologna; Yugoslavia—Martin Schrenk with the assistance of the International Center for Public Enterprises in Developing Countries, Ljubljana.

Completion date: The country studies on India and Italy have been completed in draft form and are undergoing final revision. The Yugoslav country study is available (see Reports below). A final report that will synthesize the three studies and summarize their findings is expected to be completed in March 1984.

Reports

Bhatt, V. V. "Decisionmaking in the Public Sector: Case Study of Swaraj Tractor." World Bank Reprint Series: Number Ninety-six.

Khandwalla, P. N. "The Performance Determinants of Public Enterprises: Case Studies of Four Equipment Manufacturing Indian Public Enterprises." Draft. Ahmedabad: Indian Institute of Management, May 1981.

Murthy, K. R. S. "The Control Environment of Public Enterprises in India: An Evolutionary Perspective." Draft. Ahmedabad: Indian Institute of Management, October 1981.

Prodi, Romano. "Public Industrial Enterprises: The Italian Experience." Draft. Bologna (Italy): University of Bologna, December 1981.

Schrenk, M. "Managerial Structures and Practices in Public Manufacturing Enterprises: A Yugoslav Case Study." World Bank Staff Working Paper No. 455, May 1981.

Appropriate Industrial Technology (Phase II)

Ref. No. 671-77

This project examines the issue of choice of appropriate industrial technology as the problem appears to a lending institution. The study follows Phase I (Ref. No. 671-51), now completed, which quantified the effects of the appropriate choice of technology for employment and national income originating in manufacturing in a typical developing country. For a given level of investment, it was found that these effects are very significant. But the empirical studies upon which these results were based are not sufficiently detailed, particularly with respect to technical engineering issues, to permit their use in project design and evaluation. Moreover, critical issues concerning operating efficiency and industrial organization have typically not been considered. This project attempts to bridge these gaps between the existing state of the art and the needs of project decisionmakers.

Three related areas are being analyzed:

1. There will be an exhaustive delineation, with the aid of textile engineers, of technical options for the production of blended cotton textiles. Equipment produced in both developed and developing countries will be included, and an efficient set of engineering production alternatives defined.

2. The technical production relations determined in part (1) are likely to be altered in actual operation by a number of factors that cause actual operating efficiencies to differ from those specified by engineering norms. Such inefficiencies may exert different effects on the social profitability of the various technologies and alter the choice of optimum technology. An analysis of operating inefficiencies will be made for textile plants in Kenya and the Philippines whose economic and physical environments differ.

3. The effects of alternative organizations of production within the sector will be analyzed, particularly as regards the efficiency and feasibility of decentralizing operations not subject to economies of scale. The implications of decentralizing production will be considered along with the potential infrastructure and skill requirements of such dispersal.

The analytical framework to be developed in this project will be suitable for examining technological choices in other industries and in other economic and physical circumstances.

Responsibility: Development Research Department and Industry
Department—Larry E. Westphal and Magdi R. Iskander, respectively, with the collaboration of Howard Pack (consultant).

Completion date: June 1983; the completion report is in process.

The Sources of Growth and Productivity Change: A Comparative Analysis

Ref. No. 671-79

The objective of this research project is to provide a careful
quantitative and comparative analysis of industrialization and
growth in selected developing economies—the Republic of Korea,
Turkey, and Yugoslavia. The project is related to an earlier,
ongoing research project, "A Comparative Study of the Sources of
Industrial Growth and Structural Change" (Ref. No. 671-32 in
this category). The earlier project will provide a detailed analysis
of the relative importance of domestic demand growth, export
expansion, import substitution, and technological change as components of industrial growth in Colombia, Israel, Japan, Republic
of Korea, Mexico, Norway, Turkey, and Yugoslavia and in
Taiwan, China. The present project aims at extending and deepening the methodology of comparative analysis by proceeding in
two overlapping phases.

In the first phase, a consistent time series of factor inputs and
sectoral outputs are developed, linking the demand oriented analysis, carried out so far, to an analysis of the sources of growth from
the factor side. In the second phase, a general equilibrium framework of comparative modeling is used to integrate the analysis of
the interactions of sources of growth and policy.

The approach is explicitly comparative and emphasizes historical trends in terms of different starting points and different
policies. The same analysis is applied, with the linkage between
the demand side, the supply side, and the policy focused analysis
being achieved within the framework of a common general equilibrium model. Most comparative studies available have either
concentrated on growth accounting from the factor side or on
trade and incentive policies. Integrating these two concerns, however, is crucial for a correct evaluation of policy and a comprehensive analysis of the sources of growth.

The same model structure is applied to different countries and to archetypal semi-industrial economies. The aim is not to build country models, but to extend the comparative methodology and data base developed in the earlier project on sources of industrial growth to allow for a more formal policy-oriented comparative analysis of industrialization processes. The general equilibrium modeling framework will help to ensure consistency, comparability, and rigor in the analysis.

Responsibility: Development Research Department—Sherman Robinson (on leave at the University of California at Berkeley) in collaboration with Jaime de Melo, Development Research Department; Kemal Dervis and Mieko Nishimizu, Industry Department; Anne O. Krueger, Vice President, Economics and Research Staff; Baran Tuncer, Eastern Africa Regional Office; and Yuji Kubo (consultant), Tsukuba University (Japan).

Completion date: December 1983.

Reports

de Melo, Jaime; Kubo, Yuji; Lewis, Jeffrey D.; and Robinson, Sherman. "Multisector Models and the Analysis of Alternative Development Strategies." World Bank Staff Working Paper No. 563, 1983.

de Melo, Jaime, and Robinson, Sherman. "Trade Adjustment Policies and Income Distribution in Three Archetype Developing Economies." World Bank Staff Working Paper No. 442, December 1980. Also in *Journal of Development Economics* (February 1982):67–92.

_____. "Trade Policy and Resource Allocation in the Presence of Product Differentiation." *Review of Economics and Statistics* (May 1981):169–77.

Dervis, Kemal; de Melo, Jaime; and Robinson, Sherman. "A General Equilibrium Analysis of Foreign Exchange Shortages in a Developing Economy." World Bank Staff Working Paper No. 443, January 1981. *Economic Journal* (December 1981):891–906.

Dervis, Kemal, and Robinson, Sherman. "A General Equilibrium Analysis of the Causes of a Foreign Exchange Crisis: The Case of Turkey." *Weltwirtschaftliches Archiv*, Bd. 118(2), (1982):259–80.

Krueger, Anne O., and Tuncer, Baran. "Growth of Factor Productivity in Turkish Manufacturing Industries." *Journal of Development Economics* (December 1982):307–25.

Nishimuzu, Mieko, and Page, John M., Jr. "Total Factor Productivity Growth, Technical Progress, and Technical Efficiency Change: Dimensions of Productivity Change in Yugoslavia, 1965–78." *Economic Journal* (December 1982).

Nishimuzu, Mieko, and Robinson, Sherman. "Trade Policies and Productivity Changes in Semi-Industrialized Countries." Development Research Department Discussion Paper No. 52. The World Bank, March 1983.

A Statistical Analysis of the Efficiency of the Indonesian Manufacturing Sector

Ref. No. 672-12

Developing countries often employ a number of policies that restrict trade or interfere with the free functioning of factor markets. As elsewhere in the developing world, one result of the combination of these restrictive policies in Indonesia is a widely varying level of incentives to industrial processes. The purpose of this research project is to conduct a statistical analysis of the efficiency of the Indonesian manufacturing sector.

There are indications that significant intrasectoral variations in capital/labor and skill/labor ratios exist in most of the country's manufacturing activities. This implies that the social efficiency of producing identical units of output may vary across firms. Thus, a major aspect of the analysis will be to investigate the sources of variation in the social cost of production and its components by relating them to firm and, in certain cases, to sector characteristics. These characteristics will include ownership (foreign, private, and government); location, age, and size of the firm; the nature of the special incentives provided; and barriers to competition and restrictions to international trade.

The objective of the research is to calculate the social benefit-cost indicators for individual Indonesian manufacturing firms and analyze the comparative advantage of alternative industrial activities. An appropriate measure for socially evaluating alternative activities is the domestic resource cost. By making use of a large and unusual set of existing microeconomic data, domestic resource costs will be calculated for a large number of Indonesian industrial enterprises. Based on econometrically estimated frontier production functions, measured domestic resource costs for individual firms will be decomposed into the social costs of technical inefficiency, the social cost of suboptimal factor proportions, and the domestic resource cost of socially inefficient production. These calculations will be used to rank alternative individual activities to investigate the socially optimal choice of technique and to examine the relationship between domestic resource cost, technical inefficiency, and the characteristics of firms and sectors.

It is expected that results from this study will contribute to the Bank's industrial policy dialogue with the Government of Indonesia and provide direction to its lending program in the industrial sector.

Responsibility: Country Policy Department—Armeane M. Choksi. The principal researcher is Professor Mark Pitt. The Institute of Economic and Social Research, University of Indonesia, and the Central Bureau of Statistics, Indonesia, are collaborating in the research.

Completion date: December 1983.

Programming in the Manufacturing Sector: A GAMS Application

Ref. No. 672–22A

The research project on "Programming in the Manufacturing Sector" (Ref. No. 670–24 in this category) addressed issues related to the analysis of investments in the presence of increasing returns to scale, with special emphasis on process industries such as fertilizers, forestry products, and steel. With the preparation of a series of manuals, currently under way, this project is being completed. However, in order to promote its wider use, it is believed that a series of field applications with training is required to disseminate the planning methodology effectively to prospective users.

The present project provides the organizational framework for a number of applications, one being a model of the Indian fertilizer sector. This model is the product of a joint effort by the Bank's Development Research Department and Industry Department and the Government of India which intends to use the model to assist in planning and developing policies and projects related to large investments in fertilizer production and distribution. To transfer the model to India, the Bank will train a nucleus of specialists.

Responsibility: Development Research Department—Alexander Meeraus, with assistance from the *Industry Department*—William Sheldrick.

Completion date: February 1984.

Reports

Bumb, Balu. "A Survey of the Fertilizer Sector in India." World Bank Staff Working Paper No. 331, 1979.
Choksi, Armeane M., and Meeraus, Alexander. "A Programming Approach to Fertilizer Sector Planning." World Bank Staff Working Paper No. 305, 1978.

Analysis of Small-Scale Enterprise Lending in Kenya

Ref. No. 672-34

This project builds upon some of the initial results emerging from the World Bank's research project on "Small-Scale Enterprise Development" (Ref. No. 671-59 in this category), in order to develop operationally useful and effective techniques for screening loans to small enterprises.

Problems inherent in lending to small-scale enterprises have been approached mostly from the point of view of the enterprises, and research has been based on data collected from them. The investigations have identified a range of constraints upon the borrowers that have prevented most lending programs from being truly effective. Other studies, focusing specifically on the provision of capital and associated technical assistance, have evaluated the policies and performance of individual lending institutions. A third avenue of inquiry—the one to be explored in this project— focuses narrowly on the lending process and the analysis of differential loan performance.

It seeks to provide an answer to a single question: How can an institution lending to small-scale enterprises discriminate among its customers so as to identify those projects and their entrepreneurs that have the highest probability of success?

There are essentially two steps in the analysis. The first is developing a measure of success for each loan based on some combination of loan repayment performance and other evidence of profitable operation. The second step is correlating this observed performance with various explanatory variables—attributes of either the project or the entrepreneur that have been uncovered by the research project referred to above or elsewhere as likely factors. In this context, relevant questions to be asked include:

- whether the project is a new one or an expansion of an old project;
- whether the industrial activity to which it will contribute is a new one or an already established industry;
- whether the loan is intended predominantly for investment in fixed assets or for working capital.

Other potentially significant characteristics to be tested would consist of the previous and present occupation of the entrepreneur; the proportion of the entrepreneur's time devoted to the enterprise; the entrepreneur's equity as a proportion of total capital invested; the degree of collateral coverage; the time taken by the lending institution to process the loan; the extent of loan repayment follow-up (letters, visits, legal action) by the lending institution.

The project proposed here is an application of this methodology (employing multiple regression analysis) to the loan portfolio of Kenya Industrial Estates, Ltd., the principal development agency for small industry in Kenya.

Responsibility: Development Research Department. The principal researcher is Professor Peter Kilby of Wesleyan University at Wesleyan (Connecticut), in collaboration with the Kenya Industrial Estates Ltd., Nairobi.

Completion date: June 1984.

Protection and Incentive Systems in the Turkish Manufacturing Sector

Ref. No. 672-36A

The objective of this research project is to analyze the system of industrial incentives and the structure of comparative advantage in the Turkish manufacturing sector. This is being done to the basis of firm-level data and will provide the framework for a comprehensive reform of policies dealing with such issues. The methodology has been developed in an earlier project undertaken in the Development Research Department at the World Bank. It permits the computation from firm-level data of estimates of effective protection, effective subsidy, and domestic resource cost coefficients, as well as economic rates of return on capital.

The team carrying out the study has obtained a consistent set of data for 124 firms, which were reviewed in July 1983. A second set of estimates, incorporating agreed-upon changes in some of the assumptions, were prepared for the Turkish government and the Bank, together with technical papers on the definitions used, the underlying assumptions, price comparisons, and the overall findings. A workshop was held in August 1983, in which the Turkish Industrial Development Bank (TSKB) participated, to review the firm-by-firm estimates. The final estimates and drafts of the evaluation of the results and the policy papers are being prepared. The final version is expected in January 1984.

The results of the research project will form the basis for a series of policy papers that will contain a set of recommendations to the Government of Turkey and the Bank on the reform of the system of industrial incentives in Turkey. These recommendations will cover the system of quantitative import restrictions, the structure of tariffs, price controls, and export subsidies. They will be implemented in the framework of subsequent structural adjustment programs undertaken by the Turkish government with the support of the Bank.

Responsibility: Europe, Middle East, and North Africa Country Programs Department II—Jayanta Roy and Katrine W. Saito, with the overall advice of Bela Balassa in the *Development Research Department.* The research is to be carried out by a team led by Professor M. Hic, Istanbul University, and consisting of Professor F. Yagci, Bosphorus University; Professor M. Genceli, Istanbul University; and Professor I. Birdal, Yildaz Polytechnical Academy.

Completion date: January 1984.

The World Aluminum Industry Study

Ref. No. 672-43A

This research project investigates in depth the long term prospects of the world aluminum industry. The study assesses the long-term trends in production costs and prices; the probable structural shifts resulting from the likely changes in the geographical distribution and production costs of electrical energy and bauxite supplies; and the effects of all these on the supply of and demand for aluminum.

The study develops a linear programming model using the General Algebraic Modeling System (GAMS), developed by the Development Research Department (see Ref. No. 671–58 in category 1—Development Poicy and Planning) as the model generator. A similar approach was used in a previous research project, "Natural Resources and Planning: Issues in Trade and Investment" (Ref. No. 671–09), now completed.

The model is used to simulate sectoral developments under different assumptions concerning the price of inputs, stripping ratios in bauxite mining, levies and tariffs, and transport costs. Although this approach does not incorporate directly nonquantifiable aspects, such as potential investors' assessment of risks that may occur within a country or market diversification, an attempt is made to include some of these factors by introducing constraints and changing parameter values in some versions of the model.

This research will enhance the Bank's understanding of the economics of the world aluminum industry and provide a framework for analyzing specific aspects of the industry. It will be useful to the operational departments of the Bank Group in their work in evaluating large aluminum plants and power projects related to aluminum production.

Responsibility: Economic Analysis and Projections Department-—Kenji Takeuchi in conjunction with Ardy Stoutjesdijk, Europe, Middle East, and North Africa Programs Department II. The principal researchers are Alfredo Dammert, Economic Analysis and Projections Department, and Alexander Meeraus, Development Research Department, in collaboration with the Industry Department and the Energy Department, and Martin Brown of the Development Center of the Organisation for Economic Cooperation and Development (OECD).

Completion date: February 1983; the completion report is in process.

Reports

Brown, M.; Dammert, A.; Meeraus, A.; and Stoutjesdijk, A.
"Worldwide Investment Analysis: The Case of Aluminum."
World Bank Staff Working Paper No. 603, 1983.

Experimental Support Unit for Work on Industrial Incentives and Comparative Advantage (INCA)

Ref. No. 672–44A

Over the years, a major portion of research, supported by the World Bank, on industry in developing countries has been devoted to the quantitative analysis of incentive systems and comparative advantage (INCA analysis). In the course of this research, a considerable body of knowledge has been built up on all aspects of this kind of analysis. At the same time, there has been a steady increase in the demand for such studies from governments of member countries and operating departments of the Bank, which have come to perceive these studies to be directly relevant for incentive policy reforms and for improving the economic efficiency of new investment.

For a considerable time, staff members involved in INCA research have been giving advice and assistance to operational staff responsible for applied INCA studies on an ad hoc basis. It became apparent that this assistance could be more cost-effective, if it were to some degree formalized by the establishment of a unit that would centralize the needed specialized skills. Accordingly, under this project an Industrial Incentives and Comparative Advantage (INCA) unit was established on an experimental basis for a two-year period. The unit is working on methodologies and techniques (including computer programs and software), developed in the course of past research in this field, to make them more useful for operational work. It provides support to operating departments of the Bank and to the Bank's affiliate, the International Finance Corporation (IFC), for their work in this area.

A major objective of the unit, which is part of the Industrial Strategy and Policy Division of the Industry Department, is to assist the regional operating departments in building up the capability of national institutions to undertake INCA analysis.

Apart from support for longer-term studies and the development of more operational techniques, the unit supports INCA related work at the Bank and IFC by providing methodologies, software and computer programs, information on consultants, and other relevant data, including sources of information on international prices. It also assists industry sector missions (including IFC missions) in analyzing industrial incentives, and has a role in coordinating the use of shadow prices in sector and project work.

If the experiment is successful, it is envisaged that the work of the unit will be absorbed into and become a permanent part of the activities of the Industry Department. The unit is involved in INCA work undertaken by government agencies and research organizations in about fourteen member countries.

A series of technical manuals of computer programs for estimating incentives and comparative advantage indicators are available through the Bank's INCA unit.

Responsibility: Industry Department—Garry Pursell, in collaboration with the Productivity Division of the *Development Research Department,* and with Neil Roger and Yoon Joo Lee (consultants).

Completion date: October 1983; the completion report is in process.

Reports

"Manual on Incentives and Comparative Advantage Studies." Draft. INCA Unit, Strategy and Policy Division. The World Bank: Industry Department, October 1983.

The Acquisition of Technological Capability

Ref. No. 672-48

Technological change is now generally recognized as essential to industrial development. In the research community, considerable effort has been addressed to issues of choice of technique, appropriate technology, technology transfer, and more recently to technological change at the individual firm level. Nevertheless, there is little understanding of what technological change in developing countries means.

Despite the lack of research that might guide policy, governments in many developing countries have attempted to create local technological capability by intervening directly and indirectly. Partly as a result of these interventions, different developing countries have achieved varying levels of technological capability, yet there is no systematic evidence for appraising the success or the benefits of promoting such capability. The sequence of activities that a developing country should undertake at different points in its industrial development to build up its technological capability is unclear.

This research project is intended to yield an overview of technological capability in industry to develop an understanding of what technological capability consists of and how it is acquired. It will seek cross-country comparative information, in order to get a broad appreciation of different country experiences and of different relations between local technological capability, industrial development, and government policies. The project has links with other current research at the World Bank on trade and industry. However, it focuses explicitly on technological change and, thus, represents an evolution from past Bank research on technology, which concentrated mostly on choice of techniques.

The study seeks information at two levels. Phase I mapped the extent and nature of technology exports from a selected group of developing countries. Technology exports were chosen as the initial focus because they give presumptive evidence of underlying technological capability and a prima facie indication of world standards of competence. The findings of Phase I confirm that focusing on technology exports is a useful way of identifying areas where local technological capability has been developed. Technology exports tend to reveal differences between countries in the areas of expertise and in the ways that technological capability has been established. Phase II, now under way, studies the acquisition of technological capability in some of the key firms and sectors identified in Phase I. The sectors include cement, steel, textiles, and pulp and paper.

The World Bank's project covers three countries—India, the Republic of Korea, and Mexico. The Inter-American Development Bank, which participated in the initial design of this project, has concurrently carried out research similar to that of Phase I for Brazil and Argentina, and is planning comparable work in other Latin American countries.

The World Bank's project will produce a summary monograph as well as individual country reports. Currently, there are interim reports summarizing the results of Phase I for the project as a whole as well as for each country, and outlining the methodology and strategy for Phase II.

Responsibility: Development Research Department—Carl J. Dahlman and Larry E. Westphal. Responsibility for the individual country studies is as follows: India—Sanjaya Lall, Oxford Institute of Economics and Statistics; Korea—Alice Amsden, Graduate School of Business Administration, Harvard University, and Linsu Kim, Korea Advanced Institute of Science and Technology; Mexico—Carl Dahlman of the World Bank, and Eduardo Montaño, Universidad Nacional Autónoma de Mexico; and Luis Alberto Perez Aceves (consultant).

Completion date: Phase I—November 1982; Phase II—September 1984.

Reports

Dahlman, Carl J. "The Acquisition of Technological Capability: Results from Phase I." Mimeo. The World Bank: Development Research Department, October 1982.

Dahlman, Carl J., and Cortes, Mariluz. "Technology Exports from Mexico as a Starting Point in the Study of Technological Capability." Mimeo. The World Bank: Development Research Department, August 1983.

Dahlman, Carl J., and Sercovich, Francisco. "Exports of Technology from Semi-Industrial Economies." *Journal of Development Economics* (forthcoming, 1984).

Dahlman, Carl J., and Westphal, Larry E. "The Meaning of Technological Mastery in Relation to Transfer of Technology." In Alan W. Heston and Howard Pack (eds.), *The Annals of the American Academy of Political and Social Science, Technology Transfer: New Issues, New Analysis*, vol. 458 (November 1981):12–26. Also available as World Bank Reprint Series: Number 217.

———. "Technological Effort in Industrial Development—An Interpretative Survey of Recent Research." In Frances Stewart and Jeffrey James (eds.), *The Economics of New Technology in Developing Countries.* London: Frances Printer Ltd., 1982. Also available as World Bank Reprint Series: Number 263.

Lall, Sanjaya. "Exports of Technology by India." Mimeo. The World Bank: Development Research Department, June 1982.

Westphal, Larry E.; Amsden, Alice; Kim, Linsu; and Rhee, Yung W. "The Deployment of Korea's Technological Capability in Production and Investment Overseas." Mimeo. The World Bank: Development Research Department, May 1982.

Westphal, Larry E.; Rhee, Yung W.; and Pursell, Garry. "Korean Industrial Competence: Where it Came From." World Bank Staff Working Paper No. 469, July 1981.

Productivity Change in Infant Industry (Phase I)

Ref. No. 672-86

In its simplest form, the argument for public intervention in infant industry rests on two empirical propositions: First, although the initial production costs of newly established industrial activities may exceed internationally competitive levels, they will decline over time to such an extent that the present social value of the eventual cost savings will exceed the early excess costs. And second, because of market failures due to external factors or differing social and private rates of discount or evaluations of risk, private and social evaluations of the benefits to the development of infant industry may differ.

Notwithstanding its long history in both economic policy and theory, there is surprisingly little evidence concerning either empirical proposition of the infant industry argument. For this reason, economists continue to have difficulty in answering such basic questions regarding infant industries as: What is the appropriate level of promotion for infant industries? Which sectors should be promoted? What are the appropriate instruments for the promotion of infant industry and how long should they be applied? The proposed research is an effort to begin accumulating a body of evidence on the nature and sources of changes in production costs over time in infant industries and to improve our understanding of the types and importance of market failures affecting the development of infant industries.

The research project has three objectives: (1) to measure changes in production costs in terms of total factor productivity changes in new industrial enterprises; (2) to identify important sources of total factor productivity change and, in particular, those sources which are unique to infant firms or industries; and (3) to determine the extent to which the sources of total factor productivity change are linked to market failures.

The research will apply the quantitative methodology of productivity analysis, supplemented by case studies and engineering analyses, to a sample of firms that are distinguished by technological characteristics, policy regimes and production environments in several developing countries. Proposed countries for field studies are the Arab Republic of Egypt and Thailand. A coordinating research project is being undertaken on Japan, funded by the Japanese Government, and is expected to provide valuable comparative data. A similar research project on the United Kingdom is also planned, subject to United Kingdom funding.

Responsibility: Industry Department—Mieko Nishimizu and John M. Page, Jr., with collaboration in the following countries: Egypt—Heba Handoussa, the Ministry of Industry and Mineral Wealth, and the American University in Cairo; Ahmed Seif El Din Khorshid and Yousseff O. Sharnoubi, Omar Seif El Din & Sons Engineers & Consultants. Thailand—Narongchai Akrasanee, National Economic and Social Development Board, and Industrial Management Co. of Thailand; Nattapol Chavalitcheevin, Industrial Finance Corporation of Thailand; Sunthorn Thamruanglerd, Industrial Management Co. of Thailand. Japan—Yuji Kubo, Tsukuba University; Toru Yanagihara, Institute of Developing Economies. United Kingdom—Martin Bell and Donald Scott-Kemmis, Science Policy Research Unit, the University of Sussex.

Completion date: June 1984.

Reports

Handoussa, Heba; Nishimizu, Mieko; and Page, John. "Productivity Change in Egyptian Public Sector Industries After The Opening 1973–1979." Mimeo. The World Bank: Development Research Department and Industry Department, May 1983.

5

Transportation and Telecommunications

Substitution of Labor and Equipment in Civil Construction

Ref. No. 670–26

Civil works are important for developing countries, but they are often built with equipment-intensive methods, even though there may be an abundant supply of unemployed labor. In 1971, the World Bank launched "The Study of Labor and Capital Substitution in Civil Construction" as a framework for research and implementation related to construction methods that are more appropriate for the socioeconomic environment of labor-abundant and capital-scarce countries.

Phase I of the study (February–October 1971) reviewed the available literature. It established the technical feasibility of factor substitution for a wide range of construction activities. However, a number of variations were noted in productivity rates reported in the literature with respect to both labor and equipment. Hence, Phase I indicated the need for an extensive collection of field data.

Phase II (November 1971–October 1973) collected field data at 30 road, dam, and irrigation sites in India and Indonesia where labor-based construction methods have been used for centuries. Data collection focused on the social, physical, and managerial parameters which might explain variations in labor/equipment productivity. Two major conclusions emerged: (1) as practiced in 1972 in India and Indonesia, traditional labor-based methods were not competitive with modern equipment-based methods; (2) labor productivity (and, hence, improved efficiency and competitiveness) could be markedly improved through better organization and management, through better tools and light equipment, and through the upgrading of the health and nutritional status of the workers.

Phase III (November 1973–August 1976) focused on experimental work in India on both road and irrigation projects and demonstrated the possibility of significant productivity increases through the introduction of improved procedures at the site level. At that point, the importance of the distinction between site and program became evident. A site is one of (possibly) many geographically dispersed points where construction takes place. A program is the aggregation of a number of sites into a plan of action for the improvement of technically similar infrastructure facilities. Programs are conceived and implemented by a central agency that plans, finances, and supervises the work carried out at the individual sites.

Phase III showed that improvements in management, tools, and the health/nutritional status of the labor force could significantly increase productivity at the site level. But it also suggested that improved procedures for planning, financing, staff training, and monitoring of progress should be implemented at the program level, if labor-based methods are to be competitive with equipment at a large scale of operations.

Findings of Phases I and II were summarized in two reports; findings and conclusions from specific aspects of the work of Phase III were summarized in three papers whose appearance marked the beginning of a wider dissemination of study-related material (see under "Reports"). In 1975, the study team initiated a series of technical memoranda, totaling 28 titles, to report on important or novel aspects of labor-based construction operations.

Starting in 1976, the study team became increasingly more involved in the planning and implementation of labor-based demonstration projects in Benin, Dominican Republic, Honduras, Lesotho, and the Philippines. Dissemination within the Bank of the findings of the study included a three-day seminar in 1977. Dissemination of findings of the study outside the Bank included a series of two-day seminars organized by the study team in Washington, Cologne, Copenhagen, London, and Tokyo in May–June 1978. A review of the study appeared in *World Bank Research News*, vol. 1, no. 2 (May 1980), which contains a discussion of the different phases of the study and of the conclusions that emerged from each.

Independently of the study, a report has been prepared with the collaboration of members of the study team on competitive bidding on construction projects in labor-abundant economies. Many governments have embarked on programs of labor-based public works construction out of political and social necessity, usually without full consideration of the economic factors involved. Because force account operations are readily adaptable to any desired mix of labor and equipment, they have tended to monopolize the construction of public works in many countries. To improve cost effectiveness and efficiency, a shift in policy by governments toward executing more construction projects by competitive bidding among contractors is desirable, while at the same time retaining and encouraging the opportunities for labor-based operations. This report (listed below) discusses the general requirements of modified procedures for bid evaluation on construction projects in labor-surplus economies, describes possible alternative procedures for shadow pricing of inputs, and discusses a system for bid evaluation using discounted wage rates.

Lessons from the research and field work carried out within the context of the study have been summarized in *Labor-Based Construction Programs: A Practical Guide for Planning and Management* (New Delhi: Oxford University Press, 1983). The book contains pragmatic guidelines for the planning, execution, and monitoring of labor-based civil construction programs in capital-scarce and labor-abundant developing countries.

Apart from the resources allocated to it by the World Bank, the study has been financially supported by the governments of Canada, Denmark, Finland, the Federal Republic of Germany, Japan, Norway, Sweden, the United Kingdom, and the United States.

Responsibility: Transportation Department—Helmut S. Kaden. The British consulting firm of Scott, Wilson, Kirkpatrick and Partners and the consulting firm of GITEC in the Federal Republic of Germany have participated extensively in the study. The Overseas Development Ministry of the United Kingdom has provided a number of specialists who assisted at different stages of the study. Extensive field support has been provided by the governments of Honduras, India, Kenya, and Lesotho.

Completion date: All research and field work has been completed. The project's findings are being disseminated through publications and scheduled seminars.

Reports

Bose, Swadesh R. "Some Aspects of Unskilled Labor Markets for Civil Construction in India: Observations Based on Field Investigation" (Phase III). World Bank Staff Working Paper No. 223, November 1975.

Coukis, Basil P., et al. *Labor-Based Construction Programs: A Practical Guide for Planning and Management.* New Delhi: Oxford University Press, 1983.

Coukis, Basil P., and Grimes, Orville F., Jr. "Labor-Based Civil Construction." *Finance and Development* 17 (March 1980):32–35.

"A Guide to Competitive Bidding on Construction Projects in Labor-Abundant Economies." Washington and London: The World Bank and Scott, Wilson, Kirkpatrick and Partners, 1978.

"Labor-Intensive Construction Techniques: Report of a World Bank Seminar." The World Bank: Transportation and Water Department, 1977.

"Scope for the Substitution of Labor and Equipment in Civil Construction—A Progress Report" (Phase III). New Delhi: Indian Roads Congress, December 1979.

"Some Aspects of the Use of Labor-Intensive Methods for Road Construction" (Phase III). New Delhi: Indian Roads Congress, December 1976.

"The Study of Labor and Capital Substitution in Civil Engineering Construction: Report on the World Bank-sponsored Seminars in Washington, Cologne, Copenhagen, London, and Tokyo." The World Bank: Transportation and Water Department, September 1978.

Highway Design Maintenance Standards Study (Phase II)

Ref. No. 670–27

Assistance by the World Bank for highway development is focused on lower-income, capital-scarce countries with widely varying climates. In these countries, the trade-offs between initial construction cost and future maintenance and road-user costs may well dictate strategies for highway design and maintenance that are different from those prevailing in North America and Europe. Developing countries spend more than $10 billion annually on their highway systems and much larger amounts for the ownership and operation of the vehicles using these highways. Thus, there is a clear need for research to support an analysis of trade-offs among major cost components in evaluating alternative highway design and maintenance standards.

Phase I of the Highway Design Study, completed in 1971, developed a conceptual framework for analyzing relationships between design standards, maintenance standards, and vehicle operating costs. But it concluded that empirical data to estimate many of the cost relationships necessary to determine optimum strategies were lacking.

Phase II of the research has, therefore, focused on the collection and analysis of primary data on the underlying physical and economic relationships necessary to calculate cost trade-offs under various conditions. A major field study was undertaken in Kenya from 1971 to 1974 to cover road, traffic, and environmental conditions typical of Eastern Africa. A parallel study in Brazil has extended the data base with respect to vehicle operating costs and road deterioration (including alternative maintenance policies) for conditions typical of much of Latin America. Finally, a study of vehicle operating costs in India has addressed the special construction methods and traffic patterns encountered there, and the final stages of this work encompassing traffic speed flow relationships are to be completed in December 1983.

A significant feature of these field studies is the combination of a road-user survey (which collects comprehensive cost data on vehicle operation, fuel and oil consumption, tire wear, crew costs, and vehicle maintenance, utilization, and depreciation) with experimental work on speed and fuel consumption. The studies in Brazil, India, and Kenya have quantified, for the first time, the effects of various road surface conditions on vehicle speeds and operating costs. Relationships have been established between major decision variables (vertical and horizontal alignment, type of road curve, and condition of the road) and vehicle speed, fuel consumption, and certain other components of vehicle operation costs. Also, an improved information base on the deterioration and maintenance of gravel roads and roads with a cement-modified base and double bituminous surface treatment has been developed. Continuing long-term follow-up studies in Kenya and Brazil will yield more complete information on the deterioration of asphalt concrete pavements and alternative overlay designs.

The development of management decision models has paralleled the field research. Most features of two earlier models, developed initially at the Massachusetts Institute of Technology (MIT) and subsequently at the Transport and Road Research

Laboratory (TRRL) in the United Kingdom, have now been incorporated in a new model—Highway Design and Maintenance (HDM). Cost figures are obtained by first estimating physical quantities and then applying prices or unit costs; either economic or financial prices may be used. The models can determine the total life-cycle transportation costs, provide economic comparisons for large numbers of alternative designs and maintenance policies, and can, thus, be used to search for the lowest total cost alternative.

Designed as a tool for project planning, the HDM model is already used at the prefeasibility and feasibility stages of planning in many countries by government agencies and consultants as well as by the World Bank, particularly in the planning of highway maintenance programs. Its use is now being extended to highway sector planning under budget constraints.

Phase III of the study (1980–84) concentrates on a systematic and comprehensive analysis of the entire new data set and its application to decisions concerning highways. Several publications are planned, including a revised edition of Jan de Weille's *Quantification of Road User Savings* (Baltimore and London: The Johns Hopkins University Press, 1966, 3rd printing 1970, out of print) and a book evaluating the major options in road design and maintenance strategies.

Responsibility: Transportation Department—Clell G. Harral, Per E. Fossberg, and Thawat Watanatada. The work in Kenya was done by the Transport and Road Research Laboratory of the United Kingdom, in collaboration with the Ministry of Works. The study in Brazil was undertaken by the Brazilian Transport Planning Agency (GEIPOT), with technical assistance from the University of Texas, Austin, and financial support from the United Nations Development Programme (UNDP). The study in India is being conducted by the Central Road Research Institute, New Delhi, in collaboration with the Indian Institute of Technology, Kanpur, and the Indian Institute of Statistics. The Swedish National Traffic and Road Research Institute (VTI) and the Australian Road Research Board are also providing technical assistance in the research on traffic speed/flow relationships.

Completion date: The basic work in Kenya has been completed. The HDM computer model, merging most features of the TRRL and MIT models except the construction cost submodel, is now available. The model is revised and extended as results from ongoing research become available. The study in Brazil, except for long-term monitoring of paved road experiments, was completed in December 1982, and that in India, including speed-flow simulations modeling, is expected to be completed in December 1983.

Reports

Harral, Clell G., and Agarwal, Surendra. "Highway Design Standards Study." Paper presented at the (First) International Conference on Low Volume Roads. Special Report 160. U.S. Transportation Research Board, 1975.

Harral, Clell G.; Fossberg, Per E.; and Watanatada, Thawat. "Evaluating the Economic Priority of Highway Maintenance." Paper presented at the Pan-African Conference on Highway Maintenance, Accra (Ghana), November 1977.

_____. "The Highway Design and Maintenance Standards Model." Paper presented at the Second International Conference on Low Volume Roads, Ames (Iowa), August 1979.

Hide, H., et al. The Kenya Road Transport Cost Study: Research on Vehicle Operating Costs. TRRL Laboratory Report 672. Crowthorne (United Kingdom): Transport and Road Research Laboratory, 1975.

Hodges, J. W., et al. The Kenya Road Transport Cost Study: Research on Road Deterioration. TRRL Laboratory Report 673. Crowthorne (United Kingdom): Transport and Road Research Laboratory, 1975.

Moavenzadeh, Fred, et al. "Highway Design Study, Phase I: The Model." World Bank Staff Working Paper No. 96, January 1971 (out of print).

Watanatada, Thawat. "The Highway Design and Maintenance Standards Model: Model Description and User's Manual (Release II)." The World Bank: Transportation and Water Department, December 1981.

Watanatada, Thawat, and Harral, Clell G. "Determination of Economically Balanced Highway Expenditure Programs under Budget Constraints: A Practical Approach." Paper presented at the World Conference on Transport Research, London, April 1980.

The Determinants of Railway Traffic, Freight Transport, and the Choice of Transport Modes

Ref. No. 672–07

An in-house review of railways supported by the World Bank revealed some causes for concern in three broad areas: volumes and types of traffic, operating efficiency, and finances. The last two raise institutional questions that are being investigated in the course of the Bank's operational work.

In planning railway investments in developing countries, demand for railway traffic has often been extremely difficult to forecast. Future freight traffic has often been overestimated and passenger traffic has been underestimated, sometimes with unfortunate consequences. The research project on the "Economic Role of Railways" (Ref. No. 671–50), now completed, has investigated determinants of the pace and pattern of shifts between different modes of transportation. Its findings suggest that the share of railways in total freight transport has been declining (despite some increases in absolute volumes); that railways are increasingly becoming specialized carriers used for relatively large shipments over long distances; and that the share of railways has been declining irrespective of the relative prices of different transport modes. But though this research is yielding hypotheses about shippers' choice of modes and the factors governing this choice, the data available do not permit these to be rigorously formulated and tested.

A further phase of research, approved in October 1979, uses information collected by the Netherlands Institute of Transport for a study of freight traffic in the European Economic Community and Spain, since data are not available in sufficient detail for developing countries. A detailed analysis of this data base should sharpen understanding of the comparative advantage of railways as against other modes of transport in different circumstances and of the factors governing shippers' choice of transport modes, for specified groups of commodities. It is expected to yield rigorously formulated hypotheses that can be tested in studies of individual developing countries.

Responsibility: Transportation Department—Pedro N. Taborga. Most of the work will be undertaken by the Netherlands Institute of Transport, from which a major part of the funding for this project has recently been made available.

Completion date: June 1984.

Demand for Personal Travel in Developing Countries

Ref. No. 673-05

The opportunity for personal travel—whether for work or to satisfy social or private needs—the fares, and the quality and amount of service are sensitive social and political issues, according to the experience of many developing countries. The broad objective of this research project is to bring modern consumer theory to bear on the analysis and prediction of demand for personal travel in developing countries. Consumer demand analysis will be applied to urban and rural data to estimate models that can simultaneously serve as the basis for forecasting, policy analysis, and the assessment of the distributional consequences of changes in travel opportunity. By analyzing the determinants of travel expenditure and ownership of vehicles, projections of broad categories of demand for travel will be facilitated and a framework for discussion of issues of transport policy, such as pricing, taxation, subsidization, and provision of services and infrastructure, will be provided.

During the two decades 1950–70, the volume of personal travel by road and rail within countries appears to have grown in most parts of the world at a faster rate than the transport of goods, and faster than either population growth or the level of recorded real income. In the few developing countries where similar calculations have been attempted, the evidence is substantially the same. There is also evidence that the growth of personal travel is not simply linked to the rate of urbanization: a comparison of road and rail travel in nine countries for which estimates are available fails to suggest such a correlation. Rather, a correlation between the demand for personal travel and the level of gross national product per capita is suggested by the data.

Personal travel has been considered by many investigators and governments to be a luxury item, yet some level of transportation is found to be indispensable to the average household, even at very low levels of income. A deterioration in the opportunity for travel, which need not be reflected in the expenditure on transport, can act like a tax on poor households.

The organizing principle of the "utility-based" model to be employed in this study is that consumers make rational and consistent choices. The model will be applied to answer these questions:

1. How can the demand for travel be predicted?
2. What parameters of demand can be estimated for use in a wide range of circumstances?
3. How can the level of ownership of vehicles be predicted?
4. How can the responses of owners of vehicles and users of vehicles be predicted in the face of certain policy changes?
5. Given various options in transport policy, including the provision of roads, public transport services, prices of vehicles and fuel, taxes and regulations regarding vehicle ownership, how can the impact of these policies be gauged in terms of the welfare and income of socioeconomic groups within the population?

The study is expected to be based on data already available in selected developing countries, supplemented by surveys of travel behavior and household surveys. Household surveys in the context of transportation issues typically have data on the total expenditure for transportation, sometimes distinguishing the mode of travel—rail, bus, or private vehicles. Such surveys also provide information on household income and total expenditure and on economic and demographic characteristics, all of which are partial determinants of expenditure on transportation. Data on location, work status, and the possession of durable goods, especially cars, bicycles, and carts, are important conditioning variables. Price, location, fuel costs, and maintenance costs are also important factors in the ownership levels of various types of vehicles.

Travel surveys, on the other hand, are not collected from households, but from individual travelers—on a train, on a bus, or along the road—and are, therefore, not random across a population. As data sources, the two types of survey are complementary; combined, they will allow for more specific and detailed analysis, as required by World Bank staff in project appraisal, and be representative and reliable in forecasting demand.

Responsibility: Transportation Department—Esra Bennathan; *Water Supply and Urban Development Department*—Alan Armstrong-Wright; and *Development Research Department* —Gregory K. Ingram.

Completion date: June 1985.

6

Energy

Standards of Rural Electrification

Ref. No. 671–86

Rural electrification schemes in developing countries are estimated to absorb about $50 billion during the next decade. Many of the Bank's borrowers, particularly those that are in the early stages of rural electrification, are looking to the Bank for guidance in this crucial and capital-intensive area of rural infrastructure. This research project is helping to develop a methodology for improving the efficiency of investments in rural electrification and establish guidelines that should aid in formulating and appraising projects in this subsector.

Phase I of the study consists of a critical evaluation of design criteria and standards of rural electrification in 12 developing countries. It includes a review of previous studies and relevant practices in the developed countries and describes the results of field trips. Concurrently, a combined economic/engineering methodology was developed to optimize the design of a rural electrification network, based on variations in the quality of supply. The approach used in this study considered system costs as well as costs incurred by consumers due to poor quality of supply and, therefore, subsumed the conventional criterion in power system planning of minimizing only the supply costs. All the usual economic techniques applicable to developing countries —in particular, shadow pricing—were used. Theoretical models of the activities of various types of electricity users were also developed.

Following the methodology developed in the first phase, the net economic benefits for two rural electrification networks (in India and Costa Rica) are maximized in Phase II. Particular attention is being paid to alternative qualities of supply and their impact on the type of usage and on the growth of load. Surveys have been made to verify the accuracy of the theoretical framework of user activity, the value users place on electricity, and the willingness to pay for electricity supply of various qualities.

Responsibility: Energy Department—Karl Jechoutek with the previous substantive contribution of Mohan Munasinghe, in collaboration with Walter G. Scott (consultant) to assist with the engineering aspects of the study.

Completion date: A final report is in process.

Reports

Munasinghe, Mohan. "The Optimal Planning of Rural Electric Systems and the Quality of Supply." Paper presented at a Development Policy Staff Microeconomics Seminar. The World Bank: Energy Department, May 6, 1980.

Investment Planning in the Power Sector in Indonesia

Ref. No. 672-54A

The study's objective is to develop a coherent and consistent framework for formulating and evaluating investment decisions in the power sector in Indonesia. The study will make use of mathematical programming models developed under "Programming in the Manufacturing Sector" (Ref. No. 670-24 in category 4—Industry) and the computational facilities developed under "A General Algebraic Modeling System (GAMS)" (Ref. No. 671-58 in category 1—Development Policy and Planning). The focus is on defining an "optimal" investment program that will incorporate issues of scale, location, timing and choice of technology, and reliability associated with major investments exhibiting strong economies of scale. This model is to be used as a tool for project and program selection, as well as a simulation device to evaluate the costs and benefits of alternate policies and government proposals.

In Indonesia, only about 6 percent to 7 percent of the population is estimated to have access to electricity. Power sales of the national power utility, PLN, have grown at over 20 percent a year since 1978, and long waiting lists exist for supply, especially in Java. Tentative forecasts indicate demand growth of 22 percent a year until 1985, tapering to 16 percent by 1990. There is little doubt that PLN's sales will be limited only by its ability to supply electricity, and this implies considerable investments in power generation, transmission, and distribution. Given the Bank's past and expected future involvement (of about $1 billion over the next five years) in investments in the power sector, developing an appropriate long-term investment strategy is crucial for both Indonesia and the Bank. Moreover, given Indonesia's natural resource endowments, namely oil, natural gas, coal, hydropower, geothermal and nuclear energy, the scope for technological substitution is vast. Therefore, a crucial question to be addressed by this project is: What is the most efficient way for Indonesia to meet its future demand for electricity? The answer requires not only investment planning analysis, but also investigation of the financing of alternate investment programs.

In the analysis, the importance of factors such as world market prices, availability and prices of domestic energy resources, and factors of production, including labor, capital, foreign exchange, and exogenous demand parameters, will be evaluated. For example, alternate investment programs can be determined under differing assumptions of the demand for power. Or, for any given forecast of the demand for power, the appropriate choices of technology for power generation under different assumptions of energy prices can be determined.

Moreover, the model will be used in the evaluation of the costs and benefits of alternate policies by simulating various government investment proposals or policies for energy prices. The evaluation will be performed by comparing the optimal investment program to that of the proposed strategy and determining whether there is a cost or a benefit associated with the proposal. In this manner, certain institutional constraints can also be evaluated. For example, if a decision is made to construct a power plant at a particular location or to use a particular energy resource which, in fact, turns out not to be optimal, then it would be possible to determine the total opportunity cost to the sector of this nonoptimal decision. Policy questions of interest to the Bank and the Government of Indonesia regarding power generation, transmission, regional location, and choice of energy resources may be investigated within this framework.

Since each of the alternative investment programs will be evaluated with the aid of the same, internally consistent technique, this approach should provide an effective mode of communication between the Bank, PLN, and other interested parties concerning the desirable long-term development path of the Indonesian power sector. The analysis is also expected to have important implications for the Bank's lending operations in the power sector in general.

Responsibility: Country Policy Department, Development Research Department, and *East Asia and Pacific Country Programs Department*—Armeane M. Choksi, Alexander Meeraus, and Michael Walton, respectively.

Completion date: December 1983.

Development and Application of a Minimum Standard Energy Demand Model for Developing Countries

Ref. No. 672–63

In recent years, the World Bank's energy projections have become an increasingly important element in the preparation of its global economic outlook. Traditionally, these energy projections were based on detailed country-by-country projections of energy balances. In the past, the focus of much of the research on energy demand had been on the industrial countries: first, because published data on noncommercial energy, energy efficiency, sectoral energy demand and interfuel substitution were not readily available in most developing countries, and second, because these countries accounted for less than 20 percent of the global demand for energy.

The steep increase in the price of petroleum in 1973–74 led in many countries to a careful examination of the way energy resources were used. These efforts triggered a flow of information that can now be used to arrive at more precise energy projections for a growing number of developing countries. In addition, long-term energy projections have shown that energy consumption in these countries could reach about 80 percent of the projected consumption in industrial countries. Hence, there is clearly a need to focus more sharply on the trends and behavior of energy demand in developing countries.

The main objective of this research study is to develop an analytical framework that will make it possible to analyze and project the demand for energy—in terms of the major fuels used —in the main economic sectors of developing countries. The research aims at developing a minimum standard energy demand model that can be applied—with minimal adjustments—to a large number of countries. The concept and rationale for developing such a minimum standard model for the analysis of energy demand is similar to the minimum standard macroeconomic models that have been developed in the Bank for country economic analysis. The minimum standard model will eventually be extended as more information about developing countries' energy sectors becomes available. In this respect, it would serve as a focal point for systematically assembling relevant data and information that is generated inside and outside the Bank.

The primary purpose of the study is to acquire a proper understanding of the scope of the demand for energy in developing countries and, thus, of the magnitude of the economic implications caused by rising energy costs. It is also intended to incorporate the estimated energy demand models into the global energy projections model of the Bank's Economic Analysis and Projections Department.

The proposed minimum standard model will consist of an economic module and an energy module. The purpose of the economic module is to translate exogenously projected changes in final demand into the corresponding changes of gross output using an input-output approach. The energy module converts the changes in gross output into corresponding changes in final and primary energy consumption in the industrial sector, the transport sector, agriculture, and the commercial and residential sectors. The model will consider six categories of final energy products: oil, gas, coal, electricity, firewood, and charcoal and biomass.

The work will be carried out in two stages. The thrust of the first stage will be to develop a minimum standard energy demand model. This model will be applied in four developing countries—- Brazil, India, Kenya, and Malaysia. Of these four countries, three are net oil importers; the fourth country, Malaysia, is a net oil exporter. It is expected that the differences in energy-use patterns and in endowments of energy resources of these countries will provide a sufficient test for the appropriateness of a single minimum standard energy demand model. Research institutes in the four countries have indicated their willingness to participate in the estimation and testing of the country-specific models. During the second stage, the model will be applied to estimating energy demand in the remaining developing countries.

The research is expected to take two years. An interim report on the first stage has been completed. The final product of this research will consist of a series of working papers and a monograph describing the minimum standard model and the estimated energy demand models for developing countries.

Responsibility: Economic Analysis and Projections Department —Peter Pollak. The research project is carried out by Professor Lutz Hoffmann and Dr. Lorenz Jarass of the University of Regensburg, Federal Republic of Germany.

Completion date: The first stage—September 1983; the second stage—December 1984.

The Welfare Implications of Eliminating Energy Subsidies in Indonesia

Ref. No. 672-70

The objective of this study is to evaluate the welfare implications of eliminating energy subsidies in Indonesia for different groups of consumers distinguished by income, geographical region, household size, and other characteristics that are relevant to the determination of demand patterns. The rationale stems from the Bank's advice to the Government of Indonesia to reduce and eventually to eliminate subsidies on the domestic consumption of oil products, which currently amount to about 3.5 percent of gross domestic product (GDP). Clearly, an important aspect of such a policy recommendation is its differential impact on different groups of households in the economy. For obvious reasons, this analysis is of major concern to policymakers and, as part of its ongoing policy dialogue with the government, the Bank would now like to provide answers to important questions, such as: Which groups are likely to benefit the most from this policy change? Which groups are likely to benefit the least? How do the distributions of welfare among different groups of households compare before and after the implementation of the suggested policy?

Due to the obvious political ramifications of eliminating subsidies, it is essential for the government to have some understanding of the welfare implications of such recommendations. The basic welfare measure used in this exercise is the net "compensating variation"—that is, the minimum amount of additional expenditure required to enable a group to maintain the same level of utility service after the elimination of subsidies, as it had before the policy changes. The "compensating variation" will, in general, be different for each group, thus reflecting the differential needs and tastes of these groups. The computation of the compensating variation also takes into account adjustments by consumers in response to changes in price and income.

Alternate policy changes—defined by varying (increased) price levels of energy and time-paths for the elimination of subsidies—will be developed to determine their welfare implications for the households and to identify those consumer groups that are most significantly affected by different policy regimes. This also will provide useful information for targeting conservation efforts towards specific groups. In addition, since unique group-specific demand functions can be derived from the model, it can be used to project group-specific consumption patterns in response to changes in prices, incomes, quantity constraints, and other government policies.

Moreover, the model can also focus on the quantity of aggregate consumption. In this case, it can be used to generate a projection of aggregate consumption, given the prices, incomes, and information on the joint distribution of household incomes and attributes. No simulation at the microeconomic level is required. In addition, the model can directly assimilate information on demographic shifts and changes in income distribution that may be highly relevant for medium- to long-term projections. The impact of different policies can be analyzed in terms of direct effects on consumption, such as conservation efforts and rationing, and in terms of indirect effects through changes in prices and incomes. These policies may be introduced into the model at the regional as well as the national level.

Responsibility: Country Policy Department—Armeane M. Choksi. The researchers include Professor Lawrence Lau in collaboration with Dennis Framholzer, both of Stanford University, Professors Mark Pitt and Lung-Fei Lee, both of the University of Minnesota. The Central Bureau of Statistics, Indonesia, is also involved.

Completion date: December 1983.

Adjustment in Oil-Importing Countries

Ref. No. 672-74

Oil-importing developing countries were significantly affected in the 1970s by the twin external shocks of deteriorating terms of trade and a reduction in the growth of export volumes arising from the recession in the industrial market economies. These effects called for both national and international adjustment—that is, the transfer of either real resources or claims on future resources to oil-exporting countries. This research studies the different ways in which national adjustment has been effected. It will identify the broad features of adjustment through cross-country comparative analysis; isolate the key relationships that must underlie models of macroeconomic adjustment; and assemble policy-focused case studies of archetypal countries distinguished by the structure of production and trade. The project is intended to contribute towards the formal incorporation of adjustment analysis in the Bank's country economic work.

The *World Development Report 1981* uses a common analytical framework to impose order on the diversity of country experience and to interpret the process of adjustment in selected countries.[1] The methodology compares the actual performance of import and export prices and quantities against counterfactual trends. The deviations from trend are then decomposed into those effects arising from changes in exogenous variables and those due to changes in a nation's economic performance. This leads to a "patterns of adjustment" analysis covering a large number of countries, in which the relative reliance on different modes of adjustment—trade adjustment (export expansion, import substitution), financial adjustment (additional external financing), and slower growth—may be related to production and trade characteristics, the development strategy pursued, and the magnitude of external shocks.

The research project has developed a macroeconometric modeling framework which goes beyond the purely accounting-based approach characteristic of earlier comparative work. This

---

[1] The World Bank, *World Development Report 1981* (New York: Oxford University Press), Chapter 6, pp. 64–96, and Technical Appendix, pp. 121–123.

has the advantage that "external" variables such as imports and exports can be determined simultaneously with "internal" variables such as consumption and taxes, so that the methodology offers a unified treatment of the major aspects of the adjustment process. The modeling framework is purposively simple and parsimonious in terms of data requirements so that it can be estimated for a large number of developing countries. The results may be used to generate a decomposition of shocks and adjustment, the latter into categories such as export expansion, import substitution, public and private resource mobilization, slowdown in investment demand, and additional external financing. This was done for 13 semi-industrial countries (see "Reports" below). Brief accounts of adjustment in each of the countries, in light of the chosen framework of analysis, are included.

The decomposition output is used for statistical analysis of the association of growth performance pre-1973 and post-1973 with different modes of adjustment. The following results are available for semi-industrial countries:

1. Countries that had favorable growth performance after 1973, compared to the previous decade, adjusted principally through trade adjustment and improved domestic resource mobilization. Additional external financing was used to help the time phasing of those modes of adjustment, but it was eliminated over a number of years. This pattern of adjustment did not require significant cuts in investment spending nor any prolonged interruption in economic growth.

2. Improvements in growth performance after 1973 relative to the previous decade are significantly related to improved domestic resource mobilization. Furthermore, there is a significant relationship between growth performance and public resource mobilization.

3. Reliance on slowdown in investment expenditure and additional external financing to effect adjustment was associated with both a worsening growth performance and deteriorating domestic resource mobilization.

4. There does not appear to be any statistically significant relationship between the magnitude of external shocks and a country's post-1973 growth performance relative to that in 1963-1973. Nor, when controlling for external shocks, are the effects of alternative modes of adjustment on growth performance significantly modified.

The above methodology has been applied to a number of the poorer oil-importing developing countries; it is being updated to analyze the 1979–80 round of external shocks in countries where the data till 1981 are available. The data base for the study presently contains nearly fifty developing countries.

The basic modeling framework is being extended to study the adjustment experiences of perhaps four countries drawn from subgroups of oil-importing developing countries—a semi-industrial country; a middle-income primary producing country; a large, partially industrialized low-income country; and a sub-Saharan African country. These studies will focus on three sets of questions: First, the links between policy instruments and adjustment targets will be explicitly articulated, with a view to attributing various components of adjustment to policy actions. Second, the studies will attempt to relate the sequencing of trade adjustment, domestic resource mobilization, investment and additional external financing to trade, production, and fiscal characteristics of an economy. The study of time phasing is based on the idea that while various rigidities limit the effectivenes of adjustment policy, such policy in turn can modify structural characteristics over the medium to longer term. Third, the case studies will pay some attention to the distributional consequences of alternative modes of adjustment to external shocks in terms of broad categories, namely rural versus urban, wage versus nonwage, and public versus private.

The adjustment methodology described so far has been used to interpret historical developments. It could also be applied to country projections. The research seeks to show that differences between alternative future scenarios may be decomposed into the effects of exogenous factors and national economic performance, using the language and categories of adjustment analysis. The approach has the potential of being formally integrated with the Revised Minimum Standard Model used by the Bank for country economic projections.

Responsibility: Development Research Department—Pradeep K. Mitra.

Completion date: June 1984.

Reports

Mitra, P. "Accounting for Adjustment in Selected Primary Producing Countries." Mimeo. The World Bank: Development Research Department, October 1983.

_____. "Accounting for Adjustment in Selected Semi-Industrial Countries." Mimeo. The World Bank: Development Research Department, May 1983.

_____. "World Bank Research on Adjustment to External Shocks." *World Bank Research News*, vol. 4, no. 3 (Fall/Winter 1983), (forthcoming).

Pricing and Taxing Transport Fuels in Developing Countries

Ref. No. 672-83

In developing countries, transport accounts typically for over one-half of all the oil consumed and takes a much larger share of total commercial energy than in developed countries. Given the role of oil imports in the balance of payments of many countries, the pricing of fuels is thus important not only for energy and transport policy, but also for macroeconomic policy. The evidence from many developing countries, however, shows that transport fuel pricing, which is under government control practically everywhere, has been changing erratically over the past decade. The object of the research is, therefore, to provide a logically sound and empirically manageable method for setting prices and taxes on transport fuels and vehicles, bearing in mind the circumstances of the individual transport sector and the general objectives of the governments concerned. The World Bank's advice to countries on this matter, sought and given in connection with transport sector work, energy missions, and structural adjustment lending, would thereby be placed on surer foundations.

The general nature of the problem of setting the right tax on transport fuels is described by two requirements: To strike the right balance between improved resource allocation and various distributional goals, and between considerations of public revenue and efficiency in the use of transport resources. There are, in addition, various complicating factors. Since the Bank often advises in circumstances in which only piecemeal changes in taxation are feasible, many other prices are not optimal, and government revenue from the transport sector must be maintained, the problem is one of choosing the second-best set of prices and taxes. In addition, fuels are typically both final consumption goods and intermediate goods, and considerable interfuel substitution possibilities exist. For all these reasons, the structure of the rest of the tax system is important for the design of transport taxes. Finally, transport fuels are a logical base on which to levy road-user charges.

The analytical basis for the investigation of fuel price policy will be the recently developed theory of optimal commodity taxation, somewhat simplified and adapted to the special features of the problem. In particular, the model to be constructed will have to take account of the linkages between industries that use transport and transport fuels. The distributional impact of changes in transport prices will be explored with an econometrically estimated demand system that, together with the input-output table, will yield estimates of the parameters needed for the choice of the tax structure. The study will demonstrate the consequences for tax design of ignoring distributional considerations or attaching varying degrees of importance to them.

A separate component of the research will present the methodology for estimating the cost of road use, establish order-of-magnitude estimates on the basis of the major recent empirical work in that area, and propose methods for charging for these costs.

The intended output of the research is a methodology for pricing and taxing fuels that can be applied in developing countries, each differing in its endowment of statistical data, and in the degree of fiscal flexibility. It will also provide order-of-magnitude estimates of the critical parameters and variables.

The research began by developing analytical models of the social costs incurred by vehicles on roads, building on the relationships identified by the "Highway Design Maintenance Standard Study" (Ref. No. 670-27 in category 5—Transportation and Telecommunications). The most interesting finding to date is that, under certain conditions, the marginal social cost is equal to the average cost borne by the Highways Department, even though the major part of the total social cost of highway use is the increase in subsequent vehicle operating costs caused by the increased roughness of roads. Concurrently, the impact of changes in fuel price on prices and income distribution in Thailand and Tunisia has been explored by a model based on an input-output table and a consumer budget survey. The next stage will be to calibrate the analytical road-user charge model to Tunisia, using data collected by consultants for the government, and then to combine the various components of the work into an illustrated methodology of setting taxes and vehicle license fees.

Responsibility: Development Research Department—Pradeep Mitra, with the contribution of David Newbery, currently of Churchill College, Cambridge University (United Kingdom), and *Transportation Department*—Esra Bennathan, with the assistance of Clell G. Harral and in collaboration with Gordon Hughes, Cambridge University, and W. D. Paterson (consultants).

Completion date: July 1984.

7
Urbanization and Regional Development

Strategic Planning to Accommodate Rapid Growth in Cities of Developing Countries ("The City Study")

Ref. No. 671-47

In the past few decades, many large cities in developing countries have experienced extremely high population growth, which has created the need for massive public investment and the expansion of public services. In response, the World Bank has increased its share of lending for projects on low-income segments of the urban population. Designing projects and programs that provide more urban infrastructure and serve the needs of the poor has strained available knowledge about how cities in less developed countries function. Projects are typically analyzed on a sectoral basis, and relatively little is known about their impact on development within a city, including residential and employment location, travel patterns, and the demand for public services. The study's principal objectives are to analyze the determinants of urban development patterns, the effects of urban projects on these patterns and their effects on the welfare of urban households.

Urban phenomena are difficult to analyze, chiefly because many aspects of the urban economy are interrelated. For example, changes in employment location will affect housing markets, employment opportunities, transport flows, and the need for public services. At the same time, each aspect has an identity and an analytical basis of its own that permits a separate examination. In this study, five such components of the urban economy are identified: housing, transporation, employment location, labor force, and public finance.

Within each of the five categories, three major research tasks are being carried out. First, the study is providing, to the extent permitted by the data, a systematic description of the current state and recent changes in the economy of a city and its spatial patterns. Second, it is producing estimates of behavioral parameters, such as price and income elasticities of demand, that are useful inputs in determining the impact of policies. Finally, these parameter estimates are being incorporated in analytical procedures that can be used to carry out analyses of the effects of specific policies. The analytical tools are expected to prove useful to the staff of the World Bank in the design and implementation of projects in urban areas, as well as to planning officials and decisionmakers in the developing countries.

The research has been carried out in the form of a case study of Bogota, Colombia. Portions of the study have been extended to the Colombian city of Cali, in order to test the transferability of the parameter estimates and behavioral relations. The basic data sources for the project are the national population and economic censuses, various sample surveys of the 1972 Phase II Bogota Urban Development Study, a 1978 household survey, a survey of industrial establishments, and case studies of several barrios.

The data collection and descriptive phases of the project are complete, as is the work on the estimation of behavioral parameters and the development of analytic tools. Numerous papers are available in the Bank's Urban and Regional Report series, in the working paper series of the Corporación Centro Regional de Población in Bogota, and as part of other publications. The final output of the project will be contained in a series of six research monographs to be produced in 1984.

Responsibility: Development Research Department—Gregory K. Ingram, and *Water Supply and Urban Development Department* —Andrew M. Hamer, and Kyu Sik Lee; staff members Johannes F. Linn and Rakesh Mohan have been working on the project. Corporación Centro Regional de Población (CCRP) in Bogota is the project's main collaborating institution, and the CCRP staff members principally involved include Ramiro Cardona, José Fernando Piñeda, Alvaro Pachon, and Rodrigo Villamizar. The Chamber of Commerce of Bogota has been actively involved in disseminating the project's results and has supported additional analysis in Bogota. The Urban and Regional Development Section of the Colombian National Planning Office has provided general assistance. In Cali, the Departmental and the Municipal Planning Office have participated directly in the project.

Completion date: July 1984.

Reports

Carroll, A. "Pirate Subdivisions and the Supply of Residential Lots in Bogota." World Bank Staff Working Paper No. 435, October 1980.

Cifuentes, J., and Hernandez, A. "Urban Transportation in Bogota." Urban and Regional Report No. 79-7. The World Bank, June 1978.

Fields, G. "How Segmented is the Bogota Labor Market?" World Bank Staff Working Paper No. 434, October 1980.

Hamer, A. M. "Bogota's Unregulated Subdivisions." Urban and Regional Report No. 81-19. The World Bank, August 1981.

_____. "Households and Housing: Residential Mobility, Tenure Choice, and Space Consumption in the Developing Metropolis." Urban and Regional Report No. 81-20. The World Bank, December 1981.

Ingram, G. K. "Housing Demand in the Developing Metropolis: Estimates from Bogota and Cali, Colombia." Urban and Regional Report No. 81-11. The World Bank, April 1981.

_____. "Land in Perspective: Its Role in the Structure of Cities." In M. Cullen and S. Woolery (eds.), Proceedings of World Congress on Land Policy. Lexington (Massachussetts): D. C. Heath, 1982. Also available as Urban and Regional Report No. 80-9. The World Bank, November 1980.

Ingram, G. K., and Carroll, A. "The Spatial Structure of Latin American Cities." Journal of Urban Economics, vol. 9, no. 2, (March 1981).

Ingram, G. K.; Pachon, A.; and Piñeda, J. F. "Summary of Results and Policy Implications of the City Study." Urban Development Discussion Paper. The World Bank, November 1982.

Kozel, V. "Travel Demand Models for Developing Countries: The Case of Bogota, Colombia." Urban and Regional Report No. 81-26. The World Bank, December 1981.

Latorre, E. "TASSIM-Cali: El Modelo de Demanda de Transporte para Cali." Documento de Trabajo No. 10. Bogota: Corporación Centro Regional de Población (CCRP), July 1980.

Lee, K. S. "Determinants of Intra-Urban Location of Manufacturing Employment: An Analysis of Survey Results for Bogota, Colombia." Urban and Regional Report No. 81-3. The World Bank, March 1981.

_____. "Intra-Urban Location of Manufacturing Employment in Colombia," Journal of Urban Economics, vol. 19, no. 2 (March 1981).

————. "A Model of Intra-Urban Employment Location: An Application to Bogota, Colombia." *Journal of Urban Economics,* vol. 12, no. 3 (November 1982).

Lee, Y. J. "The City Study: The Available Data, Vol. III." Urban and Regional Report No. 81-15. The World Bank, July 1981.

————. "The City Study: The Available Data, Vol. II." Urban and Regional Report No. 79-13. The World Bank, August 1979.

————. "The Spatial Development of Brazil Metropolitan Areas". Urban and Regional Report No. 81-12. The World Bank, July 1981.

Linn, J. F. "Administración y Financiamiento de Servicios Públicos en el Distrito Especial de Bogotá." Documento de Trabajo No. 11. Bogota: Corporación Centro Regional de Población (CCRP), April 1981.

Linn, J. F. (ed.). "Essays on Urban Public Finance in Colombia." Urban Development Discussion Paper. The World Bank, October 1983.

Mohan, R. "An Anatomy of the Distribution of Urban Incomes." Urban Development Discussion Paper. The World Bank, August 1983.

————. "The Determinants of Labor Earnings in Developing Metropoli: Estimates from Bogota and Cali, Colombia." World Bank Staff Working Paper No. 498, October 1981.

————. "The People of Bogota: Who They Are, What They Earn, Where They Live." World Bank Staff Working Paper No. 390, May 1980.

Mohan, R.; Garcia, J.; and Wagner, W. "Measuring Malnutrition and Poverty: A Case Study of Bogota and Cali, Colombia." World Bank Staff Working Paper No. 447, April 1981.

Mohan, R., and Hartline, N. "The Poor of Bogota: Who They Are, What They Do, and Where They Live." Urban and Regional Report No. 80-6. The World Bank, July 1980.

Mohan, R., and Villamizar, R. "The Evolution of Land Values and Urban Structure in the Context of Rapid Urban Growth: A Case Study of Bogota and Cali, Colombia." In M. Cullen (ed.), *Proceedings of World Congress on Land Policy.* Lexington (Massachussetts): D. C. Heath, 1981. Also available as Urban and Regional Report No. 80-10. The World Bank, October 1980.

Pachon, A. "El Automóvil en dos Metropolis del Tercer Mundo." Documento de Trabajo No. 17. Bogota: Corporación Centro Regional de Población (CCRP), July 1981.

_____. "Household Transportation Decisions in the Developing Metropolis." Paper presented at Latin American Meetings of the Econometric Society, Rio de Janeiro (Brazil), July 1981.

_____. "El Impacto Redistributivo de la Intervencion del Gobierno en el Transporte Urbano." Documento de Trabajo No. 19. Bogota: Corporación Centro Regional de Población (CCRP), September 1981.

_____. "Situación del Transporte en Cali y Bogotá—Década de los Setenta." Documento de Trabajo No. 18. Bogota: Corporación Centro Regional de Población (CCRP), September 1981.

Paredes, L. R. "Colombia's Urban Legal Framework." Urban and Regional Report No. 81-18. The World Bank, April 1980.

Piñeda, J. F. "Residential Location Decisions of Multiple Worker Households in Bogota, Colombia." Paper presented at Eastern Economic Association Meetings, Philadelphia (Pennsylvania), April 1981.

Reyes, L. "El Area Metropolitana de Cali." Documento de Trabajo No. 3. Bogota: Corporación Centro Regional de Población (CCRP), May 1980.

Stevenson, R. "Housing Programs and Policies in Bogota." Urban and Regional Report No. 79-8. The World Bank, June 1978.

Valverde, N. "The City Study: The Available Data, Vol. I." Urban and Regional Report No. 79-6. The World Bank, June 1978.

Villamizar, R. "The Behavior of Land Prices: Its Determinants and Effects on Urban Structure." Paper presented at Latin American Meetings of the Econometric Society, Rio de Janeiro (Brazil), July 1981.

_____. "Land Prices in Bogota between 1955 and 1978." In V. Henderson (ed.), Research in Urban Economics, vol. 2. Greenwich (Connecticut): JAI Press, 1981. Also available as Urban and Regional Report No. 80-2. The World Bank, April 1980.

Wagner, W. M. "Vacant Lots, Land Prices and Assessment Practices: The Case of Bogota, Colombia." Urban and Regional Report No. 81-14. The World Bank, July 1981.

Wiesner, G. "Cien Años de Desarrollo Histórico de los Precios de la Tierra en Bogotá." Documento de Trabajo No. 4. Bogota: Corporación Centro Regional de Población (CCRP), May 1980.

The Urban and Regional Reports are available from the Bank Research Documentation Center (BRDC) and the Urban Development Discussion Papers are available from the Water Supply and Urban Development Department, both of the World Bank. Several papers are also available in Spanish in the working paper series of the Corporación Centro Regional de Población (CCRP), Bogota, Colombia, and in Vols. 41, 42, 43, 45 and 46 of *Revista*, Cámara de Comercio de Bogotá.

National Spatial Policies: Brazil

Ref. No. 672-13

Policymakers in various countries are concerned about the degree to which population and economic activity are concentrated in a few urban centers. Many countries have experience with policies aimed at deconcentrating such activity. In the process, governments, as well as the Bank's operational staff, have become aware that substantive conceptual and empirical work on this subject is lacking, especially as it relates to developing countries. This research was the first project in a program aimed at responding to some of the more important of these concerns.

The project focused on spatial issues in Brazil, in particular those related to the patterns of urban and industrial growth in Greater Sao Paulo and its regional hinterland. Further case studies were undertaken; preparatory work on the Republic of Korea took place in 1981 and led to a second study. A program was also developed with collaborating institutions in India.

The project in Brazil had three major aspects. The first included a review of the state-of-the art in the economies of systems of cities, leading to the development of a framework for an international comparison of patterns of urban concentration. It indicated the extent to which economic analysis can explain the varying conditions found worldwide in urban development. This framework contributed to a general review of spatial development and policies in Brazil and provided the foundation for an econometric model tested with data gathered from cities in southern Brazil. The first set of tasks also included a series of background studies on demographic and industrial changes in Greater Sao Paulo and its hinterland that complemented the cited econometric work and provided useful background for the other components of the project. In particular, the degree to which the process of concentrated population growth has begun to experience a reversal has been reviewed. In addition, one study analyzed the importance of branch plants and transfers in the rapid growth of secondary cities in Greater Sao Paulo's hinterland.

The second and major component of the study was an analysis of the determinants of the behavior of industrial firms in deciding where to locate. This included an attempt to identify the effects that different types of spatial policy instruments have on the location of enterprises. An extensive survey of 600 new branch plants and independent firms in Sao Paulo State provided the principal data for this exercise. The communities where surveyed firms are located were studied. These areas differ in size and are at varying distances from metropolitan Sao Paulo. Using secondary data, an attempt was made to determine the degree to which the level of urban services varies over space. This examination served to place in context the responses of surveyed firms about the adequacy of services at the municipal level. Some effort was also made to understand the behavior of factor markets that condition the responses found in the survey. Aside from gathering information on land and freight costs at different distances from Greater Sao Paulo, the spatial variation of wages was analyzed.

The effectiveness of national spatial policies is often reduced by nonspatial policies in the public sector that have spatial biases embedded within them. The project's third component, therefore, traces the spatial impact of selected nonspatial policies in Brazil, concentrating primarily on industrial sector programs (trade, fiscal incentives, credit subsidies) and on intergovernmental relations. In particular, the net protection afforded to different industrial sectors by the public sector's tariff, fiscal, and credit policies was calculated. Through an analysis of the regional distribution of each output of each industrial sector, the value of implicit subsidies to different regions was determined.

Data limitations and budgetary constraints did not permit empirical analyses to be made of the adjustments that may be expected in the location of economic activity resulting from changes in the present set of policies in the public sector. Such adjustments can, however, be traced analytically, by adapting models from international trade theory. The spatial implications of Brazil's system of intergovernmental relations, particularly those relating to tax and expenditure policies at the federal, state, and municipal level, were examined. In both sets of tasks, an effort was made to review the impact of such policies on the relations between major agglomerations in southern Brazil, especially metropolitan Sao Paulo, and the hinterland extending over a radial distance of several hundred miles. An important concern was whether public sector policies tend to promote or hinder any process of deconcentration that might take place, whether spontaneous or induced by specific spatial incentives.

The summary of conclusions of the study, which looks at the system of cities across stages of economic growth, is as follows: First, the potential size of a city at any one point in time is insensitive to most actions by local public officials. At the same time, economic development brings in its wake a transformation of the man-made resources that are available in secondary urban centers, as well as checks to further accelerated growth in preeminent centers. Second, for most secondary urban centers there is little opportunity to profit from a transfer of dynamism from the metropolis in the form of relocations and new metropolitan-based branches, due to the limited search for locational alternatives by firm managers, which restricts geographical mobility. Attractive secondary urban centers can, however, count on growth of existing plants and the generation of new, locally based firms to promote local development. Finally, local officials should concentrate on providing for the rapid, coordinated introduction of public services at the local level, as well as on finding ways to increase the availability of leasable space for smaller businesses. Beyond that, the initiative rests with the national government, for which the best spatial policy is to develop and implement a set of efficient sectoral policies.

Responsibility: Water Supply and Urban Development Department—Andrew M. Hamer, in collaboration with William Dillinger. Principal consultants are Vernon Henderson and Peter Townroe.

Secondary data were gathered and analyzed primarily with the aid of the Fundação Instituto Brasileiro de Geografia e Estatistica. The analyses of the impact of the public sector on cities of different sizes relied on the collaboration of the National Planning Secretariat, through its Instituto de Planajamento Econômico e Social. Work on the component on industrial location was conducted jointly with the Fundação Instituto de Pesquisas Econômicas of the University of Sao Paulo.

Completion date: June 1983; the completion report is in process.

Reports

Dillinger, W. "Implicit Spatial Policies—The Case of Fiscal System in Sao Paulo State." Urban and Regional Report No. 81-27. The World Bank, Development Economics Department, November 1981.

Dillinger, W., and Hamer, A. "Sources of Growth in Manufacturing Employment in Non-metropolitan Areas." Urban Development Department Discussion Paper No. 13. The World Bank, October 1982.

Fundação Instituto de Pesquisas Econômicas. "The Coding Manual and the Simple Frequency Distributions of Responses to the 1980 Sao Paulo Industrial Survey." Urban and Regional Report No. 81-9. The World Bank: Development Economics Department, May 1981.

Hamer, A. "Brazilian Industrialization and Economic Concentration in Sao Paulo: A Survey." Urban Development Department Discussion Paper No. 14. The World Bank, October 1982.

_____. "Decentralized Development and Industrial Location Behavior in Sao Paulo, Brazil: A Synthesis of Research Issues and Conclusions." Water Supply and Urban Development Department Discussion Paper. The World Bank (forthcoming).

_____. "Limited Search Procedures and Manufacturing Location Behavior: A Case Study of Sao Paulo, Brazil." Urban and Regional Report No. 81-23. The World Bank: Development Economics Department, November 1981 (revised October 1982).

Hamer, A., and Dillinger, W. "Labor Market Behavior in Sao Paulo State." Water Supply and Urban Development Department Discussion Paper. The World Bank (forthcoming).

Hansen, E. "Why Do Firms Locate Where They Do?: An Empirical Analysis of the Productivity, Wages, and Location of New Manufacturing Plants in Sao Paulo State, Brazil." Water Supply and Urban Development Department Discussion Paper. The World Bank (forthcoming).

Henderson, J. V. "A Framework for International Comparisons of Systems of Cities." Urban and Regional Report No. 80-3. The World Bank: Development Economics Department, March 1980.

_____. "Urban Development City Size and Population Composition." Water Supply and Urban Development Department Discussion Paper. The World Bank (forthcoming).

_____. "Urban Economics of Scale in Brazil." Urban Development Department Discussion Paper No. 17. The World Bank, November 1982.

Keen, D., and Luscome, W. "Urbanization Patterns and Industrial Location in Sao Paulo State, Brazil: An Atlas." Urban Development Department Discussion Paper No. 9. The World Bank, July 1982.

Townroe, P. "A Framework for the Study of New Industrial Locations within the City Region." Urban and Regional Report No. 81-7. The World Bank: Development Economics Department, January 1981.

_____. "Employment Decentralization Policy for a Major Metropolis: The Case of Sao Paulo, Brazil." Water Supply and Urban Development Department Discussion Paper. The World Bank (forthcoming).

_____. "Location Factors for Industry Decentralizing from Metropolitan Sao Paulo, Brazil." Urban and Regional Report No. 81-8. The World Bank: Development Economics Department, May 1981.

Townroe, P., and Keen, D. "Polarization Reversal in the State of Sao Paulo, Brazil." Urban and Regional Report No. 81-16. The World Bank: Development Economics Department, July 1981.

Townroe, P., and Roseman, J. "Sectoral Influences on Spatial Changes in Manufacturing: Sao Paulo, Brazil, 1960-1975." Urban Development Department Discussion Paper No. 15. The World Bank, October 1982.

Townroe, P., and Thomas, V. "The Location of Industry and Pollution Control Policies: A Case Study of Sao Paulo, Brazil." Urban Development Department Discussion Paper No. 8. The World Bank, March 1982.

Tyler, W. "Sectoral Policies and the Spatial Concentration of Industrial Activities in Sao Paulo, Brazil." Water Supply and Urban Development Department Discussion Paper. The World Bank (forthcoming).

Redwood, J. "Industrialization Policy, Fiscal Incentives and Extra-regional Establishments in Northeast Brazil: A Characterization based on the SUDENE/BNB Survey." Urban Development Department Discussion Paper No. 16. The World Bank, November 1982.

Ruane, F. "Sectoral Policies and Spatial Concentration of Industrial Activities. A Factor Market Adjustment Approach."

Urban Development Department Discussion Paper No. 12.
The World Bank, September 1982.

Identifying the Urban Poor: A Case Study of Brazil

Ref. No. 672-37

A basic objective of the World Bank's project lending is to
transfer benefits as directly as possible to the poor. In middle-
income countries, "target groups" for projects are identified on the
basis of relative poverty: one third of the national income per
head—adjusted for price differences between rural and urban
areas—gives an income threshold below which an individual is
considered poor.

Difficulties are frequently encountered in using this income
threshold to identify the poor for the Bank's operations. First, the
use of an indicator of individual income can be misleading, since
most people live in family groups and what defines poverty is the
income available to be shared among the household members.
Second, a household poverty threshold, if it can be established,
must be converted into units that are commonly used in local
statistical tabulations. Third, especially in large countries, geographical variations in income and price levels may seriously
compromise the use of a single, national indicator of poverty.
Finally, where rapid inflation is not offset by adjustments in wage
levels, indicative income levels may quickly become outdated.

For lending projects in Brazil, the urban poverty threshold has
been defined as equivalent to a family income of three minimum
salaries. The minimum salary is defined by law and regionally
differentiated; it is the unit used in most Brazilian income statistics. This threshold is used on a national basis. However, if the
regional minimum salaries do not adequately reflect regional price
differences, the living standard represented by three minimum
salaries may vary substantially between regions. It is also possible
that very few people in Curitiba, for example, live in the kind of
poverty found in Sao Luis, even though the Bank's urban poverty
threshold identifies many families in both cities as being below the
poverty line.

As a result of these uncertainties, the Latin America and the
Caribbean Projects Department investigated the degree to which
the use of a single urban poverty threshold in Brazil may bias the
design and evaluation of projects. This study examined a set of

indicators of the quality of life represented by three minimum salaries: for example, food consumption, type of housing, education, and mortality rates. The research investigated the potential of (1) regionally based income thresholds of the same type and (2) other possible indicators of poverty. It also analyzed procedures for regularly updating the poverty indicators.

Though the study focused on Brazil, the method developed is generally applicable in countries that have regional variations in prices and incomes. The results of the study should make it easier to design and evaluate projects to reach the urban poor, and also reduce the costs of collecting and using data on urban poverty.

Responsibility: Latin America and the Caribbean Projects Department—Peter L. Watson. The study was carried out by James Hicks and David Vetter of PLANPUR, a consulting firm based in Rio de Janeiro.

Completion date: Mid-1982; the final report is available as a World Bank Staff Working Paper (listed below), and the completion report is in process.

Reports

Hicks, James F., and Vetter, David M. "Identifying the Urban Poor in Brazil." World Bank Staff Working Paper No. 565, 1983.

Housing Demand and Housing Finance in Developing Countries (Phase I)

Ref. No. 672-46

Housing-related projects have constituted an important component of the World Bank's urban lending program during the past decade. This study is intended to shift the focus of research on housing from issues connected with project planning to those at the sectoral level, in consonance with a similar shift in the lending program.

The work plan consists of three closely related clusters of analysis, all of which build upon existing work: "Analyzing the Effects of Urban Housing Policy in Developing Countries" (Ref. No. 671-37, now completed) and "The City Study" (Ref. No. 671-47 in this category). The first two clusters constituted Phase I of the program. The first cluster involved an extension of studies of housing demand to data sets from several developing countries. It examined whether a similarity in demand parameters indicated by recent evidence gathered in Colombia, El Salvador, and the Republic of Korea, holds across a broader range of developing countries and, if not, whether the differences can be explained. A second objective was to obtain a clear idea of the magnitude of the relevant parameters, which are useful both at the project and sector level. In the context of projects, for example, demand parameters are used in decisions about the affordability of a project for target groups of households; in the sector context, they are used to evaluate the impact of market interventions such as tax or subsidy changes on the demand for housing.

The second cluster of analysis concentrated on the demand for particular attributes of the housing bundle such as lot size, the level of public services, or dwelling type. The work focused especially on those attributes that are essentially fixed at the design stage of a housing development and are subsequently difficult to modify, in order to minimize misjudgments concerning such attributes which can be particularly costly.

Data needs of Phase I were met by household-level surveys of samples selected at random from the relevant urban populations in Colombia, Arab Republic of Egypt, El Salvador, Ghana, Republic of Korea, and the Philippines. The surveys covered socioeconomic characteristics of the households, including household size, age, sex, occupations and monthly incomes of household members, and ownership of the dwelling units, as well as characteristics of the dwelling units, such as size, number of rooms, materials used, utilities, location, value of the unit, and rent paid. Existing data sets were used to the extent possible.

As tentatively planned, in Phase II of the project, a series of comparative analyses of government intervention in urban land and housing markets will be conducted, and the way in which the availability of housing finance affects a household's choice of tenure (renting, owning, squatting), its consumption and choice of housing, and neighborhood attributes will be examined. Issues of particular concern for the econometric work include the relation between financing and home-ownership rates in cities, the relation between financing and levels of housing consumption, and the interaction between housing finance and price increases in housing markets. Data from India, Indonesia, Kenya, Republic of

Korea, Malaysia, and the Philippines will permit comparison among countries and analysis of additional aspects of housing market behavior that were absent from the earlier surveys. The project's methods will be refined and simplified for use in operational work. A series of workshops aimed primarily at operational staff of the Bank will be held to disseminate the results. The conceptual and methodological advances on tenure choice and finance will be very useful in guiding urban sector work.

Responsibility: Water Supply and Urban Development Department—Stephen Mayo, with the assistance of Stephen Malpezzi. James Follain of Syracuse University and Emmanuel Jimenez of the University of Western Ontario are principal consultants to the research project.

Completion date: June 1985.

Reports

Follain, James; Gross, David; Jimenez, Emmanuel; and Malpezzi, Stephen. "Annotated Bibliography of Housing Characteristic Demand Studies." Water Supply and Urban Development Discussion Paper. The World Bank, September 1983.

Follain, James, and Jimenez, Emmanuel. *The Demand for Housing Characteristics in Three Developing Countries: Colombia, Korea and the Philippines.* Metropolitan Studies Program Occasional Paper No. 67. Syracuse (New York): Syracuse University, March 1983.

————. "Willingness to Pay for Housing Characteristics: A Survey." Metropolitan Studies Program Occasional Paper. Syracuse (New York): Syracuse University (forthcoming).

Follain, James; Jimenez, Emmanuel; Kang, Sungyong; Malpezzi, Stephen; and Mayo, Stephen. "Housing in Korea: Recent Trends and Recurrent Problems." In Gill-Chin Lim (ed.), *Urban Planning and Spatial Srategies in Rapidly Changing Societies.* Princeton (New Jersey): Consortium on Urban and Regional Policy in Developing Countries, 1983.

Hackenberg, Robert. "Ecology of Poverty in Davao City, 1972–79: Impact on Income, Employment and Housing." The World Bank: Urban Development Department, 1982.

Jimenez, Emmanuel. "Tenure Security Among Urban Squatter Households in Developing Countries." Mimeo. University of Western Ontario, February 1983.

Malpezzi, Stephen; Bamberger, Michael; and Mayo, Stephen.
"Planning an Urban Housing Survey: Key Issues for Re-
searchers and Program Managers in Developing Countries."
The World Bank: Urban Development Department, November
1982.
Mayo, Stephen, with Malpezzi, Stephen, and Kang, Sungyong.
Housing Demand in Developing Countries. Mimeo. The World
Bank: Urban Development Department, March 1983.
Tipple, Graham. "Asante Culture and Low-Income Housing Poli-
cies: An Examination of Antithesis." Mimeo. University of
Newcastle-on-Tyne, March 1983.

An Evaluation of Industrial Location Policies
for Urban Deconcentration (Phase II)

Ref. Nos. 672-58 and 672-91

Rapid urbanization in developing countries has produced a
heavy concentration of population and economic activity in large
urban centers. This trend has generated concern that the largest
cities will become unmanageable, and some governments have
initiated policies aimed at deconcentrating economic activity from
city centers to outlying areas. Even though such policies have
been implemented with varying degrees of success, their impact
has been little measured or understood. The main objective of this
study is to produce analytical capabilities for quantitatively evaluating the efficiency of spatial policies.

Since the extent of urbanization and spatial concentration
depends on the changing location patterns of employment opportunities, the study focuses on the policy instruments intended to influence the location patterns of industries. Until now, most studies on
industrial location have dealt with behavioral aspects without measuring the effect of government policies, which generally have
attempted to relocate industries from the center to the periphery in
metropolitan regions and to induce new industries to settle there. In
the Seoul region of the Republic of Korea, which has been selected
as the study area, the Korean government has applied specific policy
instruments to disperse employment from the center. For example,
the Industrial Location Act prohibits new industries from locating in
Seoul and enables the government to issue relocation orders to
manufacturing firms. There are also financial and fiscal incentive
schemes regarding choices of locations by firms.

The study is conducted incrementally in two phases: Phase I, which ended in June 1982, documented changes in the location patterns of employment in the Seoul region, reviewed the historical evolution of industrial location policies, and established a methodological framework to be used for empirical analysis in the next research phase. Phase II of the research program will evaluate empirically the efficiency of industrial location policies. It will involve testing relative efficiencies of alternative policy instruments and assessing welfare losses that might result from such policies. An in-depth empirical study will be made of the Seoul region, and, in addition, some cross-country comparisons will be made.

The objective of the research effort on spatial policies is to produce analytical capabilities for responding to client countries' concerns about the desirability of decentralization policies, and for assessing project locations in the Bank's country programs. Informed assessments of the probable spatial impact in the context of national development policies will be useful in the Bank's lending operations.

Responsibility: Water Supply and Urban Development Department—Kyu Sik Lee, with the assistance of Diane Reedy. Principal consultants are: Michael Murray of Claremont Graduate School (California), and the Rand Corporation; Sang-Chuel Choe and Byung-Nak Song, Seoul National University (Republic of Korea), of which the Environmental Planning Institute is the project's main collaborating institution; and Won-Yong Kwon of the Korea Research Institute for Human Settlements. The Korean National Bureau of Statistics has provided general assistance in data-related work.

Completion date: Phase I was completed in 1982; Phase II—December 1984.

Reports

Choe, Sang-Chuel, and Song, Byung-Nak. "An Evaluation of Industrial Location Policies for Urban Deconcentration in the Seoul Region." Urban Development Department Discussion Paper No. 7. The World Bank, August 1982.

Lee, Kyu Sik. "Changing Location Patterns of Manufacturing Employment in the Seoul Region." Draft. Urban Development Department Discussion Paper. The World Bank, May 1982.

_____. "Decentralization Trends of Employment Location and Spatial Policies in LDC Cities." Urban Development Department Discussion Paper No. 20. The World Bank, May 1983. Also in George S. Tolley (ed.), *Urbanization Processes and Policies in Developing Countries.* The University of Chicago (forthcoming).

Meyer, John R. "Report on Proposed Korean Spatial Study." Urban and Regional Report No. 81–1. The World Bank, March 1981.

Murray, Michael P. "Here, There, Where?: A Strategy for Evaluating Industrial Relocation Policies in Korea." Urban Development Department Discussion Paper No. 6. The World Bank, May 1982. Also in George S. Tolley (ed.), *Urbanization Processes and Policies in Developing Countries.* The University of Chicago (forthcoming).

Reedy, Diane E. "The Spatial Content of Bank Urban Sector Work." Urban Development Department Discussion Paper No. 21. The World Bank, March 1983.

Song, Byung-Nak, and Choe, Sang-Chuel. "Review of Urban Trends and Policies in Korea." Urban and Regional Report No. 81–2. The World Bank, May 1981. Also in *International Handbook on Land Use Planning.* Westport (Connecticut): Greenwood Press (forthcoming).

Participant/Observer Evaluation of Urban Projects

Ref. No. 672–59

The World Bank has, since 1974, pioneered the development of several types of poverty-oriented urban investment, most notably sites-and-services, slum upgrading, and credit schemes for small-scale enterprises. Exceptional efforts were made to evaluate some of the first urban projects, which involved relatively expensive statistical overview methods. Partly as a result of those evaluations, major design changes were made in more recent projects. These are now making their impact felt among the urban poor. Also, current evaluation efforts should give particular attention to the interaction of the projects with their ultimate beneficiaries.

The grassroots effects of urban and rural development projects are crucial. But some aspects of the impact of such projects among their thousands of intended beneficiaries are not likely to be adequately reported by project agencies using statistical overview methods. It is thought that they could be more fully assessed by a trained observer living in a project area.

The Bank has, therefore, undertaken a participant/observer evaluation project in La Paz, Bolivia, and Guayaquil, Ecuador. Its broad objectives are (1) to use the anthropological methodology of participant/observation to supplement the knowledge derived from other types of evaluation in the evaluation of urban projects in Bolivia and Ecuador; and (2) to determine whether the benefits and relatively low cost of participant/observer evaluation would justify its use elsewhere as a supplement or substitute for more elaborate and expensive methods of evaluating new-style urban and rural development projects.

In doing so, the Bank expects to gain a more complete understanding of the social processes associated with its urban projects. A book is intended to be published in order to provide a wider and better understanding of what the Bank is doing and of the policies it advocates in the area of urban development. The experience with participant/observer evaluation would also provide the Bank with a basis for designing evaluation programs for other new-style projects.

Specific topics covered by the study included:

1. How are the participating communities organized? Does the community power structure influence the distribution of project benefits? How can community-based organizations be involved in project planning, implementation, maintenance, and operation?

2. How could interactions between public officials and community residents be improved?

3. What are the effects of financial charges and changing rental values on migration in and out of project areas? Who benefits? Does anyone suffer?

4. Are technologies introduced by the project appropriate?

5. To what extent does the project stimulate housing consolidation and affect density?

6. What is the project's impact on economic activity and employment in the area?

7. Are there indications of changes in attitudes, personal habits, family patterns, or other social structures that may be related to the project? Are there effects, for example, on extended families or child-rearing practices when families move to a sites-and-services area?

8. What flaws in project design and implementation are apparent from the perspective of the project neighborhoods that administrators might not have otherwise noted?

A consultant with experience in project administration and anthropological field work lived in one of the slums being upgraded in La Paz and in one of the sites-and-services projects in Guayaquil. Observing and interviewing individuals and small groups, with a view to answering the questions listed above, the consultant participated with his neighbors in some of the activities the project entails for them.

Preliminary results of the study are sufficiently encouraging to recommend provision of Bank resources and support for dissemination of lessons learned to date and for an evaluation of the cost effectiveness of the participant/observation methodology solely using local personnel. To this end, a supplementary request for additional funding has been approved by the Bank's Research Committee to fund the final preparation of the proposed monograph and Bank seminars, and to evaluate the cost effectiveness of the methodology developed under the project in Bolivia and Ecuador and test the methodology in two additional countries and cultural environments, probably Thailand and Brazil.

The study is viewed primarily as a complement, not as a substitute for survey-based, statistically precise evaluation methods. But in three broad areas—project management and local politics, cultural and attitudinal factors, and generating hypotheses for further study—the study is expected to provide better information than can be derived from statistical methods.

Responsibility: Latin America and the Caribbean Projects Department—Neil E. Boyle, in coordination with the *Water Supply and Urban Development Department*—Michael Bamberger. Lawrence F. Salmen is the anthropologist/urban planner who conducted the study and also trained local researchers in Bolivia and Ecuador. Collaborating institutions in Ecuador include the National Housing Bank of Ecuador and National Housing Board (Banco Ecuatoriano de la Vivienda and Junta Nacional de la Vivienda BEV/JNV) and the Municipality of Guayaquil; in Bolivia, the collaborating institution is the Municipality of La Paz, in Brazil—the National Council for Urban Development (CNDU), and in Thailand—the National Housing Authority. Institutions in Ecuador, Bolivia, and Brazil are defraying part of the costs of the original project and the supplementary request.

Completion date: June 1984.

National and State Analysis of Indian Urban Development

Ref. No. 672-64

This project aims at analyzing trends, prospects, and government policies concerning urban growth and management over the medium and long term in order to clarify the role of urbanization in the process of economic development and to provide a framework in which national urban and locational policies of India may be developed and refined.

It is intended to provide a national perspective for India's urbanization through intercountry and historical comparisons, to clarify the implications of the current government policies on urbanization and industrial location, to raise the level of debate on urban issues in India, and to provide a foundation for future cooperative research undertakings between the World Bank and national institutions in India. The project consists of two parts: an examination of selected topics related to urbanization, and the development of a computable general equilibrium model for India with which the impact of alternative policies are estimated and evaluated.

Three background papers dealing with industrial location, housing, and public finance have been written by researchers in India, and a series of papers on selected topics on urbanization have been substantively completed. They cover the relationship of urbanization and economic development, a historical analysis of urbanization and the growth of cities, the relationship of urbanization and productivity in manufacturing, the relationship of the growth of cities with particular characteristics of cities, and the implications of urbanization for income distribution in the country (see "Reports" below).

A computable general equilibrium model is being developed and policy experiments with it are presently under way. The model is an extension of the Kelley Williamson model for a representative developing country, specifically tailored to India, having ten sectors and four factors of production. Particular attention will be paid to describing urban service sectors in detail. Experiments will be undertaken, for example, with respect to the allocation of public investment by sector and by urban versus rural location; policies for urban public services; and wage, education, and taxation policies. The impact of a policy will be examined relative to urbanization, economic growth, income distribution, and other macroeconomic indicators.

Responsibility: Water Supply and Urban Development Department—Koichi Mera, in collaboration with Edwin S. Mills, Jeffrey G. Williamson, Charles M. Becker, and Satyendra Verma (consultants). Earlier consultants were A. Uday Sekhar, Devendra B. Gupta, and Abhijit Datta.

Completion date: December 1983.

Reports

Becker, Charles M.; Knight, William; and Mills, Edwin S. "Income Distribution and Urbanization in India." Urban Development Department Discussion Paper. The World Bank (forthcoming).

Becker, Charles M.; Mills, Edwin, S; and Williamson, Jeffrey G. "Public Policy, Urbanization and Development: An Introduction to A Computable General Equilibrium Simulation Model of the Indian Economy." Urban Development Department Discussion Paper No. 22. The World Bank, November 1982.

Gupta, Devendra B. "Some Aspects of Urban Housing in India." Urban Development Department Discussion Paper. The World Bank (forthcoming).

Mera, Koichi. "The National and State Analysis of the Indian Urban Development: RPO 672–64, Interim Summary Report." Urban Development Department Discussion Paper No. 23. The World Bank, May 1983.

Mills, Edwin S., and Becker, Charles M. "Historical Analysis of Indian Urbanization." Urban Development Department Discussion Paper No. 2. The World Bank, January 1983.

————. "Indian City Sizes and City Growth." Urban Development Department Discussion Paper No. 4. The World Bank, February 1983.

————. "Indian Government Programs to Alter City Sizes." Urban Development Department Discussion Paper No. 3. The World Bank, February 1983.

————. "The Relationship Between Urbanization and Economic Development." Urban Development Department Discussion Paper No. 1. The World Bank, January 1983.

————. "Urbanization and City Characteristics in India." Urban Development Department Discussion Paper. The World Bank, March 1983.

Sekhar, A. Uday. "Industrial Location Policy: The Indian Experience." Urban Development Department Discussion Paper. The World Bank (forthcoming).

Verma, Satyendra. "Urbanization and Productivity in Indian States." Urban Development Department Discussion Paper. The World Bank (forthcoming).

Development of a Model for Urban Land and Infrastructure Pricing, Costing, and Design

Ref. No. 672-81

This research project is building on an existing model for analyzing the affordability of land use and engineering standards in residential urban projects. The existing model, called the "Bertaud Model," has been used widely in developing countries to analyze the trade-offs between land use and cost parameters within the affordability constraints provided by financial parameters. The proposed extended submodel, to be programmed for microcomputers, would use much more detailed assumptions for unit cost and site layout to find an acceptable combination of infrastructure and design standards that would be consistent with the affordable cost and design parameters yielded by the existing affordability model. The model will be tested in India.

Urban development in many developing countries is constrained by a number of land-use, building, and engineering regulations, and by practices that tend to inflate the cost of new development and make legal land and shelter unaffordable for most low-income households and small businesses.

The proposed research would aim at developing a comprehensive model for the pricing of urban land and infrastructure and for costing and design. It will draw upon (1) extensive field experience over the past couple of years in the use of a similar partial model and (2) related research being done by the Housing and Urban Development Corporation of India (HUDCO), which is participating in the development and testing of the model. It is expected that the proposed model would become widely used by urban development agencies for urban planning and design, initially in India and later in other countries.

The proposed extension of the existing model would be based on the accounting relationships between many of the basic parameters of urban design, including aspects of land use and infrastructure design. This makes it possible to assess the trade-offs between the principal design parameters and helps to develop an understanding of which design parameters have the most impact on costs and benefits. Through repeated iteration, the most acceptable mix of values for design parameters is determined, taking into account overall cost constraints and how to maximize benefits, including benefits that the minimum standards were originally intended to ensure. The model would also produce schematic drawings of alternative designs. This iterative process of measuring the trade-offs between the major design variables and gradually narrowing the scope of decision until an acceptable solution is found is similar in approach to the existing Affordability and Differential Land Pricing Sub-Model used by the Bank.

The main output of the project will be the model written in BASIC for Hewlett Packard 85 and 87 microcomputers and a manual for the use of the model. The project will also produce reports on "Affordability of Land Use Regulations and Engineering Specifications" and "Urban Land Use and Infrastructure Design Process and Economic Efficiency." The first report will describe a case study from a city to be selected in India where the model will be tested in an evaluation of local land-use regulations and engineering standards. The second report will present the findings of an evaluation of the urban design process and an analysis of the economic efficiency of alternative designs.

Responsibility: South Asia Projects Department—James O. Wright, Jr. and Chandra Godavitarne, in collaboration with Alain C. Bertaud and Marie-Agnes Bertaud (consultants) who are developing the model. The model will be field tested in India by L. Laksmanan, D. Singh, and B. N. Singh (consultants).

Completion date: July 1984.

8

Population and Human Resources

8-A. Education

Education and Rural Development
in Nepal and Thailand

Ref. No. 671-49

The level of formal schooling of farmers is correlated with their efficiency as farm managers, and exposure of farmers to extension education improves agricultural efficiency. There are also indications that the formal schooling level of rural women is often correlated with the number of children they bear. Changes in agricultural productivity and population growth are two important dimensions of rural development. To the extent that education and adult information services do influence these variables, alternative governmental education policies may affect the course of rural development.

The existing literature leaves two important questions unanswered. The first is: To what extent do the observed correlations result not from the effects of education, but from attributes of individuals correlated with, but not caused by, their having received education? The second, closely related, question is: Through which of their outcomes do schooling and extension have whatever effects they do have? This study explores these relationships by designing appropriate survey instruments, conducting surveys in Nepal and Thailand, and drawing conclusions from the data.

The survey instruments were designed to obtain two categories of data that were previously unavailable. The first assesses data on the family background of the head of the farm household and that person's spouse. The second measures the ability, academic achievement, and modernity of attitudes of adult members of the households surveyed. Both sets of data are being used to ascertain the extent to which the apparent contribution of education to productivity results not from education itself, but rather from such correlates of education as ability or family background. Results from the tests are being used to quantify the contribution of each of education's measured outcomes to an increase in productivity and a decline in fertility.

Inclusion in the sample of villages exposed to reformed extension services and unexposed villages with similar populations and agricultural conditions allows a quantitative assessment of the benefits of extension. Data on farmers' agricultural knowledge and practices are permitting analysis of the mechanisms through which extension education is having its effects.

The basic tools for analyzing the effects of extension and formal education on agricultural productivity are production, profit, and factor demand functions. The magnitude and significance of the coefficients of the various education variables in these functions are the principal measures of their impact.

The detailed income data contained in these two data sets permit the determination of education's relationship to fertility, taking account of income. In addition, it is possible to show how education influences the biological determinants of the number of children (e.g., through improving maternal and child health and nutrition, or raising the age at marriage), as well as both husbands' and wives' demand for children. In Nepal, more emphasis is being placed on the biological supply of children than on the demand, since evidence indicates that actual fertility is constrained by biological factors. In Thailand, equal emphasis is being given to supply and demand. In Nepal, data have been gathered on the health and nutritional status of young children in the households sampled, allowing examination of the effect of their parents' education on these variables.

Responsibility: Population, Health, and Nutrition Department—Dean T. Jamison and Susan H. Cochrane, in collaboration with Bal Gopal Baidya, Nirmala Joshi, Lawrence J. Lau, Pichit Lertamrab, Joanne Leslie, Marlaine Lockheed, Peter R. Moock, François Orivel, Rajendra Shrestha, Manu Seetisarn, and other consultants.

Completion date: December 1983.

Reports

Baidya, B. G.; Chou, E. C.; Jamison, D. T.; Moock, P. R.; and Shrestha, R. "Evaluating the Impact of Communications on Agricultural Development: General Observations and a Case Study from Nepal." In M. Jussawalla and D. Lamberton (eds.), *Economics of Communication*. London: Pergamon Press, 1982.

Cochrane, S. H. "The Determinants of Fertility and Child Survival in the Nepal Terai." Population and Human Resources Division Discussion Paper No. 81-34. The World Bank, 1981.

Cochrane, S. H., and Jamison, D. T. "Factors Influencing Educational Attainment in Northern Thailand." In A. Summers (ed.), *New Directions for Testing and Measurement: Measurement of Educational Productivity*. Washington, D.C.: Jossey-Bass (forthcoming).

Cochrane, S. H.; Joshi, N.; and Nandwani, K. "Fertility Attitudes and Behavior in the Terai." Population and Human Resources Division Discussion Paper No. 81-9. The World Bank, 1981.

Cochrane, S. H., and Nandwani, K. "The Determinants of Fertility in 22 Villages of Northern Thailand." Population and Human Resources Division Discussion Paper No. 81-59. The World Bank, 1981.

Jamison, D. T.; Baidya, B. G.; and Leslie, J. "Determinants of the Literacy and Numeracy of Adults in the Terai Region of Nepal." Paper presented at the Eastern Economic Association Meetings, Boston (Massachusetts), May 1979.

Jamison, D. T., and Moock, P. R. "Farmer Education and Farm Efficiency in Nepal: The Role of Schooling, Extension Services, and Cognitive Skills." Population and Human Resources Division Discussion Paper No. 81-60. The World Bank, 1981.

Leslie, J.; Baidya, B. G.; and Nandwani, K. "Prevalence and Correlates of Childhood Malnutrition in the Terai Region of Nepal." Population and Human Resources Division Discussion Paper No. 81-35. The World Bank, 1981.

Leslie, J., and Jamison, D. T. "Maternal Ability and Child Malnutrition in Nepal." The World Bank: Development Research Department, 1978.

Lockheed, M. E., and Jamison, D. T. "Some Determinants of School Participation in the Terai Region of Nepal." The World Bank: Development Research Department, 1979.

Economics of Educational Radio

Ref. No. 671-54

In 1975, the World Bank's Education Department began a review of experience with educational radio. This review, the results of which were published in 1977, generated several conclusions relevant to the Bank's educational lending:

1. Radio can be used, if programmed with care, to improve the quality of instruction at the elementary level.
2. Radio, combined with correspondence materials and occasional face-to-face instruction, can be a low cost alternative to traditional means of providing secondary and higher education. Used in this way for distance teaching, radio appears capable of educating hitherto excluded groups.
3. Few instances appear to exist where educational television is superior to radio.

That study also identified two areas in which additional research would be beneficial. The first was research on the economics of radio for distance teaching. Despite a widespread impression that distance teaching is much less expensive than traditional instruction, little empirical information exists on its cost and cost effectiveness. The second research area identified by the study was the impact of in-school radio on student dropout and repetition rates. If radio resulted in even a modest reduction in repetition rates, it could more than pay for itself through reducing costs.

The present research centers around the potential of educational radio in its two most promising uses: distance teaching and the improvement of quality in schools. The study of the economics of radio for distance teaching provided information on costs and effectiveness of distance teaching for a wide range of experience: the preparation of adults for equivalency examinations at the beginning secondary level in Brazil; university instruction in Israel; teacher training in Kenya; and secondary education in the Repulic of Korea, Malawi, and Mauritius. The purpose of distance teaching systems is remarkably constant from country to country. These systems are principally designed to extend the access to formal education to groups of people who were excluded from traditional schooling, either geographically or because of the need to maintain jobs during school hours in order to support themselves. A related purpose of distance teaching systems is to reduce the cost of providing instruction. Because of the apparently well-established potential of distance teaching simultaneously to improve equity and reduce costs, provision of substantial amounts of new information on the cost effectiveness of distance learning systems was viewed as useful. The distance teaching study was substantially completed in 1978 and a supplementary case study on Brazil was finished in February 1980.

A second aspect of the project is an in-depth examination of the cost effectiveness of the Nicaragua Radio Mathematics Project. Statistical determinants and economic consequences of changes in dropout and repetition rates, with particular emphasis on the impact of introducing radio, are being examined.

This research will be useful in two important ways. Its principal purpose is to assist in the formulation of the World Bank's education projects. The information that this research will generate is designed to provide answers to remaining questions in project economics and to produce additional paradigms for use as project models.

More generally, the project will substantially increase the quantitative knowledge of the impact of educational radio both in school and through distance teaching; as educational planners are increasingly turning to nontraditional options, this knowledge should be useful to them. In order to make the research results of maximal value outside the Bank, preliminary results were presented at a conference, sponsored by Unesco in June 1978, at the University of Dijon (France). This conference brought together educational planners and policymakers from all over the world to discuss the planning and economics of the use of electronic media for formal and nonformal education.

Responsibility: Education Department and *Population, Health, and Nutrition Department*—Shigenari Futagami and Dean T. Jamison, respectively, in collaboration with David Hawkridge (United Kingdom), François Orivel (France), John Nkinyanji and Peter Kinyanji (Kenya) for work on Kenya; Joao Oliveira and Mariza Oliveira (Brazil), François Orivel and Associação Brasileira de Teleducação for work on Brazil; Bernard Braithwaite (United Kingdom) and Korean Educational Development Institute for work on Korea; Arthur Melmed (United States), Uriel Turniansky and B. Ellenbogen (Israel), and Everyman University for work on Israel; Barbara Searle and Eduard George (United

States) for work on Nicaragua; and Hilary Perraton and Anthony Bates (United Kingdom) for the overview. Unesco contributed to the travel expenses of these consultants.

Completion date: December 1983.

Reports

Batista, J., *et al.* Telecurso Secundo Gran. Rio de Janeiro: Associação Brasileira de Technologia Educacional, May 1980.

George, E. I. "Exploring the Effects of the Radio Mathematics Project on School-related Variables." In J. Friend, B. Searle, and P. Suppes (eds.), *Radio Mathematics in Nicaragua.* Stanford (California): Stanford University, Institute for Mathematical Studies in the Social Sciences, 1980.

Jamison, Dean. "Radio Education and Student Failure in Nicaragua: A Further Note." In J. Friend, B. Searle, and P. Suppes (eds.), *Radio Mathematics in Nicaragua.* Stanford (California): Stanford University, Institute for Mathematical Studies in the Social Sciences, 1980.

_____. "Radio Education and Student Repetition in Nicaragua." In P. Suppes, B. Searle, and J. Friend (eds.), *The Radio Mathematics Project: Nicaragua 1976–77.* Stanford (California): Stanford University, Institute for Mathematical Studies in the Social Sciences, 1978. Also World Bank Reprint Series: Number Ninety-one.

Perraton, Hilary (ed.). *Alternative Routes to Formal Education: Distance Teaching for School Equivalency.* Baltimore and London: The Johns Hopkins University Press, 1982.

International Study of the Retention of Literacy and Numeracy

Ref. No. 671–55

This project is concerned with the measurement of the determinants of educational achievement and the relationship between acquired levels of skill and school leaving at the primary stage of education. Previous studies have suggested that the attenuation of literacy and numeracy skills among school leavers is a significant source of inefficiency in education systems. It has been suggested that "threshold" levels of learning exist—beyond which retention of some skills is assured. However, such conclusions have usually been based on small, cross-sectional samples and the methods employed have ignored the linkage between in-school achievement and the decision by the child or the family to leave school. The purpose of this project is to test the so-called "educational wastage" hypothesis directly, using a longitudinal methodology that permits the joint determination of the acquisition of skills and the decision to drop out. Subsidiary purposes of the study are to measure the productivity of educational inputs from the home and from the school system, and to examine the consequences of the repetition of grades for achievement and school leaving. The results of the research are of fundamental interest to policymakers who, in the face of severe financial constraints and strong social pressure for schooling, are required to set and maintain minimum basic education requirements. Sponsorship of this research project reflects the high priority placed by the Bank, as well as by the Bellagio Group of donors, on basic education in developing countries.

The field work for the project has been carried out in the Arab Republic of Egypt. After completion of a pilot study in Cairo in 1977–78, a two phase study was begun. Phase I was a nationwide cross-sectional study of 60 elementary schools. Two thirds of the rural students and one-half of the urban students (8,370 students or 54 percent of the enrollment in grades 3–6) were tested to establish national norms of performance. Fifteen months later, 1,792 "dropouts" from the sample of 60 schools were traced and tested, using all the instruments applied to the in-school students.

Preliminary analysis of the cross-sectional sample revealed that a large proportion of the dropouts and some of the students from grades 3 and 4 were unable to achieve a positive score on the harder tests, whereas a few students from the higher grades got perfect scores. This led to a decision to model skill-specific achievement levels as censored normal variates. A general program for estimating censored and truncated regression functions was developed in August 1980. One of the consequences of modeling the censored distribution is that the differences in skill levels between grades, holding other individual characteristics constant, are shown to be far larger than conventional analysis of variance models reveal.

In Phase II, a follow-up study retested the original dropouts, new dropouts, and one-third of the remaining students in school.

The longitudinal study permits a more accurate assessment, at the level of the individual, of the influence of time on the erosion of basic skills. The probability of dropping out at specific grade levels can also be estimated.

Data from the follow-up study have been used to revise the skill-specific achievement measures from the cross-sectional study. By classifying students who were in school in 1978–79 as either "continuing" or "leaving," it is possible to distinguish the skill levels of would-be school leavers from those of students continuing in school. Would-be dropouts are shown to have skill levels far closer to those of students already out of school than their continuing classmates. A plausible interpretation of these results is that "wastage" is caused not by the decision to drop out, but by the failure of some students to acquire skills in school. At the present time, work is continuing on the development of a joint model of skill acquisition and the dropout decision.

The field work for the project has been conducted with the assistance of the National Centre for Educational Research (NCER) of the Ministry of Education in Cairo. NCER participated in developing and testing survey instruments and was largely responsibile for planning and executing the field work. Assistance was also received from faculty members of the University of Cairo, Ain-Shams University, and American University in Cairo.

Responsibility: Europe, Middle East, and North Africa Projects Department and *Development Research Department*—James A. Socknat and Michael J. Hartley, respectively, in collaboration with Eric Swanson (consultant). Michael J. Wilson, Stephen P. Heyneman, and Mulugueta Wodajo were actively involved in the initial stages of the project. In the Ministry of Education of Egypt, the responsible official is Dr. Youssef Khalil Youssef, Director, National Center for Educational Research.

Completion date: The final report is scheduled for January 1984.

Reports

Hartley, M. J.; Poirier, D. J.; and Bencivenga, V. "A Statistical Methodology for the Egyptian Literacy Retention Study." Project Discussion Paper No. 1. The World Bank: Development Research Department, August 1979.

Hartley, M. J., and Swanson, E. V. "The Complete ANOVA Model of Learning and Retention." Project Discussion Paper No. 8. The World Bank: Development Research Department, March 1983.

_____. "Maximum Likelihood Estimation of the Censored and Truncated Normal Regression Model." Project Discussion Paper No. 3. The World Bank: Development Research Department, November 1980.

_____. "The Measurement of Learning and Retention Curves for Basic Skills in Egyptian Primary Education: An Application of Censored Analysis of Variance." Project Discussion Paper No. 2. The World Bank: Development Research Department, August 1980.

Kheiralla, Sayed. "An Inventory and Evaluation of Intelligence and Achievement Tests in Arabic Available in Egypt." The World Bank: Education Department, December 1977.

Saad, S. L., with Makary, Khalil and N. "Dropout and Enroll ment Statistics of the Sampled Schools." Cairo: National Centre for Educational Research (NCER), 1980.

Sheffield, James R. "Retention of Literacy and Basic Skills: A Review of the Literature." The World Bank: Education Department, June 1977.

Swanson, E. V., et al. "The Retention of Literacy/Numeracy Skills: An Overview for Basic Education in Egypt." Project Discussion Paper No. 4. The World Bank: Development Research Department, May 1981. Also in *Basic Education in Egypt: Theory and Practise.* Studies and papers presented to the Conference on Basic Education, Cairo, April 21–25, 1981. Sirs-el-Layyan, Egpyt: The Regional Centre for Functional Literacy in Rural Areas (ASFEC), 1981.

Swanson, E. V., and Hartley, M. J. "The Decision to Leave School." Project Discussion Paper No. 7. The World Bank: Development Research Department, February 1983.

_____. "The Egyptian Data Sample: Design and Collection." Project Discussion Paper No. 6. The World Bank: Development Research Department, December 1982.

_____. "The Egyptian Primary Education System." Project Discussion Paper No. 5. The World Bank: Development Research Department, November 1982.

Textbook Availability and Educational Quality

Ref. No. 671-60

The quality of education in low-income countries is consistently low. This contributes to the fact that, on average, school children from low-income countries appear to learn far less than do children in industrialized societies. The difference is believed to affect later technical and economic competence. Policy alternatives for improving the quality of education are few, and many proposals (such as reduction in class size) are costly and of dubious efficacy. But one approach that appears to be effective is to improve the availability of textbooks and general reading materials.

The purpose of this research project is to attempt to replicate earlier findings of the effectiveness of textbooks, to obtain quantitative estimates of students' achievements in response to interventions that make textbooks available, and to extend the analysis of effectiveness studies to other variables, countries, and conditions.

Phase I, completed in 1979, analyzed data from three separate sources. The 1972 Primary School Quality Project in Uganda had already produced findings of interest in the fields of sociology and education. While this project, among others, showed that textbooks have an important influence on academic quality, this influence had not been isolated from other parallel influences within the classroom, such as teacher quality and physical facilities. The present research project explored the independent influence of textbooks and weighed this influence against others with investment potential.

In Nicaragua, funds were made available to provide each child in 40 randomly selected classrooms—20 in Grade 1 and 20 in Grade 4—with an up-to-date mathematics textbook. Conducted jointly by the Institute for Mathematical Studies in the Social Sciences at Stanford University and the Nicaraguan Ministry of Education, the experiment had two purposes. The first purpose was to see whether mathematics achievement was increased by giving each child a textbook and whether the increase was significantly greater than the mathematics learned over the same period of time by a randomly selected control group that was not receiving textbooks through the experiment. The second purpose was to compare the achievement gains of children who, in the same period, were exposed to instruction in mathematics by educational radio.

The World Bank's Third Education Project in the Philippines provided for a large increase in the number of textbooks available to children in public schools. As a result of this project, the average student to textbook ratio (in each school subject) declined from 10:1 to 2:1. The loan agreement stipulated that the Government of the Philippines undertake an evaluation of the project's impact. In addition, funds were included to provide additional texts to a small, randomly selected subsample of primary schools, further to lower the student-to-textbook ratio in the subsample from 2:1 to 1:1. The research project assisted the evaluation in the Philippines by bringing one of the individuals responsible for the data collection to the World Bank, where the data were further analyzed and compared with data from Uganda and elsewhere.

Significant quantities of information on educational quality have been collected in the last few years but have not been analyzed efficiently. In Phase II, approved by the Bank's Research Committee in December 1978, the project has been analyzing cross-sectional surveys of primary schools in Argentina, Bolivia, Botswana, Brazil (Brasilia State only), Chile, Colombia, Arab Republic of Egypt, El Salvador, India, Islamic Republic of Iran, Mexico, Paraguay, Peru, Thailand, and Uganda. The findings from these 15 developing countries have been contrasted with results from similar primary school surveys conducted in fourteen industrialized nations. Three questions were asked of each data set: (1) which school resources (including textbook availability) have, statistically, the greatest impact on academic achievement; (2) how equitable is the distribution of school resources; (3) do school resources in developing countries have more effect on academic achievement than they do in the United States and Western Europe, and do socioeconomic background characteristics have less effect?

Responsibility: Education Department and *Population, Health, and Nutrition Department*—Stephen P. Heyneman and Dean T. Jamison, respectively, in collaboration with William Loxley, Jorge Sanguinetty, Xenia Montenegro, and Ana-Maria Arriagada (consultants).

The organizations that have been collaborating in the sampling, instrument design, data collection, and analysis are: Regional Testing Centre, Gaborone (Botswana); Programa de Estudios Conjunctos de Integração Econômica da America Latina (ECIEL), Rio de Janeiro (Brazil); National Centre for Educational Research, Cairo (Egypt); Oficina de Planeamiento y Organización (ODEPR), San Salvador (El Salvador); Education Projects Implementing Task Force (EDPITAF), Manila (Philippines); Institute of International Education, University of Stockholm (Sweden); International Association for the Evaluation of Educational Achievement, Department of Comparative Education, University of Hamburg (Federal Republic of Germany); National Institute of Education, Makerere University, Kampala (Uganda); Institute for Mathematical Studies in the Social Sciences, Stanford University, Stanford (California); and Program in Applied Labor Economics, American University, Washington, D.C.

Completion date: Phase II—December 1983.

Reports

Arriagada, Ana-Maria. "Determinants of Sixth Grade Student Achievement in Colombia." Mimeo. The World Bank: Education Department, July 1981.

_____. "Determinants of Sixth Grade Student Achievement in Peru." Mimeo. The World Bank: Education Department, June 1981.

Heyneman, S. P.; Farrell, J. P.; and Sepulveda-Stuardo, M. "Textbooks and Achievement: What We Know." World Bank Staff Working Paper No. 298 (also in Spanish and French), October 1978. Also in *The Journal of Curriculum Studies* 3 (1981): 227–46.

Heyneman, S. P., and Jamison, D. T. "Student Learning in Uganda: Textbook Availability and Other Factors." *Comparative Education Review* 24 (June 1980):206–20.

Heyneman, S. P.; Jamison, D. T.; and Montenegro, X. "Textbooks in the Philippines: Evaluation of the Pedagogical Impact of a Nation-wide Investment." Mimeo. The World Bank: Education Department, March 1983.

Heyneman, S. P., and Loxley, W. "The Distribution of School Quality Within High and Low Income Countries." *Comparative Education Review* 27 (February 1983):108–18.

_____. "The Impact of School Quality on Science Achievement Across 29 High and Low Income Countries." *American Journal of Sociology* 88 (May 1983):1162–94.

_____. "The Influence of School Resources on Learning Out-
comes in El Salvador." Paper presented at the Annual Meeting of the Comparative and International Education Society,
Tallahassee (Florida), March 1981.

_____. "Influences on Academic Achievement Across High and
Low Income Countries: A Re-Analysis of IEA Data." *Sociology of Education* (January 1982).

Heyneman, S. P.; Loxley, W.; and Sanguinetty, J. "Codebook:
School Achievement Survey for Brazil." The World Bank:
Education Department, June 1981.

_____. "Codebook: School Achievement Survey for Six Spanish-
Speaking Countries in Latin America" (available in English
and Spanish). The World Bank: Education Department, June
1981.

Jamison, D. T.; Searle, B; Galda, K.; and Heyneman, S. P. "Improving Elementary Mathematics Education in Nicaragua: An
Experimental Study of the Impact of Textbooks and Radio on
Achievement." *Journal of Educational Psychology* 73 (August
1981):556–67.

Loxley, W. "The 'Husen Methodology' in the Context of School
Effects Research Currently Under Way in the Education Department." The World Bank: Education Department, February 1980.

_____. "The Impact of Primary School Quality on Learning in
Egypt." *International Journal of Educational Development*
(forthcoming).

Education and Other Determinants of Farm
Household Response to External Stimuli

Ref. No. 671-78

The objective of this study is to examine empirically the
determinants of the quantitative response (changes in production,
consumption, and, possibly, migratory behavior) of farm households to external stimuli. Data from a sample of individual farm
households in Thailand, observed over a period of time, will be
used. External stimuli include prices of farm outputs and inputs,
wage rates, capital and land endowments, taxes, rents, availability
of credit, irrigation, and size and composition of the household.
The determinants that will be considered include degree of literacy; levels of education, nutrition, and health; availability and

type of agricultural extension; proximity to markets; age, sex, religion, and other demographic and ethnic characteristics.

The framework is that of household utility maximization, although that assumption will be explicitly tested with the actual data. Previous studies conducted by the principal consultant suggest that the hypothesis of household utility maximization is consistent with actual data in a large number of developing countries.

A knowledge of the determinants of the quantitative responses of farm households in a developing country, or region within a country, can be extremely useful to economic and social policymakers. For example, predicting the response to an increase in the government support price of farm output may be important in deciding on the advisability of the price increase. The degree of response, however, may also depend on a complex of cultural, institutional, and societal factors, some of which can be controlled or influenced by a given policy. Thus, in order to assess whether a price increase is desirable, one must consider the possible effects of accompanying policies that may change the environment sufficiently to influence the characteristics of the response. For example, whether a price increase has a positive response may depend on the presence or absence of agricultural extension work or on the level and distribution of education in a locality.

The research project, therefore, proposes not only to study the characteristics of the responses of farm households to external stimuli under static conditions, but also to investigate the way in which characteristics of the responses may be modified as a result of changes in the underlying environment. The final product will include an improved methodology for the construction of sectoral, regional, or country models for the purpose of project appraisals in agriculture. This project is using the data set on farms in Thailand gathered under the research project "Education and Rural Development in Nepal and Thailand" (Ref. No. 671-49 in this category).

Responsibility: Population, Health, and Nutrition Department—Dean T. Jamison and Susan H. Cochrane. The principal researcher is Professor Lawrence J. Lau, Department of Economics, Stanford University, with the assistance of Erwin C. Chou (researcher).

Completion date: December 1983.

The Labor Market Consequences of Educational Expansion

Ref. No. 672-01

This research project is an evaluation of the massive investments in postprimary education made by developing countries over the last several decades. The first phase consists of case studies of Kenya and Tanzania. Sampling and survey methods to generate data on adjustments in the labor market have been developed, as have various analytical tools to be applied to the data. The study addresses such questions as:

1. Has educational expansion compressed the structure of earnings and reduced the inequality of pay?
2. Has educational expansion increased the productivity of wage labor?
3. Has expansion improved the distribution of educational opportunities and increased mobility between generations?
4. Has the expansion of postprimary education affected, through such mechanisms as migration and remittance flows, income levels and the distribution of income in regions from which migrants come to the large cities?

The principal analytical tool for the first part of the study is the wage function. An attempt is made to assess the impact of a country's education and labor market policies on the structure of wages. For Kenya and Tanzania, simulation models are estimated that allow the use of counterfactual analysis to assess the efficacy of these policy regimes and to forecast the consequences of future educational expansion. The wage function analysis is then coupled with aggregate measures of dispersion, in order to examine the effect of these policy regimes on the inequality of pay.

The second part of the study relies mainly on the results of the ability and achievement tests administered to a subsample of the workers interviewed. Ability and years of school are the input, and cognitive skills the output, of education. By distinguishing the effects of these variables on wages, it is possible to interpret the role that credentials, ability, screening, and human capital play in the determination of wages.

The third portion of the analysis relies on information on the educational attainment of three generations: the worker, his parents, and his children. It is assumed that the children of the well-educated will most probably gain access to postprimary education and increasingly to postsecondary education as well. This implies that the access of children from lower socioeconomic groups to secondary and university education depends both on the size of these systems and on the demand they must meet from the well-to-do. It is hoped to establish how tight a relationship this is and to investigate whether there are policy steps that would make the mobility of lower socioeconomic groups less dependent on the rate of the overall expansion of education.

Since a very large proportion of urban workers are migrants from rural areas or smaller urban centers, the fourth part of the project studies the migration process, absorption into the urban labor force, and current socioeconomic ties with the areas from where the migrants come. Remittance functions are estimated and other links are analyzed to examine some of the effects of education beyond the larger urban centers.

The main source of information for this study is a specially designed survey of wage employees in randomly selected establishments. It is supplemented by available sources of information on the labor market and the effects of education on earnings and their distribution. Interviews with employers are used to provide an understanding of their criteria for hiring and promoting employees. Discussions with government officials are also taking place to aid in the research.

These methods and tools developed in Eastern Africa are yielding answers to the four categories of questions cited above with a reasonable degree of statistical rigor. The answers, in turn, provide a basis for assessing the nature and magnitude of the benefits derived from the educational investment programs of the countries concerned and for establishing priorities for investing in education in the next decade.

Responsibility: Development Research Department—Richard H. Sabot, in collaboration with A. Berry of the University of Toronto, A. Hazlewood and J. Knight of Oxford University (consultants), and J. Armitage and M. Boissiere of the Massachusetts Institute of Technology (researchers).

Completion date: June 1984.

Mass Media and Rural Development

Ref. No. 672-09

This project, which follows the research project "The Economics of Educational Radio" (Ref. No. 671-54 in this category), studies the use of mass media for rural development. It focuses on two ways in which mass media have been used: (1) to supplement existing agricultural extension services, either through the upgrading of agents or by communicating directly to farmers; and (2) to offer learning activities of various kinds to rural groups created for this purpose (for example, farm forums, radio listening groups, and radiophonic schools).

While much education or information for rural adults is supplied face-to-face by the extension agents, mass media are used increasingly as a supplement or even an alternative to this method. The research reviews the available evidence on such projects and summarizes the literature in this field. In particular, the research considers the benefits from these projects, including to what extent they contribute to women's development; assesses what factors make them effective; and determines what their costs are relative to alternatives.

The provisional conclusions were tested against field conditions by carrying out a limited number of case studies of rural education projects in Africa that Unesco had agreed to fund. The overview papers are to be revised in the light of the data gathered in the case studies.

Responsibility: Education Department and *Population, Health, and Nutrition Department*—Shigenari Futagami and Dean T. Jamison, respectively. The principal collaborator is Hilary Perraton of the International Extension College (United Kingdom).

Completion date: December 1983.

Reports

Perraton, H.; Jamison, Dean; Jenkins, Janet; Orivel, François; and Wolff, Laurence. "Basic Education and Agricultural Extension: Costs, Effects and Alternatives." World Bank Staff Working Paper No. 564, 1983.

Diversified Secondary Curriculum Study (DISCUS)

Ref. No. 672-45   ▪

Educational authorities in a large number of developing countries have committed themselves, to some degree, to diversifying the curricula in secondary schools. Such diversification, in which practical and/or occupational subjects are introduced into an otherwise completely academic program, has been endorsed by the education community at large and is extensively supported by the Bank. (It is a feature of half the education projects approved by the Bank in the last fifteen years.) Its broad objective is to match the skills and aspirations of the majority of secondary school graduates more closely to the job opportunities open to them. There are two models of such diversification: one model introduces practical subjects as a component of a general curriculum with no direct occupational aims; the second introduces vocationally oriented subjects that aim at specific occupations as subjects in which students may specialize.

Experience with curricular diversification reveals several recurrent problems, notably in the training of teachers of vocational subjects, the use and maintenance of facilities, and the attitudes of staff and students. A more fundamental problem is raised by evidence that conventional academic secondary education may have been dismissed too quickly—it may, in itself, be an invaluable form of vocational training. Also, some recent innovations in postprimary education and training may be more cost-effective and useful alternatives to traditional secondary education than the diversification of conventional curricula.

A study, managed by the Bank's Education Department, tested some of the assumptions that underlie diversification and evaluated the outcomes of practical/vocational curricula. The first study to undertake comprehensive and rigorous tests of the efficacy of diversification, it evaluated its effects according to the two models on the internal efficiency of schools (measured through tests of school graduates' cognitive abilities and attitudes) and external efficiency (measured in terms of school graduates' experience of unemployment or their job performance).

Case studies were undertaken in two countries whose experience with diversified curricula was lengthy enough to be evaluated meaningfully—Tanzania for the first model and Colombia for the second. To assess the effects of diversification on the internal and external efficiency of schools, the study used cost-benefit analysis; data on earnings were gathered from recent school graduates, and the analysis of costs measured differences in the social cost between diversified and conventional schools. To supplement the quantitative analysis, existing and newly gathered data were used to compare the broad features of diversified and conventional schooling, measured in terms of enrollments, dropout and graduation rates, and the postsecondary school choices made by school leavers.

The data collected covered the costs of schooling under the two models; the socioeconomic background of students; the characteristics of communities, schools, and teachers; and the aspirations of students and their subsequent attainments. A subset of the graduates and school leavers was traced one year after leaving school to assess to what extent their experiences differed according to the type of school they had attended. Field work was completed in May 1983 in both countries.

Regression models were used to assess the impact of socioeconomic status, age, sex, and aptitude, on cognitive outcomes for each curriculum program. Logit analysis was used to assess secondary schooling's impact on the decisions to work and study after graduation. The final report is currently in draft stage.

The conclusions drawn from the study on the feasibility and effectiveness of diversification in different circumstances are intended to help provide a policy framework for the Bank's operations in secondary education and aid government decision-making on curricula.

Responsibility: Education Department—George Psacharopoulos, *Latin America and the Caribbean Projects Department*—Ralph W. Harbison, and —*Eastern Africa Projects Department*—Laurence Wolff, in collaboration with the Colombian Ministry of Education and the Instituto SER de Investigación and the Tanzanian Ministry of Education and the Department of Education, University of Dar es Salaam.

Completion date: December 1983.

Reports

"Diversification of Secondary School Curriculum Study: Guidebook." The World Bank: Education Department, 1983.

Returns to Investment in School Quality in Rural Brazil

Ref. No. 672-93

Governments of developing countries, often seriously strapped for funds to improve education, have scant evidence, and hence little scientific basis, for choosing among possible approaches to investments in rural primary schooling. Yet, they continue to invest in rural primary education to the extent possible, more from a sense of equity than from confidence in the returns to the investment. This research project is a modest effort to assist in closing this gap in policy evaluation.

The project's universe includes 400 rural primary schools in the poorest region of Brazil, a fast growing middle-income developing country.[1] As part of a World Bank loan to Brazil (EDURURAL), primary schools in 268 counties in nine northeastern Brazilian states were earmarked for investment in quality improvements, such as the provision of textbooks and classroom materials, more training and better pay for teachers, improvements in the way schools are administered, and better standards for classroom size and capacity.

As part of the loan, about $1.1 million (representing 1.2 percent of total project costs) was allocated for an evaluation of the project's contribution to increasing primary school enrollments, reducing the repetition and drop-out rates, and improving the efficiency of learning. This research project, recognizing the importance of the government's evaluation, has been designed to assist the local effort by providing technical assistance and sharing gains in experience from analyzing similar questions in other contexts and countries. The first phase of the research will be conducted by World Bank staff, consultants, and by Brazilian counterparts at the Federal University of Ceara in Fortaleza. Together they will pretest hypotheses and refine the analytical techniques to be used in the evaluation scheme in an effort to enhance the policy implications of the findings.

In Brazil, primary enrollment rose from 10 million pupils in 1965 to 21 million in 1978. Real expenditure per pupil by the government increased by 47 percent from 1970 to 1976, and by 37 percent from 1976 to 1980. Yet, the portion of those expenditures that went for nonwage items declined in real terms from between $7 to $9 per pupil in 1970 to $4 in 1980. In the United States, by comparison, the nonwage expenditure per primary pupil in 1980 was $220. At the same time, within Brazil, there were also vast discrepancies in the level of per pupil expenditure.

---

[1] For basic indicators of growth by country, see *World Development Report 1983* (Washington, D.C.: The World Bank), p. 149.

In southeastern Brazil, for example, per pupil expenditure was four times greater than in the northeast where the project is being conducted; and within the northeast itself, urban schools spent three times as much per pupil as did rural schools.

A typical youth in rural Brazil is exposed to less than four years of primary schooling. The essential question to be addressed by the analysts of the project data is: Which particular improvement in educational quality or mix of such improvements introduced by the project was most cost effective in terms of gains in learning? Developing measurements of changes in learning over a limited time as a result of the project is a major responsibility of the researchers. Undergirding the research's exploration of the costs and benefits or improvements in the quality of education in the rural Brazilian classroom is the Bank's conviction that school attendance is only among the first of many steps to be taken toward providing a sufficient base of human capital for development.

Data will be collected in four rounds; the years covered will be between a preproject year—1981 and 1987. The sample will be randomly chosen from second and fourth grade pupils in three selected Brazilian states—Pernambuco, Ceara, and Piaui—among the nine states incorporated in the project. It is expected that some pupils will feature in more than one round of data.

Responsibility: Latin American and the Caribbean Projects Department—Ralph Harbison, and *Education Department*—Stephen P. Heyneman, in collaboration with Donald B. Holsinger, Center for Research on Education of the State University of New York at Albany (consultant), and Jane Armitage (consultant) who will reside in Fortaleza; Raimundo Hélio Leite of the Federal University of Ceara in Fortaleza (Brazil) will direct the Brazilian research team responsible for conducting the evaluation. The Brazilian Ministry of Education and the Carlos Chagas Foundation are collaborating in the evaluation project as a whole.

Completion date: First phase—June 1984.

World Bank Seminar on the Quality of Education in Developing Countries

Ref. No. 673-10

During the past five years, the World Bank has conducted a series of research projects on educational quality in developing countries, addressing such phenomena as rising enrollments in the face of decreasing capital resources and higher expectations regarding the variety and sophistication of cognitive skills to be acquired from schooling. Through its lending program, the Bank has broadened its experience with projects designed to improve educational quality, including the provision and distribution of textbooks, improved equipment and facilities, and the strengthening of educational administration.

More than 40 operational and research staff of the Bank participated in this seminar on the quality of education in developing countries between May 15 and 17, 1983, at Harpers Ferry (West Virginia). The seminar had been designed to reflect on what the Bank had learned from its research and lending programs to improve educational quality. Policy issues on school management, the financial implications of the specifications of alternative curricula, and the trade-offs between expanding schools or improving the quality of schools were explored in depth. The seminar provided an opportunity for theoreticians and practitioners to share their experiences in the field of managing investments in educational quality.

Twelve sessions, eight focusing on operational problems and four on research problems, were held. The sessions on research included discussions on school quality and economic efficiency; retention of cognitive skills and literacy; socioeconomic status and economic achievement; and the distribution of school quality within countries.

As a result of the seminar, two products are anticipated: a paper on the status of educational quality in developing countries, to be written by staff of the World Bank's Education Department, and an edited volume on World Bank research on education.

Responsibility: Education Department—Stephen Heyneman, with the contribution of Benjamin Makau, Examinations Unit, Ministry of Education (Kenya); Anthony Somerset, Institute of Development Studies, Sussex (United Kingdom); Henry Levin, Stanford University School of Education, California; Philip Altbach, State University of New York at Buffalo; Birger Fredriksen, University of Oslo (Norway); and C. E. Beeby, New Zealand Council for Educational Research, Wellington.

Completion date: The paper and summary volume are in process.

8-B. Labor and Employment

Employment Models and Projections

Ref. No. 671–06

Although a considerable amount of research is under way on labor force absorption and other aspects of employment in developing countries, a standard methodology for assessing trends in sectoral employment growth, the factors contributing to these trends, and the outlook for employment has yet to emerge. The objective of this study is to develop, apply, and evaluate such a methodology on the basis of case studies in India and Zambia.

Monographs based on field work in India and Zambia will consist of:

1. An analysis of trends in sectoral employment and unemployment, supplemented by information on the growth of output, changes in capital intensity, demand mix, and factor prices.
2. A paper on the sources of employment growth, using input-output techniques to decompose sectoral employment growth into the relative and absolute contributions of final demand growth, changes in the final demand mix across sectors and expenditure categories, usage of material input, and labor productivity.
3. A macroeconomic model of each economy.
4. A report on macroeconomic and employment projections that will estimate future labor absorption under alternative assumptions about investment, foreign exchange constraints, technical change, and the demand mix.
5. A policy statement derived from the foregoing that outlines feasible fiscal and other direct measures to influence the growth of final demand, the choice of technique, and the product mix so as to increase productive labor absorption.

Responsibility: Development Research Department—Ardy Stoutjesdijk, currently of the Europe, Middle East, and North Africa Programs Department II. The principal researcher is Raj Krishna of the Planning Commission, Government of India, in collaboration with Malcolm McPherson, Harvard University.

Completion date: June 1983; the completion report is in process.

Reports

Krishna, Raj. "Rural Unemployment: A Survey of Concepts and
   Estimates for India." World Bank Staff Working Paper No. 234,
   April 1976.
McPherson, Malcolm. "A Study of Employment in Zambia."
   Mimeo. The World Bank: Development Research Department,
   May 1978.

Structure of Rural Employment, Income, and Labor Markets

Ref. No. 671-30

Agriculture and rural development projects assisted by the
World Bank are usually directed toward improving the lot of farm
households by a variety of means, ranging from the construction of
irrigation facilities to the provision of subsidized inputs. Many
households in rural areas, however, have no access to land and are,
therefore, not directly affected by such projects. Others that have
land must make production and consumption decisions jointly.
These family farms or agricultural households combine two fundamental units of microeconomic analysis—the household and the
firm. Although traditional economic theory has dealt with each
separately, in developing agriculture dominated by peasant family
farms, it is their interdependence that is of crucial importance. The
purpose of the present research is to quantify the extent to which
the World Bank's agricultural projects could benefit landless or near
landless rural households that depend on wage employment as their
main source of income. Also to be developed is a theory to integrate
the firm (production) and household (consumption) aspects of decisionmaking in agricultural households that depend upon both wage
employment and farm production for their incomes.

The first stage of the research consisted of a critical review of
the large body of empirical studies on this topic that exists in India
and a comparative analysis of the impact of technological change
over time and space on labor demand and supply and on wage rates
for selected areas in India. This phase of the research is complete
and two reports have been issued.

The second stage involved the analysis of multipurpose farm
household data for the Republic of Korea. The objective was to
estimate household labor demand and supply curves in the context

of a model that incorporates aspects of consumption and production behavior in a theoretically consistent fashion. A theoretical model that integrates farm and household decisions in a multicrop environment has been developed and its empirical estimation has been completed. This work was done jointly with the Korea Rural Economics Institute, which provided detailed farm household data for nearly 1,200 farms obtained from a nationwide survey. A report outlining the results and their implications for agricultural policies has been issued.

The final stage of the project applies the models developed earlier to a World Bank investment project being executed in Nigeria. The Northern Nigeria Agricultural Projects Monitoring, Evaluation, and Planning Unit (APMEPU) has completed a detailed household survey combining income, expenditure, and labor usage, based on weekly interviews over three years (1976–79) of a sample of about 800 households from the Gusau and Funtua project areas, where improved seed and extension services are being provided to approximately 80,000 households. The project is tied closely to the now completed research project "Adoption of Farm Technology in Northern Nigeria" (Ref. No. 671–88). A model of short-run household behavior has been estimated to explain household consumption of both goods and leisure. This model serves as a means for predicting the response of household labor supply to different forms of project interventions. In addition, it allows the estimation of the impact of new production opportunities on household incomes and hence consumption, as well as the opposite impact of household choices between labor and leisure on farm production.

Finally, the research attempts to assess the operation of the rural labor market to determine how changes in the supply of family labor, as predicted by these household models, may be expected to affect wage employment and wage rates. In addition, the implications of integrating farm and household decisions in a unified model of the behavior of agricultural households are being examined.

Responsibility: Eastern Africa Regional Office—Inderjit Singh. Kalpana Bardhan conducted the Indian phase of the project, and Professor Choong Yong Ahn of Choong Ang University, Republic of Korea, assisted with analysis of the Korean data. In addition, the Korea Rural Economics Institute cooperated in, and will continue the analysis of, the Korean data as subsequent surveys are completed and processed. The data for the Nigeria component of the study have been generated by the field evaluation unit established as part of the Bank's Gusau, Funtua, and Gombe Agricultural Projects in Nigeria. Janakiram Subramanian (consultant) assisted with the modeling and analysis. Professor Edi Karni from Tel Aviv University (Israel), assisted with the theoretical part of the model.

Completion date: The Indian and Korean components of the research project have been completed. The estimation of the Nigerian component has been completed and a report will be available in December 1983.

Reports

Ahn, C. Y.; Singh, Inderjit; and Squire, Lyn. "A Model of the Agricultural Household in a Multi-Crop Economy: The Case of Korea." *Review of Economics and Statistics*, vol. 63, no. 4 (November 1981).

Bardhan, K. "Rural Employment and Wages and Labor Markets in India: A Survey of Research." Sections I, II, and III. *Economic and Political Weekly* XII, nos. 26, 27, and 28 (1977).

_____. "Rural Employment and Wages with Agricultural Growth in India: Some Intertemporal and Cross-Section Analyses." Studies in Employment and Rural Development No. 38. The World Bank, March 1977.

Karni, Edi. "A Model of an Agricultural Household in a Multi-Crop Environment with Production Uncertainty." Studies in Employment and Rural Development No. 50. The World Bank, September 1979.

Singh, Inderjit, and Squire, Lyn. "A Model of the Agricultural Household: Some Implications for Nutrition Policies in Rural Areas." Studies in Employment and Rural Development No. 49. The World Bank, September 1978.

Wage and Employment Trends and Structures in Developing Countries

Ref. No. 671–84

This project was formulated to provide a better foundation for analyses of change in wages and employment in individual countries; for the systematic compilation of comparable series on wages, employment, and other labor market phenomena such as labor force participation, hours of work, skill formation, and mobility; and for the development of analytical tools or models of the behavior of labor markets to appraise specific issues of employment and income policies.

Traditionally, the World Bank has been much concerned, particularly in the formulation of its lending programs and the preparation of its projects in developing countries, with allocative efficiency and, hence, with the relative rewards for different types of labor and their implications for labor efficiency. With the recent emphasis on problems of poverty alleviation and income distribution, attention has increasingly been focused both on the structure of relative wages and incomes, and on the rate at which the low-income work force can be employed in increasingly productive and remunerative activities.

At the operational level in the Bank, these concerns with the efficiency and equity aspects of labor market phenomena need to be reflected in the design and evaluation of specific projects and in the presentation of analyses and recommendations of sector and country economic reports, as well as in broader development policy studies, such as the *World Development Report*. Moreover, some governments of developing countries are moving toward the use of wage and income policies to tackle distributional and poverty problems. The formulation and implementation of such policies presuppose a well-founded basis for explaining the determinants of existing wage structures and the means of controlling them.

The first component of the study reviewed the data collected to follow the labor market in developing countries and examined the problems that varying conceptual and statistical characteristics pose for estimating time trends and making intercountry comparisons. In addition, the study sought a more comprehensive empirical assessment of aggregative trends in employment, unemployment, real wages, and labor incomes in developing countries, and explored comparative patterns and changes over time of wage and employment relationships between major economic sectors. This descriptive analysis updates and augments earlier inquiries into employment aspects of development to allow for better judgments about the areas where statistical improvements are most urgently needed.

In the second component, studies of the evolution of the labor market were undertaken in India, Kenya, and Mexico. The purpose of these studies is to analyze the relation of wage trends and structures to the experience of different types of developing countries, and to the effects of government policy interventions on wages and incomes. Many past country studies of labor markets have concentrated on their most recent manifestations and on various projections into the future. In contrast, this project looks at the evolution of labor markets in the light of a longer period of development experience. (A fourth study on Brazil had to be cut short with the departure from the Bank of the principal researcher responsible, Richard Webb.) A special study on unemployment in India by Professor Raj Krishna of the Delhi School of Economics is analyzing trends in rural and urban unemployment of males and females over the period 1959–78.

Responsibility: Country Policy Department—Mark W. Leiserson has overall responsibility for the project. Swadesh R. Bose was responsible for the aggregative cross-country component of the research. Peter Gregory is consultant for the Mexico study and Deepak Lal for the India and Kenya studies. The Bureau of Statistics of the International Labour Office (ILO), Geneva, collaborated in assembling and documenting time series on wages in major economic sectors in individual developing countries.

Other consultants and collaborators include: Professor Dharma Kumar and Bhaskar Dutta of the Delhi School of Economics and Professor Kanta Ahuja of the HCM State Institute of Public Administration, Jaipur, on the India study; Paul Collier, Oxford Institute of Statistics, on the Kenya study; Isaac Kerstenetzky, Instituto Brasileiro de Geografia e Estatistica (IBGE) on the Brazil study; Professor Peter Gregory, University of New Mexico, on the Mexico study; Professor Raj Krishna, Delhi School of Economics, on the study of unemployment in India.

Completion date: June 1984.

Reports

Bose, Swadesh. "Changes in Sectoral Wages in Developing Countries: Compilation of Data." Draft. The World Bank: Development Economics Department, September 1980.

———. "Employment, Unemployment and Wages in Some African Countries: A Review of Evidence for Recent Decades." Draft. The World Bank: Development Economics Department, May 1980.

———. "Trends in Employment, Unemployment and Wages in Developing Countries: A Review of Recent Decades." Draft.

The World Bank: Development Economics Department. November 1980.

Collier, Paul, and Lal, Deepak. "Coercion, Compassion and Competition: Wages and Employment Trends and Structures in Kenya 1800–1980." Employment and Income Distribution Division Paper No. 64. The World Bank: Development Economics Department, September 1980.

Dutta, Bhaskar. "Industrial Wage Structures in India: A Survey." Employment and Rural Development Division Paper No. 61. The World Bank: Development Economics Department, May 1980.

Gregory, Peter. "Economic Development and the Labor Market in Mexico." Draft book manscript. January 1982.

_____. "Economic Development and the Labor Market in Mexico." Employment and Rural Development Division Paper No. 70. The World Bank: Development Economics Department, August 1981.

Krishna, Raj. "A Three Sector Time Series Model of the Labour Market in India." Draft. The World Bank: Country Policy Department, May 1983.

_____. "The Growth of Aggregate Unemployment in India: Trends, Sources and Macro Policy Options." Draft. The World Bank: Country Policy Department, June 1983.

Kumar, Dharma, and Krishnamurthy, J. "The Evolution of Labour Markets in India, 1857–1947." Draft. Employment and Rural Development Division Paper No. 72. The World Bank: Development Economics Department, May 1981.

Lal, Deepak. "Cultural Stability and Economic Stagnation: India 1500 B.C.–1800—Wage and Employment Trends and Structures." Draft. The World Bank: Development Economics Department, June 1981.

_____. "Wages and Employment in the Philippines." Employment and Rural Development Division Paper No. 57. The World Bank: Development Economics Department, October 1979.

Pfefferman, Guy Pierre, and Webb, Richard. "The Distribution of Income in Brazil." World Bank Staff Working Paper No. 356, September 1979.

Satyanarayana, Y. "Trends in Employment and Unemployment in India—An Analysis, Discussion and Compilation of Data." Draft. The World Bank: Development Economics Department, August 1980.

234   Population and Human Resources

_____. "Wage Trends in India: 1830 to 1976—An Analysis,
Discussion and Compilation of Data." Employment and Rural
Development Division Paper No. 74. The World Bank: Devel-
opment Economics Department, August 1980.

Structure of Employment and Sources of Income by Socioeconomic Groups and Regions in Peru

Ref. No. 672-40

In the face of unemployment amounting to over 7 percent of
the labor force and falling real household incomes among the poor,
Peru's government has attached a high priority to programs to
create employment and to alleviate poverty. But this effort is
hindered by a lack of basic knowledge of the behavior of households with regard to labor supply and income generation. The
present research aims at filling this gap through a detailed study of
the problem by concentrating on the household as the unit of
analysis. This approach has been adopted because, in the Peruvian
context, it is the household that makes the decisions on how much
to spend and how much to save—needs that determine the
amount of income desired. The latter has a primary influence on
decisions about the number of household members entering the
labor force under differing circumstances. The study is intended
as a complement at the micro level to the Peru component of an
earlier research project on "Urban Labor Markets in Latin America" (Ref. No. 671-48), now completed.

The data base is the ENCA survey (National Survey of Food
Consumption) carried out in Peru in 1971-72. Cross-sectional
analysis of this data will provide an insight into household behavior under conditions that vary widely, including those that prevail
at present. Thus, the project is expected to produce detailed
information on the working and income-generating behavior of
Peruvian households, which would help in the design of income,
employment, and education policies.

The specific objectives of the research are (1) to identify factors
underlying income differentials among workers such as education,
age, and the number of working hours; (2) to examine household
strategies aimed at earning a higher income, and workers' expectations as to future income according to type of occupation; (3) to
determine levels of underemployment by estimating potential

working hours from household units in each of the occupational categories analyzed; and (4) to determine regional income differences and the characteristics of the productive structure in each of the regions according to the degree of urbanization.

Responsibility: Latin America and the Caribbean Regional Office—Ulrich R. W. Thumm, Resident Representative in Peru, in coordination with the *Development Research Department*—Constantino P. Lluch, and in collaboration with Carlos Amat and Hector Leon, Universidad del Pacífico, and Luis Monroy, Ministry of Economy and Finance (Peru).

Completion date: December 1983; the empirical work has been completed, and the final report is in process.

8–C. Population, Health, and Nutrition

Population Growth and Rural Poverty

Ref. No. 671–02

High growth rates of population hinder the improvement of living standards in developing countries, especially among lower income families. In a number of the poorer countries, family planning programs have been adopted, but many of these have not yet succeeded in significantly reducing the rate of population increase. This situation requires further research on the determinants of fertility and the economic costs and benefits of larger families for rural households. Such information may shape policies in other realms (e.g., education, employment, and social security), whose impact on fertility might be considered an explicit benefit.

The level of fertility in any society reflects ingrained and interrelated socioeconomic factors. The World Bank believes that these factors need to be analyzed in a variety of ways—by the study of fertility differentials at one point in time, by longitudinal assessment of the impact of development projects, and by a detailed study of small communities.

Under this research project, comparative anthropological studies of eight villages in India, Kenya, Nigeria, and Sri Lanka are being prepared. While each of the studies has its own distinct emphasis and focus, all have the common element of considering the social and private forces that may affect fertility (such as the economic roles of children), the effects of rapid population growth on the local economy and social fabric, the perceptions held in the community about such change, and the reaction to it. A comparative overview of these common elements will be prepared by the project director.

Preliminary results were discussed at a mid-project conference held in December 1975. The papers, now published, include socioeconomic and demographic background studies on the villages and some initial findings on fertility patterns.

Responsibility: Development Research Department—Timothy King. The study is directed by Professor Scarlett Epstein of the Institute of Development Studies, University of Sussex (United Kingdom). The field investigations have been carried out by eight graduate students from the selected countries who are currently attending the university, each of whom has spent more than a year in one of the villages. The Population Council and the Overseas Development Administration (United Kingdom) have joined the World Bank in financing this project.

Completion date: December 1982; the completion report is in process.

Reports

Epstein, Scarlett, and Jackson, Darrel (eds.). *The Feasibility of Fertility Planning: Micro Perspectives.* London: Pergamon Press, 1977.

————. *Some Social Aspects of Population Growth: Cross Country Studies.* Bombay: MacMillan, Ltd., 1975.

Case Studies of Determinants of Recent Fertility Decline in Sri Lanka and South India

Ref. No. 671-70

The recent decline in fertility in Sri Lanka and in the State of Kerala in south India has attracted worldwide attention for a number of reasons. The decline has been fairly rapid and significant. Between 1960 and 1974, the birthrate in Sri Lanka declined from 37 births to about 27 births per thousand population; in some parts of Kerala (India), the birthrate fell to 22 per thousand or even lower. These declines are all the more remarkable because they took place in seemingly unfavorable circumstances. The per capita gross national product of Sri Lanka is about $270. In Kerala, it is substantially lower, even lower than the all-India average of $240. In neither area have vast amounts been spent on family planning.

Fertility declines of the magnitude observed in Sri Lanka and Kerala are virtually without precedent in such poor populations. It is in the context of these unique circumstances and in view of the potential pay off from a study of the experience of this region, that these case studies on the determinants of fertility decline in Sri Lanka and Kerala have been undertaken by the World Bank. For comparative purposes, Karnataka State in India, where the fertility decline has been relatively small, was also reviewed.

The principal objective of the study is to understand the process of change in fertility, in order to identify and measure the impact of the factors that caused its decline in the region. Changes in marriage patterns seem to have played a major role in bringing about a decline in the birth rate in Kerala and Sri Lanka. The study is, therefore, equally concerned with the determinants of age at marriage.

The study is based on sample survey data specially collected for the purpose from about 5,000 households in Sri Lanka and 3,000 households each in Kerala and Karnataka. The topics covered in the survey are: demography, fertility, family planning, marriage, household assets and income, and socioeconomic characteristics. In Sri Lanka, somewhat similar data were collected four years ago on the same households for the World Fertility Survey; it is, therefore, possible to analyze changes in fertility in terms of changes in socioeconomic characteristics. In Kerala and Karnataka, few data are available and the study is based mostly on the data from the surveys.

The output of the study consists of several discussion papers, and three country reports, written by Bank staff, consultants, and staff from the collaborating institutions. Findings from these reports are integrated into a regional report to give a comparative analysis of the determinants of fertility behavior in the region.

The study showed that fertility decline was very significant for all three populations; the decline was largest in Kerala and least in Karnataka. The decline was shared by all the socioeconomic groups—rich and poor, illiterate and educated, high caste and low caste.

Fertility decline in the region was caused by an optimum sequence of commonly recognized determinants of fertility. The decline began with improvements in health and education, and it gathered momentum as a result of subsequent policy interventions, such as official family planning programs and welfare programs for the poor. Land reform, wage reforms, and other redistributive policies were particularly relevant for Kerala.

The experience with fertility decline in Kerala, Karnataka, and Sri Lanka demonstrates the feasibility of bringing about a substantial reduction in fertility, even among the poor and the illiterate, through an efficient family planning program.

Responsibility: Population, Health, and Nutrition Department—K. C. Zachariah, in collaboration with N. K. Namboodiri, University of North Carolina (consultant), and A. Thavarajah and S. L. N. Rao of the United Nations Fund for Population Activities. The project is being carried out in collaboration with these local research institutions: the Department of Census and Statistics, Government of Sri Lanka, Colombo; the Bureau of Economics and Statistics, Kerala Government, Trivandrum; and the Institute for Social and Economic Change, Bangalore, Karnataka.

Completion date: December 1983. The three country reports and the first draft of the comparative analysis have been completed. A final draft is expected by December 1983.

Reports

Namboodiri, N. Krishnan, et al. "Determinants of Recent Fertility Decline in Sri Lanka." Population, Health and Nutrition Technical Series, Research No. 5. The World Bank, 1983.

Rao, N. Baskara; Kulkarni, P. M.; and Rayappa, P. Hanumantha. "Determinants of Fertility Decline in Rural Karnataka." Population, Health and Nutrition Technical Series, Research No. 4. The World Bank, 1983.

Zachariah, K. C. "Anomaly of Fertility Decline in Kerala." Population, Health and Nutrition Technical Series, Research No. 2. The World Bank, 1983.

"Age at Marriage in Sri Lanka." Population and Human Resources Division Discussion Paper No. 81-54. The World Bank, October 1981.

"Anomaly of the Fertility Decline in Kerala: Social Change, Agrarian Reforms or Family Planning Programs?" Population

and Human Resources Division Discussion Paper No. 81-17.
The World Bank, May 1981.

"Determinants of Fertility in Sri Lanka." Population and Human
Resources Division Discussion Paper No. 81-53. The World
Bank, September 1981.

"Trends and Determinants of Infant and Child Mortality in Kerala." Population and Human Resources Division Discussion Paper No. 82-2. The World Bank, January 1982.

Kenya: Health, Nutrition, Worker Productivity, and Child Development Studies

Ref. No. 671-73

An earlier research project "Effects of Health and Nutrition
Standards on Worker Productivity" (Ref. No. 671-15), carried out
in 1976-77, investigated health and nutrition factors related to the
productivity of road workers, as well as the relationship of parasitic
infestation to the health and growth of children, in certain parts of
Kenya. That research indicated that both caloric undernutrition and
anemia were common among road workers and that this affected
work output. Separately, it was also demonstrated that roundworm
infestations retard the growth of children.

The present project, by the same group, has been undertaken to
evaluate a number of possible public health interventions to address
these problems. The follow up studies, which were initiated in
Kenya in January 1978 and were extended through 1980, had the
following objectives:

1. Further evaluation of health and nutrition effects on the
   productivity of casual laborers in rural civil works. In this
   study, the effects of different caloric interventions on work
   output were to be determined in more detail. (Study No. 1)
2. Evaluation of practical interventions to improve health and
   worker productivity. In a series of studies, economic evaluations were to be undertaken of alternative methods of feeding
   and treating the workers and of routinely providing iron and
   calorie-rich foods or medicinal iron to road workers. An
   investigation was also made of the prevalence of parasitic
   diseases and their relation to anemia, and an evaluation of the
   feasibility of routine parasitic control was carried out. (Study
   No. 2)

3. Surveys of health and nutrition factors in two additional areas. This investigation at road sites in two ecological areas not covered during the 1976 research was to determine how health and nutrition problems vary in different regions and, therefore, provide a better basis for planning interventions throughout Kenya. (Study No. 3)
4. Evaluation of the feasibility and effectiveness of a parasite control program. This continuation of the study on roundworms and other intestinal parasites in children was designed to maintain control in two villages, investigate reinfection rates, and evaluate the long-term feasibility of treatment that is likely to be applicable elsewhere in Kenya. (Study No. 4)

The results of Study No. 1 revealed that workers, given 1,000 calories per day, had a small (4 percent) but significant increase in work output as compared to control groups given only 200 calories. The improvement in work output also correlated with improvement in anthropometric measurements such as weight for height and arm circumference. The research confirmed earlier studies that anemia significantly limits work output.

Study No. 2, which evaluated the feasibility and costs of different food delivery systems for road workers, showed that workers were willing voluntarily to pay for the full costs of a nutritious snack provided to them by local entrepreneurs. This study also showed that when these snacks had a high food iron and vitamin C content, the result was a significant rise in hemoglobin (blood iron) as compared to diets low in these nutrients. This is of particular significance in areas where anemia is a problem, and where routine administration of medicinal iron is not feasible. Other research carried out under Study No. 2 showed that treatment for schistosomiasis, malaria, and hookworm also resulted in a rise in blood hemoglobin.

The results of Study No. 3 revealed, as expected, that important differences in nutritional status existed among laborers in four different ecological zones of Kenya, which must be taken into account in planning future national health and nutrition programs.

Study No. 4 showed that routine deworming over a period of four years on 1,500 preschool and primary school-age children using local community participation was extremely popular, effective, and acceptable. Preliminary recommendations for nationwide worker feeding and deworming programs were made.

Following completion of the scientific work, analysis of the costs and benefits of reducing anemia was undertaken by Professor Henry Levin (consultant), Stanford University.

Responsibility: Population, Health, and Nutrition Department and *Transportation Department*—Alan Berg and Clell G. Harral, respectively. Primary researchers were Michael C. Latham and Lani Stephenson Latham, Cornell University, in association with the Rural Access Roads Programs, Ministry of Works (Kenya), and the Overseas Development Administration (United Kingdom).

Completion date: December 1983; the completion report is in process.

Reports

Basta, Samir S., and Churchill, Anthony. "Iron Deficiency Anemia and the Productivity of Adult Males in Indonesia." World Bank Staff Working Paper No. 175, April 1974.

Basta, Samir S., and Karyadi, Darwin. "Nutrition and Health of Indonesian Construction Workers: Endurance and Anemia." World Bank Staff Working Paper No. 152, April 1973.

Basta, Samir S., and Latham, Michael. "The Relationship of Nutrition and Health to Worker Productivity in Kenya." Technical Memorandum No. 26. The World Bank: Transportation and Water Department, May 1977.

Hall, Andrew. "Intestinal Parasitic Infections of Men in Four Regions of Rural Kenya." *Transactions of the Royal Society of Tropical Medicine and Hygiene,* vol. 76, no. 6 (1982):728–33.

Latham, Lani; Latham, Michael C.; and Basta, Samir S. "The Nutritional and Economic Implications of Ascaris Infection in Kenya." World Bank Staff Working Paper No. 271, September 1977.

Latham, Michael C., *et al.* "A Comparative Study of the Nutritional Status, Parasitic Infections and Health of Male Roadworkers in Four Areas of Kenya." *Transactions of the Royal Society of Tropical Medicine and Hygiene,* vol. 76, no. 6 (1982):734–40.

———. "Nutritional Status, Parasitic Infections and Health of Roadworkers in 4 Areas of Kenya: Part 1 Kwale District—Coastal Lowlands." *East African Medical Journal* (January 1983):2–10.

_____. "Parasitic Infections, Anaemia and Nutritional Status: A Study of Their Inter-relationships and the Effect of Prophylaxis and Treatment on Workers in Kwale District, Kenya." *Transactions of the Royal Society of Tropical Medicine and Hygiene*, vol. 77, no. 1 (1983):41–48.

Latham, Michael C., and Stephenson, Lani. "Kenya Health, Nutrition, Worker Productivity and Child Development Studies, Final Report." The World Bank, January 1981 (being revised for publication).

The Economics of Schistosomiasis Control

Ref. No. 671-74

Schistosomiasis is a tropical parasitic infection victimizing an estimated 250 million people in 71 developing countries. Already one of the most prevalent water-related diseases, schistosomiasis is spreading at an alarming rate, as the habitat of the intermediate host (a snail) is increasing with the development of irrigated agriculture, hydroelectric power, and fisheries. Since 1971, the Bank has directly addressed the schistosomiasis problem in 30 development projects in 18 countries.

The present study examines strategies of control and is concerned with constructing the most economical and efficient strategy, using drug therapy, pesticides, and sanitary water supply. With settlement of an irrigation scheme, the magnitude of the infected population, and hence the cost of drug therapy, changes. At the same time, the scale of the snail-infested water habitat is modified by irrigation, drainage, and snail control activities. Thus, the problem is to select a method, or combination of methods, of control that minimizes the prevalence of the disease, given a budget and any prior investments in equipment, facilities, or infrastructure.

The analytical model is constructed from three modules: The first module predicts prevalence of the infection and the probable effects of control activities. In the second module, the investment and recurrent costs of these control activities are econometrically estimated. The third module introduces optimization criteria. The modules are components of a larger planning model, but may be operated independently of each other.

The model has three stages of operation. The first stage corresponds to a precontrol period in which the spread of the infection is simulated as a function of increases in the snail habitat and the population in the project area, as well as the resulting increase in water contact. Stage two incorporates control activities and, thus, identifies the cost-effective combination and scheduling of these activities. The third stage simulates the epidemiology of the disease, following the application of control activities.

The empirical results indicate that a strategy combining three methods of control—drug therapy, the application of pesticides (mollusciciding), and sanitary water supply—is the most effective, but also the most costly. Drug therapy together with mollusciciding is the second most effective strategy, followed by chemotherapy alone, mollusciciding plus water supply, mollusciciding alone, and finally water supply alone. Sensitivity analyses with respect to different sets of parameter values of the transmission and cost modules indicate that the above ranking of strategies by effectiveness of control is robust.

From the point of view of cost effectiveness, chemotherapy alone is the optimal strategy for a control target of more than 67 cases per 100,000 population. Chemotherapy plus mollusciciding is the optimal strategy if the degree of control effectiveness desired is between 50 cases and 67 cases per 100,000 population. All three control methods become optimal only for programs seeking to reduce prevalence to fewer than 50 cases per 100,000 population.

Analyses of the empirical results of the study reveal that several widely accepted practices are not economically rational. First, as indicated, the gains from simultaneously operating several control measures rather than chemotherapy alone are very small and, as a practical matter, do not justify the additional costs that they impose. Second, the collection of extensive baseline data to be used to plan intervention is not justified. The resources expended on data collection and the concomitant delay in achieving control together reduce the overall effectiveness of a program operating under the constraint of a fixed budget. Program managers should initiate case finding and chemotherapy immediately. Third, control based upon chemotherapy was found to be fairly robust in the event of temporary interruption of the program, while other methods of control were highly vulnerable. These findings argue for implementation of simple control programs using chemotherapy rather than the elaborate schemes widely employed at present.

*Responsibility: Water Supply and Urban Development Depart-
ment*—Fredrick L. Golladay and Abraham Bekele (consultant).

Completion date: December 1983; the completion report is in
process.

Determinants of Fertility in Egypt

Ref. No. 671-81

This study is a data collection project that is being carried out in
collaboration with the Central Agency for Public Mobilization and
Statistics (CAPMAS) of the Government of the Arab Republic of
Egypt and the World Fertility Survey (WFS). The project will be
phased to follow the Egyptian Fertility Survey which will collect data
from 8,900 women. For the second round, 30 percent of the 8,900
households will be selected and the male heads of those households
will be interviewed under the World Bank project.

This data set will be one of the few having fertility data on
both husbands and wives, which will make it possible to compare
attitudes toward family size and contraception. In addition, economic data on family income and labor supply will be collected
from the male heads of households. Therefore, the data set will
contain a unique combination of economic and fertility data.

While the analysis of the data is not covered under this project
and will not begin until after all data have been collected and edited,
it is expected to determine not only what factors are related to the
preferences for large families among men and women, but also what
policies can be used to encourage a reduction in family size and to
achieve smaller families through effective contraception.

Responsibility: Population, Health, and Nutrition Department
—Susan H. Cochrane; and *Development Research Department*
—Timothy King, in collaboration with the staff of the Central
Agency for Public Mobilization and Statistics, Cairo, and the
World Fertility Survey, London.

Completion date: June 1983; the completion report is in process.

Narangwal Population and Nutrition (Phase II)

Ref. No. 672-03

The purpose of this study is to use household data, collected
from 1966 to 1974 in Narangwal (Punjab), India, to analyze fertil-

ity, family planning, nutrition, and health behavior, and the efficiency of service delivery systems. Within a controlled experimental design, groups of villages were provided with various combinations of health, family planning, and nutrition services, and households in each group were observed over time.

The analysis of the nutrition data explored the relative effects of poor nutrition and other socioeconomic factors on the growth and development of preschool children. Determinants and associated factors of the demand for nutrition services were also studied.

Analysis of the population data addressed issues of policy significance, such as the influence of household socioeconomic and community characteristics on the use of health and family planning services, and the perception of child mortality on family planning acceptance, possible trade-offs between alternative levels of health and family planning services, and the relationship between contraceptive practices and fertility.

This analysis (Phase I), now completed, indicated that integrating family planning with health services was not only more effective than providing family planning in isolation, but was also efficient in terms of cost. Integration of these services produced better results in terms of the quality of contraceptive protection and a more equal distribution of services among various socioeconomic groups of users. Certain characteristics of the potential clients (such as education, communication with spouse) were found significant in predisposing them to accept contraception. The analysis has also identified a two way relationship between the use of health services and the acceptance of family planning.

The health services added significantly to the acceptance of family planning. Experience in contraception before the program was a factor that facilitated acceptance of contraception during the program period, and its contribution seemed to be greater in the case of health services initiated by the program than those by the client.

Although the full impact of a program of contraception on fertility will go beyond the life of the project, significant declines in fertility were already observed. Births to acceptors covered by a program of family planning were substantially fewer than to nonacceptors.

In Phase II, analysis of relationships over time between the practice of family planning, use of health services, and other predisposing characteristics is continuing. The main goal is to identify criteria for determining the most appropriate population groups and the best timing of efficient service combinations that will produce a specific cost-effective and/or equitable impact on the practice of family planning and on fertility. With this goal in view, Narangwal research in Phase II comprises the following tasks:

1. Input and output measures of the Narangwal services will be refined.
2. Further multivariate analyses will be done within experimental groups (across socioeconomic classes), as well as within a socioeconomic class across experimental groups.
3. Alternative hypothetical intervention strategies will be analyzed in a simulation framework to derive an optimal mix of service components for comprehensive health and family planning objectives.
4. Features of the Narangwal experiment that may be replicable in other Bank programs will be identified.

Responsibility: Population, Health, and Nutrition Department —K. C. Zachariah, with the assistance of Rashid R. Faruqee, Western Africa Country Programs Department I. The collaborating research team from The John Hopkins University consists of Dr. Carl E. Taylor, Dr. Robert L. Parker, and Dr. William A. Reinke.

Completion date: Phase I—mid-1982; Phase II—March 1984.

Reports

Chernichovsky, D. "The Economic Theory of the Household and Impact of Measurement of Nutrition and Health Related Programs." World Bank Staff Working Paper No. 302, October 1978.

Faruqee, R. "Analyzing the Impact of Health Services: Project Experiences from India, Ghana and Thailand." World Bank Staff Working Paper No. 546, 1982.

———. "Family Planning and Health: The Narangwal Experiment." *Finance & Development* (June 1983).

———. "Integrating Family Planning with Health Services." World Bank Staff Working Paper No. 515, April 1982.

Faruqee, R., and Johnson, E. "Health, Nutrition, and Family Planning: A Survey of Experiments and Special Projects in India." World Bank Staff Working Paper No. 507, February 1982.

Kielmann, A. A., et al. *Child and Maternal Health Services in Rural India: The Narangwal Experiment.* Vol. 1: *Integrated Nutrition and Health Care.* Baltimore and London: The Johns Hopkins University Press, 1983.

Taylor, C. E.; Faruqee, R.; Sarma, R. S. S.; Parker, R.; and Reinke, W. *Child and Maternal Health Services in Rural India: The Narangwal Experiment.* Vol. 2. *Integrated Family Planning and Health Care.* Baltimore and London: The Johns Hopkins University Press (forthcoming).

Health and Rural Development in Nepal

Ref. No. 672–10

This project will examine data on health and nutrition from farm families in various locations of Nepal's Terai and Hill regions. Links will be established between environmental background variables and health status, and between health and a broad range of outcomes.

One aspect of the project will be to follow the progress of children who were of preschool age at the time of a 1978 survey of farm families in two rural districts of the Terai (see Ref. No. 671–49 in this category). Information on the children's physical growth and a history of diarrheal and respiratory disease will be combined with information on their cognitive development and family characteristics. This research will add to a growing literature on the relation between a child's mental and physical development. Findings of the effects of malnutrition on cognitive development and the effects of both of these on the propensity to enter and stay in school are expected to be of general relevance for policy. The enrollment issue is of particular relevance in Nepal at present, since the government plans substantially to increase participation (and particularly that of girls) in schools.

A second aspect of this research project will be to study the extent to which indoor cooking and heating fires contribute to chronic obstructive pulmonary disorders. It is hoped that this study will yield insights, useful for sector studies, on the general economic losses caused by a high prevalence of respiratory diseases.

Responsibility: Population, Health, and Nutrition Department—Dean T. Jamison, in collaboration with Peter R. Moock, Bal Gopal Baidya, Kathleen Hebbeler, Susan Horton, Joanne Leslie,

Marlaine Lockheed, Dr. Mrigendra R. Pandey and the Cor Pulmo-
nale Project, Dr. Robert L. Parker, Rajendra P. Shrestha, Dr.
Melvyn S. Tockman, Suan Ying, and other consultants.

Completion date: December 1983.

Reports

Martorell, R.; Leslie, J.; and Moock, P. R. "Characteristics and
Determinants of Child Nutritional Status in Nepal." Population
and Human Resources Division Discussion Paper. The World
Bank, 1982.
Moock, P. R., and Leslie, J. "Childhood Malnutrition and School-
ing in the Terai Region of Nepal." Population and Human
Resources Division Discussion Paper. The World Bank, 1982.

Poverty, Fertility, and Human Resources in Indonesia

Ref. No. 672-19

Between 1971 and 1976, a sharp reduction in fertility rates took
place in Indonesia, mainly in Java and Bali. This is noteworthy for
two reasons. First, the reduction in fertility rates took place at
relatively low levels of income and social development, although
these had been improving rapidly. Second, this coincided with the
implementation of the family planning program. Given that the
Indonesian government has set an ambitious target for further
reduction in fertility, two issues are of concern to it: how to
maintain the momentum of the family planning program in these
islands, and whether the success of the program in Java and Bali
can be repeated in the Outer Islands.

This research project aims at clarifying the following population issues:

1. To understand the process of fertility decline and to project
   the probable future growth rate of the population of
   Indonesia.
2. To assess the relative contribution of the family planning
   program to this decline, as compared with the contribution
   of accompanying socioeconomic change.
3. To identify target populations with high fertility by their
   socioeconomic characteristics and location.
4. To identify policy options other than family planning to
   maintain the current pace of fertility decline.

As regards the country's socioeconomic characteristics, the poverty issues in Indonesia were identified in a study based on the findings of a World Bank mission to the country in early 1978.[1] The report concluded that, first, the recent rapid growth of aggregate income in Indonesia had been clouded by a controversy concerning the extent to which this growth had been shared by the poorest groups. Second, it appears that urban rural disparities in consumption are growing and that overall inequality in both consumption and income is increasing. Third, irrespective of recent changes, Indonesia faces a severe problem of poverty, with 50 million people unable to maintain the very low consumption standard of $90 a year. This research program will, therefore, also attempt to advance the understanding of poverty in Indonesia by addressing the following issues:

1. To establish broad trends in consumption levels over time by updating the work in the abovementioned study, by taking into account data that have become available in the meantime.

2. To obtain a better description of the poor in terms of various distinguishing features, such as demographic characteristics, consumption patterns and caloric intakes; housing conditions and access to social services; and concentration by region and urban/rural area of residence. Such a description will be helpful in the design of policies to assist the poor directly through subsidies or the provision of social services.

3. To understand the difference between the poor and the less poor in production characteristics, that is, their participation in the labor force and income earning activities and their ownership of assets. In this way, it is hoped that some of the causes of poverty and the mechanisms of escape from it will be identified.

Two major data sets will be used in the present study: the second round of the Intercensal Population Survey, 1976 (SUPAS II) and the Multi-Purpose Household Survey, 1978/79 (SUSENAS 1978/79). These data sets contain household-level data on the socioeconomic characteristics of household members, living conditions, incomes and consumption expenditures, fertil-

---

[1] Mark Leiserson, et al., *Indonesia: Employment and Income Distribution in Indonesia*, A World Bank Country Study (July 1980).

ity behavior, and family planning practice. In addition, information at the community level, indicating the availability of family planning and other government services, will be used.

For the research on fertility, the initial focus will be on individual key relationships that will become building blocks for a more complete model of fertility behavior in Indonesia. To overcome the simultaneity problem inherent in the estimation of these relationships, subsamples will be used that control for other factors not under consideration in the particular relationship that is being focused on. The sample is large enough to seek information on the number of children born during the past year, instead of the total number of children ever born, as a measure of fertility. Multivariate regression analysis will be used.

Initially, four factors will be studied, which preliminary analysis suggests are the most relevant in explaining the number of children ever born: household income, age at first marriage, female economic activity, and knowledge of contraception. In addition, because of the large size of the sample, the effect of the family planning program will be estimated directly by considering women of identical characteristics from two similar communities, one with an active family planning program and one without it. The difference in fertility between these communities should give an indication of the impact of the program. Women of high fertility and nonusers of family planning will also be identified by their socioeconomic characteristics.

The research on the issues of poverty will develop an analytical framework that will be based on a model of household decision-making concerning the allocation of household members' time, their incomes, and the consumption of various commodities, in which children appear as an argument in the household's utility function. Given this framework, the following parameters will be studied: (1) household income, expenditures, and possibly savings; (2) participation in the labor force; (3) the demand for children and family planning; and (4) investments in child education and health.

Cross-tabulations will be obtained that will describe trends in average household consumption levels over time and give a poverty profile of the poor by analyzing their demographic and socioeconomic characteristics, consumption of major categories of goods and services, housing conditions, and access to public services. Then, in order to understand why poor households stay poor or, put differently, why the slightly better-off households are not poor, some tabulations will be generated that will classify households belonging to different income classes by the activities (work and nonwork) of different household members and the sources of their incomes. Earlier work suggests that nonagricultural opportunities in rural areas may have raised some households out of poverty. If this is borne out by the evidence, the characteristics of the rural areas in which these opportunities are available will need to be identified.

Responsibility: Country Policy Department—Oey Astra Meesook, in collaboration with Dov Chernichovsky of Ben-Gurion University (Israel), and with the Central Bureau of Statistics, Indonesia.

Completion date: March 1984.

Reports

Chernichovsky, Dov, and Meesook, Oey Astra. "Female Labor Force Participation in Indonesia." Population and Human Resources Division Discussion Paper No. 81–57. The World Bank, October 1981.

_____. "Poverty in Indonesia: A Profile." Population and Human Resources Division Discussion Paper No. 81–58. The World Bank, November 1981.

_____. "Regional Aspects of Family Planning and Fertility Behavior in Indonesia." World Bank Staff Working Paper No. 462, May 1981.

Meesook, Oey Astra. "Financing and Equity in the Social Sectors in Indonesia." Country Policy Department Discussion Paper No. 1983–5. The World Bank, May 1983.

Policy Analysis of Fertility and Family Planning in Kenya

Ref. No. 672–35A

A World Bank Country Study, *Kenya: Population and Development* (Rashid Faruqee et al., July 1980) has highlighted the serious adverse impact that rapid population growth (estimated at 4 percent per year in 1980) is having on the Kenyan economy. While mortality has been reduced significantly, fertility rates have remained high and recently have even shown signs of increasing slightly.

The Bank study, however, shows that significant variations in fertility rates exist among different population groups. Among some groups of the Kenyan population, fertility has declined in recent years; among others, it has increased. In the recent past, increases were probably larger than decreases with the result that the aggregate fertility rate has increased. In the future this may change, especially if the forces that have influenced fertility decline among some groups could be further strengthened and broadened. Kenya has been the first sub Saharan country to adopt an official family planning program (in 1967); the program, however, has faced two persistent problems—low effective demand for family planning and the high rate at which family planning acceptors drop out.

The purpose of this "research application" project was to follow-up on the Bank's country study in two areas of population research: the determinants of fertility and the evaluation of Kenya's family planning programs.

First, multivariate analysis of fertility determinants and family size preferences were conducted to provide insights about the socioeconomic forces that explain high fertility in Kenya. This was done by using more recent data—the World Fertility Survey for Kenya (1979) and the 1979 Census. The overall results show the overwhelming importance of intermediate (biological) factors in explaining the high fertility rate in Kenya. The effects of socioeconomic factors on fertility through the intermediate factors were very weak, because there was not much variation among women in most of the characteristics identified. However, a few subcategories of specific variables (for example, the education of women and urbanization) showed significant relationships. Average female education even among the youngest cohort of married women is still below five years, and husbands' average education is below seven years. While it is expected that female employment outside the home will have increasingly modernizing effects on their attitudes toward childbearing, the transition toward increased employment outside the home appears very slow. Less than a quarter of younger cohorts worked outside the home before marriage and even fewer are currently employed. High norms of family size, reflected in the variable on the desire for additional children, underscores the low motivation among Kenyan women to regulate fertility. In fact, among the oldest marriage cohort (those married 20 years or more) with an average parity of

8.1, more than one-third (39.6 percent) still want more children. These observations adequately explain the poor contraceptive coverage achieved so far by the official family planning program.

The second objective was to evaluate the family planning program in Kenya using the master file containing the records of clients' visits to the maternal and child health/family planning clinics between 1973 and 1979. The socioeconomic profile of acceptors was examined and an attempt was made to provide an explanation for the low retention rates among acceptors. It is evident that acceptors, in recent years, are on average younger and better educated than acceptors in earlier years of the program, suggesting perhaps that the use of contraception to achieve spacing between births is growing—a factor which could be crucial in lowering fertility rates in the short run, despite the persistence of high fertility norms. However, acceptors on average have higher fertility than the average population, suggesting that generally women with higher parity demand fertility regulation. The low retention rates among acceptors visiting the clinics were partly attributable to problems of institutional infrastructure and the quality of service and personnel. Inadequate service delivery points, for example, were observed to have partly accounted for the marked regional variations in the success of the program in achieving acceptor targets.

The analysis under the reserach project is complete.

Responsibility: Population, Health, and Nutrition Department—K. C. Zachariah, with assistance from Rashid R. Faruqee, Western Africa Country Programs Department I.

Completion date: October 1983; the final report is being written.

Determinants of Fertility in Egypt: An Analysis of the Second Round of the Egyptian Fertility Survey

Ref. No. 672-42

Economic models of fertility for developing countries have evolved substantially from the simple demand models of the 1960s. It is increasingly recognized that in many developing countries fertility is constrained by the biological supply of children rather than the demand for children. This is particularly true in countries with high infant and child mortality and poor maternal health. Easterlin (1980) has developed a model of fertility determination explaining how supply and demand interact and jointly determine contraceptive use.[2] This model has been applied to a number of data sets of the World Fertility Survey (WFS) and has been used as an organizing framework in Cochrane (1979).[3] The research proposed here goes beyond the earlier theoretical and empirical work by including husbands as well as wives in the determination of the demand for children and including data on income and employment as explanatory variables, which are not usually well captured in fertility surveys.

The data for testing this model have been collected explicitly for this purpose in a collaboration between the World Bank and the World Fertility Survey (WFS) and the Central Agency for Public Mobilization and Statistics (CAPMAS), Cairo (see Ref. No. 671–81 in this category). The source of these data is a nationwide sample of 8,900 women and a subsample of 2,300 husbands in 100 clusters. Egypt offers an ideal environment for testing this model, since other data show that there is a large number of couples in each of the four groupings defined by the Easterlin model.

The objectives of this research are to investigate:

1. The relative importance of husbands and wives in determining the desired family size and adoption of contraception. This would permit a better targeting of information, education, and communication programs, as well as family planning delivery services.
2. The effect of access to family planning services on usage.
3. The relationship between education and fertility in Egypt and the effect of school access, relative to parental demand for schooling on school participation, particularly of females.
4. The relationship between the availability of health facilities, family characteristics, and infant and child mortality and the effect of such mortality on fertility through demand and supply variables.

---

[2] R. A. Easterlin, Population and Economic Change in Developing Countries (Chicago and London: The University of Chicago Press, 1980).

[3] S. H. Cochrane, Fertility and Education, What Do We Really Know? (Baltimore and London: The Johns Hopkins University Press, 1979).

In addition to these policy variables, the analysis will also explore the relationship between wages and employment opportunities for women and children and fertility, as well as the effect of family income on both the biological supply and the demand for children.

The basic model to be tested is block-recursive. The major blocks are demand for children, the biological supply of living children, and the availability of contraception. Contraceptive usage is the ultimate dependent variable. Within each of these major blocks, there are submodels such as age at marriage, income determination, and child survival. The block-recursive model will also be used to organize the work. The three major collaborators will agree on the details of the model, then will separately estimate their blocks, and finally combine their results to trace the effect of exogenous variables on the primary dependent variable, as well as secondary variables such as school participation and survival of the most recent child born.

The major output of the work will be two monographs. The first monograph will be a descriptive report similar to the first country reports of the WFS. The second will be a more detailed estimation of the model discussed above; it will take approximately two years to complete.

Responsibility: Population, Health, and Nutrition Department —Susan H. Cochrane, in collaboration with Richard A. Easterlin and Eileen Crimmins of the University of Southern California, and M. Ali Khan of The Johns Hopkins University (consultants). The major institutions participating in the project are the World Fertility Survey, London, and the Central Agency for Public Mobilization and Statistics, Cairo.

Completion date: July 1984.

The Determinants of Fertility in Rural Bangladesh

Ref. No. 672-60

The Government of Bangladesh has committed a substantial amount of its limited resources to its population program in an effort to reduce the country's population growth rate, which is 2.6 percent a year, according to the 1981 census. Among the countries to which the World Bank lends for population projects, Bangladesh has received the largest credit in the population sector from the Bank's concessional affiliate, the International Development Association (IDA). Notwithstanding the involvement of the Bank and other aid agencies in the population sector, the consensus is that more effective programs and policies are needed to bring about a decline in fertility in Bangladesh. An apparent stumbling block is the lack of adequate information on what socioeconomic factors influence fertility and how fertility is regulated in Bangladesh. The purpose of this research project is to provide this policy-relevant information.

The study's focus is on the relationship between poverty and fertility in rural Bangladesh. Particular attention is given to earnings from different sources, expenditures and savings, women's participation in the labor force, and expenditures on child education and health, which may reflect a conscious choice between having many poorly educated and poorly nourished children or fewer, more privileged children. Multivariate analysis is being used to examine the influence of household characteristics on fertility. The relationship between fertility and child mortality, as well as the effect of access to services, notably health care, family planning, education, and agricultural credit, on fertility are being studied in detail. The results will help in assessing the effects of maternal and child health services and of schooling on fertility. The assumption is that if living children have a better chance of surviving and being educated, parents may plan fewer additions to the family. The results will also point to the socioeconomic circumstances, including, for example, the family's access to non-farm jobs and the equality of land distribution in the village, that may induce parents to limit their fertility.

The data used in the research project cover about 4,000 households in four contrasting areas. The Bangladesh Institute of Development Studies (BIDS) collected the data in several rounds, starting in 1976; some subrounds were completed in 1981. The data were collected under IDA's first population project credit to the country, and research funds from the World Bank were used to help process and analyze the data under this project.

A national working group of planners and researchers in Bangladesh has been constituted to guide and review the research under the project.

Responsibility: Population, Health, and Nutrition Department—K. C. Zachariah with assistance from Rashid R. Faruqee, Western Africa Country Programs Department I.

Completion date: March 1984.

Demand for and Willingness to Pay for Services in Rural Mali

Ref. No. 672-72

How do households respond to policy interventions that change the availability of public services? There is growing agreement that to predict the demand for public services, data from household surveys need to be supplemented by information on what services are available in a community and by regional data on the labor market to discover the "prices" households face for public services, as well as for their own labor time.

Specifying demand for public services is particularly important in sub-Saharan Africa, where levels of health and education lag behind those elsewhere in the world, and where the fiscal burden of improving and extending public services is very large. Services as they are now constituted and financed would be impossibly expensive to extend to the whole population. To choose among other options—for example, to increase efficiency for the same level of spending or to introduce user charges to recover some of the costs—it is necessary to know about the determinants and structure of demand. An important question is whether the introduction of user charges would constrain demand among the lower-income groups who may need the services most.

The project is a study of household demand for a range of services in rural Mali, particularly for health (traditional and modern medical care and drugs), schooling, and the supply of clean water. Analysis is based on household expenditure data collected in 1981 in preparation for a World Bank investment project in water supply and health and on a follow-up survey of villages, schools, health posts, and drug outlets in the project area. Analysis to date has suggested how household survey data, when complemented by village-level information on service fees, quality, and accessibility to potential users, can be used in the design of public programs in health, education, and water supply in poor rural areas of Africa.

The analysis includes three parts. The first part, in which the demand for services is quantified, uses standard methods of consumer demand analysis, taking into account local prices collected in the survey of services. The second is an examination at the village level of the services actually available and of attitudes toward them. Its main purpose is to establish whether there are important supply constraints on the use of services—for example, rationing by ethnic group or lack of access due to prohibitive distance. The third part is a comparison of the professed willingness of households to pay for services with their effective demand for them, as measured by their expenditures.

Responsibility: Country Policy Department—Nancy Birdsall (currently assigned to the *World Development Report*), in collaboration with François Orivel (consultant) of the University of Dijon (France).

Completion date: December 1984.

Reports

Ainsworth, Martha. "The Demand for Health and Schooling in Mali: Results of the Community and Service Provider Survey." Country Policy Department Discussion Paper. The World Bank, July 1983.

Ainsworth, Martha; Orivel, François; and Chuhan, Punam. "Cost Recovery for Health and Water Projects in Rural Mali: Household Ability to Pay and Organizational Capacity of Villages." In "Three Studies on Cost Recovery in Social Sector Projects." Country Policy Department Discussion Paper. The World Bank, July 1983.

Birdsall, Nancy. "Demand for Primary Schooling in Rural Mali: Should User Fees Be Increased?" In "Three Studies on Cost Recovery in Social Sector Projects." Country Policy Department Discussion Paper. The World Bank, July 1983.

Birdsall, Nancy, and Chuhan, Punam. "Willingness to Pay for Health and Water in Rural Mali: Do WTP Questions Work?" In "Three Studies on Cost Recovery in Social Sector Projects." Country Policy Department Discussion Paper. The World Bank, July 1983.

Indexes

Country/Regional Index

Numerical Index

Offices of The World Bank

Headquarters: 1818 H Street, N.W., Washington, D.C. 20433, U.S.A.
New York Office:
The World Bank Mission to the United
Nations/New York Office
747 Third Avenue (26th floor)
New York, N.Y. 10017, U.S.A.

European Office: The World Bank, 66, avenue d'Iéna, 75116 Paris, France
London Office: The World Bank, New Zealand House (15th floor),
London SW1 Y4TE, United Kingdom
Geneva Office: World Bank Representative to United Nations
Organizations—Geneva, ITC Building, 54 Rue de Montbrillant,
Geneva, Switzerland; *mailing address*—The World Bank, P.O. Box 104,
1211 Geneva 20 CIC, Switzerland
Tokyo Office: The World Bank, Kokusai Building (Room 916), 1-1,
Marunouchi 3-chome, Chiyoda-ku, Tokyo 100, Japan

Eastern Africa: Regional Mission in Eastern Africa, The World Bank,
Reinsurance Plaza (5th and 6th floors), Taifa Road, Nairobi, Kenya;
mailing address—P.O. Box 30577
Western Africa: Regional Mission in Western Africa, The World Bank,
Immeuble Shell, 64, Avenue Lamblin, Abidjan 01, Ivory Coast; *mailing
address*—B.P. 1850
Thailand: Regional Mission, The World Bank, Udom Vidhya Building, 956
Rama IV Road, Sala Daeng, Bangkok 5, Thailand

Bangladesh: Resident Mission, The World Bank, 222 New Eskaton Road,
Dhaka, Bangladesh; *mailing address*—G.P.O. Box 97
Bolivia: Banco Mundial, Edificio BISA (4º Piso), Avenida 16 de julio 1628,
La Paz, Bolivia; *mailing address*—Casilla 8692
Burundi: The World Bank, 45, Avenue de la Poste, Bujumbura, Burundi;
mailing address—B.P. 2637
Cameroon: The World Bank, Immeuble Kennedy, Avenue Kennedy,
Yaoundé, Cameroon; *mailing address*—B.P. 1128
Colombia: Banco Mundial, Edificio "Aseguradora del Valle," Carrera 10,
No. 24-55 (Piso 17), Bogotá D.E., Colombia; *mailing address*—Banco
Mundial, Apartado Aereo 10229
Ethiopia: The World Bank, I.B.T.E. New Telecommunications Building
(first floor), Churchill Road, Addis Ababa, Ethiopia; *mailing address*—
P.O. Box 5515
Ghana: The World Bank, c/o Royal Guardian Exchange Assurance
Building, Head Office, High Street, Accra, Ghana; *mailing address*—
P.O. Box M27
India: Resident Mission, The World Bank, New Delhi, India; *mailing
address*—P.O. Box 416
Indonesia: Resident Staff in Indonesia, The World Bank, Arthaloka
Building (8th floor), 2 Jalan Jendral Sudirman, Jakarta, Indonesia;
mailing address—P.O. Box 324/JKT

Madagascar: The World Bank, 1, rue Patrice Lumumba, Antananarivo 101, Madagascar; *mailing address*—Banque Mondiale, B.P. 4140

Mali: The World Bank, Quartier du Pont, rue Square Lumumba, Bamako, Mali; *mailing address*—B.P. 1864

Nepal: The World Bank, R.N.A.C. Building (first floor), Kathmandu, Nepal; *mailing address*—P.O. Box 798

Niger: The World Bank, Immeuble El Nasr (12e étage-escalier A), Niamey, Niger; *mailing address*—Banque mondiale, B.P. 12402

Nigeria: The World Bank, 30 Macarthy Street, Lagos, Nigeria; *mailing address*—P.O. Box 127

Pakistan: The World Bank, Islamabad, Pakistan; *mailing address*— P.O. Box 1025

Peru: Banco Mundial, Avenida Central 643 (1º Piso), Lima, Peru; *mailing address*—Apartado 4480

Rwanda: The World Bank, Kigali, Rwanda; *mailing address*—P.O. Box 609

Saudi Arabia: Resident Mission, The World Bank, Riyadh, Saudi Arabia; *mailing address*—P.O. Box 5900

Senegal: The World Bank, Immeuble S.D.I.H., 3, Place de l'Indépendance, Dakar, Senegal; *mailing address*—B.P. 3296

Somalia: The World Bank, c/o Somali Commercial & Savings Bank Building (4th floor), Mogadishu, Somalia; *mailing address*— P.O. Box 1825

Sri Lanka: The World Bank, People's Bank, Head Office (10th floor), Colombo 2, Sri Lanka; *mailing address*—P.O. Box 1761

Sudan: The World Bank, 28 Block 2H, Baladia Street, Khartoum, Sudan; *mailing address*—P.O. Box 2211

Tanzania: The World Bank, N.I.C. Building (7th floor, B), Dar es Salaam, Tanzania; *mailing address*—P.O. Box 2054

Togo: The World Bank, Immeuble BTCI (8e étage), 169, Boulevard Circulaire, Lomé, Togo; *mailing address*—B.P. 3915

Uganda: The World Bank, Kampala, Uganda; *mailing address*— P.O. Box 4463

Upper Volta: The World Bank, Immeuble BECEA (3e étage), Ouagadougou, Upper Volta; *mailing address*—B.P. 622

Zaire: The World Bank, Building UZB, Avenue des Aviateurs, Kinshasa 1, Republic of Zaire; *mailing address*—P.O. Box 14816

Zambia: The World Bank, CMAZ Building, Ben Bella Road, Lusaka, Zambia; *mailing address*—P.O. Box 35410

Also by Gordon R. Dickson:

ARCTURUS LANDING
DORSAI!
HOME FROM THE SHORE
MASTERS OF EVERON
ON THE RUN
PRO
SOLDIER, ASK NOT
THE SPACE SWIMMERS
SPACIAL DELIVERY
THE SPIRIT OF DORSAI
NAKED TO THE STARS

All from ACE Science Fiction

LOST DORSAI

SF
ace books
A Division of Charter Communications Inc.
A GROSSET & DUNLAP COMPANY
51 Madison Avenue
New York, New York 10010

LOST DORSAI

GORDON R. DICKSON

Afterword by Sandra Miesel
Illustrations by Fernando

LOST DORSAI

I am Corunna El Man.

I brought the little courier vessel down at last at the spaceport of Nahar City on Ceta, the large world around Tau Ceti. I had made it from the Dorsai in six phase shifts to transport, to the stronghold of Gebel Nahar, our Amanda Morgan—she whom they call the Second Amanda.

Normally I am far too senior in rank to act as a courier pilot. But I had been home on leave at the time. The courier vessels owned by the Dorsai Cantons are too expensive to risk lightly, but the situation required a contracts expert at Nahar more swiftly than one could safety be gotten there. They had asked me to take on the problem, and I had solved it by stretching the possibilities on each of the phase shifts, coming here.

The risks I had taken had not seemed to bother Amanda. That was not surprising, since she was Dorsai. But neither did she talk to me much on the trip; and that was a thing that had come to be, with me, a little unusual.

For things had been different for me after Baunpore. In the massacre there following the siege, when the North Freilanders finally overran the town, they cut up my face for the revenge of it; and they killed Else, for no other reason than that she was my wife. There was nothing left of her then but incandescent gas, dissipating throughout the universe; and since there could be no hope of a grave, nothing to come back to, nor any place where she could be remembered, I rejected surgery then, and chose to wear my scars as a memorial to her.

It was a decision I never regretted. But it was true that with those scars came an alteration in the way other people reacted to me. With some I found that I became almost invisible; and nearly all seemed to relax their natural impulse to keep private their personal secrets and concerns.

It was almost as if they felt that somehow I was now beyond the point where I would stand in judgment on their pains and sorrows. No, on second thought, it was something even stronger than that. It was as if I was like a burnt-out candle in the dark room of their inner selves—a lightless, but safe, companion whose presence reassured them that their privacy was still unbreached. I doubt very much that Amanda and those I was to meet on this trip to Gebel Nahar would have talked to me as freely as they later did, if I had met them back in the days when I had had Else, alive.

We were lucky on our incoming. The Gebel Nahar is more a mountain fortress than a palace or government center; and for military reasons Nahar City, near it, has a spaceport capable of handling deep-space ships. We debarked, expecting to be met in the terminal the minute we entered it through its field doors. But we were not.

The principality of Nahar Colony lies in tropical latitudes on Ceta, and the main lobby of the terminal was small, but high-ceilinged and airy; its floor and ceiling tiled in bright colors, with plants growing in planter areas all about; and bright, enormous, heavily-framed paintings on all the walls. We stood in the

middle of all this and foot traffic moved past and around us. No one looked directly at us, although neither I with my scars, nor Amanda—who bore a remarkable resemblance to those pictures of the first Amanda in our Dorsai history books—were easy to ignore.

I went over to check with the message desk and found nothing there for us. Coming back, I had to hunt for Amanda, who had stepped away from where I had left her.

"El Man—" her voice said without warning, behind me. "Look!"

Her tone had warned me, even as I turned. I caught sight of her and the painting she was looking at, all in the same moment. It was high up on one of the walls; and she stood just below it, gazing up.

Sunlight through the transparent front wall of the terminal flooded her and the picture, alike. She was in all the natural colors of life—as Else had been—tall, slim, in light blue cloth jacket and short cream-colored skirt, with white-blond hair and that incredible youthfulness that her namesake ancestor had also owned. In contrast, the painting was rich in garish pigments, gold leaf and alizarin crimson, the human figures it depicted caught in exaggerated, melodramatic attitudes.

Leto de muerte, the large brass plate below it read. *Hero's Death-Couch,* as the title would roughly translate from the bastard, archaic Spanish spoken by the Naharese. It showed a great, golden bed set out on an open plain in the aftermath of the battle. All about were corpses and bandaged officers standing in gilt-encrusted uniforms. The living surrounded the bed

10

and its occupant, the dead Hero, who, powerfully muscled yet emaciated, hideously wounded and stripped to the waist, lay upon a thick pile of velvet cloaks, jewelled weapons, marvellously-wrought tapestries and golden utensils, all of which covered the bed.

The body lay on its back, chin pointing at the sky, face gaunt with the agony of death, still firmly holding by one large hand to its naked chest, the hilt of an oversized and ornate sword, its massive blade darkened with blood. The wounded officers standing about and gazing at the corpse were posed in dramatic attitudes. In the foreground, on the earth beside the bed, a single ordinary soldier in battle-torn uniform, dying, stretched forth one arm in tribute to the dead man.

Amanda looked at me for a second as I moved up beside her. She did not say anything. It was not necessary to say anything. In order to live, for two hundred years we on the Dorsai have exported the only commodity we owned—the lives of our generations—to be spent in wars for others' causes. We live with real war; and to those who do that, a painting like this one was close to obscenity.

"So that's how they think here," said Amanda.

I looked sideways and down at her. Along with the appearance of her ancestor, she had inherited the First Amanda's incredible youthfulness. Even I, who knew she was only a half-dozen years younger than myself—and I was now in my mid-thirties—occasionally forgot that fact, and was jolted by the realization that she thought like my generation rather than like the stripling she seemed to be.

"Every culture has its own fantasies," I said. "And

this culture's Hispanic, at least in heritage."

"Less than ten percent of the Naharese population's Hispanic nowadays, I understand," she answered. "Besides, this is a caricature of Hispanic attitudes."

She was right. Nahar had originally been colonized by immigrants—Gallegos from the northwest of Spain who had dreamed of large ranches in a large open Territory. Instead, Nahar, squeezed by its more industrial and affluent neighbors, had become a crowded, small country which had retained a bastard version of the Spanish language as its native tongue and a medley of half-remembered Spanish attitudes and customs as its culture. After the first wave of immigrants, those who came to settle here were of anything but Hispanic ancestry, but still they had adopted the language and ways they found here.

The original ranchers had become enormously rich —for though Ceta was a sparsely populated planet, it was food-poor. The later arrivals swelled the cities of Nahar, and stayed poor—very poor.

"I hope the people I'm to talk to are going to have more than ten per cent of ordinary sense," Amanda said. "This picture makes me wonder if they don't prefer fantasy. If that's the way it is at Gebel Nahar. . ."

She left the sentence unfinished, shook her head, and then—apparently pushing the picture from her mind—smiled at me. The smile lit up her face, in something more than the usual sense of that phrase. With her, it was something different, an inward lighting deeper and greater than those words usually indicate. I had only met her for the first time, three days earlier, and Else was all I had ever or would ever want; but now I could see what people had meant on the

Dorsai, when they had said she inherited the first Amanda's abilities to both command others and make them love her.

"No message for us?" she said.

"No—" I began. But then I turned, for out of the corner of my eye I had seen someone approaching us.

She also turned. Our attention had been caught because the man striding toward us on long legs was a Dorsai. He was big. Not the size of the Graeme twins, Ian and Kensie, who were in command at Gebel Nahar on the Naharese contract; but close to that size and noticeably larger than I was. However, Dorsai come in all shapes and sizes. What had identified him to us—and obviously, us to him—was not his size but a multitude of small signals, too subtle to be catalogued. He wore a Naharese army bandmaster's uniform, with warrant officer tabs at the collar; and he was blond-haired, lean-faced, and no more than in his early twenties. I recognized him.

He was the third son of a neighbor from my own canton of High Island, on the Dorsai. His name was Michael de Sandoval, and little had been heard of him for six years.

"Sir—Ma'm," he said, stopping in front of us. "Sorry to keep you waiting. There was a problem getting transport."

"Michael," I said. "Have you met Amanda Morgan?"

"No, I haven't." He turned to her. "An honor to meet you, ma'm. I suppose you're tired of having everyone say they recognize you from your great-grandmother's pictures?"

"Never tire of it," said Amanda cheerfully; and gave

15

him her hand. "But you already know Corunna El Man?"

"The El Man family are High Island neighbors," said Michael. He smiled for a second, almost sadly, at me. "I remember the Captain from when I was only six years old and he was first home on leave. If you'll come along with me, please? I've already got your luggage in the bus."

"Bus?" I said, as we followed him toward one of the window-wall exits from the terminal.

"The band bus for Third Regiment. It was all I could get."

We emerged on to a small parking pad scattered with a number of atmosphere flyers and ground vehicles. Michael de Sandoval led us to a stubby-framed, powered lifting body, that looked as if it could hold about thirty passengers. Inside, one person saved the vehicle from being completely empty. It was an Exotic in a dark blue robe, an Exotic with white hair and a strangely ageless face. He could have been anywhere between thirty and eighty years of age and he was seated in the lounge area at the front of the bus, just before the compartment wall that divided off the control area in the vehicle's nose. He stood up as we came in.

"Padma, Outbond to Ceta," said Michael. "Sir, may I introduce Amanda Morgan, Contracts Adjuster, and Corunna El Man, Senior Ship Captain, both from the Dorsai? Captain El Man just brought the Adjuster in by courier."

"Of course, I know about their coming," said Padma.

He did not offer a hand to either of us. Nor did he

rise. But, like many of the advanced Exotics I have
known, he did not seem to need to. As with those others, there was a warmth and peace about him that the
rest of us were immediately caught up in, and any behavior on his part seemed natural and expected.

We sat down together. Michael ducked into the control compartment, and a moment later, with a soft vi-
bration, the bus lifted from the parking pad.

"It's an honor to meet you, Outbond," said Amanda. "But it's even more of an honor to have you meet
us. What rates us that sort of attention?"

Padma smiled slightly.

"I'm afraid I didn't come just to meet you," he said
to her. "Although Kensie Graeme's been telling me all
about you; and—" he looked over at me, "even I've
heard of Corunna El Man."

"Is there anything you Exotics don't hear about?" I
said.

"Many things," he shook his head, gently but seriously.

"What was the other reason that brought you to the
spaceport, then?" Amanda asked.

He looked at her thoughtfully.

"Something that has nothing to do with your coming," he said. "It happens I had a call to make to
elsewhere on the planet, and the phones at Gebel
Nahar are not as private as I liked. When I heard
Michael was coming to get you, I rode along to make
my call from the terminal, here."

"It wasn't a call on behalf of the Conde of Nahar,
then?" I asked.

"If it was—or if it was for anyone but myself—" he
smiled. "I wouldn't want to betray a confidence by

admitting it. I take it you know about El Conde? The titular ruler of Nahar?"

"I've been briefing myself on the Colony and on Gebel Nahar ever since it turned out I needed to come here," Amanda answered.

I could see her signalling me to leave her alone with him. It showed in the way she sat and the angle at which she held her head. Exotics were perceptive, but I doubted that Padma had picked up that subtle private message.

"Excuse me," I told them. "I think I'll go have a word with Michael."

I got up and went through the door into the control section, closing it behind me. Michael sat relaxed, one hand on the control rod; and I sat down myself in the copilot's seat.

"How are things at home, sir?" he asked, without turning his head from the sky ahead of us.

"I've only been back this once since you'd have left, yourself," I said. "But it hasn't changed much. My father died last year."

"I'm sorry to hear that."

"Your father and mother are well—and I hear your brothers are all right, out among the stars," I said. "But, of course, you know that."

"No," he said, still watching the sky ahead. "I haven't heard for quite a while."

A silence threatened.

"How did you happen to end up here?" I asked. It was almost a ritual question between Dorsais away from home.

"I heard about Nahar. I thought I'd take a look at it."

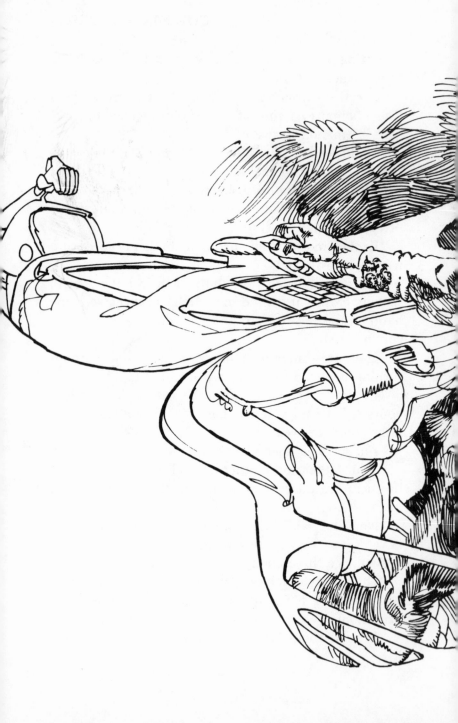

"Did you know it was as fake Hispanic as it is?"

"Not fake," he said. "Something . . . but not that."

He was right, of course.

"Yes," I said, "I guess I shouldn't use the word fake. Situations like the one here come out of natural causes, like all others."

He looked directly at me. I had learned to read such looks since Else died. He was very close in that moment to telling me something more than he would probably have told anyone else. But the moment passed and he looked back out the windshield.

"You know the situation here?" he said.

"No. That's Amanda's job," I said. "I'm just a driver on this trip. Why don't you fill me in?"

"You must know some of it already," he said, "and Ian or Kensie Graeme will be telling you the rest. But in any case . . . the Conde's a figurehead. Literally. His father was set up with that title by the first Naharese immigrants, who're all now rich ranchers. They had a dream of starting their own hereditary aristocracy here, but that never really worked. Still, on paper, the Conde's the hereditary sovereign of Nahar; and, in theory, the army belongs to him as Commander-in-Chief. But the army's always been drawn from the poor of Nahar—the city poor and the *campesinos;* and they hate the rich first-immigrants. Now there's a revolution brewing and the army doesn't know which way it'll jump."

"I see," I said. "So a violent change of government is on the way, and our contract here's with a government which may be out of power tomorrow. Amanda's got a problem."

"It's everyone's problem," Michael said. "The only

reason the army hasn't declared itself for the revolutionaries is because its parts don't work together too
well. Coming from the outside, the way you have, the
ridiculousness of the locals' attitudes may be what
catches your notice first. But actually those attitudes

are all the non-rich have, here, outside of a bare existence—this business of the flags, the uniforms, the music, the duels over one wrong glance and the idea of dying for your regiment—or being ready to go at the throat of any other regiment at the drop of a hat."

"But," I said, "what you're describing isn't any practical, working sort of military force."

"No. That's why Kensie and Ian were contracted in here, to do something about turning the local army into something like an actual defensive force. The other principalities around Nahar all have their eyes on the ranchlands, here. Given a normal situation, the Graemes'd already be making progress—you know Ian's reputation for training troops. But the way it's turned out, the common soldiers here think of the Graemes as tools of the ranchers, the revolutionaries preach that they ought to be thrown out, and the regiments are non-cooperating with them. I don't think they've got a hope of doing anything useful with the army under present conditions; and the situation's been getting more dangerous daily—for them, and now for you and Amanda, as well. The truth is, I think Kensie and Ian'd be wise to take their loss on the contract and get out."

"If accepting loss and leaving was all there was to it, someone like Amanda wouldn't be needed here," I said. "There has to be more than that to involve the Dorsai in general."

He said nothing.

"How about you?" I said. "What's your position here? You're Dorsai too."

"Am I?" he said to the windshield, in a low voice.

I had at last touched on what had been going unspoken between us. There was a name for individuals like Michael, back home. They were called "lost Dorsai." The name was not used for those who had chosen to do something other than a military vocation. It was reserved for those of Dorsai heritage who seemed to have chosen their life work, whatever it was, and then—suddenly and without explanation—abandoned it. In Michael's case, as I knew, he had graduated from the Academy with honors; but after graduation he had abruptly withdrawn his name from assignment and left the planet, with no explanation, even to his family.

"I'm Bandmaster of the Third Naharese Regiment," he said, now. "My regiment likes me. The local people don't class me with the rest of you, generally—" he smiled a little sadly, again, "except that I don't get challenged to duels."

"I see," I said.

"Yes." He looked over at me now. "So, while the army is still technically obedient to the Conde, as its Commander-in-Chief, actually just about everything's come to a halt. That's why I had trouble getting transportation from the vehicle pool to pick you up."

"I see—" I repeated. I had been about to ask him some more; but just then the door to the control compartment opened behind us and Amanda stepped in.

"Well, Corunna," she said, "how about giving me a chance to talk with Michael?"

She smiled past me at him; and he smiled back. I did not think he had been strongly taken by her—whatever was hidden in him was a barrier to anything like that. But her very presence, with all it implied of home, was plainly warming to him.

"Go ahead," I said, getting up. "I'll go say a word or two to the Outbond."

"He's worth talking to," Amanda spoke after me as I went.

I stepped out, closed the door behind me, and rejoined Padma in the lounge area. He was looking out the window beside him and down at the plains area that lay between the town and the small mountain from which Gebel Nahar took its name. The city we had just left was on a small rise west of that mountain, with suburban and planted areas in between. Around and beyond that mountain—for the fort-like residence that was Gebel Nahar faced east—the actual, open grazing land of the cattle plains began. Our bus was one of those vehicles designed to fly ordinarily at about tree-top level, though of course it could go right up to the limits of the atmosphere in a pinch, but right now we were about three hundred meters up. As I stepped out of the control compartment, Padma took his attention from the window and looked back at me.

"Your Amanda's amazing," he said, as I sat down facing him, "for someone so young."

"She said something like that about you," I told him. "But in her case, she's not quite as young as she looks."

"I know," Padma smiled. "I was speaking from the viewpoint of my own age. To me, even you seem young."

I laughed. What I had had of youth had been far back, some years before Baunpore. But it was true that in terms of years I was not even middle-aged.

"Michael's been telling me that a revolution seems to be brewing here in Nahar," I said to him.

"Yes." He sobered.

"That wouldn't be what brings someone like you to Gebel Nahar?"

His hazel eyes were suddenly amused.

"I thought Amanda was the one with the questions," he said.

"Are you surprised I ask?" I said. "This is an out of the way location for the Outbond to a full planet."

"True." He shook his head. "But the reasons that bring me here are Exotic ones. Which means, I'm afraid, that I'm not free to discuss them."

"But you know about the local movement toward a revolution?"

"Oh, yes." He sat in perfectly relaxed stillness, his hands loosely together in the lap of his robe, light brown against the dark blue. His face was calm and unreadable. "It's part of the overall pattern of events on this world."

"Just this world?"

He smiled back at me.

"Of course," he said gently, "our Exotic science of ontogenetics deals with the interaction of all known human and natural forces, on all the inhabited worlds. But the situation here in Nahar, and specifically the situation at Gebel Nahar, is primarily a result of local, Cetan forces."

"International planetary politics."

"Yes," he said. "Nahar is surrounded by five other principalities, none of which have cattle-raising land like this. They'd all like to have a part or all of this Colony in their control."

"Which ones are backing the revolutionaries?"

He gazed out the window for a moment without

speaking. It was a presumptuous thought on my part to imagine that my strange geas, that made people want to tell me private things, would work on an Exotic. But for a moment I had had the familiar feeling that he was about to open up to me.

"My apologies," he said at last. "It may be that in my old age I'm falling into the habit of treating everyone else like—children."

"How old are you, then?"

He smiled.

"Old—and getting older."

"In any case," I said, "you don't have to apologize to me. It'll be an unusual situation when bordering countries don't take sides in a neighbor's revolution."

"Of course," he said. "Actually, all of the five think they have a hand in it on the side of the revolutionaries. Bad as Nahar is, now, it would be a shambles after a successful revolution, with everybody fighting everybody else for different goals. The other principalities all look for a situation in which they can move in and gain. But you're quite right. International politics is always at work, and it's never simple."

"What's fueling this situation, then?"

"William," Padma looked directly at me and for the first time I felt the remarkable effect of his hazel eyes. His face held such a calmness that all his expression seemed to be concentrated in those eyes.

"William?" I asked.

"William of Ceta."

"That's right," I said, remembering. "He owns this world, doesn't he?"

"It's not really correct to say he owns it," Padma said. "He controls most of it—and a great many parts

29

of other worlds. Our present-day version of a merchant prince, in many ways. But he doesn't control everything, even here on Ceta. For example, the Naharese ranchers have always banded together tightly to deal with him; and his best efforts to split them apart and gain a direct authority in Nahar, haven't worked. He controls after a fashion, but only by manipulating the outside conditions that the ranchers have to deal with."

"So he's the one behind the revolution?"

"Yes."

It was plain enough to me that it was William's involvement here that had brought Padma to this backwater section of the planet. The Exotic science of ontogenetics, which was essentially a study of how humans interacted, both as individuals and societies, was something they took very seriously; and William, as one of the movers and shakers of our time would always have his machinations closely watched by them.

"Well, it's nothing to do with us, at any rate," I said, "except as it affects the Graeme's contract."

"Not entirely," he said. "William, like most gifted individuals, knows the advantage of killing two, or even fifty, birds with one stone. He hires a good many mercenaries, directly and indirectly. It would benefit him if events here could lower the Dorsai reputation and the market value of its military individuals."

"I see—" I began; and broke off as the hull of the bus rang suddenly—as if to a sharp blow.

"Down!" I said, pulling Padma to the floor of the vehicle and away from the window beside which we had been sitting. One good thing about Exotics—they trust you to know your own line of work. He obeyed me instantly and without protest. We waited . . . but there was no repetition of the sound.

"What was it?" he asked, after a moment, but without moving from where I had brought him.

"Solid projectile slug. Probably from a heavy hand weapon," I told him. "We've been shot at. Stay down, if you please, Outbond."

I got up myself, staying low and to the center of the bus, and went through the door into the control compartment. Amanda and Michael both looked around at me as I entered, their faces alert.

"Who's out to get us?" I asked Michael.

He shook his head.

"I don't know," he said. "Here in Nahar, it could be anything or anybody. It could be the revolutionaries or simply someone who doesn't like the Dorsai; or someone who doesn't like Exotics—or even someone who doesn't like me. Finally, it could be someone drunk, drugged, or just in a macho mood."

"—who also has a military hand weapon."

"There's that," Michael said. "But everyone in Nahar is armed; and most of them, legitimately or not, own military weapons."

He nodded at the windscreen.

"Anyway, we're almost down," he said.

I looked out. The interlocked mass of buildings that was the government seat called Gebel Nahar was sprawled halfway down from the top of the small mountain, just below us. In the tropical sunlight, it looked like a resort hotel, built on terraces that descended the steep slope. The only difference was that each terrace terminated in a wall, and the lowest of the

walls were ramparts of solid fortifications, with heavy weapons emplaced along them. Gebel Nahar, properly garrisoned, should have been able to dominate the countryside against surface troops all the way out to the horizon, at least on this side of the mountain.

"What's the other side like?" I asked.

"Mountaineering cliff—there's heavy weapon emplacements cut out of the rock there, too, and reached by tunnels going clear through the mountain," Michael answered. "The ranchers spared no expense when they built this place. Gallego thinking. They and their families might all have to hole up here, one day."

But a few moments later we were on the poured concrete surface of a vehicle pool. The three of us went back into the body of the bus to rejoin Padma; and Michael let us out of the vehicle. Outside, the parking area was abnormally silent.

"I don't know what's happened—" said Michael as we set foot outside. We three Dorsai had checked, instinctively, ready to retreat back into the bus and take off again if necessary.

A voice shouting from somewhere beyond the ranked flyers and surface vehicles, brought our heads around. There was the sound of running feet, and a moment later a soldier wearing an energy sidearm, but dressed in the green and red Naharese army uniform with band tabs, burst into sight and slid to a halt, panting before us.

"Sir—" he wheezed, in the local dialect of archaic Spanish. "Gone—"

We waited for him to get his breath; after a second, he tried again.

"They've deserted, sir!" he said to Michael, trying to pull himself to attention. "They've gone—all the regiments, everybody!"

"When?" asked Michael.

"Two hours past. It was all planned. Certainly, it was planned. In each group, at the same time, a man stood up. He said that now was the time to desert, to show the *ricones* where the army stood. They all marched out, with their flags, their guns, everything. Look!"

He turned and pointed. We looked. The vehicle pool was on the fifth or sixth level down from the top of the Gebel Nahar. It was possible to see, from this as from any of the other levels, straight out for miles over the plains. Looking now we saw, so far off no other sign was visible, the tiny, occasional twinkles of reflected sunlight, seemingly right on the horizon.

"They are camped out there; waiting for an army they say will come from all the other countries around, to reinforce them and accomplish the revolution."

"Everyone's gone?" Michael's words in Spanish brought the soldier's eyes back to him.

"All but us. The soldiers of your band, sir. We are the Conde's Elite Guard, now."

"Where are the two Dorsai Commanders?"

"In their offices, sir."

"I'll have to go to them right away," said Michael to the rest of us. "Outbond, will you wait in your quarters, or will you come along with us?"

"I'll come," said Padma.

The five of us went across the parking area, between the crowded vehicles and into a maze of corridors. Through these at last we found our way finally to a

large suite of offices, where the outward wall of each room was all window. Through the window of the one we were in, we looked out on the plain below, where the distant and all but invisible Naharese regiments were now camped. We found Kensie and Ian Graeme together in one of the inner offices, standing talking before a massive desk large enough to serve as a conference table for a half-dozen people.

They turned as we came in—and once again I was hit by the curious illusion that I usually experienced on meeting these two. It was striking enough whenever I approached one of them. But when the twins were together, as now, the effect was enhanced.

In my own mind I had always laid it to the fact that in spite of their size—and either one is nearly a head taller than I am—they are so evenly proportioned physically that their true dimensions do not register on you until you have something to measure them by. From a distance it is easy to take them for not much more than ordinary height. Then, having unconsciously underestimated them, you or someone else whose size you know approaches them; and it is that individual who seems to change in size as he, or she, or you get close. If it is you, you are very aware of the change. But if it is someone else, you can still seem to shrink somewhat, along with that other person. To feel yourself become smaller in relationship to someone else is a strange sensation, if the phenomenon is entirely subjective.

In this case, the measuring element turned out to be Amanda, who ran to the two brothers the minute we entered the room. Her home, Fal Morgan, was the homestead closest to the Graeme home of Foralie and the three of them had grown up together. As I said, she was not a small woman, but by the time she had reached them and was hugging Kensie, she seemed to have become not only tiny, but fragile; and suddenly—again, as it always does—the room seemed to orient itself about the two Graemes.

I followed her and held out my hand to Ian.

"Corunna!" he said. He was one of the few who still called me by the first of my personal names. His large hand wrapped around mine. His face—so different, yet so like, to his twin brother's—looked down into mine. In truth, they were identical, and yet there was all the difference in the universe between them. Only it was not a physical difference, for all its powerful effect on the eye. Literally, it was that Ian was lightless, and all the bright element that might have been in him was instead in his brother, so that Kensie radiated double the human normal amount of sunny warmth. Dark and light. Night and day. Brother and brother.

And yet, there was a closeness, an identity, between them of a kind that I have never seen in any other two human beings.

"Do you have to go back right away?" Ian was asking me. "Or will you be staying to take Amanda back?"

"I can stay," I said. "My leave-time to the Dorsai wasn't that tight. Can I be of use, here?"

"Yes," Ian said. "You and I should talk. Just a minute, though—"

He turned to greet Amanda in his turn and tell Michael to check and see if the Conde was available for a visit. Michael went out with the soldier who had met us at the vehicle pool. It seemed that Michael and

his bandsmen, plus a handful of servants and the Conde himself, added up to the total present population of
Gebel Nahar, outside of those in this room. The ramparts were designed to be defended by a handful of
people, if necessary; but we had barely more than a
handful in the forty members of the regimental band
Michael had led, and they were evidently untrained in
anything but marching.

We left Kensie with Amanda and Padma. Ian led
me into an adjoining office, waved me to a chair, and
took one himself.

"I don't know the situation on your present contract—" he began.

"There's no problem. My contract's to a space force
leased by William of Ceta. I'm leader of Red Flight
under the overall command of Hendrik Galt. Aside
from the fact that Gault would understand, as any other Dorsai would, if a situation like this warranted it,
his forces aren't doing anything at the moment. Which
is why I was on leave in the first place, along with half
his other senior officers. I'm not William's officer. I'm
Gault's."

"Good," said Ian. He turned his head to look past
the high wing of the chair he was sitting in and out
over the plain at where the little flashes of light were
visible. His arms lay relaxed upon the arms of the
chair, his massive hands loosely curved about the ends
of those chair arms. There was, as there always had
been, something utterly lonely but utterly invincible
about Ian. Most non-Dorsais seem to draw a noticeable comfort from having a Dorsai around in times of
physical danger, as if they assumed that any one of us
would know the right thing to do and so do it. It may

41

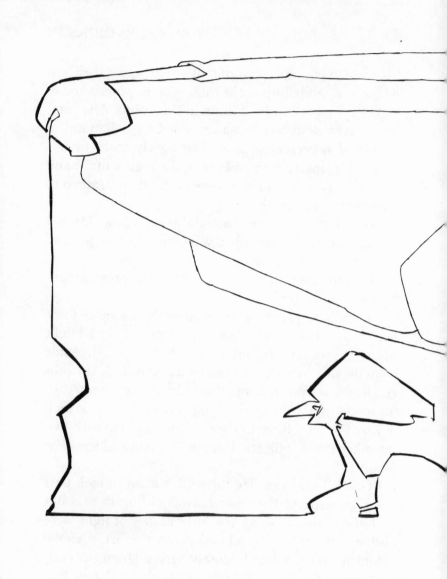

sound fanciful, but I have to say that in somewhat the same way as the non-Dorsai reacted to the Dorsai, so did most of the Dorsai I've known always react to Ian.

But not all of us. Kensie never had, of course. Nor, come to think of it, had any of the other Graemes to my knowledge. But then, there had always been something—not solitary, but independent and apart—about each of the Graemes. Even Kensie. It was a characteristic of the family. Only, Ian had that double share of it.

"It'll take them two days to settle in out there," he said now, nodding at the nearly invisible encampments on the plain. "After that, they'll either have to move against us, or they'll start fighting among themselves. That means we can expect to be overrun here in two days."

"Unless what?" I asked. He looked back at me.

"There's always an unless," I said.

"Unless Amanda can find us an honorable way out of the situation," he said. "As it now stands, there doesn't seem to be any way out. Our only hope is that she can find something in the contract or the situation that the rest of us have overlooked. Drink?"

"Thanks."

He got up and went to a sideboard, poured a couple of glasses half-full of dark brown liquor, and brought them back. He sat down once more, handing a glass to me, and I sniffed at its pungent darkness.

"Dorsai whiskey," I said. "You're provided for, here."

He nodded. We drank.

"Isn't there anything you think she might be able to use?" I asked.

"No," he said. "It's a hope against hope. An honor problem."

"What makes it so sensitive that you need an Adjuster from home?" I asked.

"William. You know him, of course. But how much do you know about the situation here in Nahar?"

I repeated to him what I had picked up from Michael and Padma.

"Nothing else?" he asked.

"I haven't had time to find out anything else. I was asked to bring Amanda here on the spur of the moment, so on the way out I had my hands full. Also, she was busy studying the available data on this situation herself. We didn't talk much."

"William—" he said, putting his glass down on a small table by his chair. "Well, it's my fault we're into this, rather than Kensie's. I'm the strategist, he's the tactician on this contract. The large picture was my job, and I didn't look far enough."

"If there were things the Naharese government didn't tell you when the contract was under discussion, then there's your out, right there."

"Oh, the contract's challengeable, all right," Ian said. He smiled. I know there are those who like to believe that he never smiles; and that notion is nonsense. But his smile is like all the rest of him. "It wasn't the information they held back that's trapped us, it's this matter of honor. Not just our personal honor—the reputation and honor of all Dorsai. They've got us in a position where whether we stay and die or go and live, it'll tarnish the planetary reputation."

I frowned at him.

"How can they do that? How could you get caught

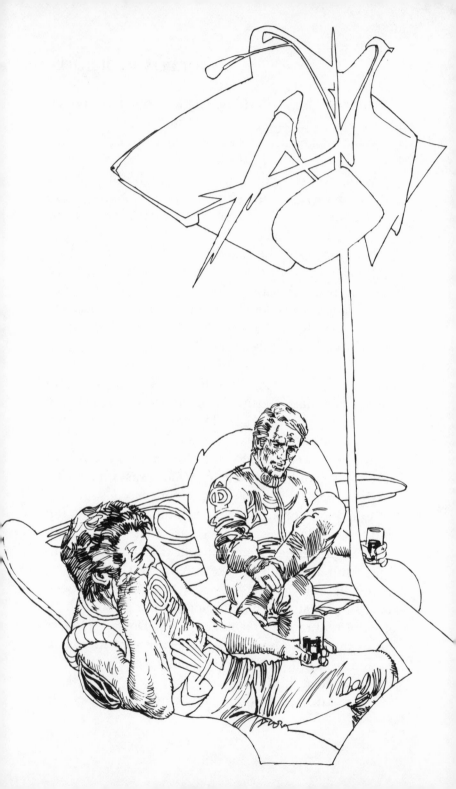

in that sort of trap?''

"Partly," Ian lifted his glass, drank, and put it back down again, "because William's an extremely able strategist himself—again, as you know. Partly, because it didn't occur to me, or Kensie, that we were getting into a three-party rather than a two-party agreement."

"I don't follow you."

"The situation in Nahar," he said, "was always one with its built-in termination clause—I mean, for the ranchers, the original settlers. The type of country they tried to set up was something that could only exist under uncrowded, near-pioneering conditions. The principalities around their grazing area got settled in, some fifty Cetan years ago. After that, the neighboring countries got built up and industrialized; and the semi-feudal notion of open plains and large individual holdings of land got to be impractical, on the international level of this world. Of course, the first settlers, those Gallegos from Galicia in northwest Spain, saw that coming from the start. That was why they built this place we're setting in."

His smile came again.

"But that was back when they were only trying to delay the inevitable," he said. "Sometime in more recent years they evidently decided to come to terms with it."

"Bargain with the more modern principalities around them, you mean?" I said.

"Bargain with the rest of Ceta, in fact," he said. "And the rest of Ceta, nowadays, is William—for all practical purposes."

"There again, if they had an agreement with William that they didn't tell you about," I said, "you've every excuse, in honor as well as on paper, to void the contract. I don't see the difficulty."

"Their deal they've got with William isn't a written, or even a spoken contract," Ian answered. "What the ranchers did was let him know that he could have the control he wanted here in Nahar—as I said, it was obvious they were going to lose it eventually, anyway —if not to him, to someone or something else—if he'd meet their terms."

"And what were they after in exchange?"

"A guarantee that their life style and this pocket culture they'd developed would be maintained and protected."

He looked under his dark brows at me.

"I see," I said. "How did they think William could do that?"

"They didn't know. But they didn't worry about it. That's the slippery part. They just let the fact be known to William that if they got what they wanted they'd stop fighting his attempts to control Nahar directly. They left it up to him to find the ways to meet their price. That's why there's no other contract we can cite as an excuse to break this one."

I drank from my own glass.

"It sounds like William. If I know him," I said, "he'd even enjoy engineering whatever situation was needed to keep this country fifty years behind the times. But it sounded to me earlier as if you were saying that he was trying to get something out of the Dorsai at the same time. What good does it do him if you have to make a penalty payment for breaking this contract? It won't bankrupt you Graemes to pay it, will it? And even if you had to borrow from general Dorsai contingency funds, it wouldn't be more than a pinprick against those funds. Also, you still haven't explained this business of your being trapped here, not by the contract, but by the general honor of the Dorsai."

Ian nodded.

"William's taken care of both things," he said. "His plan was for the Naharese to hire Dorsai to make their army a working unit. Then his revolutionary agents would cause a revolt of that army. Then, with matters out of hand, he could step in with his own non-Dorsai officers to control the situation and bring order back to Nahar."

"I see," I said.

"He then would mediate the matter," Ian went on, "the revolutionary people would be handed some limited say in the government—under his outside control, of course—and the ranchers would give up their absolute local authority but little of anything else. They'd stay in charge of their ranches, as his managers, with all his wealth and forces to back them against any real push for control by the real revolutionary faction; which would eventually be tamed and brought in line, also—the way he's tamed and brought in line all the rest of this world, and some good-sized chunks of other worlds."

"So," I said, thoughtfully, "what he's after is to show that his military people can do things Dorsai can't?"

"You follow me," said Ian. "We command the price we do now only because military like ourselves are in limited supply. If they want Dorsai results—military

situations dealt with at either no cost or a minimum cost, in life and material—they have to hire Dorsai. That's as it stands now. But if it looks like others can do the same job as well or better, our price has to go down, and the Dorsai will begin to starve."

"It'd take some years for the Dorsai to starve. In that time we could live down the results of this, maybe."

"But it goes farther than that. William isn't the first to dream of being able to hire all the Dorsai and use them as a personal force to dominate the worlds. We've never considered allowing all our working people to end up in one camp. But if William can depress our price below what we need to keep the Dorsai free and independent, then he can offer us wages better than the market—survival wages, available from him alone—and we'll have no choice but to accept."

"Then you've got no choice, yourself," I said. "You've got to break this contract, no matter what it costs."

"I'm afraid not," he answered. "The cost looks right now to be the one we can't afford to pay. As I said, we're damned if we do, damned if we don't—caught in the jaws of this nutcracker unless Amanda can find us a way out—"

The door to the office where we were sitting opened at that moment and Amanda herself looked in.

"It seems some local people calling themselves the Governors have just arrived—" Her tone was humorous, but every line of her body spoke of serious concern. "Evidently, I'm supposed to go and talk with them right away. Are you coming, Ian?"

"Kensie is all you'll need," Ian said. "We've trained

them to realize that they don't necessarily get both of us on deck every time they whistle. You'll find it's just another step in the dance, anyway—there's nothing to be done with them."

"All right." She started to withdraw, stopped. "Can Padma come with us?"

"Check with Kensie. I'd say it's best not to ruffle the Governors' feathers by asking to let him sit in, right now."

"That's all right," she said. "Kensie already thought not, but he said I should ask you."

She went out.

"Sure you don't want to be there?" I asked him.

"No need." He got up. "There's something I want to show you. It's important you understand the situation here thoroughly. If Kensie and myself should both be knocked out, Amanda would only have you to help her handle things—and if you're certain about being able to stay?"

"As I said," I repeated, "I can stay."

"Fine. Come along, then. I wanted you to meet the Conde de Nahar. But I've been waiting to hear from Michael as to whether the Conde's receiving, right now. We won't wait any longer. Let's go see how the old gentleman is."

"Won't he—the Conde, I mean—be at this meeting with Amanda and the Governors?"

Ian led the way out of the room.

"Not if there's serious business to be talked about. On paper, the Conde controls everything but the Governors. They elect him. Of course, aside from the paper, they're the ones who really control everything."

We left the suite of offices and began to travel the

53

corridors of Gebel Nahar once more. Twice we took lift
tubes and once we rode a motorized strip down one
long corridor; but at the end Ian pushed open a door
and we stepped into what was obviously the orderly
room fronting a barracks section.

The soldier bandsman seated behind the desk there
came to his feet immediately at the sight of us—or perhaps it was just at the sight of Ian.

"Sirs!" he said, in Spanish.

"I ordered Mr. de Sandoval to find out for me if the
Conde would receive Captain El Man here, and myself," Ian said in the same language. "Do you know
where the Bandmaster is now?"

"No, sir. He has not come back. Sir—it is not
always possible to contact the Conde quickly—"

"I'm aware of that," said Ian. "Rest easy. Mr. de
Sandoval's due back here shortly, then?"

"Yes, sir. Any minute now. Would the sirs care to
wait in the Bandmaster's office?"

"Yes," said Ian.

The orderly turned aside, lifting his hand in a de-
cidedly non-military gesture to usher us past his desk
through a farther entrance into a larger room, very orderly and with a clean desk, but crowded with filing
cabinets and with its walls hung with musical instruments.

Most of these were ones I had never seen before,
although they were all variants on string or wind
music-makers. There was one that looked like an early
Scottish bagpipe. It had only a single drone, some sev-
enty centimeters long, and a chanter about half that
length. Another was obviously a keyed bugle of some
sort, but with most of its central body length wrapped

with red cord ending in dependent tassels. I moved about the walls, examining each as I came to it, while Ian took a chair and watched me. I came back at length to the deprived bagpipe.

"Can you play this?" I asked Ian.

"I'm not a piper," said Ian. "I can blow a bit, of course—but I've never played anything but regular highland pipes. You'd better ask Michael if you want a demonstration. Apparently, he plays everything— and plays it well."

I turned away from the walls and took a seat myself.

"What do you think?" asked Ian. I was gazing around the office.

I looked back at him and saw his gaze curiously upon me.

"It's . . . strange," I said.

And the room was strange, for reasons that would probably never strike someone not a Dorsai. No two people keep an office the same way; but just as there are subtle characteristics by which one born to the Dorsai will recognize another, so there are small signals about the office of anyone on military duty and from that world. I could tell at a glance, as could Ian or any one of us, if the officer into whose room we had just stepped was Dorsai or not. The clues lie, not so much with what was in the room, as in the way the things there and the room itself was arranged. There is nothing particular to Dorsai-born individuals about such a recognition. Almost any veteran officer is able to tell you whether the owner of the office he has just stepped into is also a veteran officer, Dorsai or not. But in that case, as in this, it would be easier to give the answer than to list the reasons why the answer was what it was.

So, Michael de Sandoval's office was unmistakably the office of a Dorsai. At the same time it owned a strange difference from any other Dorsai's office, that almost shouted at us. The difference was a basic one, underneath any comparison of this place with the office of a Dorsai who had his walls hung with weapons, or with one who kept a severely clean desktop and message baskets, and preferred no weapon in sight.

"He's got these musical instruments displayed as if they were fighting tools," I said.

Ian nodded. It was not necessary to put the implication into words. If Michael had chosen to hang a banner from one of the walls testifying to the fact that he would absolutely refuse to lay his hands upon a weapon, he could not have announced himself more plainly to Ian and myself.

"It seems to be a strong point with him," I said. "I wonder what happened?"

"His business, of course," said Ian.

"Yes," I said.

But the discovery hurt me—because suddenly I identified what I had felt in young Michael from the first moment I had met him, here on Ceta. It was pain, a deep and abiding pain; and you cannot have known someone since he was in childhood and not be moved by that sort of pain.

The orderly stuck his head into the room.

"Sirs," he said, "the Bandmaster comes. He'll be here in one minute."

"Thank you," said Ian.

A moment later, Michael came in.

"Sorry to keep you waiting—" he began.

"Perfectly all right," Ian said. "The Conde made

you wait yourself before letting you speak with him, didn't he?"

"Yes sir."

"Well, is he available now, to be met by me and Captain El Man?"

"Yes sir. You're both most welcome."

"Good."

Ian stood up and so did I. We went out, followed by Michael to the door of his office.

"Amanda Morgan is seeing the Governors, at the moment," Ian said to him as we left him. "She may want to talk to you after that's over. You might keep yourself available for her."

"I'll be right here," said Michael. "Sir—I wanted to apologize for my orderly's making excuses about my not being here when you came—" he glanced over at the orderly who was looking embarrassed. "My men have been told not to—"

"It's all right, Michael," said Ian. "You'd be an unusual Dorsai if they didn't try to protect you."

"Still—" said Michael.

"Still," said Ian. "I know they've trained only as bandmen. They may be line troops at the moment— all the line troops we've got to hold this place with— but I'm not expecting miracles."

"Well," said Michael. "Thank you, Commander."

"You're welcome."

We went out. Once more Ian led me through a maze of corridors and lifts.

"How many of his band decided to stay with him when the regiments moved out?" I asked as we went.

"All of them," said Ian.

"And no one else stayed?"

Ian looked at me with a glint of humor.

"You have to remember," he said, "Michael did graduate from the Academy, after all."

A final short distance down a wide corridor brought us to a massive pair of double doors. Ian touched a visitor's button on the right-hand door and spoke to an annunciator panel in Spanish.

"Commander Ian Graeme and Captain El Man are here with permission to see the Conde."

There was the pause of a moment and then one of the doors opened to show us another of Michael's bandsmen.

"Be pleased to come in, sirs," he said.

"Thank you," Ian said as we walked past. "Where's the Conde's majordomo?"

"He is gone, sir. Also most of the other servants."

"I see."

The room we had just been let into was a wide lobby filled with enormous and magnificently-kept furniture but lacking any windows. The bandman led us through two more rooms like it, also without windows, until we were finally ushered into a third and finally window-walled room, with the same unchanging view of the plains below. A stick-thin old man dressed in black was standing with the help of a silver-headed cane, before the center of the window area.

The soldier faded out of the room. Ian led me to the old man.

"El Conde," he said, still in Spanish, "may I introduce Captain Corunna El Man. Captain, you have the honor of meeting El Conde de Nahar, Macias Francisco Ramón Manuel Valentin y Compostela y Abente."

"You are welcome, Captain El Man," said the Con-

de. He spoke a more correct, if more archaic, Spanish than that of the other Naharese I had so far met; and his voice was the thin remnant of what once must have been a remarkable bass. "We will sit down now, if you please. If my age produces a weakness, it is that it is wearisome to stand for any length of time."

We settled ourselves in heavy, overstuffed chairs with massively padded arms—more like thrones than chairs.

"Captain El Man," said Ian, "happened to be on leave, back on the Dorsai. He volunteered to bring Amanda Morgan here to discuss the present situation with the Governors. She's talking to them now."

"I have not met. . ." the Conde hesitated over her name, "Amanda Morgan."

"She is one of our experts of the sort that the present situation calls for."

"I would like to meet her."

"She's looking forward to meeting you."

"Possibly this evening? I would have liked to have had all of you to dinner, but you know, I suppose, that most of my servants have gone."

"I just learned that," said Ian.

"They may go," said the Conde. "They will not be allowed to return. Nor will the regiments who have deserted their duty be allowed to return to my armed forces."

"With the Conde's indulgence," said Ian, "we don't yet know all the reasons for their leaving. It may be that some leniency is justified."

"I can think of none." The Conde's voice was thin with age, but his back was as erect as a flagstaff and his dark eyes did not waver. "But, if you think there is some reason for it, I can reserve judgment momentarily."

"We'd appreciate that," Ian said.

"You are very lenient." The Conde looked at me. His voice took on an unexpected timbre. "Captain, has the Commander here told you? Those deserters out there—" he flicked a finger toward the window and the plains beyond, "under the instigation of people calling themselves revolutionaries, have threatened to take over Gebel Nahar. If they dare to come here, I and what few loyal servants remain will resist. To the death!"

"The Governors—" Ian began.

"The Governors have nothing to say in the matter!" the Conde turned fiercely on him. "Once, they—their fathers and grandfathers, rather—chose my father to be El Conde. I inherited that title and neither they, nor anyone else in the universe has the authority to take it from me. While I live, I will be El Conde; and the only way I will cease to be El Conde will be when death takes me. I will remain, I will fight—alone if need be —as long as I am able. But I will retreat, never! I will compromise, *never!*"

He continued to talk, for some minutes; but although his words changed, the message of them remained the same. He would not give an inch to anyone who wished to change the governmental system in Nahar. If he had been obviously uninformed or ignorant of the implications of what he was saying, it would have been easy to let his words blow by unheeded. But this was obviously not the case. His frailty was all in the thin old body. His mind was not only clear but fully aware of the situation. What he announced was simply an unshakable determination never to yield in spite of reason or the overwhelming odds against him.

After a while he ran down. He apologized graciously for his emotion, but not for his attitude; and, after a few minutes more of meaninglessly polite conversation on the history of Gebel Nahar itself, let us leave.

"So you see part of our problem," said Ian to me when we were alone again, walking back to his offices.

We went a little distance together in silence.

"Part of that problem," I said, "seems to lie in the difference between our idea of honor, and theirs, here."

"And William's complete lack of it," said Ian. "You're right. With us, honor's a matter of the individual's obligation to himself and his community —which can end up being to the human race in general. To the Naharese, honor's an obligation only to their own soul."

I laughed, involuntarily.

"I'm sorry," I said, as he looked at me. "But you hit it almost too closely. Did you ever read Calderon's poem about the Mayor of Zalamea?"

"I don't think so. Calderon?"

"Pedro Calderon de la Barca, seventeenth century Spanish poet. He wrote a poem called *El Alcalde de Zalamea*."

I gave him the lines he had reminded me of.

> *Al Rey la hacienda y la vida*
> *Se ha de dar; pero el honor*
> *Es patrimonio del alma*
> *Y el alma soló es de Dios.*

" '—*Fortune and life we owe to the King*,' " murmured

Ian, " *'but honor is patrimony of the soul and the soul belongs to God alone.'* I see what you mean."

I started to say something, then decided it was too much effort. I was aware of Ian glancing sideways at me as we went.

"When did you eat last?" he asked.

"I don't remember," I said. "But I don't particularly need food right now."

"You need sleep, then," said Ian, "I'm not surprised, after the way you made it here from the Dorsai. When we get back to the office, I'll call one of Michael's men to show you your quarters, and you'd better sleep in. I can make your excuses to the Conde if he still wants us all to get together tonight."

"Yes. Good," I said. "I'd appreciate that."

Now that I had admitted to tiredness, it was an effort even to think. For those who have never navigated between the stars, it is easy to forget the implications in the fact that the danger increases rapidly with the distance moved in a single shift—beyond a certain safe amount of light-years. We had exceeded safe limits as far as I had dared push them on each of the six shifts that had brought Amanda and myself to Ceta.

It's not just that danger—the danger of finding yourself with so large an error in destination that you cannot recognize any familiar star patterns from which to navigate. It is the fact that even when you emerge in known space, a large error factor requires infinitely more recalculation to locate your position. It is vital to locate yourself to a fine enough point so that your error on the next shift will not be compounded and you will find yourself lost beyond repair.

For three days I had had no more than catnaps be-

tween periods of calculation. I was numb with a fatigue I had held at bay until this moment with the body adrenalin that can be evoked to meet an emergency situation.

When the bandsman supplied by Ian had shown me at last to a suite of rooms, I found I wanted nothing more than to collapse on the enormous bed in the bedroom. But years of instinct made me prowl the quarters first and check them out. My suite consisted of three rooms and bathroom; and it had the inevitable plains-facing window wall—with one difference. This one had a door in it to let me out onto a small balcony that ran the length of this particular level. It was divided into a semi-private outdoor area for each suite by tall plants in pots which acted as screens at each division point.

I checked the balcony area and the suite, locked the doors to the hall and to the balcony, and slept.

It was sometime after dark when I awoke, suddenly. I was awake and sitting up on the edge of the bed in one reflex movement before it registered that what had roused me had been the sound of the call chime at the front door of my suite.

I reached over and keyed on the annunciator circuit. "Yes?" I said. "Who is it?"

"Michael de Sandoval," said Michael's voice, "can I come in?"

I touched the stud that unlocked the door. It swung open, letting a knife-blade sharp swath of light from the corridor into the darkness of my sitting room, as seen through the entrance from my bedroom. I was up on my feet now, and moving to meet him in the sitting room. He entered and the door closed behind him.

"What is it?" I asked.

"The ventilating system is out on this level," he said; and I realized that the air in the suite was now perfectly motionless—motionless and beginning to be a little warm and stuffy. Evidently Gebel Nahar had been designed to be sealed against outside atmosphere.

"I wanted to check the quarters of everyone on this level," Michael said. "Interior doors aren't so tight that you would have asphyxiated; but the breathing could have got a little heavy. Maybe by morning we can locate what's out of order and fix it. This is part of the problem of the servant staff taking off when the army did. I'd suggest that I open the door to the balcony for you, sir."

He was already moving across the room toward the door he had mentioned.

"Thanks," I said. "What was the situation with the servants? Were they revolutionary sympathizers, too?"

"Not necessarily." He unlocked the door and propped it open to the night air, which came coolly and sweetly through the aperture. "They just didn't want their throats cut along with the Conde's, when the army stormed its way back in here."

"I see," I said.

"Yes." He came back to me in the center of the sitting room.

"What time is it?" I asked. "I've been sleeping as if I was under drugs."

"A little before midnight."

I sat down in one of the chairs of the unlighted lounge. The glow of the soft exterior lights spaced at ten meter intervals along the outer edge of the balcony came through the window wall and dimly illuminated the room.

"Sit for a moment," I said. "Tell me. How did the meeting with the Conde go this evening?"

He took a chair facing me.

"I should be getting back soon," he said. "I'm the only one we've got available for a duty officer at the moment. But—the meeting with the Conde went like a charm. He was so busy being gracious to Amanda he almost forgot to breathe defiance against the army deserters."

"How did Amanda do with the Governors, do you know?"

70

I sensed, rather than saw, a shrug of his shoulders in the gloom.

"There was nothing much to be done with them," he said. "They talked about their concern over the desertion of the regiments and wanted reassurances that Ian and Kensie could handle the situation. Effectively, it was all choreographed."

"They've left, then?"

"That's right. They asked for guarantees for the safety of the Conde. Both Ian and Kensie told them that there was no such thing as a guarantee; but we'd protect the Conde, of course, with every means at our disposal. Then they left."

"It sounds," I said, "as if Amanda could have saved her time and effort."

"No. She said she wanted to get the feel of them." He leaned forward. "You know, she's something to write home about. I think if anyone can find a way out of this, she can. She says herself that there's no question that there is a way out—it's just that finding it in the next twenty-four to thirty-six hours is asking a lot."

"Has she checked with you about these people? You seem to be the only one around who knows them at all well."

"She talked with me when we flew in—you remember. I told her I'd be available any time she needed me. So far, however, she's spent most of her time either working by herself, or with Ian or Padma."

"I see," I said. "Is there anything I can do? Would you like me to spell you on the duty officer bit?"

"You're to rest, Ian says. He'll need you tomorrow. I'm getting along fine with my duties." He moved toward the front door of the suite. "Good night."

"Good night," I said.

He went out, the knife of light from the corridor briefly cutting across the carpeting of my sitting room and vanishing again as the door opened, then latched behind him.

I stayed where I was in the sitting room chair, enjoying the gentle night breeze through the propped-open door. I may have dozed. At any rate I came to, suddenly, to the sound of voices from the balcony. Not from my portion of the balcony, but from the portion next to it, beyond my bedroom window to the left.

". . . yes," a voice was saying. Ian had been in my mind; and for a second I thought I was hearing Ian speak. But it was Kensie. The voices were identical; only, there was a difference in attitude that distinguished them.

"I don't know. . ." it was Amanda's voice answering, a troubled voice.

"Time goes by quickly," Kensie said. "Look at us. It was just yesterday we were in school together."

"I know," she said, "you're talking about it being time to settle down. But maybe I never will."

"How sure are you of that?"

"Not sure, of course." Her voice changed as if she had moved some little distance from him. I had an unexpected mental image of him standing back by the door in a window wall through which they had just come out together; and one of her, having just turned and walked to the balcony railing, where she now stood with her back to him, looking out at the night and the starlit plain.

"Then you could take the idea of settling down under consideration."

"No," she said. "I know I don't want to do that."

Her voice changed again, as if she had turned and come back to him. "Maybe I'm ghost-ridden, Kensie. Maybe it's the old spirit of the first Amanda that's ruling out the ordinary things for me."

"She married—three times."

"But her husbands weren't important to her, that way. Oh, I know she loved them. I've read her letters and what her children wrote down about her after they were adults themselves. But she really belonged to everyone, not just to her husbands and children. Don't you understand? I think that's the way it's going to have to be for me, too."

He said nothing. After a long moment she spoke again, and her voice was lowered, and drastically altered.

"Kensie! Is it that important?"

His voice was lightly humorous, but the words came a fraction more slowly than they had before.

"It seems to be."

"But it's something we both just fell into, as children. It was just an assumption on both our parts. Since then, we've grown up. You've changed. I've changed."

"Yes."

"You don't need me. Kensie, you don't need *me*—" her voice was soft. "Everybody loves you."

"Could I trade?" The humorous tone persisted. "Everybody for you?"

"Kensie, don't!"

"You ask a lot," he said; and now the humor was gone, but there was still nothing in the way he spoke that reproached her. "I'd probably find it easier to

74

stop breathing."

There was another silence.

"Why can't you see? I don't have any other choice," she said. "I don't have any more choice than you do. We're both what we are, and stuck with what we are."

"Yes," he said.

The silence this time lasted a long time. But they did not move, either of them. By this time my ear was sensitized to sounds as light as the breathing of a sparrow. They had been standing a little apart, and they stayed standing apart.

"Yes," he said again, finally—and this time it was a long, slow *yes,* a tired *yes.* "Life moves. And all of us move with it, whether we like it or not."

She moved to him, now. I heard her steps on the concrete floor of the balcony.

"You're exhausted," she said. "You and Ian both. Get some rest before tomorrow. Things'll look different in the daylight."

"That sometimes happens." The touch of humor was back, but there was effort behind it. "Not that I believe it for a moment, in this case."

They went back inside.

I sat where I was, wide awake. There had been no way for me to get up and get away from their conversation without letting them know I was there. Their hearing was at least as good as mine, and like me they had been trained to keep their senses always alert. But knowing all that did not help. I still had the ugly feeling that I had been intruding where I should not have been.

There was no point in moving now. I sat where I was, trying to talk sense to myself and get the ugly

feeling under control. I was so concerned with my own feelings that for once I did not pay close attention to the sounds around me, and the first warning I had was a small noise in my own entrance to the balcony area; and I looked up to see the dark silhouette of a woman in the doorway.

"You heard," Amanda's voice said.

There was no point in denying it.

"Yes," I told her.

She stayed where she was, standing in the doorway.

"I happened to be sitting here when you came out on the balcony," I said. "There was no chance to shut the door or move away."

"It's all right," she came in. "No, don't turn on the light."

I dropped the hand I had lifted toward the control studs in the arm of my chair. With the illumination from the balcony behind her, she could see me better than I could see her. She sat down in the chair Michael had occupied a short while before.

"I told myself I'd step over and see if you were sleeping all right," she said. "Ian has a lot of work in mind for you tomorrow. But I think I was really hoping to find you awake."

Even through the darkness, the signals came loud and clear. My geas was at work again.

"I don't want to intrude," I said.

"If I reach out and haul you in by the scruff of the neck, are you intruding?" Her voice had the same sort of lightness overlying pain that I had heard in Kensie's. "I'm the one who's thinking of intruding—of intruding my problems on you."

"That's not necessarily an intrusion," I said.

"I hoped you'd feel that way," she said. It was strange to have her voice coming in such everyday tones from a silhouette of darkness. "I wouldn't bother you, but I need to have all my mind on what I'm doing here and personal matters have ended up getting in the way."

She paused.

"You don't really mind people spilling all over you, do you?" she said.

"No," I said.

"I thought so. I got the feeling you wouldn't. Do you think of Else much?"

"When other things aren't on my mind."

"I wish I'd known her."

"She was someone to know."

"Yes. Knowing someone else is what makes the difference. The trouble is, often we don't know. Or we don't know until too late." She paused. "I suppose you think, after what you heard just now, that I'm talking about Kensie?"

"Aren't you?"

"No. Kensie and Ian—the Graemes are so close to us Morgans that we might as well all be related. You don't usually fall in love with a relative—or you don't think you will, at least, when you're young. The kind of person you imagine falling in love with is someone strange and exciting—someone from fifty light years away."

"I don't know about that," I said. "Else was a neighbor and I think I grew up being in love with her."

"I'm sorry." Her silhouette shifted a little in the darkness. "I'm really just talking about myself. But I know what you mean. In sober moments, when I was younger, I more or less just assumed that some day I'd wind up with Kensie. You'd have to have something wrong with you not to want someone like him."

"And you've got something wrong with you?" I said.

"Yes," she said. "That's it. I grew up, that's the trouble."

"Everybody does."

"I don't mean I grew up, physically. I mean, I matured. We live a long time, we Morgans, and I suppose we're slower growing up than most. But you know how it is with young anythings—young animals as well as young humans. Did you ever have a wild animal as a pet as a child?"

"Several," I said.

"Then you've run into what I'm talking about. While the wild animal's young, it's cuddly and tame; but when it grows up, the day comes it bites or slashes at you without warning. People talk about that being part of their wild nature. But it isn't. Humans change just exactly the same way. When anything young grows up, it becomes conscious of itself, its own wants, its own desires, its own moods. Then the day comes when someone tries to play with it and it isn't in a playing mood—and it reacts with *'Back off! What I want is just as important as what you want!'* And all at once, the time of its being young and cuddly is over forever."

"Of course," I said. "That happens to all of us."

"But to us—to our people—it happens too late!" she said. "Or rather, we start life too early. By the age of seventeen on the Dorsai we have to be out and working like an adult, either at home or on some other world. We're pitchforked into adulthood. There's never any time to take stock, to realize what being adult is going to turn us into. We don't realize we aren't cubs any more until one day we slash or bite someone without warning; and then we realize that we've changed —and they've changed. But it's too late for us to adjust to the change in the other person because we've already been trapped by our own change."

She stopped. I sat, not speaking, waiting. From my experience with this sort of thing since Else died, I assumed that I no longer needed to talk. She would carry the conversation, now.

"No, it wasn't Kensie I was talking about when I first came in here and I said the trouble is you don't know someone else until too late. It's Ian."

"Ian?" I said, for she had stopped again, and now I felt with equal instinct that she needed some help to continue.

"Yes," she said. "When I was young, I didn't understand Ian. I do now. Then, I thought there was nothing to him—or else he was simply solid all the way through, like a piece of wood. But he's not. Everything you can see in Kensie is there in Ian, only there's no light to see it by. Now I know. And now it's too late."

"Too late?" I said. "He's not married, is he?"

"Married? Not yet. But you didn't know? Look at

the picture on his desk. Her name's Leah. She's on Earth. He met her when he was there, four years ago. But that's not what I mean by too late. I mean—it's too late for me. What you heard me tell Kensie is the truth. I've got the curse of the first Amanda. I'm born to belong to a lot of people, first; and only to any single person, second. As much as I'd give for Ian, that equation's there in me, ever since I grew up. Sooner or later it'd put even him in second place for me. I can't do that to him; and it's too late for me to be anything else."

"Maybe Ian'd be willing to agree to those terms."

She did not answer for a second. Then I heard a slow intake of breath from the darker darkness that was her.

"You shouldn't say that," she said.

There was a second of silence. Then she spoke again, fiercely.

"Would you suggest something like that to Ian if our positions were reversed?"

"I didn't suggest it," I said. "I mentioned it."

Another pause.

"You're right," she said. "I know what I want and what I'm afraid of in myself, and it seems to me so obvious I keep thinking everyone else must know too."

She stood up.

"Forgive me, Corunna," she said. "I've got no right to burden you with all this."

"It's the way the world is," I said. "People talk to people."

"And to you, more than most." She went toward the door to the balcony and paused in it. "Thanks again."

"I've done nothing," I said.

"Thank you anyway. Good night. Sleep if you can."

She stepped out through the door; and through the window wall I watched her, very erect, pass to my left until she walked out of my sight beyond the sitting room wall.

I went back to bed, not really expecting to fall asleep again easily. But I dropped off and slept like a log.

When I woke it was morning, and my bedside phone was chiming. I flicked it on and Michael looked at me out of the screen.

"I'm sending a man up with maps of the interior of Gebel Nahar," he said, "so you can find your way around. Breakfast's available in the General Staff Lounge, if you're ready."

"Thanks," I told him.

I got up and was ready when the bandsman he had sent arrived, with a small display cube holding the maps. I took it with me and the bandsman showed me to the General Staff Lounge—which, it turned out, was not a lounge for the staff of Gebel Nahar, in general, but one for the military commanders of that establishment. Ian was the only other present when I got there and he was just finishing his meal.

"Sit down," he said.

I sat.

"I'm going ahead on the assumption that I'll be defending this place in twenty-four hours or so," he said. "What I'd like you to do is familiarize yourself with its defenses, particularly the first line of walls and its weapons, so that you can either direct the men working them, or take over the general defense, if necessary."

"What have you got in mind for a general defense?"

I asked, as a bandsman came out of the kitchen area to see what I would eat. I told him and he went.

"We've got just about enough of Michael's troops to man that first wall and have a handful in reserve," he said. "Most of them have never touched anything but a handweapon in their life, but we've got to use them to fight with the emplaced energy weapons against foot attack up the slope. I'd like you to get them on the weapons and drill them—Michael should be able to help you, since he knows which of them are steady and which aren't. Get breakfast in you; and I'll tell you what I expect the regiments to do on the attack and what I think we might do when they try it."

He went on talking while my food came and I ate. Boiled down, his expectations—based on what he had learned of the Naharese military while he had been here, and from consultation with Michael—were for a series of infantry wave attacks up the slope until the first wall was overrun. His plan called for a defense of the first wall until the last safe moment, destruction of the emplaced weapons, so they could not be turned against us, and a quick retreat to the second wall with its weapons—and so, step by step retreating up the terraces. It was essentially the sort of defense that Gebel Nahar had been designed for by its builders.

The problem would be getting absolutely green and excitable troops like the Naharese bandsmen to retreat cool-headedly on order. If they could not be brought to do that, and lingered behind, then the first wave over the ramparts could reduce their numbers to the point where there would not be enough of them to make any worthwhile defense of the second terrace, to say nothing of the third, the fourth, and so on, and still

have men left for a final stand within the fortress-like walls of the top three levels.

Given an equal number of veteran, properly trained troops, to say nothing of Dorsai-trained ones, we might even have held Gebel Nahar in that fashion and inflicted enough casualties on the attackers to eventually make them pull back. But unspoken between Ian and myself as we sat in the lounge, was the fact that the most we could hope to do with what we had was inflict a maximum of damage while losing.

However, again unspoken between us, was the fact that the stiffer our defense of Gebel Nahar, even in a hopeless situation, the more difficult it would be for the Governors and William to charge the Dorsai officers with incompetence of defense.

I finished eating and got up to go.

"Where's Amanda?" I asked.

"She's working with Padma—or maybe I should put it that Padma's working with her," Ian said.

"I didn't know Exotics took sides."

"He isn't," Ian said. "He's just making knowledge —his knowledge—available to someone who needs it. That's standard Exotic practice as you know as well as I do. He and Amanda are still hunting some political angle to bring us and the Dorsai out of this without prejudice."

"What do you really think their chances are?"

Ian shook his head.

"But," he said, shuffling together the papers he had spread out before him on the lounge table, "of course, where they're looking is away out, beyond the areas of strategy I know. We can hope."

"Did you ever stop to think that possibly Michael,

with his knowledge of these Naharese, could give them some insights they wouldn't otherwise have?" I asked.

"Yes," he said. "I told them both that; and told Michael to make himself available to them if they thought they could use him. So far, I don't think they have."

He got up, holding his papers and we went out; I to the band quarters and Michael's office, he to his own office and the overall job of organizing our supplies and everything else necessary for the defense.

Michael was not in his office. The orderly directed me to the first wall, where I found him already drilling his men on the emplaced weapons there. I worked with him for most of the morning; and then we stopped, not because there was not a lot more practice needed, but because his untrained troops were exhausted and beginning to make mistakes simply out of fatigue.

Michael sent them to lunch. He and I went back to his office and had sandwiches and coffee brought in by his orderly.

"What about this?" I asked, after we were done, getting up and going to the wall where the archaic-looking bagpipe hung. "I asked Ian about it. But he said he'd only played highland pipes and that if I wanted a demonstration, I should ask you."

Michael looked up from his seat behind his desk, and grinned. The drill on the guns seemed to have done something for him in a way he was not really aware of himself. He looked younger and more cheerful than I had yet seen him; and obviously he enjoyed any attention given to his instruments.

"That's a *gaita gallega*," he said. "Or, to be correct, it's a local imitation of the gaita gallega you can still find occasionally being made and played in the province of Galicia in Spain, back on Earth. It's a perfectly playable instrument to anyone who's familiar with the highland pipes. Ian could have played it—I'd guess he just thought I might prefer to show it off myself."

"He seemed to think you could play it better," I said.

"Well. . ." Michael grinned again. "Perhaps, a bit."

He got up and came over to the wall with me.

"Do you really want to hear it?" he asked.

"Yes, I do."

He took it down from the wall.

"We'll have to step outside," he said. "It's not the sort of instrument to be played in a small room like this."

We went back out on to the first terrace by the deserted weapon emplacements. He swung the pipe up in his arms, the long single drone with its fringe tied at the two ends of the drone, resting on his left shoulder and pointing up into the air behind him. He took the mouthpiece between his lips and laid his fingers across the holes of the chanter. Then he blew up the bag and began to play.

The music of the pipes is like Dorsai whiskey. People either cannot stand it, or they feel that there's nothing comparable. I happen to be one of those who love the sound—for no good reason, I would have said until that trip to Gebel Nahar; since my own heritage is Spanish rather than Scottish and I had never before realized that it was also a Spanish instrument.

Michael played something Scottish and standard— *The Flowers of the Forest*, I think—pacing slowly up and down as he played. Then, abruptly he swung around

and stepped out, almost strutted, in fact; and played something entirely different.

I wish there were words in me to describe it. It was anything but Scottish. It was hispanic, right down to its backbones—a wild, barbaric, musically ornate challenge of some sort that heated the blood in my veins and threatened to raise the hair on the back of my neck.

He finished at last with a sort of dying wail as he swung the deflating bag down from his shoulder. His face was not young any more, it was changed. He looked drawn and old.

"What was that?" I demanded.

"It's got a polite name for polite company," he said. "But nobody uses it. The Naharese call it *Su Madre.*"

"Your Mother?" I echoed. Then, of course, it hit me. The Spanish language has a number of elaborate and poetically insulting curses to throw at your enemy about his ancestry; and the words *su madre* are found in most of them.

"Yes," said Michael. "It's what you play when you're daring the enemy to come out and fight. It accuses him of being less than a man in all the senses of that phrase—and the Naharese love it."

He sat down on the rampart of the terrace, suddenly, like someone very tired and discouraged by a long and hopeless effort, resting the gaita gallega on his knees.

"And they like me," he said, staring blindly at the wall of the barrack area, behind me. "My bandsmen, my regiment—they like me."

"There're always exceptions," I said, watching him. "But usually the men who serve under them like their Dorsai officers."

LOST DORSAI

"That's not what I mean." He was still staring at
the wall. "I've made no secret here of the fact I won't
touch a weapon. They all knew it from the day I signed
on as bandmaster."

"I see," I said. "So that's it."

He looked up at me, abruptly.

"Do you know how they react to cowards—as they
consider them—people who are able to fight but
won't, in this particular crazy splinter culture? They
encourage them to get off the face of the earth. They
show their manhood by knocking cowards around
here. But they don't touch me. They don't even challenge me to duels."

"Because they don't believe you," I said.

"That's it." His face was almost savage. "They
don't. Why won't they believe me?"

"Because you only *say* you won't use a weapon," I
told him bluntly. "In every other language you speak,
everything you say or do, you broadcast just the opposite information. That tells them that not only can
you use a weapon, but that you're so good at it none of
them who'd challenge you would stand a chance. You
could not only defeat someone like that, you could
make him look foolish in the process. And no one
wants to look foolish, particularly a macho-minded individual. That message is in the very way you walk
and talk. How else could it be, with you?"

"That's not true!" he got suddenly to his feet, holding the gaita. "I live what I believe in. I have, ever
since—"

He stopped.

"Maybe we'd better get back to work," I said, as
gently as I could.

"No!" The word burst out of him. "I want to tell someone. The oods are we're not going to be around after this. I want someone to. . ."

He broke off. He had been about to say "someone to understand. . ." and he had not been able to get the words out. But I could not help him. As I've said, since Else's death, I've grown accustomed to listening to people. But there is something in me that tells me when to speak and when not to help them with what they wish to say. And now I was being held silent.

He struggled with himself for a few seconds, and then calm seemed to flow over him.

"No," he said, as if talking to himself, "what people think doesn't matter. We're not likely to live through this, and I want to know how you react."

He looked at me.

"That's why I've got to explain it to someone like you," he said. "I've got to know how they'd take it, back home, if I'd explained it to them. And your family is the same as mine, from the same canton, the same neighborhood, the same sort of ancestry. . ."

"Did it occur to you you might not owe anyone an explanation?" I said. "When your parents raised you, they only paid back the debt they owed their parents for raising them. If you've got any obligation to anyone —and even that's a moot point, since the idea behind our world is that it's a planet of free people—it's to the Dorsai in general, to bring in interstellar exchange credits by finding work off-planet. And you've done that by becoming bandmaster here. Anything beyond that's your own private business."

It was quite true. The vital currency between worlds was not wealth, as every schoolchild knows, but the exchange of interplanetary work credits. The inhabited worlds trade special skills and knowledges, packaged in human individuals; and the exchange credits earned by a Dorsai on Newton enables the Dorsai to hire a geophysicist from Newton—or a physician from Kultis. In addition to his personal pay, Michael had been earning exchange credits ever since he had come here. True, he might have earned these at a higher rate if he had chosen work as a mercenary combat officer; but the exchange credits he did earn as bandmaster more than justified the expense of his education and training.

"I'm not talking about that—" he began.

"No," I said, "you're talking about a point of obligation and honor not very much removed from the sort of thing these Naharese have tied themselves up with."

He stood for a second, absorbing that. But his mouth was tight and his jaw set.

"What you're telling me," he said at last, "is that you don't want to listen. I'm not surprised."

"Now," I said, "you really are talking like a Naharese. I'll listen to anything you want to say, of course."

"Then sit down," he said.

He gestured to the rampart and sat down himself. I came and perched there, opposite him.

"Do you know I'm a happy man?" he demanded. "I really am. Why not? I've got everything I want. I've got a military job, I'm in touch with all the things that I grew up feeling made the kind of life one of my family ought to have. I'm one of a kind. I'm better at what I do and everything connected with it than anyone else

they can find—and I've got my other love, which was music, as my main duty. My men like me, my regiment is proud of me. My superiors like me."

I nodded.

"But then there's this other part. . ." His hands closed on the bag of the gaita, and there was a faint sound from the drone.

"Your refusal to fight?"

"Yes." He got up from the ramparts and began to pace back and forth, holding the instrument, talking a little jerkily. "This feeling against hurting anything . . . I had it, too, just as long as I had the other—all the dreams I made up as a boy from the stories the older people in the family told me. When I was young it didn't seem to matter to me that the feeling and the dreams hit head on. It just always happened that, in my own personal visions the battles I won were always bloodless, the victories always came with no one getting hurt. I didn't worry about any conflict in me, then. I thought it was something that would take care of itself later, as I grew up. You don't kill anyone when you're going through the Academy, of course. You know as well as I do that the better you are, the less of a danger you are to your fellow-students. But what was in me didn't change. It was there with me all the time, not changing."

"No normal person likes the actual fighting and killing," I said. "What sets us Dorsai off in a class by ourselves is the fact that most of the time we *can* win bloodlessly, where someone else would have dead bodies piled all over the place. Our way justifies itself to our employers by saving them money; but it also gets us away from the essential brutality of combat and keeps us human. No good officer pins medals on himself in proportion to the people he kills and wounds. Remember what Cletus says about that? He hated what you hate, just as much."

"But he could do it when he had to," Michael stopped and looked at me with a face, the skin of which was drawn tight over the bones. "So can you, now. Or Ian. Or Kensie."

That was true, of course. I could not deny it.

"You see," said Michael, "that's the difference between out on the worlds and back at the Academy. In life, sooner or later, you get to the killing part. Sooner or later, if you live by the sword, you kill with the sword. When I graduated and had to face going out to the worlds as a fighting officer, I finally had to make that decision. And so I did. I can't hurt anyone. I won't hurt anyone—even to save my own life, I think. But at the same time I'm a soldier and nothing else. I'm bred and born a soldier. I don't want any other life, I can't conceive of any other life; and I love it."

He broke off, abruptly. For a long moment he stood, staring out over the plains at the distant flashes of light from the camp of the deserted regiments.

"Well, there it is," he said.

"Yes," I said.

He turned to look at me.

"Will you tell my family that?" he asked. "If you should get home and I don't?"

"If it comes to that, I will," I said. "But we're a long way from being dead, yet."

He grinned, unexpectedly, a sad grin.

"I know," he said. "It's just that I've had this on my conscience for a long time. You don't mind?"

"Of course not."

"Thanks," he said.

He hefted the gaita in his hands as if he had just suddenly remembered that he held it.

"My men will be back out here in about fifteen minutes," he said. "I can carry on with the drilling myself, if you've got other things you want to do."

I looked at him a little narrowly.

"What you're trying to tell me," I said, "is that they'll learn faster if I'm not around."

"Something like that." He laughed. "They're used to me; but you make them self-conscious. They tighten up and keep making the same mistakes over and over again; and then they get into a fury with themselves and do even worse. I don't know if Ian would approve, but I do know these people; and I think I can bring them along faster alone. . ."

"Whatever works," I said. "I'll go and see what else Ian can find for me to do."

I turned and went to the door that would let me back into the interior of Gebel Nahar.

"Thank you again," he called after me. There was a note of relief in his voice that moved me more strongly than I had expected, so that instead of telling him that what I had done in listening to him was nothing at all, I simply waved at him and went inside.

I found my way back to Ian's office, but he was not there. It occurred to me, suddenly, that Kensie, Padma or Amanda might know where he had gone—and they should all be at work in other offices of that same suite.

I went looking, and found Kensie with his desk covered with large scale printouts of terrain maps.

"Ian?" he said. "No, I don't know. But he ought to be back in his office soon. I'll have some work for you tonight, by the way. I want to mine the approach slope. Michael's bandsmen can do the actual work, after they've had some rest from the day; but you and I are going to need to go out first and make a sweep to pick up any observers they've sent from the regiments to camp outside our walls. Then, later, before dawn

I'd like some of us to do a scout of that camp of theirs on the plains and get some hard ideas as to how many of them there are, what they have to attack with, and so on. . ."

"Fine," I said. "I'm all slept up now, myself. Call on me when you want me."

"You could try asking Amanda or Padma if they know where Ian is."

"I was just going to."

Amanda and Padma were in a conference room two doors down from Kensie's office, seated at one end of a long table covered with text printouts and with an activated display screen flat in its top. Amanda was studying the screen and they both looked up as I put my head in the door. But while Padma's eyes were sharp and questioning, Amanda's were abstract, like the eyes of someone refusing to be drawn all the way back from whatever was engrossing her.

"Just a question. . ." I said.

"I'll come," Padma said to me. He turned to Amanda. "You go on."

She went back to her contemplation of the screen without a word. Padma got up and came to me, stepping into the outside room and shutting the door behind him.

"I'm trying to find Ian."

"I don't know where he'd be just now," said Padma. "Around Gebel Nahar somewhere—but saying that's not much help."

"Not at the size of this establishment," I nodded toward the door he had just shut.

"It's getting rather late, isn't it," I asked, "for Amanda to hope to turn up some sort of legal solution?"

"Not necessarily." The outer office we were standing in had its own window wall, and next to that window wall were several of the heavily overstuffed armchairs that were a common article of furniture in the place. "Why don't we sit down there? If he comes in from the corridor, he's got to go through this office, and if he comes out on the terrace of this level, we can see him through the window."

We went over and took chairs.

"It's not exact, actually, to say that there's a legal way of handling this situation that Amanda's looking for. I thought you understood that?"

"Her work is something I don't know a thing about," I told him. "It's a specialty that grew up as we got more and more aware that the people we were making contracts with might have different meanings for the same words, and different notions of implied obligations, than we had. So we've developed people like Amanda, who steep themselves in the differences of attitude and idea we might run into, in the splinter cultures we deal with."

"I know," he said.

"Yes, of course you would, wouldn't you?"

"Not inevitably," he said. "It happens that as an Outbond, I wrestle with pretty much the same sort of problems that Amanda does. My work is with people who aren't Exotics, and my responsibility most of the time is to make sure we understand them—and they us. That's why I say what we have here goes far beyond legal matters."

"For example?" I found myself suddenly curious.

"You might get a better word picture if you said what Amanda is searching for is a *social* solution to the situation."

"I see," I said. "This morning Ian talked about Amanda saying that there always was a solution, but the problem here was to find it in so short a time. Did I hear that correctly—that there's always a solution to a tangle like this?"

"There's always any number of solutions," Padma said. "The problem is to find the one you'd prefer—or maybe just the one you'd accept. Human situations, being human-made, are always mutable at human hands, if you can get to them with the proper pressures before they happen. Once they happen, of course, they become history—"

He smiled at me.

"—And history, so far at least, is something we aren't able to change. But changing what's about to happen simply requires getting to the base of the forces involved in time, with the right sort of pressures exerted in the right directions. What takes time is identifying the forces, finding what pressures are possible and where to apply them."

"And we don't have time."

His smile went.

"No. In fact, you don't."

I looked squarely at him.

"In that case, shouldn't you be thinking of leaving, yourself?" I said. "According to what I gather about these Naharese, once they overrun this place, they're liable to kill anyone they come across here. Aren't you too valuable to Mara to get your throat cut by some battle-drunk soldier?"

"I'd like to think so," he said. "But you see, from our point of view, what's happening here has importances that go entirely beyond the local, or even the planetary situation. Ontogenetics identifies certain individuals as possibly being particularly influential on the history of their time. Ontogenetics, of course, can be wrong—it's been wrong before this. But we think the value of studying such people as closely as possible at certain times is important enough to take priority over everything else."

"Historically influential? Do you mean William?" I said. "Who else—not the Conde? Someone in the revolutionary camp?"

Padma shook his head.

"If we tagged certain individuals publicly as being influential men and women of their historic time, we would only prejudice their actions and the actions of the people who knew them and muddle our own conclusions about them—even if we could be sure that ontogenetics had read their importance rightly; and we can't be sure."

"You don't get out of it that easily," I said. "The fact you're physically here probably means that the individuals you're watching are right here in Gebel

Nahar. I can't believe it's the Conde. His day is over, no matter how things go. That leaves the rest of us. Michael's a possibility, but he's deliberately chosen to bury himself. I know I'm not someone to shape history. Amanda? Kensie and Ian?"

He looked at me a little sadly.

"All of you, one way or another, have a hand in shaping history. But who shapes it largely, and who only a little is something I can't tell you. As I say, ontogenetics isn't that sure. As to whom I may be watching, I watch everyone."

It was a gentle, but impenetrable, shield he opposed me with. I let the matter go. I glanced out the window, but there was no sign of Ian.

"Maybe you can explain how Amanda, or you go about looking for a solution," I said.

"As I said, it's a matter of looking for the base of the existing forces at work—"

"The ranchers—and William?"

He nodded.

"Particularly William—since he's the prime mover. To get the results he wants, William or anyone else has to set up a structure of cause and effect, operating through individuals. So, for anyone else to control the forces already set to work, and bend them to different results, it's necessary to find where William's structure is vulnerable to cross-pressures and arrange for those to operate—again through individuals."

"And Amanda hasn't found a weak point yet?"

"Of course she has. Several." He frowned at me, but with a touch of humor. "I don't have any objection to telling you all this. You don't need to draw me with leading questions."

"Sorry," I said.

"It's all right. As I say, she's already found several. But none that can be implemented between now and sometime tomorrow, if the regiments attack Gebel Nahar then."

I had a strange sensation. As if a gate was slowly but inexorably being closed in my face.

"It seems to me," I said, "the easiest thing to change would be the position of the Conde. If he'd just agree to come to terms with the regiments, the whole thing would collapse."

"Obvious solutions are usually not the easiest," Padma said. "Stop and think. Why do you suppose the Conde would never change his mind?"

"He's a Naharese," I said. "More than that, he's honestly an hispanic. *El honor* forbids that he yield an inch to soldiers who were supposedly loyal to him and now are threatening to destroy him and everything he stands for."

"But tell me," said Padma, watching me. "Even if *el honor* was satisfied, would he want to treat with the rebels?"

I shook my head.

"No," I said. It was something I had recognized before this, but only with the back of my head. As I spoke to Padma now, it was like something emerging from the shadows to stand in the full light of day. "This is the great moment of his life. This is the chance for him to substantiate that paper title of his, to make it real. This way he can prove to himself he is a real aristocrat. He'd give his life—in fact, he can hardly wait to give his life—to win that."

There was a little silence.

"So you see," said Padma. "Go on, then. What other ways do you see a solution being found?"

"Ian and Kensie could void the contract and make the penalty payment. But they won't. Aside from the fact that no responsible officer from our world would risk giving the Dorsai the sort of bad name that could give, under these special circumstances, neither of those two brothers would abandon the Conde as long as he insisted on fighting. It's as impossible for a Dorsai to do that as it is for the Conde to play games with *el honor*. Like him, their whole life has been oriented against any such thing."

"What other ways?"

"I can't think of any," I said. "I'm out of suggestions—which is probably why I was never considered for anything like Amanda's job, in the first place."

"As a matter of fact, there are a number of other possible solutions," Padma said. His voice was soft, almost pedantic. "There's the possibility of bringing counter economic pressure upon William—but there's no time for that. There's also the possibility of bringing social and economic pressure upon the ranchers; and there's the possibility of disrupting the control of the revolutionaries who've come in from outside Nahar to run this rebellion. In each case, none of these solutions are of the kind that can very easily be made to work in the short time we've got."

"In fact, there isn't any such thing as a solution that can be made to work in time, isn't that right?" I said, bluntly.

He shook his head.

"No. Absolutely wrong. If we could stop the clock at this second and take the equivalent of some months to study the situation, we'd undoubtedly find not only one, but several solutions that would abort the attack of the regiments in the time we've got to work with. What you lack isn't time in which to act, since that's merely something specified for the solution. What you lack is time in which to discover the solution that will work in the time there is to act."

"So you mean," I said, "that we're to sit here tomorrow with Michael's forty or so bandsmen—and face the attack of something like six thousand line troops, even though they're only Naharese line troops, all the time knowing that there is absolutely a way in which that attack doesn't have to happen, if only we had the sense to find it?"

"The sense—and the time," said Padma. "But yes, you're right. It's a harsh reality of life, but the sort of reality that history has turned on, since history began."

"I see," I said. "Well, I find I don't accept it that easily."

"No." Padma's gaze was level and cooling upon me. "Neither does Amanda. Neither does Ian or Kensie. Nor, I suspect, even Michael. But then, you're all Dorsai."

I said nothing. It is a little embarrassing when someone plays your own top card against you.

"In any case," Padma went on, "none of you are being called on to merely accept it. Amanda's still at work. So is Ian, so are all the rest of you. Forgive me, I didn't mean to sneer at the reflexes of your culture. I envy you—a great many people envy you—that inability to give in. My point is that the fact that we know there's an answer makes no difference. You'd all be doing the same thing anyway, wouldn't you?"

"True enough," I said—and at that moment we were interrupted.

"Padma?" It was the general office annunciator speaking from the walls around us with Amanda's voice. "Could you give me some help, please?"

Padma got to his feet.

"I've got to go," he said.

He went out. I sat where I was, held by that odd little melancholy that had caught me up—and I think does the same with most Dorsai away from home—at moments all through my life. It is not a serious thing, just a touch of loneliness and sadness and the facing of the fact that life is measured; and there are only so

many things that can be accomplished in it, try how you may.

I was still in this mood when Ian's return to the office suite by the corridor door woke me out of it.

I got up.

"Corunna!" he said, and led the way into his private office. "How's the training going?"

"As you'd expect," I said. "I left Michael alone with them, at his suggestion. He thinks they might learn faster without my presence to distract them."

"Possible," said Ian.

He stepped to the window wall and looked out. My height was not enough to let me look over the edge of the parapet on this terrace and see down to the first where the bandsmen were drilling; but I guessed that his was.

"They don't seem to be doing badly," he said.

He was still on his feet, of course, and I was standing next to his desk. I looked at it now, and found the cube holding the image Amanda had talked about. The woman pictured there was obviously not Dorsai, but there was something not unlike our people about her. She was strong-boned and dark-haired, the hair sweeping down to her shoulders, longer than most Dorsais out in the field would have worn it, but not long according to the styles of Earth.

I looked back at Ian. He had turned away from the window and his contemplation of the drill going on two levels below. But he had stopped, part way in his backturn, and his face was turned toward the wall beyond which Amanda would be working with Padma at this moment. I saw him in three-quarter's face, with the light from the window wall striking that quarter of his features that was averted from me; and I noticed a tiredness about him. Not that it showed anywhere specifically in the lines of his face. He was, as always, like a mountain of granite, untouchable. But something about the way he stood spoke of a fatigue—perhaps a fatigue of the spirit rather than of the body.

"I just heard about Leah, here," I said, nodding at the image cube, speaking to bring him back to the moment.

He turned as if his thoughts had been a long way away.

"Leah? Oh, yes." His own eyes went absently to the cube and away again. "Yes, she's Earth. I'll be going to get her after this is over. We'll be married in two months."

"That soon?" I said. "I hadn't even heard you'd fallen in love."

"Love?" he said. His eyes were still on me, but their attention had gone away again. He spoke more as if to himself than to me. "No, it was years ago I fell in love. . ."

His attention focused, suddenly. He was back with me.

"Sit down," he said, dropping into the chair behind his desk. I sat. "Have you talked to Kensie since breakfast?"

"Just a little while ago, when I was asking around to find you," I said.

"He's got a couple of runs outside the walls he'd like your hand with, tonight after dark's well settled in."

"I know," I said. "He told me about them. A sweep of the slope in front of this place to clear it before laying mines there, and a scout of the regimental camp

for whatever we can learn about them before tomorrow."

"That's right," Ian said.

"Do you have any solid figures on how many there are out there?"

"Regimental rolls," said Ian, "give us a total of a little over five thousand of all ranks. Fifty-two hundred and some. But something like this invariably attracts a number of Naharese who scent personal glory, or at least the chance for personal glory. Then there're perhaps seven or eight hundred honest revolutionaries in Nahar, Padma estimates, individuals who've been working to loosen the grip of the rancher oligarchy for

some time. Plus a hundred or so agents provocateurs
from outside.''

"In something like this, those who aren't trained
soldiers we can probably discount, don't you think?''

Ian nodded.

"How many of the actual soldiers'll have had any actual combat experience?" I asked.

"Combat experience in this part of Ceta," Ian said, "means having been involved in a border clash or two with the armed forces of the surrounding principalities. Maybe one in ten of the line soldiers has had that. On the other hand, every male, particularly in Nahar, has dreamed of a dramatic moment like this."

"So they'll all come on hard with the first attack," I said.

"That's as I see it," said Ian, "and Kensie agrees. I'm glad to hear it's your thought, too. Everyone out there will attack in that first charge, not merely determined to do well, but dreaming of outdoing everyone else around him. If we can throw them back even once, some of them won't come again. And that's the way it ought to go. They won't lose heart as a group. Just each setback will take the heart out of some, and we'll work them down to the hard core that's serious about being willing to die if only they can get over the walls and reach us."

"Yes," I said, "and how many of those do you think there are?"

"That's the problem," said Ian, calmly. "At the very least, there's going to be one in fifty we'll have to kill to stop. Even if half of them are already out by the time we get down to it, that's sixty of them left; and we've got to figure by that time we'll have taken at least thirty percent casualties ourselves—and that's an optimistic figure, considering the fact that these bandsmen are next thing to noncombatants. Man to man, on the kind of hardcore attackers that are going to be making it over the walls, the bandsmen that're left will be lucky to take care of an equal number of attackers. Padma, of course, doesn't exist in our defensive table of personnel. That leaves you, me, Kensie, Michael, and Amanda to handle about thirty bodies. Have you been keeping yourself in condition?"

I grinned.

"That's good," said Ian. "I forgot to figure that scar-face of yours. Be sure to smile like that when they come at you. It ought to slow them down for a couple of seconds at least, and we'll need all the help we can get."

I laughed.

"If Michael doesn't want you, how about working with Kensie for the rest of the afternoon?"

"Fine," I said.

I got up and went out. Kensie looked up from his printouts when he saw me again.

"Find him?" he asked.

"Yes. He suggested you could use me."

"I can. Join me."

We worked together the rest of the afternoon. The so-called large scale terrain maps the Naharese army library provided were hardly more useful than tourist brochures from our point of view. What Kensie needed to know was what the ground was like meter by meter from the front walls on out over perhaps a couple of hundred meters of plain beyond where the slope of the mountain met it. Given that knowledge, it would be possible to make reasonable estimates as to how a foot attack might develop, how many attackers we might be likely to have on a front, and on which parts of that front, because of vegetation, or the footing or the terrain, attackers might be expected to fall behind their fellows during a rush.

The Naharese terrain maps had never been made with such a detailed information of the ground in mind. To correct them, Kensie had spent most of the day before taking telescopic pictures of three-meter square segments of the ground, using the watch cameras built into the ramparts of the first wall. With these pictures as reference, we now proceeded to make notes on blown-up versions of the clumsy Naharese maps.

It took us the rest of the afternoon; but by the time we were finished, we had a fairly good working knowledge of the ground before the Gebel Nahar, from the viewpoint not only of someone storming up it, but from the viewpoint of a defender who might have to cover it on his belly—as Kensie and I would be doing that night. We knocked off, with the job done, finally, about the dinner hour.

In spite of having finished at a reasonable time, we found no one else at dinner but Ian. Michael was still up to his ears in the effort of teaching his bandsmen to be fighting troops; and Amanda was still with Padma, hard at the search for a solution, even at this eleventh hour.

"You'd both probably better get an hour of sleep, if you can spare the time," Ian said to me. "We might be able to pick up an hour or two more of rest just before dawn, but there's no counting on it."

"Yes," said Kensie. "And you might grab some sleep, yourself."

Brother looked at brother. They knew each other so well, they were so complete in their understanding of each other, that neither one bothered to discuss the matter further. It had been discussed silently in that one momentary exchange of glances, and now they were concerned with other things.

As it turned out, I was able to get a full three hours of sleep. It was just after ten o'clock, local time when Kensie and I came out from Gebel Nahar. On the reasonable assumption that the regiments would have watchers keeping an eye on our walls—that same watch Kensie and I were to silence so that the bandsmen could mine the slope—I had guessed we would be doing something like going out over a dark portion of the front wall on a rope. Instead, Michael was to lead us, properly outfitted and with our face

and hands blackened, through some cellarways and along a passage that would let us out into the night a good fifty meters beyond the wall.

"How did you know about this?" I asked, as he took us along the passage. "If there's more secret ways like this, and the regiments know about them—"

"There aren't and they don't," said Michael. We were going almost single file down the concrete-walled tunnel as he answered me. "This is a private escape hatch that's the secret of the Conde, and no one else. His father had it built thirty-eight local years ago. Our Conde called me in to tell me about it when he heard the regiments had deserted."

I nodded. There was plainly a sympathy and a friendship between Michael and the old Conde that I had not had time to ask about. Perhaps it had come of their each being the only one of their kind in Gebel Nahar.

We reached the end of the tunnel and the foot of a short wooden ladder leading up to a circular metal hatch. Michael turned out the light in the tunnel and we were suddenly in absolute darkness. I heard him cranking something well-oiled, for it turned almost noiselessly. Above us the circular hatch lifted slowly to show starlit sky.

"Go ahead," Michael whispered. "Keep your heads

down. The bushes that hide this spot have thorns at the end of their leaves."

We went up; I led, as being the more expendable of the two of us. The thorns did not stab me, although I heard them scratch against the stiff fabric of the black combat overalls I was wearing, as I pushed my way through the bushes, keeping level to the ground. I heard Kensie come up behind me and the faint sound of the hatch being closed behind us. Michael was due to open it again in two hours and fourteen minutes.

Kensie touched my shoulder. I looked and saw his hand held up, to silhouette itself against the stars. He made the hand signal for *move out,* touched me again lightly on the shoulder and disappeared. I turned away and began to move off in the opposite direction, staying close to the ground.

I had forgotten what a sweep like this was like. As with all our people, I had been raised with the idea of being always in effective physical condition. Of course, in itself, this is almost a universal idea nowadays. Most cultures emphasize keeping the physical vehicle in shape so as to be able to deliver the mental skills wherever the market may require them. But, because in our case the conditions of our work are so physically demanding, we have probably placed more emphasis on it. It has become an idea which begins in the cradle and becomes almost an ingrained reflex, like washing or brushing teeth.

This may be one of the reasons we have so many people living to advanced old age; apart from those naturally young for their years like the individuals in Amanda's family. Certainly, I think, it is one of the reasons why we tend to be active into extreme old age, right up to the moment of death. But, with the best efforts possible, even our training does not produce the same results as practice.

Ian had been right to needle me about my condition, gently as he had done it. The best facilities aboard the biggest space warships do not compare to the reality of being out in the field. My choice of work lies between the stars, but there is no denying that those like myself who spend the working years in ships grow rusty in the area of ordinary body skills. Now, at night, out next to the earth on my own, I could feel a sort of self-consciousness of my body. I was too aware of the weight of my flesh and bones, the effort my muscles made, and the awkwardness of the creeping and crawling positions in which I had to cover the ground.

I worked to the right as Kensie was working left, covering the slope segment by segment, clicking off these chunks of Cetan surface in my mind according to the memory pattern in which I had fixed them. It was all sand and gravel and low brush, most with built-in defenses in the form of thorns or burrs. The night wind blew like an invisible current around me in the darkness, cooling me under a sky where no clouds hid the stars.

The light of a moon would have been welcome, but Ceta has none. After about fifteen minutes I came to the first of nine positions that we had marked in my area as possible locations for watchers from the enemy camp. Picking such positions is a matter of simple reasoning. Anyone but the best trained of observers, given the job of watching something like the Gebel Nahar, from which no action is really expected to develop, would find the hours long. Particularly, when the

hours in question are cool nighttime hours out in the
middle of a plain where there is little to occupy the
attention. Under those conditions, the watcher's certainty that he is simply putting in time grows steadily;
and with the animal instinct in him he drifts automatically to the most comfortable or sheltered location
from which to do his watching.

But there was no one at the first of the positions I
came to. I moved on.

It was just about this time that I began to be aware
of a change in the way I was feeling. The exercise, the

126

adjustment of my body to the darkness and the night temperature, had begun to have their effects. I was no longer physically self-conscious. Instead, I was beginning to enjoy the action.

Old habits and reflexes had awakened in me. I flowed over the ground, now, not an intruder in the night of Nahar, but part of it. My eyes had adjusted to the dim illumination of the starlight, and I had the illusion that I was seeing almost as well as I might have in the day.

Just so, with my hearing. What had been a confusion of dark sounds had separated and identified itself as a multitude of different auditory messages. I heard the wind in the bushes without confusing it with the distant noise-making of some small, wild plains animal. I smelled the different and separate odors of the vegetation. Now I was able to hold the small sounds of my own passage—the scuff of my hands and body upon the ground—separate from the other noises that rode the steady stream of the breeze. In the end, I was not only aware of them all, I was aware of being one with them—one of the denizens of the Cetan night.

There was an excitement to it, a feeling of naturalness and rightness in my quiet search through this dim-lit land. I felt not only at home here, but as if in some measure I owned the night. The wind, the scents, the sounds I heard, all entered into me; and I recognized suddenly that I had moved completely beyond an awareness of myself as a physical body separate from what surrounded me. I was pure observer, with the keen involvement that a wild animal feels in the world he moves through. I was disembodied; a pair of eyes, a nose and two ears, sweeping invisibly through the world. I had forgotten Gebel Nahar. I had almost forgotten to think like a human. Almost—for a few moments—I had forgotten Else.

Then a sense of duty came and hauled me back to my obligations. I finished my sweep. There were no observers at all, either at any of the likely positions Kensie and I had picked out or anywhere else in the area I had covered. Unbelievable as it seemed from a military standpoint, the regiments had not even bothered to keep a token watch on us. For a second I wondered if they had never had any intention at all of at-

tacking, as Ian had believed they would; and as everyone else, including the Conde and Michael's bandsmen, had taken for granted.

I returned to the location of the the tunnel-end, and met Kensie there. His hand-signal showed that he had also found his area deserted. There was no reason why Michael's men should not be moved out as soon as possible and put to work laying the mines.

Michael opened the hatch at the scheduled time and we went down the ladder by feel in the darkness. With the hatch once more closed overhead, the light came on again.

"What did you find?" Michael asked, as we stood squinting in the glare.

"Nothing," said Kensie. "It seems they're ignoring us. You've got the mines ready to go?"

"Yes," said Michael. "If it's safe out there, do you want to send the men out by one of the regular gates? I promised the Conde to keep the secret of this tunnel."

"Absolutely," said Kensie. "In any case, the less people who know about this sort of way in and out of a place like Gebel Nahar, the better. Let's go back inside and get things organized."

We went. Back in Kensie's office, we were joined by Amanda, who had temporarily put aside her search for a social solution to the situation. We sat around in a circle and Kensie and I reported on what we had found.

"The thought occurred to me," I said, "that something might have come up to change the mind of the Naharese about attacking here."

Kensie and Ian shook their heads so unanimously

and immediately it was as if they had reacted by instinct. The small hope in the back of my mind flickered and died. Experienced as the two of them were, if they were that certain, there was little room for doubt.

"I haven't waked the men yet," said Michael, "because after that drill on the weapons today they needed all the sleep they could get. I'll call the orderly and tell him to wake them now. We can be outside and at work in half an hour; and except for my rotating them in by groups for food and rest breaks, we can work straight through the night. We ought to have all the mines placed by a little before dawn."

"Good," said Ian.

I sat watching him, and the others. My sensations, outside of having become one with the night, had left my senses keyed to an abnormally sharp pitch. I was feeling now like a wild animal brought into the artificial world of indoors. The lights overhead in the office seemed harshly bright. The air itself was full of alien, mechanical scents, little trace odors carried on the ventilating system of oil and room dust, plus all the human smells that result when our race is cooped up within a structure.

And part of this sensitivity was directed toward the other four people in the room. It seemed to me that I saw, heard and smelled them with an almost painful acuity. I read the way each of them was feeling to a degree I had never been able to, before.

They were all deadly tired—each in his or her own way, very tired, with a personal, inner exhaustion that had finally been exposed by the physical tiredness to which the present situation had brought all of them except me. It seemed what that physical tiredness had

accomplished had been to strip away the polite covering that before had hidden the private exhaustion; and
it was now plain on every one of them.

"...Then there's no reason for the rest of us to
waste any more time," Ian was saying. "Amanda, you
and I'd better dress and equip for that scout of their
camp. Knife and sidearm, only."

His words brought me suddenly out of my separate
awareness.

"You and Amanda?" I said. "I thought it was
Kensie and I, Michael and Amanda who were going to
take a look at the camp?"

"It was," said Ian. "One of the Governors who

came in to talk to us yesterday is on his way in by personal aircraft. He wants to talk to Kensie again, privately—he won't talk to anyone else."

"Some kind of a deal in the offing?"

"Possibly," said Kensie. "We can't count on it, though, so we go ahead. On the other hand we can't ignore the chance. So I'll stay and Ian will go."

"We could do it with three," I said.

"Not as well as it could be done by four," said Ian. "That's a good-sized camp to get into and look over in a hurry. If anyone but Dorsai could be trusted to get in and out without being seen, I'd be glad to take half a dozen more. It's not like most military camps, where there's a single overall headquarters area. We're going to have to check the headquarters of each regiment; and there're six of them."

I nodded.

"You'd better get something to eat, Corunna," Ian went on. "We could be out until dawn."

It was good advice. When I came back from eating, the other three who were to go were already in Ian's office, and outfitted. On his right thigh Michael was wearing a knife—which was after all, more tool than weapon—but he wore no sidearms and I noticed Ian did not object. With her hands and face blacked, wearing the black stocking cap, overalls and boots, Amanda looked taller and more square-shouldered than she had in her daily clothes.

"All right," said Ian. He had the plan of the camp laid out, according to our telescopic observation of it through the rampart watch-cameras, combined with what Michael had been able to tell us of Naharese habits.

"We'll go by field experience," he said. "I'll take two of the six regiments—the two in the center. Michael, because he's more recently from his Academy training and because he knows these people, will take two regiments—the two on the left wing that includes the far left one that was his own Third Regiment. You'll take the Second Regiment, Corunna, and Amanda will take the Fourth. I mention this now in case we don't have a chance to talk outside the camp."

"It's unlucky you and Michael can't take regiments adjoining each other," I said. "That'd give you a chance to work together. You might need that with two regiments apiece to cover."

"Ian needs to see the Fifth Regiment for himself, if possible," Michael said. "That's the Guard Regiment, the one with the best arms. And since my regiment is a traditional enemy of the Guard Regiment, the two have deliberately been separated as far as possible—that's why the Guards are in the middle and my Third's on the wing."

"Anything else? Then we should go," said Ian.

We went out quietly by the same tunnel by which Kensie and I had gone for our sweep of the slope, leaving the hatch propped a little open against our return. Once in the open we spread apart at about a ten meter interval and began to jog toward the lights of the regimental camp, in the distance.

We were a little over an hour coming up on it. We began to hear it when we were still some distance from it. It did not resemble a military camp on the eve of battle half so much as it did a large open-air party.

The camp was laid out in a crescent. The center of each regimental area was made up of the usual

beehive-shaped buildings of blown bubble-plastic that could be erected so easily on the spot. Behind and between the clumpings of these were ordinary tents of all types and sizes. There was noise and steady traffic between these tents and the plastic buildings as well as between the plastic buildings themselves.

We stopped a hundred meters out, opposite the center of the crescent and checked off. We were able to stand talking, quite openly. Even if we had been without our black accoutrements, the general sound and activity going on just before us ensured as much privacy and protection as a wall between us and the camp would have afforded.

"All back here in forty minutes," Ian said.

We checked chronometers and split up, going in. My target, the Second Regiment, was between Ian's two regiments and Michael's Two; and it was a section that had few tents, these seeming to cluster most thickly either toward the center of the camp or out on both wings. I slipped between the first line of buildings, moving from shadow to shadow. It was foolishly easy. Even if I had not already loosened myself up on the scout across the slope before Gebel Nahar, I would have found it easy. It was very clear that even if I had come, not in scouting blacks but wearing ordinary local clothing and obviously mispronouncing the local Spanish accent, I could have strolled freely and openly wherever I wanted. Individuals in all sorts of civilian clothing were intermingled with the uniformed military; and it became plain almost immediately that few of the civilians were known by name and face to the soldiers. Ironically, my night battle dress was the one outfit that would have attracted unwelcome attention

—if they had noticed me.

But there was no danger that they would notice me. Effectively, the people moving between the buildings and among the tents had neither eyes nor ears for what was not directly under their noses. Getting about unseen under such conditions boils down simply to the fact that you move quietly—which means moving all of you in a single rhythm, including your breathing; and that when you stop, you become utterly still—which means being completely relaxed in whatever bodily position you have stopped in.

Breathing is the key to both, of course, as we learn back home in childhood games even before we are school age. Move in rhythm and stop utterly and you can sometimes stand in plain sight of someone who does not expect you to be there, and go unobserved. How many times has everyone had the experience of being looked "right through" by someone who does not expect to see them at a particular place or moment?

So, there was no difficulty in what I had to do; and as I say, my experience on the slope had already keyed me. I fell back into my earlier feeling of being nothing but senses—eyes, ears, and nose, drifting invisibly through the scenes of the Naharese camp. A quick circuit of my area told me all we needed to know about this particular regiment.

Most of the soldiers were between late twenties and early forties in age. Under other conditions this might have meant a force of veterans. In this case, it indicated just the opposite, time-servers who liked the uniform, the relatively easy work, and the authority and freedom of being in the military. I found a few

field energy weapons—light, three-man pieces that were not only out-of-date, but impractical to bring into action in open territory like that before Gebel Nahar. The heavier weapons we had emplaced on the ramparts would be able to take out such as these almost as soon as the rebels could try to put them into action, and long before they could do any real damage to the heavy defensive walls.

The hand weapons varied, ranging from the best of newer energy guns, cone rifles and needle guns—in the hands of the soldiers—to the strangest assortment of ancient and modern hunting tools and slug-throwing sport pieces—carried by those in civilian clothing. I did not see any crossbows or swords; but it would not have surprised me if I had. The civilian and the military hand weapons alike, however, had one thing in common that surprised me, in the light of everything else I saw—they were clean, well-cared for, and handled with respect.

I decided I had found out as much as necessary about this part of the camp. I headed back to the first row of plastic structures and the darkness of the plains beyond, having to detour slightly to avoid a drunken brawl that had spilled out of one of the buildings into the space between it and the next. In fact, there seemed to be a good deal of drinking and drugging going on, although none of those I saw had got themselves to the edge of unconsciousness yet.

It was on this detour that I became conscious of someone quietly moving parallel to me. In this place and time, it was highly unlikely that there was anyone who could do so with any secrecy and skill except one of us who had come out from Gebel Nahar. Since it was on the side of my segment that touched the area given to Michael to investigate, I guessed it was he. I went to look, and found him.

I've got something to show you, he hand signalled me. *Are you done, here?*

Yes, I told him.

Come on, then.

He led me into his area, to one of the larger plastic buildings in the territory of the second regiment he had been given to investigate. He brought me to the building's back. The curving sides of such structures are not difficult to climb quietly if you have had some practise doing so. He led me to the top of the roof curve and pointed at a small hole.

I looked in and saw six men with the collar tabs of Regimental Commanders, sitting together at a table, apparently having sometime since finished a meal. Also present were some officers of lesser rank, but none of these were at the table. Bubble plastic, in addition to its other virtues, is a good sound baffle; and since the table and those about it were not directly under the observation hole, but over against one of the curving walls, some distance off, I could not make out their conversation. It was just below comprehension level. I could hear their words, but not understand them.

But I could watch the way they spoke and their gestures, and tell how they were reacting to each other. It became evident, after a few minutes, that there were a great many tensions around that table. There was no open argument, but they sat and looked at each other in ways that were next to open challenges and the rumble of their voices bristled with the electricity of controlled angers.

141

I felt my shoulder tapped, and took my attention from the hole to the night outside. It took a few seconds to adjust to the relative darkness on top of the structure; but when I did, I could see the Michael was again talking to me with his hands.

Look at the youngest of the Commanders—the one on your left, with the very black mustache. That's the Commander of my regiment.

I looked, identified the man, and lifted my gaze from the hole briefly to nod.

Now look across the table and as far down from him as possible. You see the somewhat heavy Commander with the gray sideburns and the lips that almost pout?

I looked, raised my head and nodded again.

That's the Commander of the Guard Regiment. He and my Commander are beginning to wear on each other. If not, they'd be seated side by side and pretending that anything that ever was between their two regiments has been put aside. It's almost as bad with the junior officers, if you know the signs to look for in each one's case. Can you guess what's triggered it off?

No, I told him, *but I suppose you do, or you wouldn't have brought me here.*

I've been watching for some time. They had the maps out earlier, and it was easy to tell what they were discussing. It's the position of each regiment in the line of battle, tomorrow. They've agreed what it's to be, at last, but no one's happy with the final decision.

I nodded.

I wanted you to see it for yourself. They're all ready to go at each other's throats and it's an explosive situation. Maybe Amanda can find something in it she can use. I brought you here because I was hoping that when we go back to rendezvous with the others, you'll support me in suggesting she come and see this for herself.

I nodded again. The brittle emotions betrayed by the commanders below had been obvious, even to me, the moment I had first looked through the hole.

We slipped quietly back down the curve of the building to the shadowed ground at its back and moved out together toward the rendezvous point.

We had no trouble making our way out through the rest of the encampment and back to our meeting spot. It was safely beyond the illumination of the lights that the regiments had set up amongst their buildings. Ian and Amanda were already there; and we stood together, looking back at the activity in the encampment as we compared notes.

"I called Captain El Man in to look at something I'd found," Michael said. "In my alternate area, there was a meeting going on between the regimental commanders—"

The sound of a shot from someone's antique explosive firearm cut him short. We all turned toward the encampment; and saw a lean figure wearing a white shirt brilliantly reflective in the lights, running toward us, while a gang of men poured out of one of the tents, stared about, and then started in pursuit.

The one they chased was running directly for us, in his obvious desire to get away from the camp. It would have been easy to believe that he had seen us and was running to us for help; but the situation did not support that conclusion. Aside from the unlikeliness of his seeking aid from strangers dressed and equipped as we were, it was obvious that with his eyes still dilated from the lights of the camp, and staring at black-dressed figures like ours, he was completely unable to see us.

All of us dropped flat into the sparse grass of the

plain. But he still came straight for us. Another shot sounded from his pursuers.

It only seems, of course, that the luck in such situations is always bad. It is not so, of course. Good and bad balance out. But knowing this does not help when things seem freakishly determined to do their worst. The fugitive had all the open Naharese plain into which to run. He came toward us instead as if drawn on a cable. We lay still. Unless he actually stepped on one of us, there was a chance he could run right through us and not know we were there.

He did not step on one of us, but he did trip over Michael, stagger on a step, check, and glance down to see what had interrupted his flight. He looked directly at Amanda, and stopped, staring down in astonishment. A second later, he had started to swing around to face his pursuers, his mouth open to shout to them.

Whether he had expected the information of what he had found to soothe their anger toward him, or whether he had simply forgotten at that moment that they had been chasing him, was beside the point. He was obviously about to betray our presence, and Amanda did exactly the correct thing—even if it produced the least desirable results. She uncoiled from the ground like a spring released from tension, one fist taking the fugitive in the adam's apple to cut off his cry and the other going into him just under the breastbone to take the wind out of him and put him down without killing him.

She had been forced to rise between him and his pursuers. But, all black as she was in contrast to the brilliant whiteness of his shirt, she would well have flickered for a second before their eyes without being

recognized; and with the man down, we could have slipped away from the pursuers without their realizing until too late that we had been there. But the incredible bad luck of that moment was still with us.

As she took the man down, another shot sounded from the pursuers, clearly aimed at the now-stationary target of the fugitive—and Amanda went down with him.

She was up again in a second.

"Fine—I'm fine," she said. "Let's go!"

We went, fading off into the darkness at the same steady trot at which we had come to the camp. Until we were aware of specific pursuit there was no point in burning up our reserves of energy. We moved steadily away, back toward Gebel Nahar, while the pursuers finally reached the fugitive, surrounded him, got him on his feet and talking.

By that time we could see them flashing around them the lights some of them had been carrying, searching the plain for us. But we were well away by that time, and drawing farther off every second. No pursuit developed.

"Too bad," said Ian, as the sound and lights of the camp dwindled behind us. "But no great harm done. What happened to you, 'Manda?"

She did not answer. Instead, she went down again, stumbling and dropping abruptly. In a second we were all back and squatting around her.

She was plainly having trouble breathing.

"Sorry. . ." she whispered.

Ian was already cutting away the clothing over her left shoulder.

"Not much blood," he said.

The tone of his voice said he was very angry with her. So was I. It was entirely possible that she might have killed herself by trying to run with a wound that should not have been excited by that kind of treatment. She had acted instinctively to hide the knowledge that she had been hit by that last shot, so that the rest of us would not hesitate in getting away safely. It was not hard to understand the impulse that had made her do it—but she should not have.

"Corunna," said Ian, moving aside. "This is more in your line."

He was right. As a captain, I was the closest thing to a physician aboard, most of the time. I moved in beside her and checked the wound as best I could. In the general but faint starlight it showed as merely a small patch of darkness against a larger, pale patch of exposed flesh. I felt it with my fingers and put my cheek down against it.

"Small caliber slug," I said. Ian breathed a little harshly out through his nostrils. He had already deduced that much. I went on. "Not a sucking wound. High up, just below the collarbone. No immediate pneumothorax, but the chest cavity'll be filling with blood. Are you very short of breath, Amanda? Don't talk, just nod or shake your head."

She nodded.

"How do you feel. Dizzy? Faint?"

She nodded again. Her skin was clammy to my touch.

"Going into shock," I said.

I put my ear to her chest again.

"Right," I said. "The lung on this side's not filling with air. She can't run. She shouldn't do anything.

We'll need to carry her."

"I'll do that," said Ian. He was still angry—irrationally, emotionally, angry, but trying to control it. "How fast do we have to get her back, do you think?"

"Her condition ought to stay the same for a couple of hours," I said. "Looks like no large blood vessels were hit; and the smaller vessels tend to be self-sealing. But the pleural cavity on this side has been filling up with blood and she's collapsed a lung. That's why she's having trouble breathing. No blood around her mouth, so it probably didn't nick an airway going through. . ."

I felt around behind her shoulder but found no exit wound.

"It didn't go through. If there're MASH med-mech units back at Gebel Nahar and we get her back in the next two hours, she should be all right—if we carry her."

Ian scooped her into his arms. He stood up.

"Head down," I said.

"Right," he answered and put her over one shoulder in a fireman's carry. "No, wait—we'll need some padding for my shoulder."

Michael and I took off our jerseys and made a pad for his other shoulder. He transferred her to that shoulder, with her head hanging down his back. I sympathized with her. Even with the padding, it was not a comfortable way to travel; and her wound and shortness of breath would make it a great deal worse.

"Try it at a slow walk, first," I said.

"I'll try it. But we can't go slow walk all the way," said Ian. "It's nearly three klicks from where we are now."

He was right, of course. To walk her back over a distance of three kilometers would take too long. I went behind him to watch her as well as could be done. The sooner I got her to a med-mech unit the better. We started off, and he gradually increased his pace until we were moving smoothly but briskly.

"How are you?" he asked her, over his shoulder.

"She nodded," I reported, from my position behind him.

"Good," he said, and began to jog.

We travelled. She made no effort to speak, and none of the rest of us spoke. From time to time I moved up closer behind Ian to watch her at close range; and as far as I could tell, she did not lose consciousness once on that long, jolting ride; Ian forged ahead, something made of steel rather than of ordinary human flesh, his gaze fixed on the lights of Gebel Nahar, far off across the plain.

There is something that happens under those conditions where the choice is either to count the seconds, or disregard time altogether. In the end we all—and I think Amanda, too, as far as she was capable of controlling how she felt—went off a little way from ordinary time, and did not come back to it until we were at the entrance to the Conde's secret tunnel, leading back under the walls of Gebel Nahar.

By the time I got Amanda laid out in the medical section of Gebel Nahar, she looked very bad indeed and was only semi-conscious. Anything else, of course, would have been surprising indeed. It does not improve the looks of even a very healthy person to be carried head down for over thirty minutes. Luckily, the medical section had everything necessary in the way of med-mechs. I was able to find a portable unit that could be rigged for bed rest—vacuum pump, power unit, drainage bag. It was a matter of inserting a tube between Amanda's lung and chest wall—and this I left to the med-mech, which was less liable to human mistakes than I was on a day in which luck seemed to be running so badly—so that the unit could exhaust the blood from the pleural space into which it had drained.

It was also necessary to rig a unit to supply her with

reconstituted whole blood while this draining process was going on. However, none of this was difficult, even for a part-trained person like myself, once we got her safely to the medical section. I finally got her fixed up and left her to rest—she was in no shape to do much else.

I went off to the offices to find Ian and Kensie. They were both there; and they listened without interrupting to my report on Amanda's treatment and my estimate of her condition.

"She should rest for the next few days, I take it," said Ian when I was done.

"That's right," I said.

"There ought to be some way we could get her out of here, to safety and a regular hospital," said Kensie.

"How?" I asked. "It's almost dawn now. The Naharese would zero in on any vehicle that tried to leave this place, by ground or air. It'd never get away."

Kensie nodded soberly.

"They should," said Ian, "be starting to move now, if this dawn was to be the attack moment."

He turned to the window, and Kensie and I turned with him. Dawn was just breaking. The sky overhead was white-blue and hard, and the brown stretch of the plain looked also stony and hard and empty between the Gebel Nahar and the distant line of the encampment. It was very obvious, even without vision amplification, that the soldiers and others in the encampment had not even begun to form up in battle positions, let alone begin to move toward us.

"After all their parties last night, they may not get going until noon," I said.

"I don't think they'll be that late," said Ian, absent-

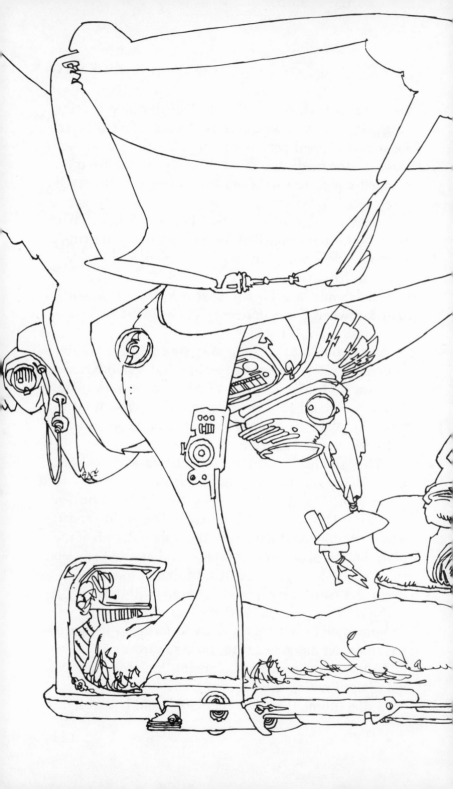

ly. He had taken me seriously. "At any rate, it gives us a little more time. Are you going to have to stay with Amanda?"

"I'll want to look in on her from time to time—in fact, I'm going back down now," I said. "I just came up to tell you how she is. But in between visits, I can be useful."

"Good," said Ian. "As soon as you've had another look at her, why don't you go see if you can help Michael. He's been saying he's got his doubts about those bandsmen of his."

"All right." I went out.

When I got back to the medical section, Amanda was asleep. I was going to slip out and leave her to rest, when she woke and recognized me.

"Corunna," she said, "how am I?"

"You're fine," I said, going back to the side of the bed where she lay. "All you need now is to get a lot of sleep and do a good job of healing."

"What's the situation outside?" she said. "Is it day, yet?"

We were in one of the windowless rooms in the interior of Gebel Nahar.

"Just dawn," I said. "Nothing happening so far. In any case, you forget about all that and rest."

"You'll need me up there."

"Not with a tube between your ribs," I said. "Lie back and sleep."

Her head moved restlessly on the pillow.

"It might have been better if that slug had been more on target."

I looked down at her.

"According to what I've heard about you," I said,

"you of all people ought to know that when you're in a hospital bed it's not the best time in the world to be worrying over things."

She started to speak, interrupted herself to cough, and was silent for a little time until the pain of the tube, rubbing inside her with the disturbance of her coughing, subsided. Even a deep breath would move that tube now, and pain her. There was nothing to be done about that, but I could see how shallowly she breathed, accordingly.

"No," she said. "I can't want to die. But the situation as it stands, is impossible; and every way out of it there is, is impossible, for all three of us. Just like our situation here in Gebel Nahar with no way out."

"Kensie and Ian are able to make up their own minds."

"It's not a matter of making up minds. It's a matter of impossibilities."

"Well," I said, "is there anything you can do about that?"

"I ought to be able to."

"Ought to, maybe, but can you?"

She breathed shallowly. Slowly she shook her head on the pillow.

"Then let it go. Leave it alone," I said. "I'll be back to check on you from time to time. Wait and see what develops."

"How can I wait?" she said. "I'm afraid of myself. Afraid I might throw everything overboard and do what I want most—and so ruin everyone."

"You won't do that."

"I might."

"You're exhausted," I told her. "You're in pain.

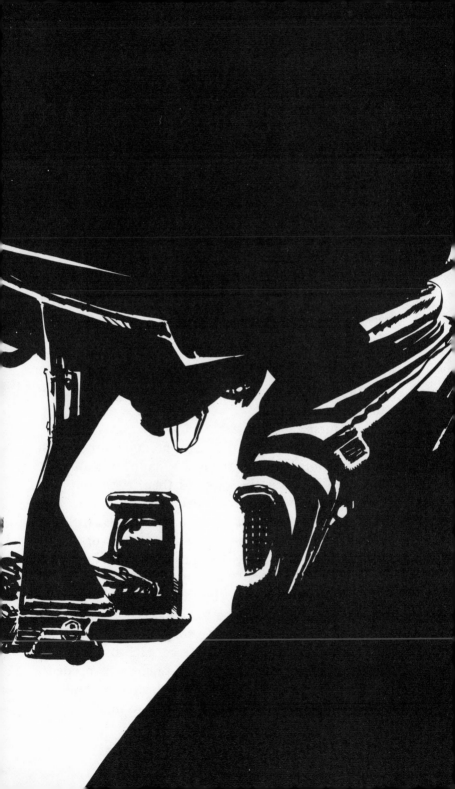

Stop trying to think. I'll be back in an hour or two to check on you. Until then, rest!"

I went out.

I took the corridors that led me to the band section. I saw no other bandsmen in the corridors as I approached their section, but an orderly was on duty as usual in Michael's outer office and Michael himself was in his own office, standing beside his desk with a sheaf of printed records in hand.

"Captain!" he said, when he saw me.

"I've got to look in on Amanda from time to time," I said. "But in between, Ian suggested you might find me useful."

"I'd always find you useful, sir," he said, with the ghost of a smile. "Do you want to come along to stores with me? I need to check a few items of supply and we can talk as we go."

"Of course."

We left the offices and he led me down other corridors and into a supply section. What he was after, it developed, was not the supplies themselves, but the automated delivery system that would keep feeding them, on command—or at regular intervals, without command, if the communications network was knocked out—to various sections of Gebel Nahar. It was a system of a sort I had never seen before.

"Another of the ways the ranchers who designed this looked ahead to having to hole up here," Michael explained as we looked at the supply bins for each of the various sections of the fortress, each bin already stocked with the supplies it would deliver as needed. He was going from bin to bin, checking the contents of each and testing each delivery system to make sure it was working.

The overhead lights were very bright, and their illumination reflected off solid concrete walls painted a utilitarian, flat white. The effect was both blinding and bleak at once; and the feeling of bleakness was reinforced by the stillness of the air. The ventilators must have been working here as in other interior parts of the Gebel Nahar, but with the large open space of the supply section and its high ceilings, the air felt as if there was no movement to it at all.

"Lucky for us," I said.

Michael nodded.

"Yes, if ever a place was made to be defended by a handful of people, this is it. Only, they didn't expect the defense to be by such a small handful as we are. They were thinking in terms of a hundred families, with servants and retainers. Still, if it comes to a last stand for us in the inner fort, on the top three levels, they're going to have to pay one hell of a price to get at us."

I watched his face as he worked. There was no doubt about it. He looked much more tired, much leaner, and older than he had appeared to me only a few days before when he had met Amanda and me at the spaceport terminal of Nahar City. But the work he had been doing and what he had gone through could not alone have been enough to cut him down so visibly, at his age.

He finished checking the last of the delivery systems and the last of the bins. He turned away.

"Ian tells me you've got some concern as to how your bandsmen may stand up to the attack," I said.

His mouth thinned and straightened.

163

"Yes," he said. There was a little pause, and then he added: "You can't blame them. If they'd been real soldier types they would have been in one of the line companies. There's security, but no chance of promotion to speak of, in a band."

Then humor came back to him, a tired but real smile.

"Of course, for someone like myself," he said, "that's ideal."

"On the other hand," I said. "They're here with us. They stayed."

"Well. . ." He sat down a little heavily on a short stack of boxes and waved me to another, "so far it hasn't cost them anything but some hard work. And they've been paid off in excitement. I think I said something to you about that when we were flying out from Nahar City. Excitement—drama—is what most Naharese live for; and die for, for that matter, if the drama is big enough."

"You don't think they'll fight when the time comes?"

"I don't know." His face was bleak again. "I only know I can't blame them—I can't, of all people—if they don't."

"Your attitude's a matter of conviction."

"Maybe theirs is, too. There's no way to judge any one person by another. You never know enough to make a real comparison."

"True," I said. "But I still think that if they don't fight, it'll be for somewhat lesser reasons than yours for not fighting."

He shook his head slowly.

"Maybe I'm wrong, all wrong." His tone was

almost bitter. "But I can't get outside myself to look at it. I only know I'm afraid."

"Afraid?" I looked at him. "Of fighting?"

"I wish it was of fighting," he laughed, briefly. "No, I'm afraid that I don't have the will *not* to fight. I'm afraid that at the last moment it'll all come back, all those early dreams and all the growing up and all the training—and I'll find myself killing, even though I'll know that it won't make any difference in the end and that the Naharese will take Gebel Nahar anyway."

"I don't think it'd be Gebel Nahar you'd be fighting for," I said slowly. "I think it'd be out of a natural, normal instinct to stay alive yourself as long as you can —or to help protect those who are fighting alongside you."

"Yes," he said. His nostrils flared as he drew in an unhappy breath. "The rest of you. That's what I won't be able to stand. It's too deep in me. I might be able to stand there and let myself be killed. But can I stand there when they start to kill someone else—like Amanda, and she already wounded?"

There was nothing I could say to him. But the irony of it rang in me, just the same. Both he and Amanda, afraid that their instincts would lead them to do what their thinking minds had told them they should not do. He and I walked back to his office in silence. When we arrived, there was a message that had been left with Michael's orderly, for me, to call Ian.

I did. His face looked out of the phone screen at me, as unchanged as ever.

"The Naharese still haven't started to move," he said. "They're so unprofessional I'm beginning to think that perhaps we can get Padma, at least, away

166

from here. He can take one of the small units from the vehicle pool and fly out toward Nahar City. My guess is that once they stop him and see he's an Exotic, they'll simply wave him on."

"It could be," I said.

"I'd like you to go and put that point to him," said Ian. "He seems to want to stay, for reasons of his own, but he may listen if you make him see that by staying here, he simply increases the load of responsibility on the rest of us. I'd like to order him out of here; but he knows I don't have the authority for that."

"What makes you think I'm the one to talk him into going?"

"It'd have to be one of the senior officers here, to get him to listen," said Ian. "Both Kensie and I are too tied up to take the time. While even if either one was capable, Michael's a bad choice and Amanda's flat in bed."

"All right," I said. "I'll go talk to him right now. Where is he?"

"In his quarters, I understand. Michael can tell you how to find them."

I reached Padma's suite without trouble. In fact, it was not far from the suite of rooms that had been assigned to me. I found Padma seated at his desk making a recording. He broke off when I stepped into his sitting room in answer to his invitation, which had followed my knock on his door.

"If you're busy, I can drop back in a little while," I said.

"No, no." He swung his chair around, away from the desk. "Sit down. I'm just doing up a report for whoever comes out from the Exotics to replace me."

"You won't need to be replaced if you'll leave now," I said. It was a blunt beginning, but he had given me the opening and time was not plentiful.

"I see," he said. "Did Ian or Kensie ask you to talk to me, or is this the result of an impulse of your own?"

"Ian asked me," I said. "The Naharese are delaying their attack, and he thinks that they're so generally disorganized and unmilitary that there's a chance for you to get safely away to Nahar City. They'll undoubtedly stop whatever vehicle you'd take, when they see it coming out of Gebel Nahar. But once they see you're an Exotic—"

His smile interrupted me.

"All right," I said. "Tell me. Why shouldn't they let you pass when they see you're an Exotic? All the worlds know Exotics are noncombatants."

"Perhaps," he said. "Unfortunately, William has made a practice of identifying us as the machiavellian practitioners at the roots of whatever trouble and evil there is to be found anywhere. At the moment most of the Naharese have an image of me that's half-demon, half-enemy. In their present mood of license, most of them would probably welcome the chance to shoot me on sight."

I stared at him. He was smiling.

"If that's the case, why didn't you leave days ago?" I asked him.

"I have my duty, too. In this instance, it's to gather information for those on Mara and Kultis." His smile broadened. "Also, there's the matter of my own temperament. Watching a situation like the one here is fascinating. I wouldn't leave now if I could. In short, I'm as chained here as the rest of you, even if it is for different reasons."

I shook my head at him.

"It's a fine argument," I said. "But if you'll forgive me, it's a little hard to believe."

"In what way?"

"I'm sorry," I told him, "but I don't seem to be able to give any real faith to the idea that you're being held here by patterns that are essentially the same as mine, for instance."

"Not the same," he said. "Equivalent. The fact others can't match you Dorsai in your own particular area doesn't mean those others don't have equal areas in which equal commitments apply to them. The physics of life works in all of us. It simply manifests itself differently with different people."

"With identical results?"

"With comparable results—could I ask you to sit down?" Padma said mildly. "I'm getting a stiff neck looking up at you."

I sat down facing him.

"For example," he said. "In the Dorsai ethic, you and the others here have something that directly justifies your natural human hunger to do things for great purposes. The Naharese here have no equivalent ethic; but they feel the hunger just the same. So they invent their own customs, their *leto de muerte* concepts. But can you Dorsais, of all people, deny that their concepts can lead them to as true a heroism, or as true a keeping of faith as your ethic leads you to?"

"Of course I can't deny," I said. "But my people can at least be counted on to perform as expected. Can the Naharese?"

"No. But note the dangers of the fact that Dorsais are known to be trustworthy, Exotics known to be per-

sonally nonviolent, the church soldiers of the Friendly Worlds known to be faith-holders. That very knowledge tends too often to lead one to take for granted that trustworthiness is the exclusive property of the Dorsai, that there are no truly non-violent individuals not wearing Exotic robes, and that the faith of anyone not a Friendly must be weak and unremarkable. We are all human and struck with the whole spectrum of the human nature. For clear thinking, it's necessary to first assume that the great hungers and responses are there in everyone—then simply go look for them in all people—including the Naharese."

"You sound a little like Michael when you get on the subject of the Naharese." I got up. "All right, have it your way and stay if you want. I'm going to leave now, myself, before you talk me into going out and offering to surrender before they even get here."

He laughed. I left.

It was time again for me to check Amanda. I went to the medical section. But she was honestly asleep now. Apparently she had been able to put her personal concerns aside enough so that she could exercise a little of the basic physiological control we are all taught from birth. If she had, it could be that she would spend most of the next twenty-four hours sleeping, which would be the best thing for her. If the Naharese did not manage, before that time was up, to break through to the inner fort where the medical section was, she would have taken a large stride toward healing herself. If they did break through she would need whatever strength she could gain between now and then.

It was a shock to see the sun as high in the sky as it was, when I emerged from the blind walls of the corridors once more, on to the first terrace. The sky was almost perfectly clear and there was a small, steady breeze. The day would be hot. Ian and Kensie were each standing at one end of the terrace and looking through watch cameras at the Naharese front.

Michael, the only other person in sight, was also at a watch camera, directly in front of the door I had come out. I went to him and he looked up as I reached him.

"They're on the move," he said, stepping back from the watch camera. I looked into its rectangular viewing screen, bright with the daylight scene it showed under the shadow of the battle armor hooding the camera. He was right. The regiments had finally formed for the attack and were now moving toward us with their portable field weapons, at the pace of a slow walk across the intervening plain.

I could see their regimental and company flags spaced out along the front of the crescent formation and whipping in the morning breeze. The Guard Regiment was still in the center and Michael's Third Regiment out on the right wing. Behind the two wings I could see the darker swarms that were the volunteers and the revolutionaries, in their civilian clothing.

The attacking force had already covered a third of the distance to us. I stepped away from the screen of the camera, and all at once the front of men I looked at became a thin line with little bright flashes of reflected sunlight and touches of color all along it, still distant under the near-cloudless sky and the climbing sun.

"Another thirty or forty minutes before they reach us," said Michael.

I looked at him. The clear daylight showed him as pale and wire-tense. He looked as if he had been whittled down until nothing but nerves were left. He was not wearing weapons, although at either end of the terrace, Ian and Kensie both had sidearms clipped to their legs, and behind us there were racks of cone rifles ready for use.

The rifles woke me to something I had subconsciously noted but not focused upon. The bays with the fixed weapons were empty of human figures.

"Where're your bandsmen?" I asked Michael.

He gazed at me.

"They're gone," he said.

"Gone?"

"Decamped. Run off. Deserted, if you want to use that word."

I stared at him.

"You mean they've joined—"

"No, no." He broke in on me as if the question I was just about to ask was physically painful to him. "They haven't gone over to the enemy. They just decided to save their own skins. I told you—you remember, I told you they might. You can't blame them. They're not Dorsai; and staying here meant certain death for them."

"If Gebel Nahar is overrun," I said.

"Can you believe it won't be?"

"It's become hard to," I said, "now that there's just us. But there's always a chance as long as anyone's left to fight. At Baunpore, I saw men and women firing from hospital beds, when the North Freilanders broke in."

I should not have said it. I saw the shadow cross his

eyes and knew he had taken my reference to Baunpore personally, as if I had been comparing his present weaponless state with the last efforts of the defenders I had seen then. There were times when my scars became more curse than blessing.

"That's a general observation, only," I told him. "I don't mean to accuse—"

"It's not what you accuse me of, it's what I accuse

me of," he said, in a low voice looking out at the on-coming regiments. "I knew what it meant when my bandsmen took off. But I also understand how they could decide to do it."

There was nothing more I could say. We both knew that without his forty men we could not even make a pretence of holding the first terrace past the moment when the first line of Naharese would reach the base of the ramparts. There were just too few of us and too many of them to stop them from coming over the top.

"They're probably hiding just out beyond the walls," he said. He was still talking about his former bandsmen. "If we do manage to hold out for a day or two, there's a slight chance they might trickle back—"

He broke off, staring past me. I turned and saw Amanda.

How she had managed to do it by herself, I do not know. But, clearly, she had gotten herself out of her hospital bed and strapped the portable drainage unit on to her. It was not heavy or much bigger than a thick book; and it was designed for wearing by an am-bulatory patient, but it must have been hell for her to rig it by herself with that tube rubbing inside her at every deep breath.

Now she was here, looking as if she might collapse at any time, but on her feet with the unit slung from her right shoulder and strapped to her right side. She had a sidearm clipped to her left thigh, over the cloth of the hospital gown; and the gown itself had been ripped up the center so that she could walk in it.

"What the hell are you doing up here?" I snarled at her. "Get back to bed!"

"Corunna—" she gave me the most level and un-yielding stare I have ever encountered from anyone in my life, "don't give me orders. I rank you."

I blinked at her. It was true I had been asked to be her driver for the trip here, and in a sense that put me under her orders. But for her to presume to tell a Captain of a full flight of fighting ships, with an edge of half a dozen years in seniority and experience that in a combat situation like this she ranked him—it was raving nonsense. I opened my mouth to explode—and found myself bursting out in laughter, instead. The situation was too ridiculous. Here we were, five people even counting Michael, facing three thousand; and I was about to let myself get trapped into an argument over who ranked who. Aside from the fact that only the accident of her present assignment gave her any claim to superiority over me, relative rank between Dorsai had always been a matter of local conditions and situations, tempered with a large pinch of common sense.

But, obviously she was out here on the terrace to stay; and obviously, I was not going to make any real issue of it under the circumstances. We both understood what was going on. Which did not change the fact that she should not have been on her feet. Like Ian out on the plain, and in spite of having been forced to see the funny side of it, I was still angry with her.

"The next time you're wounded, you better hope I'm not your medico," I told her. "What do you think you can do up here, anyway?"

"I can be with the rest of you," she said.

I closed my mouth again. There was no arguing with that answer. Out of the corner of my eyes I saw Kensie and Ian approaching from the far ends of the

terrace. In a moment they were with us.

They looked down at her but said nothing, and we all turned to look again out across the plain.

The Naharese front had been approaching steadily. It was still too far away to be seen as a formation of individuals. It was still just a line of different shade than the plain itself, touched with flashes of light and spots of color. But it was a line with a perceptible thickness now.

We stood together, the four of us, looking at the slow, ponderous advance upon us. All my life, as just now with Amanda, I had been plagued by a sudden awareness of the ridiculous. It came on me now. What mad god had decided that an army should march against a handful—and that the handful should not only stand to be marched upon, but should prepare to fight back? But then the sense of the ridiculousness passed. The Naharese would continue to come on because all their lives had oriented them against Gebel Nahar. We would oppose them when they came because all our lives had been oriented to fighting for even lost causes, once we had become committed to them. In another time and place it might be different for those of us on both sides. But this was the here and now.

With that, I passed into the final stage that always came on me before battle. It was as if I stepped down into a place of private peace and quiet. What was coming would come, and I would meet it when it came. I was aware of Kensie, Ian, Michael and Amanda standing around me, and aware that they were experiencing much the same feelings. Something like a telepathy flowed between us, binding us together in a feeling of particular unity. In my life there has been nothing like that feeling of unity, and I have noticed that those who have once felt it never forget it. It is as it is, as it always has been, and we who are there at that moment are together. Against that togetherness, odds no longer matter.

There was a faint scuff of a foot on the terrace floor, and Michael was gone. I looked at the others, and the thought was unspoken between us. He had gone to put on his weapons. We turned once more to the plain, and saw the approaching Naharese now close enough so that they were recognizable as individual figures. They were almost close enough for the sound of their approach to be heard by us.

We moved forward to the parapet of the terraces and stood watching. The day-breeze, strengthening, blew in our faces. There was time now to appreciate the sunlight, the not-yet-hot temperature of the day and the moving air. Another few hundred meters and they would be within the range of maximum efficiency for our emplaced weapons—and we, of course, within range of their portables. Until then, there was nothing urgent to be done.

The door opened behind us. I turned, but it was not Michael. It was Padma, supporting El Conde, who was coming out to us with the help of a silver-headed walking stick. Padma helped him out to where we stood at the parapet, and for a second he ignored us, looking instead out at the oncoming troops. Then he turned to us.

"Gentlemen and lady," he said in Spanish, "I have chosen to join you."

"We're honored," Ian answered him in the same

tongue. "Would you care to sit down?"

"Thank you, no. I will stand. You may go about your duties."

He leaned on the cane, watching across the parapet and paying no attention to us. We stepped back away from him, and Padma spoke in a low voice.

"I'm sure he won't be in the way," Padma said. "But he wanted to be down here, and there was no one but me left to help him."

"It's all right," said Kensie. "But what about you?"

"I'd like to stay, too," said Padma.

Ian nodded. A harsh sound came from the throat of the count, and we looked at him. He was rigid as some ancient dry spearshaft, staring out at the approaching soldiers, his face carved with the lines of fury and scorn.

"What is it?" Amanda asked.

I had been as baffled as the rest. Then a faint sound came to my ear. The regiments were at last close enough to be heard; and what we were hearing were their regimental bands—except Michael's band, of course—as a faint snatch of melody on the breeze. It was barely hearable, but I recognized it, as El Conde obviously already had.

"They're playing the *te guelo*," I said. "Announcing '*no quarter*.'"

The *te guelo* is a promise to cut the throat of anyone opposing. Amanda's eyebrows rose.

"For us?" she said. "What good do they think that's going to do?"

"They may think Michael's bandsmen are still with us, and perhaps they're hoping to scare them out," I said. "But probably they're doing it just because it's always done when they attack."

The others listened for a second. The *te guelo* is an effectively chilling piece of music; but, as Amanda had implied, it was a little beside the point to play it to Dorsai who had already made their decision to fight.

"Where's Michael?" she asked now.

I looked around. It was a good question. If he had indeed gone for weapons, he should have been back out on the terrace by this time. But there was no sign of him.

"I don't know," I said.

"They've stopped their portable weapons," Kensie said, "and they're setting them up to fire. Still out of effective range, against walls like this."

"We'd probably be better down behind the armor of our own embayments and ready to fire back when they

get a little closer," said Ian. "They can't hurt the walls from where they are. They might get lucky and hurt some of us."

He turned to El Conde.

"If you'd care to step down into one of the weapon embayments, sir—" he said.

El Conde shook his head.

"I shall watch from here," he announced.

Ian nodded. He looked at Padma.

"Of course," said Padma. "I'll come in with one of you—unless I can be useful in some other way?"

"No," said Ian. A shouting from the approaching soldiers that drowned out the band music turned him and the rest of us once more toward the plain.

The front line of the attackers had broken into a run toward us. They were only a hundred meters or so now from the foot of the slope leading to the walls of Gebel Nahar. Whether it had been decided that they should attack from that distance, or—more likely—someone had been carried away and started forward early, did not matter. The attack had begun.

For a moment, all of us who knew combat recognized immediately, this development had given us a temporary respite from the portable weapons. With their own soldiers flooding out ahead, it would be difficult for the gunners to fire at Gebel Nahar without killing their own men. It was the sort of small happenstance that can sometimes be turned to an advantage —but, as I stared out at the plain, I had no idea of what we might do that in that moment that would make any real difference to the battle's outcome.

"Look!"

It was Amanda calling. The shouting of the attacking soldiers had stopped, suddenly. She was standing right at the parapet, pointing out and down. I took one step forward, so that I could see the slope below close by the foot of the first wall, and saw what she had seen.

The front line of the attackers was full of men trying to slow down against the continued pressure of those behind who had not yet seen what those in front had. The result was effectively a halting of the attack as more and more of them stared at what was happening on the slope.

What was happening there was that the lid of El Conde's private exit from Gebel Nahar was rising. To the Naharese military it must have looked as if some secret weapon was about to unveil itself on the slope— and it would have been this that had caused them to have sudden doubts and their front line of men to dig in their heels. They were still a good two or three hundred meters from the tunnel entrance, and the first line of attackers, trapped where they were by those behind them, must have suddenly conceived of themselves as sitting ducks for whatever field-class weapon would elevate itself through this unexpected opening and zero in on them.

But of course no such weapon came out. Instead, what emerged was what looked like a head wearing a regimental cap, with a stick tilted back by its right ear . . . and slowly, up on to the level of the ground, and out to face them all came Michael.

He was still without weapons. But he was now dressed in his full parade regimentals as band officer; and the *gaita gallega* was resting in his arms and on his shoulder, the mouthpiece between his lips, the long drone over his shoulder. He stepped out on to the slope of the hill and began to march down it, toward the Naharese.

The silence was deadly; and into that silence, striking up, came the sound of the *gaita gallega* as he started to play it. Clear and strong it came to us on the wall; and clearly it reached as well to the now-silent and motionless ranks of the Naharese. He was playing *Su Madre*.

He went forward at a march step, shoulders level, the instrument held securely in his arms; and his playing went before him, throwing its challenge directly into their faces. A single figure marching against six thousand.

From where I stood, I had a slight angle on him; and with the help of the magnification of the screen on the watch camera next to me, I could get just a glimpse of his face from the side and behind him. He looked peaceful and intent. The exhausted leanness and tension I had seen in him earlier seemed to have gone out of him. He marched as if on parade, with the intentness of a good musician in performance, and all the time *Su Madre* was hooting and mocking at the armed regiments before him.

I touched the controls of the camera to make it give me a closeup look at the men in the front of the Naharese force. They stood as if paralyzed, as I panned along their line. They were saying nothing, doing nothing, only watching Michael come toward them as if he meant to march right through them. All along their front, they were stopped and watching.

But their inaction was something that could not last —a moment of shock that had to wear off. Even as I watched, they began to stir and speak. Michael was

between us and them, and with the incredible voice of the bagpipe his notes came almost loudly to our ears. But rising behind them, we now began to hear a low-pitched swell of sound like the growl of some enormous beast.

I looked in the screen. The regiments were still not advancing, but none of the figures I now saw as I panned down the front were standing frozen with shock. In the middle of the crescent formation, the soldiers of the Guard Regiment who held a feud with Michael's own Third Regiment, were shaking weapons and fists at him and shouting. I had no way of knowing what they were saying, at this distance, and the camera could not help me with that, but I had no doubt that they were answering challenge with challenge, insult with insult.

All along the line, the front boiled, becoming more active every minute. They had all seen that Michael was unarmed; and for a few moments this held them in check. They threatened, but did not offer to, fire on him. But even at this distance I could feel the fury building up in them. It was only a matter of time, I thought, until one of them lost his self-control and used the weapon he carried.

I wanted to shout at Michael to turn around and come back to the tunnel. He had broken the momentum of their attack and thrown them into confusion. With troops like this they would certainly not take up their advance where they had halted it. It was almost a certainty that after this challenge, this emotional shock, that their senior officers would pull them back and reform them before coming on again. A valuable breathing space had been gained. It could be some hours, it could be not until tomorrow they would be able to mount a second attack; and in that time internal tensions or any number of developments might work to help us further. Michael still had them between his thumb and forefinger. If he turned his back on them now, their inaction might well hold until he was back in safety.

But there was no way I could reach him with that message. And he showed no intention of turning back on his own. Instead he went steadily forward, scorning them with his music, taunting them for attacking in their numbers an opponent so much less than themselves.

Still the Naharese soldiery only shook their weapons

and shouted insults at him; but now in the screen I began to see a difference. On the wing occupied by the Third Regiment there were uniformed figures beginning to wave Michael back. I moved the view of the screen further out along that wing and saw individuals in civilian clothes, some of those from the following swarm of volunteers and revolutionaries, who were pushing their way to the front, kneeling down and putting weapons to their shoulders.

The Third Regiment soldiers were pushing these others back and jerking their weapons away from them. Fights were beginning to break out; but on that wing, those who wished to fire on Michael were being held back. It was plain that the Third Regiment was torn now between its commitment to join in the attack on Gebel Nahar and its impulse to protect their former bandmaster in his act of outrageous bravery. Still, I saw one civilian with the starved face of a fanatic who had literally to be tackled and held on the ground by three of the Third Regiment before he could be stopped from firing on Michael.

A sudden cold suspicion passed through me. I swung the view of the screen to the opposite wing; and there I saw the same situation. From behind the uniformed soldiers there, volunteers and civilian revolutionaries were trying to stop Michael with their weapons. Some undoubtedly were from the neighboring principalities where a worship of drama and acts of flamboyant courage was not part of the culture, as it was here. On this wing, also, the soldiers were trying to stop those individuals who attempted to shoot Michael. But here, the effort to prevent that firing was scattered and ineffective.

I saw a number of weapons of all types leveled at Michael. No sound could reach me, and only the sport guns and ancient explosive weapons showed any visible sign that they were being fired; but it was clear that death was finally in the air around Michael.

I switched the view hastily back to him. For a moment he continued to march forward in the screen as if some invisible armor was protecting him. Then he stumbled slightly, caught himself, went forward, and fell.

For a second time—for a moment only—the voice of the attackers stopped, cut off as if a multitude of invisible hands had been clapped over the mouths of those there. I lifted the view on the screen from the fallen shape of Michael and saw soldiers and civilians alike standing motionless, staring at him, as if they could not believe that he had at last been brought down.

Then, on the wing opposite to that held by the Third Regiment, the civilians that had been firing began to dance and wave their weapons in the air—and suddenly the whole formation seemed to collapse inward, the two wings melting back into the main body as the soldiers of the Third Regiment charged across the front to get at the rejoicing civilians, and the Guard Regiment swirled out to oppose them. The fighting spread as individual attacked individual. In a moment they were all embroiled. A wild mob without direction or purpose of any kind, except to kill whoever was closest, took the place of the military formation that had existed only five minutes before.

As the fighting became general, the tight mass of bodies spread out like butter rapidly melting down from a solid to a liquid; and the struggle spread out over a larger and larger area, until at last it covered even the place where Michael had fallen. Amanda turned away from the parapet and I caught her as she staggered. I held her upright and she leaned heavily against me.

"I have to lie down, I guess," she murmured.

I led her towards the door and the bed that was waiting for her back in the medical section. Ian, Kensie and Padma turned and followed, leaving only El Conde, leaning on his silver-headed stick and staring out at what was taking place on the plain, his face lighted with the fierce satisfaction of a hawk perched above the body of its kill.

It was twilight before all the fighting had ceased; and, with the dark, there began to be heard the small sounds of the annunciator chimes at the main gate. One by one Michael's bandsmen began to slip back to us in Gebel Nahar. With their return, Ian, Kensie and I were able to stop taking turns at standing watch, as we had up until then. But it was not until after midnight that we felt it was safe to leave long enough to go out and recover Michael's body.

Amanda insisted on going with us. There was no reason to argue against her coming with us and a good deal of reason in favor of it. She was responding very well to the drainage unit and a further eight hours of sleep had rebuilt her strength to a remarkable degree. Also, she was the one who suggested we take Michael's body back to the Dorsai for burial.

The cost of travel between the worlds was such that few individuals could afford it; and few Dorsai who died in the course of their duties off-planet had their

bodies returned for internment in native soil. But we had adequate space to carry Michael's body with us in the courier vessel; and it was Amanda's point that Michael had solved the problem by his action—something for which the Dorsai world in general owed him a debt. Both Padma and El Conde had agreed, after what had happened today, that the Naharese would not be brought back to the idea of revolution again for some time. William's machinations had fallen through. Ian and Kensie could now either make it their choice to stay and execute their contract, or legitimately withdraw from it for the reason that they had been faced with situations beyond their control.

In the end, all of us except Padma went out to look for Michael's body, leaving the returned bandsmen to stand duty. It was full night by the time we emerged once more on to the plain through the secret exit.

"El Conde will have to have another of these made for him," commented Kensie, as we came out under the star-brilliant sky. "This passage is more a national monument than a secret, now."

The night was one very much like the one before, when Kensie and I had made our sweep in search of observers from the other side. But this time we were looking only for the dead; and that was all we found.

During the afternoon all the merely wounded had been taken away by their friends; but there were bodies to be seen as we moved out to the spot where we had seen Michael go down, but not many of them. It had been possible to mark the location exactly using the surveying equipment built into the watch cameras. But the bodies were not many. The fighting had been more a weaponed brawl than a battle. Which did not alter the fact that those who had died were dead. They would not come to life again, any more than Michael would. A small night breeze touched our faces from time to time as we walked. It was too soon after the fighting for the odors of death to have taken possession of the battlefield. For the present moment under the stars the scene we saw, including the dead bodies, had all the neatness and antiseptic quality of a stage setting.

We came to the place where Michael's body should have been, but it was gone. Ian switched on a pocket lamp; and he, with Kensie, squatted to examine the ground. I waited with Amanda. Ian and Kensie were

the experienced field officers, with Hunter Team practise. I could spend several hours looking, to see what they would take in at a glance.

After a few minutes they stood up again and Ian switched off the lamp. There were a few seconds while our eyes readjusted, and then the plain became real around us once more, replacing the black wall of darkness that the lamplight had instantly created.

"He was here, all right," Kensie said. "Evidently quite a crowd came to carry his body off someplace else. It'll be easy enough to follow the way they went."

We followed the trail of scuffed earth and broken vegetation left by the footwear of those who had carried away Michael's body. The track they had left was plain enough so that I myself had no trouble picking it out, even by starlight, as we went along at a walk. It led further away from Gebel Nahar, toward where the center of the Naharese formation had been when the general fighting broke out; and as we went, bodies became more numerous. Eventually, at a spot which must have been close to where the Guard Regiment had stood, we found Michael.

The mound on which his body lay was visible as a dark mass in the starlight, well before we reached it. But it was only when Ian switched on his pocket lamp again that we saw its true identity and purpose. It was a pile nearly a meter in height and a good two meters long and broad. Most of what made it up was clothes; but there were many others things mixed in with the cloth items—belts and ornamental chains, ancient weapons, so old that they must have been heirlooms, bits of personal jewelry, even shoes and boots.

But, as I say, the greater part of what made it up

was clothing—in particular uniform jackets or shirts, although a fair number of detached sleeves or collars bearing insignia of rank had evidently been deliberately torn off by their owners and added as separate items.

On top of all this, lying on his back with his dead face turned toward the stars, was Michael. I did not need an interpretation of what I was seeing here, after my earlier look at the painting in the Nahar City Spaceport Terminal. Michael lay not with a sword, but with the *gaita gallega* held to his chest; and beneath him was the *leto de muerte*—the real *leto de muerte*, made up of everything that those who had seen him there that day, and who had fought for and against him after it was too late, considered the most valuable thing they could give from what was in their possession at the time.

Each had given the best he could, to build up a bed of state for the dead hero—a bed of triumph, actually, for in winning here Michael had won everything, according to their rules and their ways. After the supreme victory of his courage, as they saw it, there was nothing left for them but the offering of tribute; their possessions or their lives.

We stood, we three, looking at it all in silence. Finally, Kensie spoke.

"Do you still want to take him home?"

"No," said Amanda. The word was almost as a sigh from her, as she stood looking at the dead Michael. "No. This is his home, now."

We went back to Gebel Nahar, leaving the corpse of Michael with its honor guard of the other dead around him.

The next day Amanda and I left Gebel Nahar to return to the Dorsai. Kensie and Ian had decided to complete their contract; and it looked as if they should be able to do so without difficulty. With dawn, individual soldiers of the regiments had begun pouring back into Gebel Nahar, asking to be accepted once more into their duties. They were eager to please, and for Naharese, remarkably subdued.

Padma was also leaving. He rode into the spaceport with us, as did Kensie and Ian, who had come along to see us off. In the terminal, we stopped to look once more at the *leto de muerte* painting.

"Now I understand," said Amanda, after a moment. She turned from the painting and lightly touched both Ian and Kensie who were standing on either side of her.

"We'll be back," she said, and led the two of them off.

I was left with Padma.

"Understand?" I said to him. "The *leto de muerte* concept?"

"No," said Padma, softly. "I think she meant that now she understands what Michael came to understand, and how it applies to her. How it applies to everyone, including me and you."

I felt coldness on the back of my neck.

"To me?" I said.

"You have lost part of your protection, the armor of your sorrow and loss," he answered. "To a certain extent, when you let yourself become concerned with Michael's problem, you let someone else in to touch you again."

I looked at him, a little grimly.

"You think so?" I put the matter aside. "I've got to get out and start the checkover on the ship. Why don't you come along? When Amanda and the others come back and don't find us here, they'll know where to look."

Padma shook his head.

"I'm afraid I'd better say goodby now," he replied. "There are other urgencies that have been demanding my attention for some time and I've put them aside for this. Now, it's time to pay them some attention. So I'll say goodby now; and you can give my farewells to the others."

"Goodby, then," I said.

As when we had met, he did not offer me his hand; but the warmth of him struck through to me; and for the first time I faced the possibility that perhaps he was right. That Michael, or he, or Amanda—or perhaps the whole affair—had either worn thin a spot, or chipped off a piece, of that shell that had closed around me when I watched them kill Else.

"Perhaps we'll run into each other again," I said.

"With people like ourselves," he said, "it's very likely."

He smiled once more, turned and went.

I crossed the terminal to the Security Section, identified myself and went out to the courier ship. It was no more than half an hour's work to run the checkover—these special vessels are practically self-monitoring. When I finished the others had still not yet appeared. I was about to go in search of them when Amanda pulled herself through the open entrance port and closed it behind her.

"Where's Kensie and Ian?" I asked.

"They were paged. The Board of Governors showed up at Gebel Nahar, without warning. They both had to hurry back for a full-dress confrontation. I told them I'd say goodby to you for them."

"All right. Padma sends his farewells by me to the rest of you."

She laughed and sat down in the copilot's seat beside me.

"I'll have to write Ian and Kensie to pass Padma's on," she said. "Are we ready to lift?"

"As soon as we're cleared for it. That port sealed?"

She nodded. I reached out to the instrument bank before me, keyed Traffic Control and asked to be put in sequence for liftoff. Then I gave my attention to the matter of warming the bird to life.

Thirty-five minutes later we lifted, and another ten minutes after that saw us safely clear of the atmosphere. I headed out for the legally requisite number of planetary diameters before making the first phase shift. Then, finally, with mind and hands free, I was able to turn my attention again to Amanda.

She was lost in thought, gazing deep into the pin-point fires of the visible stars in the navigation screen above the instrument bank. I watched her without speaking for a moment, thinking again that Padma had possibly been right. Earlier, even when she had spoken to me in the dark of my room of how she felt about Ian, I had touched nothing of her. But now, I could feel the life in her as she sat beside me.

She must have sensed my eyes on her, because she roused from her private consultation with the stars and looked over.

"Something on your mind?" she asked.

"No," I said. "Or rather, yes. I didn't really follow your thinking, back in the terminal when we were looking at the painting and you said that now you understood."

"You didn't?" She watched me for a fraction of a second. "I meant that now I understood what Michael had."

"Padma said he thought you'd meant you understood how it applied to you—and to everyone."

She did not answer for a second.

"You're wondering about me—and Ian and Kensie," she said.

"It's not important what I wonder," I said.

"Yes, it is. After all, I dumped the whole matter in your lap in the first place, without warning. It's going to be all right. They'll finish up their contract here and then Ian will go to Earth for Leah. They'll be married and she'll settle in Foralie."

"And Kensie?"

"Kensie." She smiled sadly. "Kensie'll go on . . . his own way."

"And you?"

"I'll go mine." She looked at me very much as Padma had looked at me, as we stood below the painting. "That's what I meant when I said I'd understood. In the end the only way is to be what you are and do what you must. If you do that, everything works. Michael found that out."

"And threw his life away putting it into practise."

"No," she said swiftly. "He threw nothing away. There were only two things he wanted. One was to be the Dorsai he was born to be and the other was never to use a weapon; and it seemed he could have either

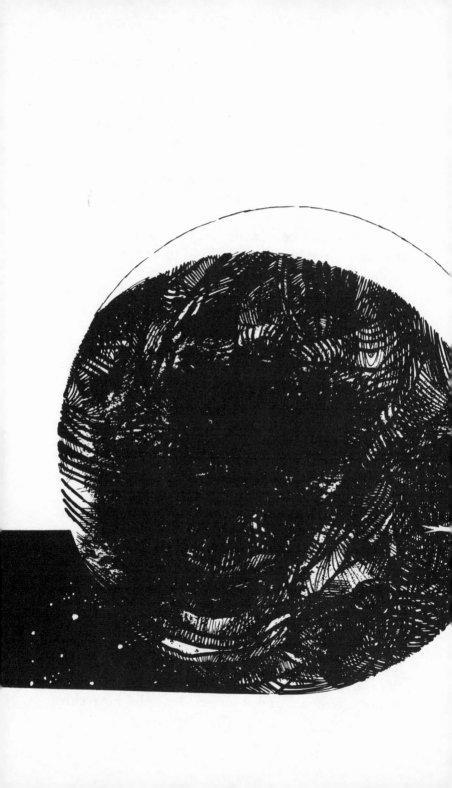

one but not the other. Only, he was true to both and it worked. In the end, he was Dorsai and unarmed—and by being both he stopped an army."

Her eyes held me so powerfully that I could not look away.

"He went his way and found his life," she said, "and my answer is to go mine. Ian, his. And Kensie, his—"

She broke off so abruptly I knew what she had been about to say.

"Give me time," I said; and the words came a little more thickly than I had expected. "It's too soon yet. Still too soon since she died. But give me time, and maybe . . . maybe, even me."

WARRIOR

The spaceliner coming in from New Earth and Freiland, worlds under the Sirian sun, was delayed in its landing by traffic at the spaceport in Long Island Sound. The two police lieutenants, waiting on the bare concrete beyond the shelter of the Terminal buildings, turned up the collars of their cloaks against the hissing sleet, in this unweatherproofed area. The sleet was turning into tiny hailstones that bit and stung all exposed areas of skin. The gray November sky poured them down without pause or mercy; the vast, reaching surface of concrete seemed to dance with their white multitudes.

"Here it comes now," said Tyburn, the Manhattan Complex police lieutenant, risking a glance up into the hailstorm. "Let me do the talking when we take him in."

"Fine by me," answered Breagan, the spaceport officer, "I'm only here to introduce you—and because it's my bailiwick. You can have Kenebuck, with his hood connections, and his millions. If it were up to me, I'd let the soldier get him."

"It's him," said Tyburn, "who's likely to get the soldier—and that's why I'm here. You ought to know that."

The great mass of the interstellar ship settled like a cautious mountain to the concrete two hundred yards off. It protruded a landing stair near its base like a metal leg, and the passengers began to disembark. The two policemen spotted their man immediately in the crowd.

"He's big," said Breagan, with the judicious appraisal of someone safely on the sidelines, as the two of them moved forward.

"They're all big, these professional military men off the Dorsai world," answered Tyburn, a little irritably, shrugging his shoulders against the cold, under his cloak. "They breed themselves that way."

"I know they're big," said Breagan. "This one's bigger."

The first wave of passengers was rolling toward them now, their quarry among the mass. Tyburn and Breagan moved forward to meet him. When they got close they could see, even through the hissing sleet, every line of his dark, unchanging face looming above the lesser heights of the people around him, his military erectness molding the civilian clothes he wore until they might as well have been a uniform. Tyburn found himself staring fixedly at the tall figure as it came toward him. He had met such professional soldiers from the Dorsai before, and the stamp of their breeding had always been plain on them. But this man was somehow more so, even than the others Tyburn had seen. In some way he seemed to be the spirit of the Dorsai, incarnate.

He was one of twin brothers, Tyburn remembered now from the dossier back at his office. Ian and Kensie were their names, of the Graeme family at Foralie, on the Dorsai. And the report was that Kensie had two men's likability, while his brother Ian, now approaching Tyburn, had a double portion of grim shadow and solitary darkness.

Staring at the man coming toward him, Tyburn could believe the dossier now. For a moment, even, with the sleet and the cold taking possession of him, he found himself believing in the old saying that, if the born soldiers of the Dorsai ever cared to pull back to

213

their own small, rocky world, and challenge the rest of humanity, not all the thirteen other inhabited planets could stand against them. Once, Tyburn had laughed at that idea. Now, watching Ian approach, he could not laugh. A man like this would live for different reasons from those of ordinary men—and die for different reasons.

Tyburn shook off the wild notion. The figure coming toward him, he reminded himself sharply, was a professional military man—nothing more.

Ian was almost to them now. The two policemen moved in through the crowd and intercepted him.

"Commandant Ian Graeme?" said Breagan. "I'm Kaj Breagan of the spaceport police. This is Lieutenant Walter Tyburn of the Manhattan Complex Force. I wonder if you could give us a few minutes of your time?"

Ian Graeme nodded, almost indifferently. He turned and paced along with them, his longer stride making more leisurely work of their brisk walking, as they led him away from the route of the disembarking passengers and in through a blank metal door at one end of the Terminal, marked *Unauthorized Entry Prohibited*. Inside, they took an elevator tube up to the offices on the Terminal's top floor, and ended up in chairs around a desk in one of the offices.

All the way in, Ian had said nothing. He sat in his chair now with the same indifferent patience, gazing at Tyburn, behind the desk, and at Breagan, seated back against the wall at the desk's right side. Tyburn found himself staring back in fascination. Not at the granite face, but at the massive, powerful hands of the man, hanging idly between the chair-arms that supported his forearms. Tyburn, with an effort, wrenched his gaze from those hands.

"Well, Commandant," he said, forcing himself at last to look up into the dark, unchanging features, "you're here on Earth for a visit, we understand."

"To see the next-of-kin of an officer of mine." Ian's voice, when he spoke at last, was almost mild compared to the rest of his appearance. It was a deep, calm voice, but lightless—like a voice that had long forgotten the need to be angry or threatening. Only . . . there was something sad about it, Tyburn thought.

"A James Kenebuck?" said Tyburn.

"That's right," answered the deep voice of Ian. "His younger brother, Brian Kenebuck, was on my staff in the recent campaign on Freiland. He died three months back."

"Do you," said Tyburn, "always visit your deceased officers' next of kin?"

"When possible. Usually, of course, they die in the line of duty."

"I see," said Tyburn. The office chair in which he sat seemed hard and uncomfortable underneath him. He shifted slightly. "You don't happen to be armed, do you, Commandant?"

Ian did not even smile.

"No," he said.

"Of course, of course," said Tyburn, uncomfortable. "Not that it makes any difference." He was looking again, in spite of himself, at the two massive, relaxed hands opposite him. "Your . . . extremities by themselves are lethal weapons. We register professional karate and boxing experts here, you know—or did you know?"

Ian nodded.

"Yes," said Tyburn. He wet his lips, and then was furious with himself for doing so. Damn my orders, he thought suddenly and whitely, I don't have to sit here

215

making a fool of myself in front of this man, no matter how many connections and millions Kenebuck owns.

"All right, look here, Commandant," he said, harshly, leaning forward. "We've had a communication from the Freiland-North Police about you. They suggest that you hold Kenebuck—James Kenebuck—responsible for his brother Brian's death."

Ian sat looking back at him without answering.

"Well," demanded Tyburn, raggedly after a long moment, "do you?"

"Force-leader Brian Kenebuck," said Ian calmly, "led his Force, consisting of thirty-six men at the time, against orders, farther than was wise into enemy perimeter. His Force was surrounded and badly shot up. Only he and four men returned to the lines. He was brought to trial in the field under the Mercenaries Code for deliberate mishandling of his troops under combat conditions. The four men who had returned with him testified against him. He was found guilty and I ordered him shot."

Ian stopped speaking. His voice had been perfectly even, but there was so much finality about the way he spoke that after he finished there was a pause in the room while Tyburn and Breagan stared at him as if they had both been tranced. Then the silence, echoing in Tyburn's ears, jolted him back to life.

"I don't see what all this has to do with James Kenebuck, then," said Tyburn. "Brian committed some . . . military crime, and was executed for it. You say you gave the order. If anyone's responsible for Brian Kenebuck's death then, it seems to me it'd be you. Why connect it with someone who wasn't even there at the time, someone who was here on Earth all the while, James Kenebuck?"

"Brian," said Ian, "was his brother."

The emotionless statement was calm and coldly reasonable in the silent, brightly-lit office. Tyburn found his open hands had shrunk themselves into fists on the desk top. He took a deep breath and began to speak in a flat, official tone.

"Commandant," he said, "I don't pretend to understand you. You're a man of the Dorsai, a product of one of the splinter cultures out among the stars. I'm just an old-fashioned Earthborn—but I'm a policeman in the Manhattan Complex and James Kenebuck is . . . well, he's a taxpayer in the Manhattan Complex."

He found he was talking without meeting Ian's eyes. He forced himself to look at them—they were dark unmoving eyes.

"It's my duty to inform you," Tyburn went on, "that we've had intimations to the effect that you're to bring some retribution to James Kenebuck, because of Brian Kenebuck's death. These are only intimations, and as long as you don't break any laws here on Earth, you're free to go where you want and see whom you like. But this *is Earth, Commandant.*"

He paused, hoping that Ian would make some sound, some movement. But Ian only sat there, waiting.

"We don't have any Mercenaries Code here, Commandant," Tyburn went on harshly. "We haven't any feud-right, no *droit-de-main.* But we do have laws. Those laws say that, though a man may be the worst murderer alive, until he's brought to book in our courts, under our process of laws, no one is allowed to harm a hair of his head. Now, I'm not here to argue whether this is the best way or not; just to tell you that that's the way things are." Tyburn stared fixedly into the dark eyes. "Now," he said, bluntly, "I know that if you're determined to try to kill Kenebuck without counting the cost, I can't prevent it."

He paused and waited again. But Ian still said nothing.

"I know," said Tyburn, "that you can walk up to him like any other citizen, and once you're within reach you can try to kill him with your bare hands before anyone can stop you. *I* can't stop you in that case. But what I can do is catch you afterwards, if you succeed, and see you convicted and executed for murder. And you *will* be caught and convicted, there's no doubt about it. You can't kill James Kenebuck the way someone like you would kill a man, and get away with it here on Earth—do you understand that, Commandant?"

"Yes," said Ian.

"All right," said Tyburn, letting out a deep breath. "Then you understand. You're a sane man and a Dorsai professional. From what I've been able to learn about the Dorsai, it's one of your military tenets that part of a man's duty to himself is not to throw his life away in a hopeless cause. And this cause of yours to bring Kenebuck to justice for his brother's death, is hopeless."

He stopped. Ian straightened in a movement preliminary to getting up.

"Wait a second," said Tyburn.

He had come to the hard part of the interview. He had prepared his speech for this moment and rehearsed it over and over again—but now he found himself without faith that it would convince Ian.

"One more word," said Tyburn. "You're a man of camps and battlefields, a man of the military; and you must be used to thinking of yourself as a pretty effective individual. But here, on Earth, those special skills

218

of yours are mostly illegal. And without them you're ineffective and helpless. Kenebuck, on the other hand, is just the opposite. He's got money—millions. And he's got connections, some of them nasty. And he was born and raised here in Manhattan Complex." Tyburn stared emphatically at the tall, dark man, willing him to understand. "Do you follow me? If you, for example, should suddenly turn up dead here, we just might not be able to bring Kenebuck to book for it. Where we absolutely could, and would, bring you to book if the situation were reversed. Think about it."

He sat, still staring at Ian. But Ian's face showed no change, or sign that the message had gotten through to him.

"Thank you," Ian said. "If there's nothing more, I'll be going."

"There's nothing more," said Tyburn, defeated. He watched Ian leave. It was only when Ian was gone, and he turned back to Breagen that he recovered a little of his self-respect. For Breagan's face had paled.

Ian went down through the Terminal and took a cab into Manhattan Complex, to the John Adams Hotel. He registered for a room on the fourteenth floor of the transient section of that hotel and inquired about the location of James Kenebuck's suite in the resident section; then sent his card up to Kenebuck with a request to come by to see the millionaire. After that, he went on up to his own room, unpacked his luggage, which had already been delivered from the spaceport, and took out a small, sealed package. Just at that moment there was a soft chiming sound and his card was returned to him from a delivery slot in the room wall. It fell into the salver below the slot and he picked it up, to read what was written on the face of it. The penciled note read:

Come on up—
K.

He tucked the card and the package into a pocket and left his transient room. And Tyburn, who had followed him to the hotel, and who had been observing all of Ian's actions from the second of his arrival, through sensors placed in the walls and ceilings, half rose from his chair in the room of the empty suite directly above Kenebuck's, which had been quietly taken over as a police observation post. Then, helplessly, Tyburn swore and sat down again, to follow Ian's movements in the screen fed by the sensors. So far there was nothing the policeman could do legally—nothing but watch.

So he watched as Ian strode down the softly carpeted hallway to the elevator tube, rose in it to the eightieth floor and stepped out to face the heavy, transparent door sealing off the resident section of the hotel. He held up Kenebuck's card with its message to a concierge screen beside the door, and with a soft sigh of air the door slid back to let him through. He passed on in, found a second elevator tube, and took it up thirteen more stories. Black doors opened before him—and he stepped one step forward into a small foyer to find himself surrounded by three men.

They were big men—one, a lantern-jawed giant, was even bigger than Ian—and they were vicious. Tyburn, watching through the sensor in the foyer ceiling that had been secretly placed there by the police the day before, recognized all of them from his files. They were underworld muscle hired by Kenebuck at word of Ian's coming; all armed, and brutal and hair-trigger—mad dogs of the lower city. After that first step into their midst, Ian stood still. And there followed a strange, unnatural cessation of movement in the room.

The three stood checked. They had been about to put their hands on Ian to search him for something, Tyburn saw, and probably to rough him up in the process. But something had stopped them, some abrupt change in the air around them. Tyburn, watching, felt the change as they did; but for a moment he felt it without understanding. Then understanding came to him.

The difference was in Ian, in the way he stood there. He was, saw Tyburn, simply . . . waiting. That same patient indifference Tyburn had seen upon him in the Terminal office was there again. In the split second of his single step into the room he had discovered the men, had measured them, and stopped. Now, he waited, in his turn, for one of them to make a move.

A sort of black lightning had entered the small foyer. It was abruptly obvious to the watching Tyburn, as to the three below, that the first of them to lay hands on Ian would be the first to find the hands of the Dorsai soldier upon him—and those hands were death.

For the first time in his life, Tyburn saw the personal power of the Dorsai fighting man, made plain without words. Ian needed no badge upon him, standing as he stood now, to warn that he was dangerous. The men about him were mad dogs; but, patently, Ian was a wolf. There was a difference with the three, which Tyburn now recognized for the first time. Dogs —even mad dogs—fight, and the losing dog, if he can, runs away. But no wolf runs. For a wolf wins every fight but one, and in that one he dies.

After a moment, when it was clear that none of the

three would move, Ian stepped forward. He passed through them without even brushing against one of them, to the inner door opposite, and opened it and went on through.

He stepped into a three-level living room stretching to a large, wide window, its glass rolled up, and black with the sleet-filled night. The living room was as large as a small suite in itself, and filled with people, men and women, richly dressed. They held cocktail glasses in their hands as they stood or sat, and talked. The atmosphere was heavy with the scents of alcohol, and women's perfumes and cigarette smoke. It seemed that they paid no attention to his entrance, but their eyes followed him covertly once he had passed.

He walked forward through the crowd, picking his way to a figure before the dark window, the figure of a man almost as tall as himself, erect, athletic-looking with a handsome, sharp-cut face under whitish-blond hair that stared at Ian with a sort of incredulity as Ian approached.

"Graeme . . . ?" said this man, as Ian stopped before him. His voice in this moment of off-guardedness betrayed its two levels, the semi-hoodlum whine and harshness underneath, the polite accents above. "My boys . . . you didn't—" he stumbled, "leave anything with them when you were coming in?"

"No," said Ian. "You're James Kenebuck, of course. You look like your brother." Kenebuck stared at him.

"Just a minute," he said. He set down his glass, turned and went quickly through the crowd and into the foyer, shutting the door behind him. In the hush of the room, those there heard, first silence then a short, unintelligible burst of sharp voices, then silence again.

Kenebuck came back into the room, two spots of angry color high on his cheekbones. He came back to face Ian.

"Yes," he said, halting before Ian. "They were supposed to . . . tell me when you came in." He fell silent, evidently waiting for Ian to speak, but Ian merely stood, examining him, until the spots of color on Kenebuck's cheekbones flared again.

"Well?" he said, abruptly. "Well? You came here to see me about Brian, didn't you? What about Brian?" He added, before Ian could answer, in a tone suddenly brutal: "I know he was shot, so you don't have to break that news to me. I suppose you want to tell me he showed all sorts of noble guts—refused a blindfold and that sort of—"

"No," said Ian. "He didn't die nobly."

Kenebuck's tall, muscled body jerked a little at the words, almost as if the bullets of an invisible firing squad had poured into it.

"Well . . . that's fine!" he laughed angrily. "You come light-years to see me and then you tell me that! I thought you liked him—liked Brian."

"Liked him? No," Ian shook his head. Kenebuck stiffened, his face for a moment caught in a gape of bewilderment. "As a matter of fact," went on Ian, "he was a glory-hunter. That made him a poor soldier and a worse officer. I'd have transferred him out of my command if I'd had time before the campaign on Freiland started. Because of him, we lost the lives of thirty-two men in his Force, that night."

"Oh." Kenebuck pulled himself together, and looked sourly at Ian. "Those thirty-two men. You've got them on your conscience—is that it?"

"No," said Ian. There was no emphasis on the word

as he said it, but somehow to Tyburn's ears above, the brief short negative dismissed Kenebuck's question with an abruptness like contempt. The spots of color on Kenebuck's cheeks flamed.

"You didn't like Brian and your conscience doesn't bother you—what're you here for, then?" he snapped.

"My duty brings me," said Ian.

"Duty?" Kenebuck's face stilled, and went rigid.

Ian reached slowly into his pocket as if he were surrendering a weapon under the guns of an enemy and did not want his move misinterpreted. He brought out the package from his pocket.

"I brought you Brian's personal effects," he said. He turned and laid the package on a table beside Kenebuck. Kenebuck stared down at the package and the color over his cheekbones faded until his face was nearly as pale as his hair. Then slowly, hesitantly, as if he were approaching a booby-trap, he reached out and gingerly picked it up. He held it and turned to Ian, staring into Ian's eyes, almost demandingly.

"It's in here?" said Kenebuck, in a voice barely above a whisper, and with a strange emphasis.

"Brian's effects," said Ian, watching him.

"Yes . . . sure. All right," said Kenebuck. He was plainly trying to pull himself together, but his voice was still almost whispering. "I guess . . . that settles it."

"That settles it," said Ian. Their eyes held together. "Good-by," said Ian. He turned and walked back through the silent crowd and out of the living room. The three muscle-men were no longer in the foyer. He took the elevator tube down and returned to his own hotel room.

Tyburn, who with a key to the service elevators, had

not had to change tubes on the way down as Ian had, was waiting for him when Ian entered. Ian did not seem surprised to see Tyburn there, and only glanced casually at the policeman as he crossed to a decanter of Dorsai whisky that had since been delivered up to the room.

"That's that, then!" burst out Tyburn, in relief. "You got in to see him and he ended up letting you out. You can pack up and go, now. It's over."

"No," said Ian. "Nothing's over yet." He poured a few inches of the pungent, dark whisky into a glass, and moved the decanter over another glass. "Drink?"

"I'm on duty," said Tyburn, sharply.

"There'll be a little wait," said Ian, calmly. He poured some whisky into the other glass, took up both glasses, and stepped across the room to hand one to Tyburn. Tyburn found himself holding it. Ian had stepped on to stand before the wall-high window. Outside, night had fallen; but—faintly seen in the lights from the city levels below—the sleet here above the weather shield still beat like small, dark ghosts against the transparency.

"Hang it, man, what more do you want?" burst out Tyburn. "Can't you see it's you I'm trying to protect —as well as Kenebuck? I don't want *anyone* killed! If you stay around here now, you're asking for it. I keep telling you, here in Manhattan Complex you're the helpless one, not Kenebuck. Do you think he hasn't made plans to take care of you?"

"Not until he's sure," said Ian, turning from the ghost-sleet, beating like lost souls against the window-glass, trying to get in.

"Sure about what? Look, Commandant," said Tyburn, trying to speak calmly, "half an hour after we heard from the Freiland-North Police about you,

225

Kenebuck called my office to ask for police protection." He broke off, angrily. "Don't look at me like that! How do I know how he found out you were coming? I tell you he's rich, and he's got connections! But the point is, the police protection he's got is just a screen—an excuse—for whatever he's got planned for you on his own. You saw those hoods in the foyer!"

"Yes," said Ian, unemotionally.

"Well, think about it!" Tyburn glared at him. "Look, I don't hold any brief for James Kenebuck! All right—let me tell you about him! We knew he'd been trying to get rid of his brother since Brian was ten—but blast it, Commandant, Brian was no angel, either—"

"I know," said Ian, seating himself in a chair opposite Tyburn.

"All right, you know! I'll tell you anyway!" said Tyburn. "Their grandfather was a local kingpin—he was in every racket on the eastern seaboard. He was one of the mob, with millions he didn't dare count because of where they'd come from. In their father's time, those millions started to be fed into legitimate businesses. The third generation, James and Brian, didn't inherit anything that wasn't legitimate. Hell, we couldn't even make a jaywalking ticket stick against one of them, if we'd ever wanted to. James was twenty and Brian ten when their father died, and when he died the last bit of tattle-tale gray went out of the family linen. But they kept their hoodlum connections, Commandant!"

Ian sat, glass in hand, watching Tyburn almost curiously.

"Don't you get it?" snapped Tyburn. "I tell you that, on paper, in law, Kenebuck's twenty-four carat gilt-edge. But his family was hoodlum, he was raised like a hoodlum, and he thinks like a hood! He didn't want his young brother Brian around to share the crown prince position with him—so he set out to get rid of him. He couldn't just have him killed, so he set out to cut him down, show him up, break his spirit, until Brian took one chance too many trying to match up to his older brother, and killed himself off."

Ian slowly nodded.

"All right!" said Tyburn. "So Kenebuck finally succeeded. He chased Brian until the kid ran off and became a professional soldier—something Kenebuck wouldn't leave his wine, women and song long enough to shine at. And he can shine at most things he really wants to shine at, Commandant. Under that hood attitude and all those millions, he's got a good mind and a good body that he's made a hobby out of training. But, all right. So now it turns out Brian was still no good, and he took some soldiers along when he finally got around to doing what Kenebuck wanted, and getting himself killed. All right! But what can you do about it? What can anyone do about it, with all the connections, and all the money and all the law on Kenebuck's side of it? And, why should you think about doing something about it, anyway?"

"It's my duty," said Ian. He had swallowed half the whisky in his glass, absently, and now he turned the glass thoughtfully around, watching the brown liquor swirl under the forces of momentum and gravity. He looked up at Tyburn. "You know that, Lieutenant."

"Duty! Is duty that important?" demanded Tyburn. Ian gazed at him, then looked away, at the ghost-sleet beating vainly against the glass of the window that held it back in the outer dark.

"Nothing's more important than duty," said Ian, half to himself, his voice thoughtful and remote.

"Mercenary troops have the right to care and protection from their own officers. When they don't get it, they're entitled to justice, so that the same thing is discouraged from happening again. That justice is a duty."

Tyburn blinked, and unexpectedly a wall seemed to go down in his mind.

"Justice for those thirty-two dead soldiers of Brian's!" he said, suddenly understanding. "That's what brought you here!"

"Yes." Ian nodded, and lifted his glass almost as if to the sleet-ghosts to drink the rest of his whisky.

"But," said Tyburn, staring at him, "You're trying to bring a civilian to justice. And Kenebuck has you out-gunned and out-maneuvered—"

The chiming of the communicator screen in one corner of the hotel room interrupted him. Ian put down his empty glass, went over to the screen and depressed a stud. His wide shoulders and back hid the screen from Tyburn, but Tyburn heard his voice.

"Yes?"

The voice of James Kenebuck sounded in the hotel room.

"Graeme—listen!"

There was a pause.

"I'm listening," said Ian, calmly.

"I'm alone now," said the voice of Kenebuck. It was tight and harsh. "My guests have gone home. I was just looking through that package of Brian's things . . ." He stopped speaking and the sentence seemed to Tyburn to dangle unfinished in the air of the hotel room. Ian let it dangle for a long moment.

"Yes?" he said, finally.

"Maybe I was a little hasty . . ." said Kenebuck.

But the tone of his voice did not match the words. The tone was savage. "Why don't you come up, now that I'm alone, and we'll . . . talk about Brian, after all?"

"I'll be up," said Ian.

He snapped off the screen and turned around.

"Wait!" said Tyburn, starting up out of his chair. "You can't go up there!"

"Can't?" Ian looked at him. "I've been invited, Lieutenant."

The words were like a damp towel slapping Tyburn in the face, waking him up.

"That's right . . ." he stared at Ian. "Why? Why'd he invite you back?"

"He's had time," said Ian, "to be alone. And to look at that package of Brian's."

"But . . ." Tyburn scowled. "There was nothing important in that package. A watch, a wallet, a passport, some other papers . . . Customs gave us a list. There wasn't anything unusual there."

"Yes," said Ian. "And that's why he wants to see me again."

"But what does he want?"

"He wants me," said Ian. He met the puzzlement of Tyburn's gaze. "He was always jealous of Brian," Ian explained, almost gently. "He was afraid Brian would grow up to outdo him in things. That's why he tried to break Brian, even to kill him. But now Brian's come back to face him."

"Brian . . . ?"

"In me," said Ian. He turned toward the hotel door.

Tyburn watched him turn, then suddenly—like a man coming out of a daze, he took three hurried strides after him as Ian opened the door.

"Wait!" snapped Tyburn. "He won't be alone up there! He'll have hoods covering you through the

229

walls. He'll definitely have traps set for you . . ."

Easily, Ian lifted the policeman's grip from his arm. "I know," he said. And went.

Tyburn was left in the open doorway, staring after him. As Ian stepped into the elevator tube, the police-man moved. He ran for the service elevator that would take him back to the police observation post above the sensors in the ceiling of Kenebuck's living room.

When Ian stepped into the foyer the second time, it was empty. He went to the door to the living room of Kenebuck's suite, found it ajar, and stepped through it. Within the room was empty, with glasses and overflowing ashtrays still on the tables; the lights had been lowered. Kenebuck rose from a chair with its back to the far, large window at the end of the room. Ian walked toward him and stopped when they were little more than an arm's length apart.

Kenebuck stood for a second, staring at him, the skin of his face tight. Then he made a short almost angry gesture with his right hand. The gesture gave away the fact that he had been drinking.

"Sit down!" he said. Ian took a comfortable chair and Kenebuck sat down in the one from which he had just risen. "Drink?" said Kenebuck. There was a de-canter and glasses on the table beside and between them. Ian shook his head. Kenebuck poured part of a glass for himself.

"That package of Brian's things," he said, abruptly, the whites of his eyes glinting as he glanced up under his lids at Ian, "there was just personal stuff. Nothing else in it!"

"What else did you expect would be in it?" asked Ian, calmly.

Kenebuck's hands clenched suddenly on the glass.

He stared at Ian, and then burst out into a laugh that rang a little wildly against the emptiness of the large room.

"No, no . . ." said Kenebuck, loudly. "I'm asking the questions, Graeme. I'll ask them! What made you come all the way here, to see me, anyway?"

"My duty," said Ian.

"Duty? Duty to whom—Brian?" Kenebuck looked as if he would laugh again, then thought better of it. There was the white, wild flash of his eyes again. "What was something like Brian to you? You said you didn't even like him."

"That was beside the point," said Ian, quietly. "He was one of my officers."

"One of your officers! He was my brother! That's more than being one of your officers!"

"Not," answered Ian in the same voice, "where justice is concerned."

"Justice?" Kenebuck laughed. "Justice for Brian? Is that it?"

"And for thirty-two enlisted men."

"Oh—" Kenebuck snorted laughingly. "Thirty-two men . . . those thirty-two men!" He shook his head. "I never knew your thirty-two men, Graeme, so you can't blame me for them. That was Brian's fault; him and his idea—what was the charge they tried him on? Oh, yes, that he and his thirty-two or thirty-six men could raid enemy Headquarters and come back with the enemy Commandant. Come back . . . covered with glory." Kenebuck laughed again. "But it didn't work. Not my fault."

"Brian did it," said Ian, "to show you. You were what made him do it."

"Me? Could I help it if he never could match up to me?" Kenebuck stared down at his glass and took a quick swallow from it then went back to cuddling it in his hands. He smiled a little to himself. "Never could even *catch* up to me." He looked whitely across at Ian. "I'm just a better man, Graeme. You better remember that."

Ian said nothing. Kenebuck continued to stare at him; and slowly Kenebuck's face grew more savage.

"Don't believe me, do you?" said Kenebuck, softly. "You better believe me. I'm not Brian, and I'm not bothered by Dorsais. You're here, and I'm facing you —alone."

"Alone?" said Ian. For the first time Tyburn, above the ceiling over the heads of the two men, listening and watching through hidden sensors, thought he heard a hint of emotion—contempt—in Ian's voice. Or had he imagined it?

"Alone—Well!" James Kenebuck laughed again, but a little cautiously. "I'm a civilized man, not a hick frontiersman. But I don't have to be a fool. Yes, I've got men covering you from behind the walls of the room here. I'd be stupid not to. And I've got this . . ." He whistled, and something about the size of a small dog, but made of smooth, black metal, slipped out from behind a sofa nearby and slid on an aircushion over the carpeting to their feet.

Ian looked down. It was a sort of satchel with an orifice in the top from which two metallic tentacles protruded slightly.

Ian nodded slightly.

"A medical mech," he said.

"Yes," said Kenebuck, "cued to respond to the heartbeats of anyone in the room with it. So you see, it wouldn't do you any good, even if you somehow knew where all my guards were and beat them to the draw. Even if you killed me, this could get to me in time to keep it from being permanent. So, I'm unkillable. Give up!" He laughed and kicked at the mech. "Get back," he said to it. It slid back behind the sofa.

"So you see . . ." he said. "Just sensible precautions. There's no trick to it. You're a military man—and what's that mean? Superior strength. Superior tactics. That's all. So I outpower your strength, outnumber you, make your tactics useless—and what are you? Nothing." He put his glass carefully aside on the table with the decanter. "But I'm not Brian. I'm not afraid of you. I could do without these things if I wanted to."

Ian sat watching him. On the floor above, Tyburn had stiffened.

"Could you?" asked Ian.

Kenebuck stared at him. The white face of the millionaire contorted. Blood surged up into it, darkening it. His eyes flashed whitely.

"What're you trying to do—test me?" he shouted suddenly. He jumped to his feet and stood over Ian, waving his arms furiously. It was, recognized Tyburn overhead, the calculated, self-induced hysterical rage of the hoodlum world. But how would Ian Graeme below know that? Suddenly, Kenebuck was screaming. "You want to try me out? You think I won't face you? You think I'll back down like that brother of mine, that . . ." he broke into a flood of obscenity in which the name of Brian was freely mixed. Abruptly, he whirled about to the walls of the room, yelling at them. "Get out of there! All right, out! Do you hear me? All of you! Out—"

Panels slid back, bookcases swung aside and four men stepped into the room. Three were those who had been in the foyer earlier when Ian had entered for the first time. The other was of the same type.

"Out!" screamed Kenebuck at them. "Everybody

out. Outside, and lock the door behind you. I'll show this Dorsai, this . . ." almost foaming at the mouth, he lapsed into obscenity again.

Overhead, above the ceiling, Tyburn found himself gripping the edge of the table below the observation screen so hard his fingers ached.

"It's a trick!" he muttered between his teeth to the unhearing Ian. "He planned it this way! Can't you see that?"

"Graeme armed?" inquired the police sensor technician at Tyburn's right. Tyburn jerked his head around momentarily to stare at the technician.

"No," said Tyburn. "Why?"

"Kenebuck is." The technician reached over and tapped the screen, just below the left shoulder of Kenebuck's jacket image. "Slug-thrower."

Tyburn made a fist of his aching right fingers and softly pounded the table before the screen in frustration.

"All right!" Kenebuck was shouting below, turning back to the still-seated form of Ian, and spreading his arms wide. "Now's your chance. Jump me! The door's locked. You think there's anyone else near to help me? Look!" He turned and took five steps to the wide, knee-high to ceiling window behind him, punched the control button and watched as it swung wide. A few of the whirling sleet-ghosts outside drove from out of ninety stories of vacancy, into the opening—and fell dead in little drops of moisture on the windowsill as the automatic weather shield behind the glass blocked them out.

He stalked back to Ian, who had neither moved nor changed expression through all this. Slowly, Kenebuck sank back down into his chair, his back to the night, the blocked-out cold and the sleet.

"What's the matter?" he asked, slowly, acidly. "You don't do anything? Maybe *you* don't have the nerve, Graeme?"

"We were talking about Brian," said Ian.

"Yes, Brian . . ." Kenebuck said, quite slowly. "He had a big head. He wanted to be like me, but no matter how he tried—how I tried to help him—he couldn't make it." He stared at Ian. "That's just the way, he never could make it—the way he decided to go into enemy lines when there wasn't a chance in the world. That's the way he was—a loser."

"With help," said Ian.

"What? What's that you're saying?" Kenebuck jerked upright in his chair.

"You helped him lose," Ian's voice was matter of fact. "From the time he was a young boy, you built him up to want to be like you—to take long chances and win. Only your chances were always safe bets, and his were as unsafe as you could make them."

Kenebuck drew in an audible, hissing breath.

"You've got a big mouth, Graeme!" he said, in a low, slow voice.

"You wanted," said Ian, almost conversationally, "to have him kill himself off. But he never quite did. And each time he came back for more, because he had it stuck into his mind, carved into his mind, that he wanted to impress you—even though by the time he was grown, he saw what you were up to. He knew, but he still wanted to make you admit that he wasn't a loser. You'd twisted him that way while he was growing up, and that was the way he grew."

"Go on," hissed Kenebuck. "Go on, big mouth."

"So, he went off-Earth and became a professional soldier," went on Ian, steadily and calmly. "Not because he was drafted like someone from Newton or a

born professional from the Dorsai, or hungry like one
of the ex-miners from Coby. But to show you you were
wrong about him. He found one place where you
couldn't compete with him, and he must have started
writing back to you to tell you about it—half rubbing
it in, half asking for the pat on the back you never gave
him."

Kenebuck sat in the chair and breathed. His eyes
were all one glitter.

"But you didn't answer his letters," said Ian. "I
suppose you thought that'd make him desperate
enough to finally do something fatal. But he didn't.
Instead he succeeded. He went up through the ranks.
Finally, he got his commission and made Force-Leader, and you began to be worried. It wouldn't be long,
if he kept on going up, before he'd be above the field
officer grades, and out of most of the actual fighting."

Kenebuck sat perfectly still, a little leaning forward.
He looked almost as if he were praying, or putting all
the force of his mind to willing that Ian finish what he
had started to say.

"And so," said Ian, "on his twenty-third birthday—
which was the day before the night on which he led his
men against orders into the enemy area—you saw that
he got this birthday card . . ." He reached into a side
pocket of his civilian jacket and took out a white,
folded card that showed signs of having been savagely
crumpled but was now smoothed out again. Ian
opened it and laid it beside the decanter on the table
between their chairs, the sketch and legend facing
Kenebuck. Kenebuck's eyes dropped to look at it.

The sketch was a crude outline of a rabbit, with a
combat rifle and battle helmet discarded at its feet,
engaged in painting a broad yellow stripe down the
center of its own back. Underneath this picture was

printed in block letters, the question—"WHY FIGHT IT?"

Kenebuck's face slowly rose from the sketch to face Ian, and the millionaire's mouth stretched at the corners, and went on stretching into a ghastly version of a smile.

"Was that all . . . ?" whispered Kenebuck.

"Not all," said Ian. "Along with it, glued to the paper by the rabbit, there was this—"

He reached almost casually into his pocket.

"No, you don't!" screamed Kenebuck triumphantly. Suddenly he was on his feet, jumping behind his chair, backing away toward the darkness of the window behind him. He reached into his jacket and his hand came out holding the slug-thrower, which cracked loudly in the room. Ian had not moved, and his body jerked to the heavy impact of the slug.

Suddenly, Ian had come to life. Incredibly, after being hammered by a slug, the shock of which should have immobilized an ordinary man, Ian was out of the chair on his feet and moving forward. Kenebuck screamed again—this time with pure terror—and began to back away, firing as he went.

"Die, you—! Die!" he screamed. But the towering Dorsai figure came on. Twice it was hit and spun clear around by the heavy slugs, but like a football fullback shaking off the assaults of tacklers, it plunged on, with great strides narrowing the distance between it and the retreating Kenebuck.

Screaming finally, Kenebuck came up with the back of his knees against the low sill of the open window. For a second his face distorted itself out of all human shape in a grimace of its terror. He looked, to right and to left, but there was no place left to run. He had been pulling the trigger of his slugthrower all this time, but now the firing pin clicked at last upon an empty chamber. Gibbering, he threw the weapon at Ian, and it flew wide of the driving figure of the Dorsai, now almost upon him, great hands outstretched.

Kenebuck jerked his head away from what was rushing toward him. Then, with a howl like a beaten dog, he turned and flung himself through the window before those hands could touch him, into ninety-odd stories of unsupported space. And his howl carried away down into silence.

Ian halted. For a second he stood before the window, his right hand still clenched about whatever it was he had pulled from his pocket. Then, like a toppling tree, he fell.

—As Tyburn and the technician with him finished burning through the ceiling above and came dropping through the charred opening into the room. They almost landed on the small object that had come rolling from Ian's now-lax hand. An object that was really two objects glued together. A small paint-brush and a transparent tube of glaringly yellow paint.

"I hope you realize, though," said Tyburn, two weeks later on an icy, bright December day as he and the recovered Ian stood just inside the Terminal waiting for the boarding signal from the spaceliner about to take off for the Sirian worlds, "what a chance you took with Kenebuck. It was just luck it worked out for you the way it did."

"No," said Ian. He was as apparently emotionless as ever; a little more gaunt from his stay in the Manhattan hospital, but he had mended with the swiftness of his Dorsai constitution. "There was no luck. It all happened the way I planned it."

Tyburn gazed in astonishment.

"Why . . ." he said, "if Kenebuck hadn't had to send his hoods out of the room to make it seem necessary for him to shoot you himself when you put your hand into your pocket that second time—or if you hadn't had the card in the first place—" He broke off, suddenly thoughtful. "You mean . . . ?" he stared at Ian. "Having the card, you planned to have Kenebuck get you alone . . . ?"

"It was a form of personal combat," said Ian. "And personal combat is my business. You assumed that Kenebuck was strongly entrenched, facing my attack. But it was the other way around."

"But you had to come to him—"

"I had to appear to come to him," said Ian, almost coldly. "Otherwise he wouldn't have believed that he had to kill me—before I killed him. By his decision to kill me, he put himself in the attacking position."

"But he had all the advantages!" said Tyburn, his head whirling. "You had to fight on his ground, here where he was strong . . ."

"No," said Ian. "You're confusing the attack position with the defensive one. By coming here, I put Kenebuck in the position of finding out whether I actually had the birthday card, and the knowledge of why Brian had gone against orders into enemy territory that night. Kenebuck planned to have his men in the foyer shake me down for the card—but they lost their nerve."

"I remember," murmured Tyburn.

"Then, when I handed him the package, he was sure the card was in it. But it wasn't," went on Ian. "He saw his only choice was to give me a situation where I might feel it was safe to admit having the card and the knowledge. He had to know about that, because Brian had called his bluff by going out and risking his neck after getting the card. The fact Brian was tried and executed later made no difference to Kenebuck. That was a matter of law—something apart from hoodlum guts, or lack of guts. If no one knew that Brian was braver than his older brother, that was all right; but if I knew, he could only save face under his own standards by killing me."

"He almost did," said Tyburn. "Any one of those slugs—"

"There was the medical mech," said Ian, calmly. "A man like Kenebuck would be bound to have something like that around to play safe—just as he would be bound to set an amateur's trap." The boarding horn of the spaceliner sounded. Ian picked up his luggage bag. "Good-by," he said, offering his hand to Tyburn.

"Good-by . . ." he muttered. "So you were just going along with Kenebuck's trap, all of it. I can't believe it . . ." He released Ian's hand and watched as the big man swung around and took the first two strides away toward the bulk of the ship shining in the winter sunlight. Then, suddenly, the numbness broke clear from Tyburn's mind. He ran after Ian and caught at his arm. Ian stopped and swung half-around, frowning slightly.

"I can't believe it!" cried Tyburn. "You mean you went up there, *knowing* Kenebuck was going to pump you full of slugs and maybe kill you—all just to square things for thirty-two enlisted soldiers under the command of a man you didn't even like? I don't believe it —you can't be that cold-blooded! I don't care how much of a man of the military you are!"

Ian looked down at him. And it seemed to Tyburn that the Dorsai face had gone away from him, somehow become as remote and stony as a face carved high up on some icy mountain's top.

"But I'm not just a man of the military," Ian said. "That was the mistake Kenebuck made, too. That was why he thought that stripped of military elements, I'd be easy to kill."

Tyburn, looking at him, felt a chill run down his spine as icy as wind off a glacier.

"Then, in heaven's name," cried Tyburn. "What are you?"

Ian looked from his far distance down into Tyburn's eyes and the sadness rang as clear in his voice finally, as iron-shod heels on barren rock.

"I am a man of war," said Ian, softly.

With that, he turned and went on; and Tyburn saw him black against the winter-bright sky, looming over all the other departing passengers, on his way to board the spaceship.

The Plume and the Sword
by
Sandra Miesel

"Fantasy abandoned by reason produces impossible monsters; united with it, she is the mother of the arts and origin of marvels."

—Goya

In life even as in art, the harmony of opposites is Gordon R. Dickson's constant goal. This man who unifies opposing principles in his fiction unites within himself the most disparate extremes of frivolity and keenness—the plume and sword alike are his to wear.

In person, Dickson's fluffiness has always made the greatest impression on the greatest number of people. He is everyone's favorite conventioneer. (During his forty years in sf fandom, he has attended hundreds of conventions.) His image as the jolly party-goer, singing and playing the guitar until dawn, led Ben Bova to parody *My Darling Clementine* in Dickson's honor. The chorus concludes: "Science fiction is his hobby/ But his main job's having fun."

Dickson is a veteran trencherman, a mainstay of epic dinner parties, but he has also been known to spend more time selecting the wine than eating the meal. His bizarre preference for drinking milk, juice, coffee, beer, and Bloody Marys at the same breakfast has been cause for comment since his student days at the University of Minnesota thirty years ago. Lately, allergies (including—alas—a mild one to wine) and a desire for waistline trimness have tempered these habits somewhat, but Dickson's zest for living remains uncommonly brisk.

Yet such pleasures are the least components of his *joie de vivre*. Dickson has a capacity for wonder that will not be worn out. It has been claimed that no one else can say "golly" quite as joyfully as he does. (Dickson's habit of burbling along in innocent schoolboy exclamations once inspired some of his friends to stage a "Gordon R. Dickson Murfle-Alike Contest.")

Enthusiasm colors everything he does. He not only admires fine craftsmanship, he quizzes craftsmen on the tools, techniques, and attitudes that support their skills. (How many men would demand to see the wrong side of embroidered fabric?) He is always eager for new knowledge and fresh experiences. Recent endeavors include lessons in bagpipe-playing and in *akido*. Moreover, he encourages the same adventurousness in others. His friends have found themselves wielding knives, making lace, or writing novels for the first time at his urging.

Dickson describes himself as "a galloping optimist," unshakably certain that "man's future is onward and upward." Right must inevitably triumph. He admits that human beings may not be quite perfectible—"Perfectible is a little too good to be true—but improvable, tremendously improvable by their own strength."

Idealism gives him confidence in his own potential as well as that of his species. After watching his own Childe Cycle gradually move from rejection to acceptance, after observing fractious humans slowly struggle to build things together, Dickson concludes that creativity can overcome all obstacles. It is the only sure key to progress.

This same confidence in creativity makes him patient with other people, no matter how unpromising they may seem. He is among the most approachable of all sf professionals. For instance, few others would have taken the time to explain the elementary rules of prosody to an aspiring ballad writer and then been on hand afterwards to applaud her first acceptable efforts. Dickson's forbearance, skill, and above all, his respect for even the grubbiest amateur's dignity, have made him a superb mentor for young authors who are serious about their art. (Among the newer names in sf who have at times listened to him are Joe Haldeman, Robert Aspirin, and Lynn Abbey.) Dickson tends to downplay his influence because he believes that "fine teaching comes as automatically as breathing" to experienced writers. Yet his inner nature is revealed by the positive effects he has on those around him. For the past three decades his encouragement of talent and his support of professionalism have worked like buds of yeast to leaven the sf field.

One thing Dickson will not endure patiently is a shoddy performance. His Victorian upbringing imbued him with high standards of excellence. He has a born aristocrat's awareness of his own prerogatives, even in trivial matters: woe to the careless waiter who serves Dickson's vichyssoise improperly chilled. But his special ire is reserved for time-wasters too lazy to develop their own talents. "Some people," he complains, "like my advice so much, they frame it and hang it on the wall instead of using it." Fortunately such failures are rare. Most of those who beseech his advice or cry on his broad shoulders put the experience to good use.

Dickson's helpfulness arouses a corresponding helpfulness in others. Whether he asks for a Puritan sermon text, an Italian menu, a sample of Gregorian chant, or medical data on battle wounds, someone will promptly provide it—fandom is a living data bank. So grateful is he for help, he attracts almost too much solicitude. At times the attentiveness of friends reduces Dickson to the status of a favorite teddy bear in danger of having all its fur petted off.

Dickson's admirers do react intensely. Women's tears over the fate of Ian Graeme in *Soldier, Ask Not* prodded him to re-examine the implications of his text and see a solution to the tragedy. Other fans want to elaborate the Cycle's background with or without the author's sanction. There was the lawyer who speculated on interstellar legal systems and the artist who tried to predict future art tastes. The most conspicuous example of this phenomenon is a non-profit organization known as the Dorsai Irregulars which provides security services at sf conventions, sometimes in costume. The author has licensed their use of the Dorsai name and insignia.

Dickson appreciates such vivid identification because he enjoys playing roles himself. The historical persona he designed to join the Society for Creative Anachronism is "Kenneth of Otterburn," a fourteenth-century border lord whose heraldic badge is the otter. This character is a bow to duality in general and to Dickson's own Anglo-Scottish heritage in particular. One earlier member of his family, Simon Fraser, the eleventh Lord Lovat, was beheaded in 1747 for supporting Bonnie Prince Charlie. The official Dickson crest is: "a hart couchant gardant proper; attired, or within two branches of laurel leaves vert in orle," which is to say, a stag with gilded horns at rest on a field bordered with green laurel leaves. The family motto is *"Cubo sed curo,"* "I lie down but I remain watchful."

More importantly, this SCA project, like so many of

Dickson's activities, is a remote preparation for the Childe Cycle. The climax of *Childe,* the concluding volume of the series, will be modeled on the Battle of Otterburn fought between the English and the Scots in 1388. Furthermore, investigating the life of an imaginary medieval nobleman will also give the author special insights into the mind of the real Sir John Hawkwood, hero of the Cycle's planned opening volume.

Dickson is never content to do his research from books, even from primary sources. Whenever possible, he must visit sites and handle actual artifacts. For example, he absorbs historical *mana* by fingering Plantagenet coins and reading gothic manuscripts. When reality is unattainable, he turns to replicas. His most ambitious plan yet is to commission the making of a complete suit of armor such as Hawkwood might have worn. (He rejects suggestions that experiments with fleas, lice, and dysentery might be equally instructive.) So far, he has acquired only the mailshirt, helmet, and a magnificent pair of armored gloves. But attired in a friend's full equippage, Dickson cut a marvelously gallant figure—six feet of russet-haired, blue-eyed knight with a bit of lace visible at his wrist to accent the steel and leather. "I feel as if I could walk through doors," he proclaimed, striding off down the motel corridor. Fortunately, no other guests disputed his passage.

But his own experience did not suffice. He wanted to observe another man's reactions as well. So he convinced a less-than-eager Kelly Freas to try on the armor next. Freas, being shorter and stockier, probably approximated a real medieval knight better than Dickson. Others might have followed suit, but by then the outfit's undergarments were disagreeably drenched with sweat. The author's zeal for medieval weaponry is so compelling that on another occasion he insisted that one notably unmartial colleague take up arms and beat on the maple trees in Dickson's back yard with a sword—all by way of sealing a business partnership.

Although mimetic research sounds amusing, it is no game to Dickson but rather a measure of his dedication to his craft. He needs to set all his senses gathering data in order to generate the authentic details his writing requires. His creativity is almost a metabolic process: information digested, art synthesized. Consider the awesome volume of material he had to process for *The Far Call*, the finest realistic novel about the space program yet written. This book's flavor comes from the author's own fervent pro-space views. Its substance is the product of many visits to Kennedy Space Center and lengthy consultations with experts on the scene. Dickson believes he must eat the bread of a place before he can truly know it.

Dickson deliberately incorporates his own interests, experiences, and values in his fiction. Take, for instance, his fascination with animal psychology. "I tend to gestalt things," he says. "I see humans and animals as illuminating one another by what they do and also humans and animals illuminating aliens and vice versa." Thus Dickson's favorite beasts show up in his pages, either wearing their own hides or disguised as extraterrestrials: bears (*Spacial Delivery, The Alien Way*), wolves (*Sleepwalker's World*), sea mammals (*Home From the Shore, The Space Swimmers*), cats (*Time Storm, The Masters of Everon*), and, of course, otters (*Alien Art*). On the other hand, Dickson lent his own antic enthusiasm and exasperating glee to the teddy bear-like Hokas (*Earthman's Burden, Star Prince Charlie* written with his old college classmate Poul Anderson). Dickson contemplating a gourmet meal or a fine guitar is the very image of a Hoka.

Guitar in hand, Dickson is a pillar of convention "filksings," gatherings of people who perform odd songs which may or may not have any bearing on sf. Although his tenor has lost its original clarity, his renditions of classics like *The Face on the Barroom Floor* or *The Three Ravens* are still enjoyable. It is even more of a treat to hear him sing his own compositions like the grim *Battle Hymn* of the Friendlies, the wistful love song from *Necromancer,* or the rollicking *Ballad of the Shoshonu.* This has inspired some of his fans to write Childe Cycle songs themselves.

Among sf writers, Dickson is second only to Poul Anderson in the ornamental use of songs and poetry. Like Anderson, Dickson was raised on folk ballads, epics, fairy tales, and the great nineteenth-century novels, although there was more of a British than a Scandinavian slant to his literary formation. Furthermore, Dickson along with Anderson, Robert A. Heinlein, Jerry Pournelle, Richard McKenna, John Brunner, and Cordwainer Smith, has been heavily influenced by Rudyard Kipling. (Kipling's impact on sf, now reaching into its second and third generation, has never been adequately investigated.) However, Dickson also cites major mainstream American and Russian authors and even Thomas Mann among his influences.

One expects a professional writer to maintain a large library and, indeed, the walls of Dickson's Richfield, Minnesota home are lined with books. But Dickson is a true bibliophile. He loves books simply as physical objects, delighting in fine bindings and crisp pages. He shows a marked preference for hardbound volumes even for works of passing interest. Accompanying him to a bookstore is like tagging behind a tornado. His ever-expanding holdings are systematically catalogued and he maintains a complete collection of his own editions.

Dickson has stronger opinions than most writers on how his work should be illustrated and collects originals of the illustrations that please him. (Wallspace in his home not devoted to books is mostly covered with art.) His feeling for visual aesthetics was deepened by years of night classes at the Minneapolis Institute of Arts. His studies taught him the difference between written and painted visions. As he ruefully observes, too often writers try to paint with their "writing equipment" while painters try to write with their "painting equipment."

Dickson's life and career are also molded by a complementary set of physical pursuits. Allergies—and time—now bar him from the camping, climbing, and other outdoor recreations he formerly enjoyed. However, on a recent trip to Florida he caught the small marlin that decorates his office wall. Still, the experiences he has had with wildlife and open spaces remain with him as raw material for creative efforts. He would not be the same man or the same writer if boyhood memories of Pacific breakers did not echo in his dreams.

Dickson's handling of nature is subtler than Anderson's lush, almost pantheistic approach. He sees it primarily as a milieu for human action. (His preference for somber, austere landscapes is most sensitively revealed in *Alien Art*.) Having lived in Western Canada as a child and in Minnesota since prompts his frequent use of these regions as story settings, either directly or as models for alien worlds. His beloved Canadian mountains, "the bones of the continent," become the cool, rocky highlands of the Dorsai. Northcountry lakes and woodlands reappear in *Pro*.

Indoors, Dickson's ardor for fitness shames his more sedentary friends. His ambition to achieve something of the high performance under stress he admires in tough old fighting men like Hawkwood led to his involvement with the martial arts—the chivalry of medieval Europe and the *bushido* of feudal Japan have much in common. Formal training has done more than impart special physical skills. It has also reinforced views he already held on self-mastery and functional beauty. Performing a clean knife pass takes the discipline of a dancer; a well-designed blade is a pleasing piece of metal sculpture.

Dickson uses the Oriental martial arts to study the attainment and control of that perennially fascinating phenomenon, the exaltation state. He can and on occasion has discussed the topic for long hours on end. What lies behind hysterical strength, stunning intuition, heroic virtue? Creativity is once again his answer. When human beings operate at the very highest levels their bodies, minds, or spirits permit, they enter a transcendant phase Dickson calls "creative overdrive." In this condition, they can direct their conscious and unconscious powers to some otherwise unreachable goal. Salvation is integration and creativity integrates.

Thus, cerebral, artistic adventure heroes are Dickson's specialty. For instance, in *The Final Encyclopedia*, Hal Mayne is a poet who has passed through previous incarnations as a soldier *(Dorsai!)* and a mystic *(Necromancer)*. Michael de Sandoval in *Lost Dorsai* is a musician and Cletus Grahame in *Tactics of Mistake* has tried painting. Dickson endows his heroes with the talents he himself esteems and lets them demonstrate overdrive by their deeds. They are offered as examples of what the entire race could achieve if only its creative energies were fully liberated.

Dickson himself is an advertisement for his theories. His memory lapses are legendary—once when making introductions, he could not recall his own brother's name. He often confuses the titles of his books, scrambles the locations of his planets, and forgets the lyrics to his own songs. Nevertheless, his mind becomes astonishingly supple and efficient when overdrive directs it in the service of his art. In this heightened state, he can move briskly through public appearances though exhausted and can soar to fresh imaginative insights. For Dickson, creativity is both the journey and the journey's end. It enables him to unite the plumy and swordlike extremes of his own nature in order to work.

He has an unparalleled sense of vocation, a commitment to his artistic mission as keen as any crusader's vow. By writing the Cycle, he hopes to bring the evolutionary progress he describes that much closer. When asked if he expects the Childe Cycle to appear on some thirtieth century list of Ten Books That Changed the Cosmos, Dickson replied with a smile, "And what are the other nine?" His idealism has been dismissed as naive in some quarters but events within and without the sf field continue to vindicate him.

Some authors stumble into their trade for lack of anything better to do; others are forced into it by economic necessity. Not so Dickson: "I've been a writer all my life, as far back as I can remember. Nobody ever told me not to until later on, by which time it was too late." His talents were encouraged by his parents, an Australian-born mining engineer and an American school teacher who met and married in Canada. His older half-brother is the distinguished Canadian novelist Lovat Dickson, but his mother's influence was the crucial formative one. Her reading him books and telling him stories are among his fondest early memories.

Maude Dickson, a wonderfully gracious and spry lady of ninety-one, modestly disputes the importance of her efforts. Nevertheless, her son was a precocious writer: a newspaper published his poem "Apple Blossoms" when he was only seven years old. In 1939, at age fifteen, he entered the University of Minnesota to major in creative writing but his studies were interrupted by military service during World War II. Army aptitude tests predicted he would have a bright future as a dentist.

Dickson graduated in 1948, planning to take his doctorate, teach, and write on the side. He abandoned this "unduly sensible" scheme to follow his gift and write full-time. It was a desperate gamble. He supported himself by selling his blood—twice as often as permitted—and subsisted on a diet of stale bread, peanut butter, and vitamin pills. His sacrifices were rewarded when his first sf story, "The Friendly Man," appeared in *Astounding* in February, 1951.

Three decades, 40 novels, and 175 shorter works later, the gamble may be said to have paid off in honors and prosperity. Dickson has won the Hugo for "Soldier, Ask Not" (1965), the Nebula for "Call Him Lord" (1966), the Jupiter for *Time Storm* (1977), and the British Fantasy Award for *The Dragon and the George* (1978) as well as receiving many other award nominations. These days, a dedicated staff including a full-time business manager and part-time secretarial and research workers assist him. Maintaining his affairs in good order requires an otter-keeper's patience but the task should become easier once the intricacies of his newly purchased computer system are unraveled.

Dickson is one master who seeks perfection in his craft and freely shares his expertise with fellow guildsmen. He served two terms as President of the Science Fiction Writers of America (1969-71) and is currently working to extend the benefits of SFWA's organizational experience to the fledgling Association of Science Fiction Artists. Much in demand as a speaker and resource person, he is one of the few non-academic professional writers in the Science Fiction Research Association. He took part in one Clarion Workshop for new writers and regularly attended the Milford Conference for established writers during the 1960's. (However, he was never known as a member of the infamous "Milford Mafia.") He has also been invited to participate in sessions of the Science Fiction Institute, a teacher-training program held annually at the University of Kansas. Thus, chat by speech, he fosters professional excellence and public understanding.

Dickson's mastery of technique combines theoretical lessons acquired in university classes taught by such people as Sinclair Lewis and Robert Penn Warren with ruthlessly practical ones learned in the low-paying sf magazine market. His faith in his own ability saw him safely through both processes. "I was a fully-formed writer long before I got my degree," he explains. "I had enough mass and momentum along the road I wanted to travel so that I couldn't be jolted off." Neither lethal classroom situations nor the pressure of gaining enough story skills to stay alive blocked his progress.

Now in the mellowness of his maturity, Dickson is reaching the destination he chose for himself half a century ago. He successfully merges style and content, polished literary form and research-based substance, into one liquid whole. Although clarity can be a handicap when critics equate obscurity with profundity, Dickson's art conceals his artfulness on purpose with a view to reaching the widest possible audience. He believes that "good fiction should become transparent so people end up reading it not so much for the words as for the ideas."

Dickson has always been a highly conscious writer. There is nothing random or spontaneous in his tightly structured prose, never a wheel misplaced, never a gear unmeshed. He seeks the optimum configuration for his fictional drive train in order to transmit messages most efficiently. Philosophical convictions generate the relentless power of his best work.

He calls his method of rendering principles in fiction the "consciously thematic novel." This technique, developed from mainstream models, enables him to argue a specific point of view without resorting to propaganda. It presents an unbiased selection of natural incidents to support its thesis. "The aim is to make the theme such an integral part of the novel that it can be effective upon the reader without ever having to be stated explicitly," says Dickson. A consciously thematic story can, of course, be read and enjoyed for its entertainment value alone. But ideally, when the reader sees all the resonances and repetitions, the author hopes that "he will do the work of looking at this slew of evidence I've laid out and will, on his own, come to the conclusion I'd like him to reach."

Dickson calls the Childe Cycle "my showpiece for the consciously thematic novel." Curiously enough, the Cycle itself originated in this very way, through a deeper interpretation of pre-existing evidence—as though the unconscious side of the author's mind were operating on the conscious side via thematic methods.

During the 1940's, Dickson started—but never finished—an historical novel entitled *The Pikeman* about a young Swiss mercenary serving in fifteenth century Italy. This plot, enhanced by ideas drawn from Rafael Sabatini's *Bellarion* and from *Astounding* editor John W. Campbell, yielded *Dorsai!* in 1959. Then during the course of a night-time asthma attack at the following summer's Milford Conference, a hitherto unsuspected pattern sprang at Dickson from the pages of *Dorsai!*. "Eureka! I had it!" he recalls. "I got up the next morning and spent three hours trying to tell Richard McKenna about it, a process by which I sorted it out in my mind. The essential structure was born full-blown at that moment."

The Childe Cycle is an epic of human evolution, a scenario for mankind's rite of passage. Over the course of a thousand years, from the fourteenth century to the twenty-fourth, interactions between three archetypical Prime Characters—the Men of Faith, War, and Philosophy—succeed in uniting the unconscious/conservative and the conscious/progressive halves of the racial psyche. The result is a fully-evolved being endowed with intuition, empathy, and creativity whom Dickson calls Ethical-Responsible Man. At that point, the human organism will no longer be a "childe" but a spurred and belted knight.

In Dickson's future universe, mankind has shattered into Splinter Cultures that develop only one facet of human nature at the expense of the others. The most important Splinter Cultures are: the Dorsai (Warriors—Body), the Exotics (Philosophers—Mind), and the Friendlies (Believers—Spirit) but none of these is fully human and none has the ultimate society. Dickson's Messianic hero Donal Graeme, first-born of the

Ethical-Responsible Men, lives three lives and thereby absorbs the best qualities of Warrior, Philosopher, and Believer. His indomitable will divides the racial psyche in order to develop it, then reunites it in order to perfect it.

When completed, the Cycle will consist of three historical, three contemporary, and six science fiction novels. *Dorsai!* (1959), *Necromancer* (1960), *Soldier, Ask Not* (1968), and *Tactics of Mistake* (1971) have already appeared and are scheduled for reissue by Ace. *The Final Encyclopedia* and *Childe* are currently in preparation. These novels are accompanied by a series of shorter works or "illuminations" that stand outside the argument of the Cycle proper but share the same settings and characters: "Warrior" (1965), "Brothers" (1973), "Amanda Morgan" (1979) and *Lost Dorsai* (1980). "Amanda Morgan" and "Brothers" have been set in a narrative frame with illustrations and published by Ace as *The Spirit of Dorsai* (1979). Although each work can stand alone, it is even more enjoyable understood in proper context. The novels are best read in order of publication rather than according to internal chronology—one should begin with *Dorsai!* to follow Donal Graeme's forays backwards and forwards in time.

The illuminations must not be lumped together with the Cycle in one amorphous mass. There is no such thing as the "Dorsai series." Dickson's subject is mankind, not the Dorsai. Indiscriminate labeling also obscures the uniqueness of Dickson's plan. He is not writing a coherent future history in the manner of Robert A. Heinlein, Poul Anderson, Larry Niven, or Jerry Pournelle. Neither is he merely re-using a familiar universe the way Andre Norton and R.A. Lafferty do. Least of all is Dickson building alien planets like

Hal Clement or alien cultures like C. J. Cherryh.

Notice the vagueness of the chronology, the improbability of the colonial locales, and the essential familiarity of the environments thanks to terraforming. Dickson's universe is not wildly futuristic despite advanced military hardware and a few props like floating chairs. The interstellar flights shown might as well be intercontinental.

Compare Dickson's approach with the exoticism of Frank Herbert. Although *Dune* postdates *Dorsai!*, it, too, features a Messianic hero surrounded by equivalents of the Dorsai, the Exotics, and the Friendlies. Herbert clothes his philosophy in fabulously intricate costumes but Dickson presents his in sleekly functional garb to reveal the form beneath the fabric. In all respects, Dickson's universe is a selected reality, neither naturalistic nor fantastic.

Dickson has staunchly resisted pressure from enthusiastic readers to elaborate the Cycle's background. He introduces new details (such as Dorsai domestic arrangements in "Amanda Morgan") only as required to tell his story. For most of the two decades between *Dorsai!* and *The Final Encyclopedia,* he carried all his notes in his head. This bred a host of small inconsistencies, now purged from these Ace editions. The artistic energy that might have otherwise gone into constructing genealogies or inventing languages powers the illuminations instead. These short works enable the author to spotlight certain characters and events within the Cycle without disturbing its structure.

The illuminations serve many purposes. They dramatize events that are off-stage in the novels: Dorsai non-combatants repelling Earth's elite troops has to be taken on faith in *Tactics of Mistake* but "Amanda

257

Morgan" makes the defense convincing. They magnify incidents: Kensie's death is a mere plot device in *Dorsai!*, attains mythic stature in *Soldier, Ask Not,* and is finally depicted in "Brothers." They bring characters into focus: Corunna El Man has only a cameo role in *Dorsai!* but serves as the roving narrator of *Lost Dorsai* and may become the hero of his own illumination someday. Above all, they elucidate principles: "Warrior" reveals the values a true man of war will live and die for.

Each illumination examines the twin moral issues of integrity and responsibility: how can human beings reconcile what they must be with what they must do? The major arena of conflict is the will—notice how little space is actually devoted to physical combat. The stakes are higher in each succeeding contest because the fates of more people are at risk: a few individuals in "Warrior," a city in "Brothers," a planet in "Amanda Morgan," and all the inhabited worlds in *Lost Dorsai.* Victory must always be bought in blood because the willingness to die is the ultimate proof of commitment. Again and again, the ancient myth of the hero's saving death is played out among the stars. Martyrdom at the hands of enemies in the illuminations complements Donal's voluntary self-sacrifices in the Cycle.

"Warrior" grew from a tiny detail in *Dorsai!*—the terrible scar on Ian's arm. This earliest and simplest of the illuminations sets the pattern for those that followed. It proclaims that fidelity to ideals and duty will ultimately prevail, whatever the odds. Vice is always vulnerable because it cannot comprehend virtue's tactics.

"Warrior" makes explicit what *Dorsai!* only implied: one of Ian's special functions as the ultimate

Man of War is to avenge sins committed by and against warriors. In this story, set a decade before the opening of *Dorsai!*, Ian is still a young commandant. He punishes a reckless officer for wasting his men's lives, then destroys the culprit's gangster brother for goading him to hunt glory. Through Ian, the lone wolf facing mad dogs, Dickson defines the honorable and dishonorable uses of force.

Ian's triumph is shown through the eyes of Tyburn, a conscientious policeman who tries to protect Ian despite his civilian distaste for the military. The reader sees what Tyburn cannot: he, too, in his humble way is a righteous Defender. The proud gifts that bloom in the Dorsai still remain in the rootstock people of Earth. Bringing the potential in all persons to harvest, not glorifying supermen, is the Cycle's goal.

Dickson uses an ordinary man as a "lens of heroic experience" even more skillfully in "Brothers." This story's first person narrator is St. Marie police chief Tomas Velt. He brings the larger-than-life Graeme twins into scale and his reactions make the epic events surrounding Kensie's death believable. Tom is stubbornly normal. He knows his own limitations but does not let them paralyze him. His balance and dedication collide with the self-hatred and thoughtlessness of his best friend and symbolic brother Pel. Pel adores Kensie yet betrays him; Tom undervalues Ian yet aids him. Responsibility is the thread tying Tom to Ian. It makes him Ian's smaller counterpart just as Tyburn was in "Warrior." The policeman and the commander cooperate to find Kensie's assassins before Dorsai wrath falls on the city where the outrage occurred.

Ian's dilemma is the cruelest. He must uphold the Dorsai ideal of restraint and at the same time obtain justice for his slain brother. He risks his life rather

259

than his principles and so gains the victory. His grief for the brother who was his "other self" is measureless in its very silence, like a scream of agony pitched too low for human ears to hear. Initially, Ian shows "no more emotion at his brother's death than he might have on discovering an incorrect Order of the Day." Yet his wordless last farewell to Kensie is fierce enough to crumple steel—and spectators' hearts.

Though Ian is left to walk in darkness all his days, dying cannot dim Kensie's godlike radiance. In retrospect, his murder becomes a sacrifice for his death saves what it was meant to destroy. When the people of St. Marie mourn this beautiful dead Balder, they are cleansed by their own tears. Kensie becomes their adopted hero. By emulating him they will achieve the self-respect and self-control their "fat little farm world" had hitherto lacked. Furthermore, Kensie's assassination interlocks with the voluntary martyrdom of Jamethon Black, the Friendly officer who gives up his life to save his troops in *Soldier, Ask Not*. Both are victims of Tam Olyn, a vengeful Earthman who negates everything they stand for. Yet, in the end this Judas is redeemed, partly through the merits of Kensie, Jamethon, and Ian. When wholeness of heart unites with devotion to duty, nothing evil can endure.

"Amanda Morgan" is as resolutely feminine as "Brothers" is masculine. *The Spirit of Dorsai*'s two components fit together as smoothly as *yin* and *yang*, as naturally as root and blossom. Ian flourishes in the high summer of Dorsai. Amanda was already there at the first signs of spring. Though a century divides them, hero and heroine are complementary halves of the same defensive shield.

As her descendant Amanda III explains, Earth-born Amanda I "was Dorsai before there was a Dorsai world. What she was, was the material out of which our people and our culture here were made." Like the matriarch in *John Brown's Body*, Amanda builds her homestead "out of her blood and bone/ With her heart for the Hall's foundation-stone." She builds well. Her household, Fal Morgan, endures until the Splinter Cultures are no more.

This dynamic heroine makes "Amanda Morgan" a major landmark in Dickson's literary development. Women simply do not exist within the pages of "Brothers"—even its underlying myths are wholly male. However, in the six years following the original publication of "Brothers," Dickson taught himself step by step to expand this "collapsed area of the continuum." Tracing the course of his progress would be an essay in itself, but *The Spirit of Dorsai* is a fine yardstick to measure the gap covered.

Sex-role reversals abound in "Amanda Morgan" without shrieking for attention—this is art, not propaganda. No capital letters announce that the Dorsai world is a *de facto* matriarchy. Initially, women had to manage planetary affairs while their men were off to the wars. (The analogy to medieval chatelaines is obvious and intended.) As economic conditions improve, the proportion of soldiers in the population declines. By Ian's time, only a minority of Dorsai—women as well as men—are professional soldiers, but planetside women still guard the continuity of the culture.

Individual merit affects the pattern as much as necessity. While avoiding the fashionable error of belittling all males to exalt all females, this story allows men to be sensitive and women tough. Minor touches carry out the theme: a reckless young girl protects a smaller, shyer boy; formidable General Khan meekly prepares sandwiches. Major examples cluster around Amanda herself. In the colony's early days, she led the fight against outlaw gangs. Years later when Earth invades the Dorsai, she is still "the best person to command" her District—even at age ninety-two. Amanda personally defies the invaders' General Amorine. (Note the unconscious word play in their names.) Neither his legions nor his shiny hardware impress her, for her strength is that of family, hearth, and the living world.

Unconquerable Amanda is both memorable and complex. Although she is Dorsai through and through, she (and her namesakes the second and third Amandas) can believe, think, and fight like the fully evolved humans of the future. Yet she is not complacent about her own excellence. Self-criticism keeps her learning and growing in her tenth decade of life. In the course of the story she achieves new insights. She discovers that "you love what you give to—and in proportion as you give." (Ian lives by the reverse principle.) She realizes that the most loving thing an integrated and responsible person can do is allow others to master these virtues for themselves. She learns how to let go after a lifetime of holding fast.

"To strive and not to yield" might be the Dorsai motto: no power can break the Dorsai will. It is the capacity to resist Wrong that defines a Dorsai, not physical might. (The one Dorsai renegade mentioned is superbly gifted.) The Dorsai spirit blazes as brightly in crippled bodies as in sound ones, as purely in Amanda as in Ian. What Dorsai indomitability protects is the right to be free. This is their practical function in interstellar politics and their metaphysical function in racial evolution. Whether they die defending their homes or attacking on some foreign battlefield, Dorsai must buy their freedom with blood. These Defenders' readiness to die—and the tactical efficiency of their dying—is their margin of survival.

Lost Dorsai couples the willingness to die with the refusal to kill. This story demonstrates that a Dorsai can even be a pacifist without repudiating his cultural ideals. Tensions between integrity and responsibility are especially severe here because of the number of characters and the intertwined complexity of the difficulties they face.

Both Michael and the second Amanda are "afraid that their instincts would lead them to do what their thinking minds had told them they should not do." His problem is war, hers, love. Her dilemma entangles Kensie, the warrior who loves her and Ian, the warrior she loves. Michael's runs parallel to that of Corunna who lost his beloved in war.

All the knots pull tight during the siege of Gebel Nahar, a "few against the many" situation so typical of Dickson. (The siege of Earth in *The Final Encyclopedia* will be the ultimate example.) This military crisis is a symptom of grave social imbalances, not only in Nahar but on Ceta and all the inhabited worlds. The web tears at a single pull. Michael's sacrifice affects far more than the lives immediately around him. He adds a bit of impetus to the forces breaking humanity free from the net that confines it.

Every issue in *Lost Dorsai* shares a common factor: the cleavage between *being* and *doing*. The troubled groups and individuals shown cannot reconcile private essence with social existence. The Naharese are obsessed with the form rather than the substance of *el honor*. They have no valid ethic to bridle their violent impulses. This morbid culture points up the healthiness of the Dorsai. It also demonstrates that in the long run, all Splinter Cultures are too distorted to be viable. The Dorsai regard Naharese martial fantasies as obscene—empty and unreal as pornography. But their judgment may be too harsh. Even these comic-opera soldiers can respond to a genuine hero when one appears.

Michael renounced his Dorsai heritage rather than compromise his non-violent beliefs. Corunna has suppressed his feelings to bury himself in his work. The Conde is the ghost of an authority figure, not a man. His underlings prefer to keep their lives instead of their honor. Ian neglects his own needs in favor of the gestalt identity he shares with his twin. Kensie tries to attain his own dream without gauging the impact on Ian. Amanda is torn between the wish to belong to one person and the need to be available to many.

Padma is the only balanced personality in the cast and the only one without a quandary. This passive observer watches and learns but does not appear to grow inwardly during the ordeal. For one dedicated to evolutionary progress, he is curiously static. There is a greater irony in the fiery Conde's unslaked thirst for martyrdom. The cup of glory goes instead to Michael, who never desired it. Paradoxically, it is Michael's refusal of his original calling that positions him for an unprecedented adventure—no other Dorsai ever defeated an army singlehandedly.

Dickson allows his hero a grand ceremonial tribute after death. There is none in the story that inspired *Lost Dorsai,* Kipling's "Drums of the Fore and Aft" (1889). There two scruffy British drummer boys turn rout into victory by charging the Afghans alone, but all the recognition they get from their shamefaced regiment is an unmarked grave.

Michael's monument, the *Leto de muerte,* is a custom Dickson invented for this story. It was suggested by the practice of throwing prizes—even personal belongings

—to successful bullfighters, something he had witnessed during travels in Mexico. (Roman gladiators may have been rewarded in the same way.) He was not thinking of the mass sacrifices of battle trophies made by the Iron Age Celts, although the gestures are similar in spirit.

Dickson modeled quasi-Hispanic Nahar partly on Galicia. The Gallegos are the Scots or Bretons of Spain —a romantic but suspicious people. Their lean country is the ancient heart of Spain and the site of its holiest shrine, Santiago de Compostela. (Coincidentally, among Galicia's cities is La Coruña—medieval Corunna—from which the story's narrator takes his name.) However, Nahar's social conditions—hungry *campesinos* and greedy *ricones*—resemble those in contemporary Latin America. The Dorsai could easily be U.S. military advisers caught in a revolution. But the merits of the two warring parties are not really at issue. What matters is preventing the tyrant William from exploiting the situation to his own advantage. Cries for justice—in Nahar and elsewhere—will not be properly answered until the Cycle's close a century hence.

Since the moment of fulfillment is not yet at hand, partial solutions are all *Lost Dorsai*'s survivors can reach. Corunna's heart is just beginning to heal. (He will seem normal when he meets Donal Graeme in *Dorsai!*.) Whatever Padma has learned, it does not include a profound understanding of the Graeme twins. But having shared the Gebel Nahar experience with them may dispose him to act on their behalf in "Brothers." Losing Amanda weakens Kensie's will to live enough to doom him in "Brothers" about five years later. The excess of fraternal love Ian shows by refusing to compete with Kensie for Amanda is precisely why he suffers so much in "Brothers" and afterwards. Amanda strikes a better balance than the men. Though the Star Maiden grieves both her twin suitors, she does win peace of soul for herself. She becomes a spiritual mother to her people as the first Amanda was a physical one.

Only Michael's victory is final because it is sealed in death. Michael is a willing sacrificial lamb. Kensie is a bright golden Achilles cut down in his prime. Ian, on the other hand, endures like a battered Herakles. He is the ultimate Dorsai, with a darkness in him so deep it bedazzles. He demonstrates how much harder it is to *live* heroically than to *die* heroically. Not for Ian the quick, sharp moment of trial. He must prove himself day in and day out through one grim moral choice after another. His leadership and example help the Dorsai survive desperate times. Thus something remains of his family and people a century later for Hal Mayne and his beloved, the third Amanda, to use in the evolutionary struggle.

Thus the illuminations, like the Childe Cycle they complement, turn on the question of balance. Though the demands of integrity and responsibility can clash, they should unite to reinforce each other. As the second Amanda concludes: " 'In the end the only way is to be what you are and do what you must. If you do that, everything works.' " Balance through union is a universal imperative for the race as well as the individual. The conscious and unconscious aspects of human nature must come together. Then evolved mankind—intuitive, empathic, creative—can win the future without losing the past.

To dramatize these principles, Dickson has in effect assembled his own set of secular-historical archetypes. The Cycle and the illuminations function like an original system of mythology that correlates with nearly every area of human experience. It has shaped the author as much as he has shaped it: life anticipates art; art elucidates life. Dickson could apply Hopkins' definition to himself: "What I do is me: for that I came." His twenty-year quest to complete the Childe Cycle has become a kind of initiation for him, both as an artist and as a man. He tried to live the unity he preaches by combining fluffy and intense traits within himself. He knows that separately, the plume is frivolous and the sword ruthless. But together they are gallant.

The plume waves. The sword flashes. The proud chevalier has pledged himself to see the journey through and will not count the cost of keeping faith.

Editor's note: *As a special bonus for readers of* Lost Dorsai, *the author has consented to the publication of an extensive excerpt from his great work-in-progress,* The Final Encyclopedia. *Penultimate novel in the Childe Cycle, Mr. Dickson feels that* The Final Encyclopedia *is his most significant work to date. It commences on the following page.*

THE FINAL ENCYCLOPEDIA: AN EXCERPT

The story up to this point:

Hal Mayne, an orphan found in a small, otherwise empty interstellar ship drifting near Earth orbit, is raised on Earth by three tutors, who are his guardians: one Dorsai, one Exotic, and one Friendly.

When he is fifteen years old his guardians are murdered by the Others, the ambitious and charismatic crossbreeds of the Splinter Cultures, who are rapidly gaining control of human societies throughout all the inhabited worlds. The historical time is approximately 100 years after the time of Dorsai! *and* Soldier, Ask Not.

Such a contingency had been foreseen by the tutors. Hal, grown, will be the natural opponent of the crossbreeds, but until grown he is no match for them. He flees, first to Coby, the mining world where he spends nearly two years, until he is located there by the Others—although the Others still do not realize his potential. Still, their second in command, Nigel Blas, has become interested enough to want to see Hal face to face.

Hal escapes from Coby and lands on Harmony, under the alias of a dead Friendly known as Howard Immanuelson. Recalcitrants are opposing the Others and their controlled governments on both Harmony and Association. As Immanuelson, Hal is befriended by a recalcitrant named Jason Rowe, whom Hal meets in the detention center where both Jason and he are being held by the local authorities under the suspicion of their being what Jason actually is.

THE FINAL ENCYCLOPEDIA:
An Excerpt

The cell door clashed open, waking them. Instinctively, Hal Mayne was on his feet by the time the guard came through the open door and he saw out of the corner of his eye that Jason Rowe was also.

"All right," said the guard. He was thin and tall—though not as tall as Hal—with a starved angry face. "Outside!"

They obeyed. Hal's tall body was still numb from sleep, but his mind, triggered into immediate overdrive, was whirring. He avoided looking at Jason in the interests of keeping up the pretense that they had not talked and still did not know each other, and he noticed that Jason avoided looking at him. Once in the corridor they were herded back the way Hal remembered being brought in.

"Where are we going?" Jason asked.

"Silence!" said the guard softly, without looking at him and without changing the expression of his gaunt, set features. "or I will hang thee by thy wrists for an hour or so after this is over, apostate whelp."

Jason said no more. His thin face was expressionless. His slight frame was held erect. They were moved along down several corridors, up a freight lift shaft, to what was again very obviously the office section of this establishment. Their guard brought them to join a gathering of what seemed to be twenty or more prisoners like themselves, waiting outside the open doors of a room with a raised platform at one end, a desk upon it and an open space before it. The flag of the

United Sects, a white cross on a black field, hung from a flagpole set upright on the stage.

Their guard left them with the other prisoners and stepped a few steps aside to stand with the five other guards present. They stood, guards and prisoners alike, and time went by.

Finally, there was the sound of footwear on polished corridor floor, echoing around the bend in the further corridor, and three figures turned the corner and came into sight. Hal's breath caught in his chest. Two were men in ordinary business suits—almost certainly local officials. But the man between them, tall above them, was Nigel Blas.

Nigel ran his glance over all the prisoners as he approached; and his eye paused for a second on Hal, but not for longer than might have been expected from the fact that Hal was noticeably the tallest of the group. Nigel came on and turned into the doorway, shaking his head at the two men accompanying him as he did so.

"Foolish," he was saying to them as he passed within arm's length of Hal, "Foolish, foolish! Did you think I was the sort to be impressed by what you could sweep off the streets, that I was to be amused like some primitive ruler by state executions or public torture-spectacles? This sort of thing only wastes energy. I'll show you how to do things. Bring them in here."

The guards were already moving in response before one of the men with Nigel turned and gestured at the prisoners. Hal and the others were herded into the room and lined up in three ranks facing the platform on which the two men now stood behind the desk and Nigel himself half-sat, half-lounged, with his weight on the further edge of that piece of furniture. To even this casual pose he lent an impression of elegant authority.

The sick coldness had returned to the pit of Hal's stomach with Nigel's appearance; and now that feeling was growing, spreading all through him. Sheltered and protected as he had been all his life, he had grown up without ever knowing the kind of fear that compresses the chest and takes the strength from the limbs. Then, all at once, he had encountered death and that kind of fear for the first time, all in one moment; and now the reflex set up by that moment had been triggered by a second encounter of the tall, commanding figure on the platform before him.

He was not afraid of the Friendly authorities who were holding him captive. His mind recognized the fact that they were only human, and he had deeply absorbed the principle that for any problem involving human interaction there should be a practical solution. But the sight of Nigel faced him with something that had destroyed the very pillars of his universe. He felt the paralysis of his fear staining all through him; and the rational part of him recognized that once it had taken him over completely he would throw himself upon the fate that would follow Nigel's identification of him—just to get it over with.

He reached for help, and the ghosts of three old men came out of his memory in response.

"He is no more than a weed that flourishes for a single summer's day, this man you face," said the harsh voice of Obadiah in his mind. "No more than the rain on the mountainside, blowing for a moment past the rock. God is that rock, and eternal. The rain passes and is as if it never was. Hold to the rock and ignore the rain."

"He can do nothing," said the soft voice of Walter Inteacher, "that I've not shown you at one time or another. He is only a user of skills developed by other

271

men and women, many of whom could use them far better than he. Remember that no one's mind and body are ever more than human. Forget the fact that he is older and more experienced than you; concentrate only on a true image of what he is, and what his limits are."

"Fear is only another weapon," said Malachi, "no more dangerous in itself than a sharpened blade is. Treat it as you would any weapon. When it approaches, turn yourself to let it pass you by, then take and control the hand that guides it at you. The weapon without the hand is only one more thing—in a universe full of things."

Up on the platform Nigel looked at them all.

"Pay attention to me, my friends," he said softly. "Look at me."

They looked, Hal with the rest of them. He saw Nigel's lean, aristocratic face and pleasant brown eyes. Then, as he looked at them, those eyes began to expand until they would entirely fill his field of vision.

Reflexively, out of his training under Walter the Inteacher, he took a step back within his own mind, putting what he saw at arm's length—and all at once it was as if he was aware of things on two levels. There was the level on which he stood with the other prisoners, held by Nigel like animals transfixed by a bright light in darkness; and there was the level in which he was aware of the assault that was being made on his free will by what was hidden behind that bright light, and on which he struggled to resist it.

He thought of rock. In his mind he formed the image of a mountainside, cut and carved into an altar on which an eternal light burned. Rock and light . . . untouchable, eternal.

"I must apologize to you, my friends and brothers,"

Nigel was saying gently to all of them. "Mistakenly, you've been made to suffer; and that shouldn't be. But it was a natural mistake and small mistakes of your own have contributed to it. Examine your conscience. Is there one of you here who isn't aware of things you know you shouldn't have done . . ."

Like mist, the beginnings of rain blew upon the light and the altar. But the light continued to burn, and the rock was unchanged. Nigel's voice continued; and the rain thickened, blowing more fiercely upon the rock and the light. On the mountainside the day darkened, but the light burned on through the darkness, showing the rock still there, still unmarked and unmoved . . .

Nigel was softly showing them all the way to a worthier and happier life, a way that trusted in what he was telling them. All that they needed to do was to acknowledge the errors of their past and let themselves be guided in the proper path in the future. His words made a warm and friendly shelter away from all storm, its door open and waiting for all of them. But, sadly, Hal must remain behind, alone, out on the mountainside in the icy and violent rain, clinging to the rock so that the wind would not blow him away; with only the pure but heatless light burning in the darkness to comfort him.

Slowly, he became aware that the increasing wind had ceased growing stronger, that the rain which had been falling ever heavier was now steady, that the darkness could grow no darker—and he, the rock and the light were still there, still together. A warmth of a new sort kindled itself inside him and grew until it shouted in triumph. He felt a strength within him that he had never felt before, and with that strength, he stepped back, merging once more the two levels, so that he looked out nakedly through his own eyes again at Nigel.

Nigel had finished talking and was stepping down from the platform, headed out of the room. All the prisoners turned to watch him go as if he walked out of the room holding one string to which all of them were attached.

"If you'll come this way, brothers," said one of the guards.

They were led, by this single guard only, down more corridors and into a room with desks, where they were handed back their papers.

* * *

Apparently, they were free to go. They were ushered out of the building and Hal found himself walking down the street with Jason at his side. He looked at the other man and saw him smiling and animated.

"Howard!" Jason said. "Isn't this wonderful? We've got to find the others and tell them about this great man. They'll have to see him for themselves."

Hal looked closely into Jason's eyes.

"What is it, brother?" said Jason. "Is something wrong?"

"No," said Hal. "But maybe we should sit down somewhere and make some plans. Is there any place around here where we can talk, away from people?"

Jason looked around. They were in what appeared to Hal to be a semi-industrial section. It was mid-morning, and the rain that had been falling when they had landed the day before was now holding off, although the sky was dark and promised more precipitation.

"This early . . ." Jason hesitated. "There's a small eating place with booths in its back room, and this time of day the back room ought to be completely empty."

"Let's go," said Hal.

The eating place turned out to be small indeed. It was hardly the sort of establishment that Hal would have found himself turning into if he had simply wanted a meal, but its front room held only one group of four and one or two customers at the square tables there; and the back room, as Jason had predicted, was empty. They took a booth in a corner and ordered coffee.

"What plans did you have in mind to make, Howard?" asked Jason, when the coffee had been brought.

Hal tasted what was in his cup, and set the cup down again. Coffee—or rather some imitation of it—was to be found on all the inhabited worlds. But its taste varied largely on any two worlds, and was often markedly different in widely distant parts of the same world. Hal had spent three years getting used to Coby coffee. He would have to start all over again with Harmony coffee.

"Have you seen this?" he asked, in turn.

From a pocket he brought out a small gold nugget encased in a cube of glass. It was the first piece of pocket gold he had found in the Yow Dee Mine; and, following a Coby custom, he had bought it back from the mine owners and had it encased in glass, to carry about as a good-luck piece. His fellow team-members would have thought him strange if he had not. Now, for the first time, he had a use for it.

Jason bent over the cube.

"Is that real gold?" he asked, with the fascination of anyone not of either Coby or Earth.

"Yes," said Hal. "See the color . . ."

He reached out across the table and took the back of Jason's neck gently and precisely between the tips of his thumb and middle finger. The skin beneath his fingertips jumped at his touch, then relaxed as he put soft pressure on the nerve endings below it.

"Easy," he said, "just watch the piece of gold . . . Jason, I want you to rest for a bit. Just close your eyes and lean back against the back of the booth and sleep for a couple of minutes. Then you can open your eyes and listen. I've got something to tell you."

With an obedience a little too ready to be natural, Jason closed his eyes and leaned back, resting his head against the hard, dark-dyed wooden panel that was the back of the booth. Hal took his hand from the other's neck and Jason stayed as he was, breathing easily and deeply for about a hundred and fifty heartbeats. Then he opened his eyes and stared at Hal as if puzzled for a second. He smiled.

"You were going to tell me something," he said.

"Yes," said Hal. "And you're going to listen to me all the way through and then not say anything until you've thought about what I've just told you. Aren't you?"

"Yes, Howard," said Jason.

"Good. Now listen closely." Hal paused. He had never done anything like this before; and there was a danger, in Jason's present unnaturally receptive state, that some words Hal used might have a larger effect than he had intended it to have. "Because I want you to understand something. Right now you think you're acting normally and doing exactly what you'd ordinarily want to do. But actually, that's not the case. The fact is, a very powerful individual's made you an attractive offer on a level where it's hard for you to refuse him, a choice to let your conscience go to sleep and leave all moral decisions up to someone else. Because you were approached on that particular level, you've no way of judging whether this was a wise decision to make, or not. Do you follow me so far? Nod your head if you do."

Jason nodded. He was concentrating just hard enough to bring a small frown line into being between his eyebrows. But otherwise his face was still relaxed and happy.

"Essentially what you've just been told," Hal said, "is that Nigel Blas, or people designated by him, will decide not only what's right for you, but what you'll want to do; and you've agreed that this would be a good thing. Because of that, you've now joined those who've already made that agreement with him; those who were until an hour ago your enemies, in that they were trying to destroy the faith you've held to all your life . . ."

The slight frown was deepening between Jason's brows and the happiness on his face was being replaced by a strained expression. Hal talked on; and when at last he stopped, Jason was huddled on the other seat, turned as far away from Hal as the close confines of the booth would allow, with his face hidden in his hands.

Hal sat, feeling miserable himself, and tried to drink his coffee. The silence between them continued, until finally Jason heaved a long, shivering sigh and dropped his hands. He turned a face to Hal that looked as if it had not slept for two nights.

"Oh, God!" he said.

Hal looked back at him, but did not try to say anything.

"I'm unclean," said Jason. "Unclean!"

"Nonsense," said Hal. Jason's eyes jumped to his face; and Hal made himself grin at the other. "What was that I seem to remember hearing when I was

young—and you must've remembered hearing, too—
about the sin of pride? What makes you feel you're
particularly evil in having knuckled under to the persuasion of Nigel Blas?"

"I lacked faith!" said Jason.

"We all lack faith to some extent," Hal said. "There
are probably some men and women so strong in their
faith that Blas wouldn't have been able to touch them.
I had a teacher once . . . but the point is, everyone else
in that room gave in to him, the same way you did."

"You didn't."

"I've had special training," said Hal. "That's what
I was telling you just now, remember? What Nigel
Blas did, he succeeded in doing because he's also had
special training. Believe me, someone without training
would have had to have been a very remarkable person
to resist him. But for someone with training, it was . . .
relatively easy."

Jason drew another deep, ragged breath.

"Then I'm ashamed for another reason," he said
bleakly.

"Why?" Hal stared at him.

"Because I thought you were a spy, planted on me
by the Accursed of God, when they decided to hold me
captive. When we heard Howard Immanuelson had
died of a lung disease in a holding station on Coby, we
all assumed his papers had been lost. The thought that
someone else of the faith could find them and use them
—and his doing it would be so secret that someone like
myself wouldn't know—that was stretching coin-
cidence beyond belief. And you were so quick to pick
up the finger speech. So I was going to pretend I was
taken in by you. I was going to bring you with me to
some place where the other brothers and sisters of the
faith could question you and find out why you were

sent and what you knew about us."

He stared burningly at Hal.

"And then you, just now, brought me back from Hell—from where I could never have come back without you. There was no need for you to do that if you had been one of the enemy, one of the Accursed. How could I have doubted that you were of the faith?"

"Quite easily," said Hal. "As far as bringing you back from Hell, all I did was hurry up the process a little. The kind of persuasion Nigel Blas was using only takes permanently with people who basically agree with him to begin with. With those who don't, his type of mind-changing gets eaten away by the natural feelings of the individual until it wears thin and breaks down. Since you were someone opposed enough to him to fight him, the only way he could stop you permanently would be to kill you."

"Why didn't he then?" said Jason. "Why didn't he kill all of us?"

"Because it's to his advantage to pretend that he only opens people's eyes to the right way to live," said Hal, hearing an echo of Walter the Inteacher in the words even as he said them. He had not consciously stopped to think the matter out, but Jason's question had automatically evoked the obvious answer. "Even his convinced followers feel safer if he is always right, always merciful. What he did with us, there, wasn't because we were important, but because the two men with him on the platform were important—to him. There're really only a handful of what you call the Belial-spawn, compared to the trillions of people on the fourteen worlds. Those like Nigel don't have the time, even if they felt like it, to control everyone personally. So, whenever possible they use the same sort of social mechanisms that've been used down the centuries when a few people wanted to command many."

Jason sat watching him.

"Who are you, Howard?" he asked.

"I'm sorry." Hal hesitated. "I can't tell you that. But I should tell you you've no obligation to call me brother. I'm afraid I lied to you. I'm not of the faith, as you call it. I've got nothing to do with whatever organization you and those with you belong to. But I am at war with Nigel Blas and his kind."

"Then you're a brother," said Jason, simply. He picked up his own cold coffee cup and drank deeply from it. "We—those the Accursed call the Children— are of every sect and every possible interpretation of the Idea of God. Your difference from the rest of us isn't any greater than our differences from each other. But I'm glad you told me this, because I'll have to tell the others about you when we reach them."

"Can we reach them?" asked Hal.

"There's no problem about that," said Jason. "I'll make contact in town here with someone who'll know where the closest band of warriors is, right now; and we'll join them. Out in the countryside we of the faith still control. Oh, they chase us, but they can't do more than keep us on the move. It's only here, in the cities, that the Belial-spawn and their minions rule."

He slid to the end of the booth and stood up.

"Come along," he said.

Out in the coldly damp air of the street, they located a callbox and coded for an autocab. In succession, they visited a clothing store, a library and a gymnasium, without Jason's recognizing anyone he trusted enough to ask for help. Their fourth try brought them to a small vehicle custom-repair garage in the northern outskirts of Citadel.

The garage itself was a dome-like temporary struc-

ture perched in an open field out where residences
gave way to small personal farm-plots rented by city
dwellers on an annual basis. It occupied an open
stretch of stony ground that was its own best demonstration of why it had not been put to personal farming
the way the land around it had. Inside the barely-
heated dome, the air of which was thick with the faintly banana-like smell of a local tree oil used for lubri-
cation hanging like an invisible mist over the half-dis-
mantled engines of several surface vehicles, they found
a single occupant—a square, short, leathery man in
his sixties, engaged in reassembling the rear support
fan of an all-terrain fourplace cruiser.

"Hilary!" said Jason, as they reached him.

"Jase—" said the worker, barely glancing up at
them. "When did you get back?"

"Yesterday," said Jason. "The Accursed put us up
overnight in their special hotel. This is Howard Immanuelson. Not of the faith, but one of our allies. From
Coby."

"Coby?" Hilary glanced up once more at Hal.
"What did you do on Coby?"

"I was a miner," said Hal.

Hilary reached for a cleansing rag, wiped his hands,
turned about and offered one of them to Hal.

"Long?" he asked.

"Three years."

Hilary nodded.

"I like people who know how to work," he said.
"You two on the run?"

"No," said Jason. "They turned us loose. But we
need to get out into the country. Who's close right
now?"

Hilary looked down at his hands and wiped them
once more on his cloth, then threw the cloth in a

wastebin.

"Rukh Tamani," he said. "She and her people're passing through, on their way to something. You know Rukh?"

"I know of her," said Jason. "She's a sword of the Lord."

"You might connect up with them. Want me to give you a map?"

"Please," said Jason. "And if you can supply us—"

"Clothes and gear, that's all," said Hilary. "Weapons are getting too risky."

"Can you take us close to her, at all?"

"Oh, I can get you fairly well in." Hilary looked again at Hal. "Anything I'll be able to give you in the way of clothes is going to fit pretty tight."

"Let's try what you've got," said Jason.

Hilary led them to a partitioned-off corner of his dome. The door they went through let them into a storeroom piled to the ceiling with a jumble of containers and goods of all kinds. Hilary threaded his way among the stacks to a pile of what seemed to be mainly clothing and camping gear, and started pulling out items.

Twenty minutes later, he had them both outfitted with heavy bush clothing including both shoulder and belt packs and camping equipment. As Hilary had predicted, Hal's shirt, jacket and undershirt were tight in the shoulders and short in the sleeves. Otherwise, everything that he had given Hal fitted well enough. The one particular blessing turned out to be the fact that there were bush boots available of the proper length for Hal's feet. They were a little too wide, but extra socks and insoles took care of that.

"Now," Hilary said when the outfitting was complete. "When did you eat last?"

Hunger returned to Hal's consciousness like a body blow. Unconsciously, once it had become obvious in the cell that there was no hope of food soon, he had blocked out his need for it—strongly enough that he had even sat in the coffee place with Jason and not thought of food, when he could have had it for the ordering. As it was, Jason answered before he did.

"We didn't. Not since we got off the ship."

"Then I better feed you, hadn't I?" grunted Hilary. He led them out of the storeroom and into another corner of the dome that had a cot, sink, foodkeeper and cooking equipment.

He fed them an enormous meal, mainly of fried vegetables, local mutton and bread, washed down with quantities of a flat, semi-sweet root beer, apparently made from a variform of the native Earth product. The heavy intake of food operated on Hal like a sedative. Once they had all piled into a battered six-place bush van, he stretched out and fell asleep.

He woke to a rhythmic sound that was the slashing of branch tips against the sides of the van. Looking out the windows on either side, he saw that they were proceeding down a forest track so narrow that the bushes on either side barely allowed the van to pass. Jason and Hilary were in mid-conversation in the front seat of the van.

". . . Of course it won't stop them!" Hilary was saying. "But if there's anything at all the Belial-spawn are even a little sensitive to, it's public opinion. If Rukh and her people can take care of the core shaft tap, it'll be a choice for them of starving Hope, Valleyvale, and the other local cities, or shifting the ship outfitting to the core tap center on South Promise. It'll save them trouble to shift. It's a temporary spoke in their wheel, that's all; but what more can we ask?"

"We can ask to win," said Jason.

"God allowed the spawn to gain control in our cities," said Hilary. "In His time, He will release us from them. Until then, our job is to testify for Him by doing all we can to resist them."

Jason sighed.

"Hilary," he said. "Sometimes I forget you're just like the other old folk when it comes to anything that looks like an act of God's will."

"You haven't lived long enough yet," Hilary said. "To you, everything seems to turn on what's happened in your own few years. Get older and look around the fourteen worlds, and you'll see that the time of Judgement's not that far off. Our race is old and sick in sin. On every world, things are falling into disorder and decay, and the coming among us of these mixed breeds who'd make everyone else into their personal cattle is only one more sign of the approach of Judgement."

"I can't take that attitude," said Jason, shaking his head. "We wouldn't be capable of hope, if hope had no meaning."

"It's got meaning," said Hilary, "in a practical sense. Forcing the spawn to change their plans to another core tap delays them; and who's to know but that very delay may be part of the battle plan of the Lord, as he girds his loins to fight this last and greatest fight?"

The noise of the branches hitting the sides and windows of the van ceased suddenly. They had emerged into an open area overgrown only by tall, straight-limbed conifers—variforms of some Earthly stock—spaced about upon uneven, rocky ground that had hardly any covering beyond patches of green moss and brown, dead needles fallen from the trees. The sun, for the first time Hal had seen it since he had arrived on Harmony, was breaking through a high-lying mass of white and black clouds, wind-torn here and there to show occasional patches of startling blue and brilliant light. The ground-level breeze blew strongly against the van; and for the first time Hal became aware that their way was uphill. With that recognition, the realization came that the plant life and the terrain indicated a considerably higher altitude than that of Citadel.

Hal sat up on the seat.

"You alive back there?" said Hilary.

"Yes," answered Hal.

"We'll be there in a few minutes, Howard," said Jason. "Let me talk to Rukh about you, first. It'll be her decision as to whether you're allowed to join her group, or not. If she won't have you, I'll come back with you, too; and we'll stay together until Hilary can find a group that'll have us both."

"You'll be on your own, if I have to take you back," said Hilary. "I can't afford to keep you around my place for fear of attracting attention."

"We know that," said Jason.

The van went up and over a rise of the terrain, and nosed down abruptly into a valley-like depression that was like a knife-cut in the slope. Some ten or twenty meters below was the bed of the valley, with a small stream running through it; the stream itself was hardly visible because of the thick cluster of small trees that grew about its moisture. The van slid down the slope of the valley wall on the air-cushion of its fans, plunged in among the trees, and came to a halt at a short distance from the near edge of the stream. From above, Hal had seen nothing of people or shelters, but suddenly they were in the midst of a small encampment.

THE FINAL ENCYCLOPEDIA: AN EXCERPT

He took it in at one glance. It was a picture that was to stay in his mind afterwards. Brightly touched by a moment of the sunlight breaking through the ragged clouds overhead, he saw a number of collapsible shelters like beehives the height of a grown man, their olive-colored side panels and tops further camouflaged by tree branches fastened about them. Two men were standing in the stream, apparently washing clothes. A woman approaching middle age, in a black, leather-like jacket, was just coming out of the trees to the left of the van. On a rock in the center of the clearing sat a gray-haired man with a cone rifle half torn down for cleaning its parts, lying on a cloth he had spread across his knees. Facing him, and turning now to face the van, was a tall, slim, dark young woman in a somber green bush jacket, its large number of square pockets bulging with their contents. Below the bush jacket, she wore heavy bush pants tucked into the tops of short boots. A gunbelt and sidearm were hooked tightly about her narrow waist, the black holster holding the sidearm with its weather flap clipped firmly down.

She wore nothing on her head. Her black hair was cut short about her ears, and her face was narrow and perfect below a wide brow and brilliant, dark eyes. In that single, arrested moment, the repressed poet in Hal woke, and he thought that she was like the dark blade of a sword in the sunlight. Then his attention was jerked from her. In a series of flashing motions the disassembled parts of the cone rifle in the hands of the gray-haired man were thrown back together, ending with the hard slap of a new tube of cones into the magazine slot below the barrel. The man was almost as swift as Hal had seen Malachi be in similar demonstrations. The movements of this man did not have the smooth, unitary flow of Malachi's—but he was almost as fast.

"All right," said the woman in the bush jacket. "It's Hilary."

The hands of the gray-haired man relaxed on the now-ready weapon; but the weapon itself still lay on the cloth over his knees, pointing in the general direction of Hal and the other two. Hilary got out of the van. Jason and Hal did the same.

"I brought you a couple of recruits," said Hilary, as coolly as if the man on the rock was holding a stick of candy. He started to walk forward and Jason moved after him. Hal followed.

"This is Jason Rowe," said Hilary. "Maybe you know him. The other's not of the faith, but a friend. He's Howard Immanuelson, a miner from Coby."

By the time he had finished saying this he was within a meter and a half of the woman and the man with Jason and Hal a step behind. Hilary stopped. The woman glanced at Jason, nodded briefly, then turned her brilliant gaze on Hal.

"Immanuelson?" she said. "I'm Rukh Tamani. This is my sergeant, James Child-of-God."

Hal found it hard to look away from her, but he turned his gaze on the face of the gray-haired man. He found himself looking into a rectangular, raw-boned set of features, clothed in skin gone leathery some years since from sun and weather. Lines radiated from the corners of the eyes of James Child-of-God; deeper lines had carved themselves in long curves about the corners of his mouth, from nose to chin, and the pale blue eyes he fastened on Hal were like the muzzles of cone rifles.

"If not of the faith," he said to them all now, in a dry, penetrating tenor voice, "he hath no right here among us."